Chinese Theories of Reading and Writing

SUNY series in Chinese Philosophy and Culture

Roger T. Ames, editor

Chinese Theories of Reading and Writing

A Route to Hermeneutics and Open Poetics

Ming Dong Gu

State University of New York Press

Published by
State University of New York Press, Albany

For information, address State University of New York Press,
90 State Street, Suite 700, Albany, NY 12207

Production by Judith Block
Marketing by Anne Valentine

Library of Congress Cataloging-in-Publication Data
Gu, Ming Dong, 1955–
    Chinese theories of reading and writing: a route to hermeneutics and open poetics/Ming Dong Gu.
        p.   cm.—(Suny series in chinese philosophy and culture)
    Includes bibliographical references and index.
    ISBN 0-7914-6423-7 (alk. paper)
    1. Chinese classics—History and criticism.   2. Hermeneutics.   I. Title.
II. Series.
PL2461. Z7G8 2005
895. 1′09—dc22

                                                            2004016207

10   9   8   7   6   5   4   3   2   1

To the memory of
my father, Gu Shirong (1929–2000)
and
my mother, Xu Hongzuo (1931–2000)

Contents

Part I Conceptual Inquiries into Reading and Openness

Contents

ix

Part IV Literary Hermeneutics

Preface

Traditional China does not lack conceptual inquiries into reading and writing, but the insights are scattered in different kinds of discourses and have never been synthesized into a clearly defined system. Whether in Chinese or other languages, a systematic study of Chinese theories of reading and writing in intellectual thought and critical practice is long overdue. This study attempts to fill that blank. It argues that the Chinese tradition has formed an implicit system of reading and writing with fascinating insights that not only predated similar ideas in the West by centuries but also anticipated contemporary ideas of hermeneutic openness and open poetics. Furthermore, it seeks to construct a Chinese system of hermeneutic theories, reflect on it from a comparative perspective, and tease out theoretical insights that may contribute to the formulation of a transcultural open poetics for textual criticism and creative composition.

Initially, however, I was motivated only by the desire to unseat hermeneutic inertia and to locate new strategies of reading. As my research deepened and broadened, it gradually dawned on me that hermeneutic openness is really a pivotal point on which different issues of criticism, hermeneutics, and literary theory in contemporary discourse intersect. In the past fifty years or so, fundamental and far-reaching changes have taken place in modern criticism and literary theory. The changes, comparable to paradigm shifts in the natural sciences, seem to focus on one central issue: the conditions of the text. For all the dazzling varieties, one of the central concerns of modern hermeneutic thought is with the question of hermeneutic openness: Is a text an enclosed space of unity, harmony, and at most a balance of opposites, which allows only for nuanced and coherent exegeses, or an open space of different views, voices, values, attitudes, and ideologies, which invites different and conflicting interpretations? As a result of this realization, such general theoretical issues as "author," "reader," "text," "context," "meaning," "intention," "signification," "semiosis," and the like, naturally became categories under my consideration.

My study undergoes another readjustment thanks to insights gained from reading some books on Chinese and Asian intellectual thought. In their series of books on Chinese thought, David Hall, Roger Ames, and other scholars of Asian intellectual thought have pioneered a comparative and dialogic approach that successfully brings about meaningful dialogues between Chinese/Asian and Western thought.[1] Their inspiring success confirms my long-held conviction that despite some unique features of Chinese hermeneutic thought, its concerns with endless meaning of a text converge with similar concerns of its Western counterpart and have a cross-cultural value. Because of this conviction, my inquiry takes another turn and becomes a comparative study of Chinese reading and writing in relation to Western hermeneutic theories and in the larger context of postmodern theories. I am convinced that if we wish to locate a bridge across the divide between Chinese and Western hermeneutic thought, hermeneutic openness is definitely a viable one. Across this bridge Chinese and Western ideas can travel in a two-way flow and engage in truly meaningful dialogues. As a result of this realization, my study of reading and writing in the Chinese tradition became a cross-cultural inquiry.

In spite of various readjustments, this study has remained focused on two interrelated critical issues: interpretive openness and the making of hermeneutic space. Here, I will dwell a little on why I have focused on these two issues. First, I am not primarily concerned with searching for texts that may be said to be open. I attempt to explain why a text is open and to explore how we can open up a text. In so doing, I am preoccupied with the poetics of reading as well as writing. Second, I believe that an exploration of the making of hermeneutic space will facilitate a balance between the two major trends in reading: the postmodern one that emphasizes the primacy of contemporary theories, and the traditional one that affirms the value of sensitive and sensible close readings. In a most recent book, *Reading after Theory* (2002), Valentine Cunningham reviews the dissemination of reading theories from the 1960s to the present day. While criticizing conservatives of reading who naively dream of natural and independent readings uncontaminated by prejudices and preconceptions and free from theories, especially postmodern theories, he, like Umberto Eco, accuses postmodern theories of encouraging textual abuse and diminishing humanly rich experiences of reading.[2] I believe that only with a balanced approach can reading and interpretation perform the multiple function of illuminating critical practice, discovering structures and conventions of textual discourse, and enriching the human experience of reading and writing.

This study grew out of a substantial portion of a doctoral dissertation at the University of Chicago. In its present form, it owes a great deal to the guidance, advice, and encouragement of my advisors, Professors Anthony C. Yu, David T. Roy, Edward L. Shaughnessy, and W. J. T. Mitchell. I consider myself fortunate in having these scholars as my mentors, who are truly worthy of that honorable name. In that intellectually stimulating institution, I was also indebted to a number of teachers and scholars, from whom I received instruction, assistance, and encouragement: Professors Françoise Meltzer, William Sibley, James Ketelaar, Judith Zeitlin, Wu Hung, Xiaobing Tang, Prasenjita Duara, Guy Allito, George C. C. Chao, and Norma Field; and to my classmates and friends from whom I received encouragement and assistance in both life and scholarship: Yiwen Li, Hongbing Zhang, David Sena, Yiqing Wu, Ke Peng, Weihong Bao, Lin Hong Lam, and Feng Li. Among these, I am most grateful to Yiwen Li, who has facilitated my access to the East Asian materials in the University of Chicago library.

I have owed an intellectual debt to scholars from other institutions. Sections of chapters 1 and 2 were presented at two panels that I organized for the Association for Asian Studies (2000 and 2002). I benefited a great deal from the comments by panel members including Professors Stephen Owen of Harvard University, Kang-I Sun Chang of Yale University, Haun Saussy of Stanford University, Pauline Yu of the University of California at Los Angeles, Anthony C. Yu of the University of Chicago, Shuen-fu Lin of the University of Michigan, Dore Levy of Brown University, and Longxi Zhang of the City University of Hong Kong. I must express my special thanks to two scholars: Professor Kang-I Sun Chang at Yale University and Professor Chung-ying Cheng of the University of Hawaii. Professor Chang, despite her own busy schedule, took the trouble to read earlier versions of chapters 7 and 8, supplied me with some useful materials, and offered detailed suggestions for revision. I did not have the honor of meeting Professor Cheng until he attended one of my presentations at a scholarly conference. After hearing my presentation, he kindly sought me out, had a long talk with me, and provided valuable guidance and suggestions for my conceptual inquiries into Chinese intellectual thought. In addition to scholars whom I know personally, I am also indebted to many scholars whom I never met but whose scholarships have influenced my study. In my early manuscript, I acknowledged my indebtedness in detailed notes and a long bibliography, but because of the compelling need to save space, I have reduced almost all long notes to mere citations and only listed works cited in my study.

Ideas and sections of this study have appeared in revised form in some scholarly journals. Materials in the introduction, chapter 2, and conclusion were incorporated into an article published in *Comparative Literature* 55.2 (2003), pp. 112–29. Sections of chapter 2 were published in revised form in *Philosophy East and West* 53.4 (2003), pp. 490–513. A shorter version of chapter 4 was published in *Journal of Chinese Philosophy*, 31.4 (2004), pp. 469–88, and an earlier version of chapter 3 appeared in *Philosophy East and West*, 55.2 (2005). I thank the editors of the journals for their permission to use the published materials. I also wish to thank two anonymous reviewers of the State University of New York Press who offered perceptive comments on my manuscript and recommended it for publication, and the press's editor, Ms. Nancy Ellegate, for her vision and encouragement. Finally, I thank my present institution, Rhodes College, for providing me with three summers of faculty development endowment grants, and my wife, Ping Lu, for her unfailing emotional support, which has helped me pull through setbacks and frustrations.

MDG
Wancheng Studio

Hermeneutic Openness: A Transcultural Phenomenon

The Rise of Hermeneutic Openness

Hermeneutics is "the art or theory of interpretation, as well as a type of philosophy that starts with questions of interpretation."[1] Even after the term has acquired a broad significance in its historical development, it is still very much concerned with textual interpretation as it once was with exegeses of canonical texts. The text-centered feature is especially prominent in literary hermeneutics, which may be loosely defined as the theory of the interpretation of literary texts. Whether it is philosophical hermeneutics or literary hermeneutics, hermeneutic experience entails a sense of openness in interpretation because, as Hans-Georg Gadamer points out, it "has its own fulfillment not in definite knowledge, but in that openness to experience that is encouraged by experience itself."[2] Gadamer views adequate interpretation as a result of the "fusion of horizons" between the reader and the text in a dialogic interaction. Since the text and reader have their historicity and intentionality, and there are generations of readers, the hermeneutic space is theoretically open, and the horizon of meaning is consequently boundless. Hence, we may say that hermeneutic experience is invariably open.

Hermeneutic openness in literary studies is called "literary openness." It is a major aesthetic issue in literary traditions, East or West. In theory, it means that a literary text is not an enclosure of words whose messages are finite and limited, but a hermeneutic space constructed with imagistic or verbal signs capable of generating unlimited interpretations.

In common sense, it means that a literary text has no "correct" interpretation, or has multiple interpretations. Literary "openness" as a theoretical concept was first proposed by Umberto Eco in his *Opera aperta* (the Open Work) in 1962,[3] but in the Chinese tradition, the idea can be traced back to high antiquity. Very early in the development of Chinese literature, Chinese writers seemed to have felt the impulse for artistic openness and toyed with the idea and practice of open work. The earliest interest in openness is found in the inquiry into the origin, nature, and function of the *Zhouyi* (*Book of Changes*) and in the composition and interpretation of the *Shijing* (*Book of Songs*). Later inquiries into openness permeated Chinese poetic criticism and interpretations of canonical works.

Origins of Openness in China

Initially, awareness of openness in China emerged from two major sources: metaphysical inquiry of the universe and interpretive practice of canonical texts. In the metaphysical inquiry into textual openness, the Chinese tradition had an earlier start than the West. As early as the fourth century BC[4] in China, there appeared in the appended verbalizations to the *Yijing* 易經, also known as the *Zhouyi* or *Book of Changes*, a famous saying, which has since become a household word for rationalizing different interpretations of the same text or phenomenon: "[In the interpretation of the Dao,] a benevolent person who sees it will say that it is benevolent; a wise person who sees it will say that it is wise."[5] In the second century BC, the Chinese Confucian thinker Dong Zhongshu 董仲舒 (c.179–c.104 BC) articulated a dictum that is directly related to literature: "[*The Book of*] *Poetry* has no constant [or thorough-going] interpretation 詩無達詁."[6] Although this dictum referred specifically to the exegesis of the *Book of Poetry* (or *Book of Songs* in Waley's popular translation), it was later extended to all poetry. Shen Deqian 沈德潛 (1673–1769), for example, in relating Dong Zhongshu's dictum broadly to all poetry, practically viewed poetry as an open hermeneutic space amenable to what contemporary theory calls reader response criticism:

> The words of ancient poets contain within themselves unlimited implications. When posterity reads them, they will come to different understandings, depending upon their dispositions, which may be shallow or deep, high or low. . . . This is what Master Dong had in mind when he said: "[*The Book of*] Poetry has no constant interpretation." Commentaries, annotations, and interpretations are all posterity's views from different quarters and corners.[7]

In critical practice, openness in the Chinese tradition emerged from critical blindness rather than conscious insight. In *Blindness and Insight*, Paul de Man examines the works of some influential European and American theorists and critics and finds in them a gap between their statements about the nature of literature and the results of their practical criticism. Paradoxically, de Man argues, their critical blindness to the gap frequently gives rise to some very fascinating insights into literature, art, culture, and hermeneutics.[8] The same may be said of the emergence of hermeneutic openness in the critical discourses by traditional Chinese thinkers and scholars. In their statements about some canonical texts, they viewed the text as an enclosure of words that contained the original intentions of the author and declared that it is the task of a commentator to ferret out those intentions that constitute meaning. But in their actual commentaries, the multifaceted interpretations of a given text not only fragmented the text but also implied that it was an open hermeneutic space. The *Shijing* (*Book of Songs*) hermeneutic tradition is a case in point. There has been a perennial search for the original intentions of the anonymous poets. While the search was aimed at discovering the original meaning that was supposed to reside in a given poem, it led to a multiplicity of interpretations that effectively open up a given poem to different and even conflicting interpretations. Take the first poem of the *Shijing*, "Guanju," for example. In a later chapter, I will show that there are, according to my incomplete statistics, eight major interpretations and many more minor readings. Of the major interpretations, the poem has been construed to cover heaven and earth, individuals and society, government and politics, mores and morality, family relations and human relations, customs and habits, physical passion and spiritual sublimation, and eulogy and satire. The interpretations are not always compatible with each other. In fact, some directly conflict and contradict each other. In terms of the multiple interpretations, we may say that the poem is practically open. This is also true of many other poems in the anthology.

I, therefore, suggest that in critical practice, hermeneutic openness in Chinese tradition emerged from critical blindness rather than conscious insight. To a large extent, the Chinese notion of openness grew out of the conflict between a canonical precept and critical practice. Confucius, who started the *Shijing* hermeneutic tradition, posited a monolithic thematic guideline: "If out of the three hundred poems one were to choose one phrase to summarize the theme, I would say: there is no evil thought."[9] Since Confucius was regarded as a sage, Confucian scholars took his words literally. But to their chagrin, they found that the anthology contains poems which not only deviate from this thematic guideline but also can be considered obscene by Confucian moral standards. To cope with this disconcerting discovery, they had to resort to various exegetical methods which led to a multiplicity of readings. As a result, although in theory they viewed a text as a closed entity, in practice, they opened it up.

Since the Confucian canon incorporates other classics in addition to the *Book of Songs*, metaphysical openness and critical openness converge in Chinese poetics. Dong Zhongshu's dictum, "Poetry has no constant interpretation," marked the convergence. It certainly grew out of the attempt to cope with deviations from the monolithic guideline and represented a search for a theoretical underpinning to justify the practice of reading the *Book of Poetry* in terms of changing circumstances. The historical circumstances in which his dictum was uttered indicate that metaphysical and critical openness gradually merged into a notion of textual openness, which differs little from the contemporary idea of hermeneutic openness. In the *Chunqiu fanlu*, someone asked why the *Spring and Autumn Annals* did not observe its stated practice of using a proper title for addressing a ruler. Dong replied: "I have heard that the *Book of Poetry* has no constant interpretation; the *Book of Changes* has no constant divination; and the *Spring and Autumn Annals* uses no constant wording. All follow changing circumstances and meanings, but all obey the heavenly principle with a unified purpose."[10] What merits our attention is not just Dong's advocacy of the necessity for recontexualization in accordance with changing circumstances of interpretation; his reasoning touches upon different aspects of hermeneutics. "The *Book of Poetry* has no constant interpretation" concerns literary openness; "The *Book of Changes* has no constant divination" addresses the making of openness, or the poetics of openness; "the *Spring and Autumn Annals* uses no constant wording" recognizes the signifying flux of language. Since the *Book of Poetry* is a writing of poetic form, the *Book of Changes* a writing composed of both verbal and semiotic signs, and the *Spring and Autumn Annals* a writing of prose form, Dong Zhongshu's dictum may be viewed as a pithy but comprehensive expression of the concept of hermeneutic openness in the Chinese tradition.

By the sixth century, the Chinese tradition already formed an inchoate theory of hermeneutic openness that centers on the seminal ideas and concepts like *yiyin* 遺音 (lingering sound), *yiwei* 遺味 (lasting flavor), *congzhi* 重旨 (literally, double intention, equivalent to multivalence), *fuyi* 復義 (literally, multiple meanings, equivalent to polysemy), *wenwai quzhi* 文外曲致 (subtle connotations beyond the text), *bujin zhiyi* 不盡之義 (endless meaning, equivalent to unlimited semiosis).[11]

Origins of Openness in the West

In the West, the idea of hermeneutic openness in the sense of multivalence and polysemy started very late. The early prejudice against poets and poetry practically nipped the idea of openness in the bud. In Plato's "Protagoras," Socrates is described as making derogative comments on differing interpretations: "No one can interrogate poets about what they say, and most often when they are introduced into the discussion some say the poet's meaning is one thing and some another, for the topic is one on which nobody can produce a conclusive argument. The best people avoid such discussions."[12] Plato's open condemnation of poets as liars further made it difficult for ideas of openness to appear in early Western literary thought. By the first century AD, in his *On the Sublime*, Longinus could only timidly suggest that if something "does not leave in the mind [of a man well versed in literature] more food for reflection than the words seem to convey, . . . it cannot rank as true sublimity because it does not survive a first hearing. For that is really great which bears a repeated examination."[13] It was not until the sixteenth century that the idea of literary openness resurfaced, and it had to assume the form of nonliteralness or metaphysical emptiness comparable to the philosophical conception of the Dao in the Chinese tradition. Philip Sidney (1554–1586), in his defense of poetry against Plato's charge of lying, declared, "the poet, he nothing affirms, and therefore never lieth." In his argument, there is already a faint notion of open hermeneutic space: "The poet never maketh any circles about your imagination, to conjure you to believe for true what he writes. He citeth not authorities of other histories, but even for his entry calleth the sweet Muses to inspire into him a good invention; in truth, no laboring to tell you what is, or is not, but what should or should not be."[14]

If in China, a strand of literary openness grew out of an exegetical desire to smooth out inconsistencies, discrepancies, and conflicting views in interpreting the canonical works, interestingly enough, an early practice of literary openness in the West emerged from similar circumstances and was based on similar theoretical rationale. The Christian allegorical interpretation of the *Song of Songs* in the Bible gave rise to a critical practice that sanctions multiple interpretations of the image of the Beloved: she stands for God, Israel, Christ, the Church, or simply an object of erotic love.[15] Just as Chinese Confucian scholars made ingenious and often far-fetched moves to interpret poems of erotic themes as canonical texts of moral virtue or metaphysical ideas, Christian exegetes made similar moves to replace the object of erotic love with morally and theologically meaningful categories. In his comparative study of the *Book of Poetry* and the *Song of Songs*, Longxi Zhang convincingly argues: "The way Christian exegetes use allegorization in order to read the *Song of Songs* as a theologically meaningful and morally edifying composition and thereby to justify its canonicity bears striking similarities to the way many traditional Chinese scholars read part of the Confucian canon, *Shi Jing* or the Book of *Poetry*."[16] The multiple interpretation evolved from a similar reading strategy to smooth out discrepancies and inconsistencies, a strategy, interestingly enough, called "allegorical reading" in both traditions. Although the Christian allegorization is not as multifaceted as the Confucian allegorical exegeses, there is no doubt that it unconsciously promoted an idea of multiplicity, which anticipates the modern idea of openness.

Inquiries into literary openness in the true sense of the word did not appear until modern times in the West, but the belated efforts have been rigorous, systematic, and profound. An interest in literary openness was inaugurated by William Empson's theory of literary ambiguity expounded in his *Seven Types of Ambiguity* and further sustained by New Critical explorations of irony, paradox, tension, and total meaning in the theoretical works of I. A. Richards, Cleanth Brooks, John Crowe Ransom, W. K. Wimsatt, and Monroe C. Beardsley.[17] The exploration of multiple interpretations then went from literary ambiguity all the way to a most radical claim that a text is only a picnic for which the author brings nothing but words while the readers bring all that makes sense.[18] However, only with the advent of Eco's *Opera aperta* [the Open Work] in 1962, the actual concept of openness was articulated for the first time as an aesthetic category that anticipated some major issues of the contemporary debates on and discussions of literature, art, and culture in general. In 1970, Tzvetan Todorov, Hélène Cixous, and Gerard Genette jointly founded an influential journal of literary criticism and literary theory, *Poétique*. In the editor's introduction to the first number of the journal, an open poetics, which embraces both open critical practice and open interpretive practice, was declared: "All play of language and writing, all rhetoric in action, every obliteration of verbal transparency, whether in folklore, in 'mass communications,' in the discourse of dream or madness, in the most modestly constructed texts or the most fortuitous encounters of words—all these enjoy full rights in the realm of modern poetics, which must be a poetics, above all, open."[19] Since then, literary openness has become quite a common word in literary criticism and evaluation, and retained its enduring power because, as one scholar puts it, it is central to two major themes of contemporary literary theory: "the insistence on the element of multiplicity, plurality, or polysemy in art, and the emphasis on the role of the reader, on literary interpretation and responses as an interactive process between reader and text."[20]

Paradoxes in Interpretive Theories

There has been a paradoxical situation with regard to the concept of literary openness in both the Chinese and Western traditions. In the West, since Eco first raised the concept of open work and explored its poetics, other theorists' work has directly or indirectly enriched this concept. Indeed, as new theoretical explorations have pushed the boundaries of hermeneutics further and further, the concept has brought on a reaction. Ironically, Eco, who first articulated on open work and poetics of openness, takes some steps backward and questions some postmodern theories that espouse unlimited interpretations. His two works, the *Limits of Interpretation* and *Interpretation and Overinterpretation*, seem to have marked some retrogression from his former positions on literary openness by their titles alone. In both works, he not only implies that there are certain limits to interpretation but also unequivocally labels some interpretations as "overinterpretation."[21] Eco's criticism of overinterpretation caused some leading theorists (Jonathan Culler for example) to come out with an open defense of overinterpretation.[22] The controversy has not been satisfactorily resolved. And such questions as What is openness? Why is a text open? How is openness achieved? To what extent is the hermeneutic space of a text open? and How can a reader open up a text to generate new interpretations? have remained unanswered.

In China, the situation is even more intriguing. While on the one hand, some thinkers and scholars advocated that poetry has no constant or thoroughgoing interpretation and one of the criteria for judging a good poem is whether it has unending meanings (*bujin zhiyi*), the whole hermeneutic tradition was dominated by an endless search for the original intention of the author, whether he was a sage, a poet, or an essayist. This is especially prominent in the exegesis of the Confucian canons. Under the aegis of various dynastic governments, traditional Chinese scholars brought out a number of so-called correct interpretations of the Confucian canons. Among them, *Wujing zhengyi* 五經正義 (Correct Meanings of the Five Classics) is perhaps the most ambitious project in the endeavor to establish correct interpretations. It is certainly representative of the Chinese hermeneutic impulse to search for the original intention of a text. Because of this dominant trend in the Chinese hermeneutic tradition, Chinese literary thought on openness has remained an unexplored undercurrent despite the fact that ideas similar to and compatible with literary openness have consistently been regarded as a most desirable characteristic feature of first-rate verbal art.

Despite an incredibly early start, up to the present day, literary openness in Chinese hermeneutic tradition has never been systematically explored. Haphazard inquiries have seldom risen to a theoretic level higher than when the seminal ideas were first formulated. Rarely have intuitive insights into openness been brought to confront opposite ideas as though they belonged to separate currents of thought that were not supposed to meet. As a result, something like an intentionalist theory has prevailed in premodern Chinese literary thought. Generally speaking, a text is usually viewed as an enclosure of words that carries the intention of the author and it is the reader's task to retrieve that intention. Mencius (372–289 BC) believed that a poet's original intention could be recovered through adequate reading, as he said: "Therefore, a commentator of the *Shijing* should not allow literary ornaments to harm the wording, nor allow the wording to harm the intent of the poet. To trace the intention of the poet with the understanding of a reader—only this can be said to have grasped the poet's intention."[23] Mencius' statement is a refutation of an interlocutor's reading of a *Shijing* poem in a different context. He was against contextualizing a poem by supplying a different context but in favor of the restoration of the original context of the poem so as to get the original meaning. From a comparative perspective, Mencius' idea reminds us of E. D. Hirsch's intentionalist theory based on Edmund Husserl's view of meaning as an "intentional object."[24] The similarity lies in that both conceive of meaning as an intentional act willed by the author and fixed in a series of signs, which may be retrieved by the use of the same system of signs.[25] Mencius' idea underlay the exegetical assumptions of traditional hermeneutics that constituted the dominant exegetical trend in the Chinese tradition. However, as James Liu rightly points out, despite the dominance of Confucian moralism and Mencian intentionalism, Chinese literary thinkers, without openly repudiating the mainstream hermeneutic thought in interpretation, "quietly developed other modes of interpretation, which were concerned with neither moralization nor authorial intent but with such linguistic aspects of poetry as prosody and verbal style, or such supralinguistic concepts as 'inspired mood [*xinqu*],' 'spirit and tone [*shenyun*],' and 'world [*jingjie*].'"[26] Ironically, while "endless meaning" has consistently been treasured as a hallmark of good poetry, modern Chinese scholars sometimes have to be reminded by similar Western ideas of the fact that the idea of multiple meaning existed in the Chinese tradition.[27]

With the appearance of Deconstruction, the view of a literary text as a closed entity has been completely shattered in the West. Nevertheless, the controversies over literary openness in reading and interpretation are far from being resolved and many related issues remain unsettled. Whether it be in the Western tradition or in the Chinese tradition, an inquiry into hermeneutic openness and open poetics has a multiple significance for cross-cultural studies of literature and art, for the theoretical consideration of hermeneutics, and for the practical uses of literary criticism and creative writing.

Two Hermeneutic Traditions in China

In a provocative book on cross-cultural studies, Roland Barthes calls Japanese culture an "empire of signs." His epithet would apply to Chinese culture equally well.[28] Indeed, traditional China is, as some scholars put it, an "empire of texts" or "empire of writing."[29] It takes pride not just in its numerous texts but also in a long tradition of hermeneutics, which centers on exegeses of various classical texts and interpretive theories on poetry, fiction, and drama. Just as in the West, hermeneutics originated from the religious need to interpret Christian classics, so in China, hermeneutics arose as a result of the doctrinal need to interpret state-approved canons. Since most canons are avowedly Confucian classics, Chinese hermeneutic tradition is predominantly Confucian with a dual emphasis on political indoctrination and moral education. There, however, has existed another more intriguing tradition. If we call the dominant tradition a politico-ethical tradition, the other may be termed a metaphysical-aesthetic tradition because it originated from metaphysical and artistic concerns with the conditions of texts. Without openly challenging the dominant tradition, the "other" tradition engages it in a dynamic interaction, which not only enriches Chinese hermeneutics as a whole but also changes the course of Chinese exegetical practice. In the interaction between the dominant and subordinate traditions, there has been a visible but little studied trend, characterized by a movement from exegetic closure required by Mencius' intentionalist theory to hermeneutic openness guided by a theory of aesthetic suggestiveness. While the Mencian theory dictated the main direction of Chinese hermeneutics, the theory of suggestiveness develops into an intriguing system of hermeneutics, the core principles of which anticipate contemporary theories of reading and interpretation, especially the ideas of literary openness and open poetics.

Objectives and Scope of Inquiry

This is a study of Chinese theories of reading and interpretation, but because reading and writing are inseparably bound and adequate interpretation depends upon substantial knowledge of language representation, it is also a study of writing. In addition to introducing the Chinese system of reading and writing theories, it is preoccupied with a cultural practice that the Chinese had been engaged in for millennia before modern times but that has been largely overlooked. In terms of "modernist" and "postmodern" interpretive practice in the West, it may be called "hermeneutic openness." Of course, the Chinese did not give that cultural practice a conceptual category; nor did they reflect on the phenomenon systematically. What I will do in this study is to give it the conceptual category of "hermeneutic openness," reflect on it systematically, and tease out conceptual insights that may contribute to the formulation of a transcultural open poetics in reading and writing.

This study examines materials of Chinese hermeneutics mostly in the premodern periods. The analytical data are chosen not only for their formative impact upon the development of Chinese literature and culture, traditional and modern, but also for the fact that over history studies of these materials have already constituted the hermeneutic mainstream in the Chinese tradition. The whole study consists of an introduction, eight chapters grouped into four parts, and an epilogue. The introduction opens the ground for the whole study, describing its nature, identifying its objectives, delimiting its scope, establishing its methodology and approach, and raising some theoretical questions to be answered by the whole research.

Part 1 consists of two chapters and will address general and conceptual issues of reading and writing in Chinese intellectual and aesthetic thought. Chapter 1 conducts a conceptual inquiry into some foundational ideas of reading and writing in the Chinese tradition from a cross-cultural perspective and argues for a reconsideration of the significance of these foundational ideas. By bringing Chinese notions of reading and writing by Confucius, Mencius, Zhuangzi, Yang Xiong, Lu Ji, Liu Xie, and other thinkers into a meaningful dialogue with similar notions by modern theorists of hermeneutics like Dilthey, Heidegger, Gadamer, Jacobson, Hirsch, and others, it attempts to chart a course of development through the scattered conceptual ideas and work out a model of reading and writing based on them.

Chapter 2 centers on an inquiry into the conceptual insights of openness in Chinese aesthetic thought. It aims at constructing a conceptual framework for exploring Chinese notions of openness in textual exegeses. This part will synthesize scattered ideas of openness from different historical periods into a system with a philosophical basis and make attempts to redefine intuitive insights in terms of conceptual categories. By examining a series of key terms, concepts, and discourses on Chinese literature in relation to contemporary Western literary theories, it argues that although literary openness is a modern concept, its connotations are by no means alien to Chinese literary thinkers. An abundance of Chinese ideas of suggestiveness not only gestures beyond aesthetic suggestiveness but also effectively forms a Chinese system of open poetics.

Chapters 3 and 4 form part 2. It focuses on the hermeneutic tradition centering on the exegeses of the *Zhouyi* or *Book of Changes*. Adopting a semiotic approach to the *Zhouyi* texts, and examining their relations to interpretations, commentaries, and exegetical methodologies, chapter 3 argues that the *Zhouyi* is an open system of representation and, after examining the mechanisms of its openness, I suggest that although the *Zhouyi* is not generally considered a literary text, *Zhouyi* hermeneutics pioneered for the Chinese tradition an open poetics of reading and writing and formulated some fundamental principles of exegesis that will help open up any text, verbal or imagistic. This chapter will also formulate a semiotic model of reading and representation based on the insights teased out. Chapter 4 focuses on the debates between the *Xiangshu* (Image-Number) school and *Yili* (Meaning-Principle) school in *Zhouyi* hermeneutics with an emphasis on Wang Bi's seminal discourse on the clarification of images. Situating the debate within the larger context of reading and interpretation in the Chinese tradition, I will explore the linguistic, philosophical, and literary significance of the debate beyond the immediate context of *Zhouyi* hermeneutics. By showing how ancient Chinese thinkers have been preoccupied with the conflict between interpretive closure and hermeneutic openness, I suggest that the debate anticipated modern debates in reading and hermeneutics, and its outcome marked a paradigm shift in reading from author-centered exegeses to reader-oriented interpretations.

Part 3 centers on another major hermeneutic tradition: the exegeses of the *Shijing* or *Book of Songs*. In chapter 5, by documenting the exegetical history of a few poems, I suggest that like the *Zhouyi*, the *Shijing* is an open classic, whose textual and extratextual elements contribute to multiple interpretations. Through an examination of the various sources of openness, I advance the notion of an open field as a complex system of signifying relations in a poem. Chapter 6 studies the major approaches to the classic and argues that the *Shijing* commentators and critics from ancient times to the present day have all been bogged down in a search for the original intention or meaning of a given poem. Their blind search, however, has led to a multiplicity of readings and a proliferation of exegetical methodologies and yielded enough insights to form an open poetics of reading and writing. Out of the foundational text in *Shijing* hermeneutics, the Great Preface, I will extract a writing model of intertextual dissemination.

Part 4 turns to textual openness in literary hermeneutics. Chapter 7 concentrates on a few chosen masterpieces from traditional Chinese poetry and makes an attempt to answer a few basic questions: Why does a poem

elicit different interpretations? What makes a poem open to different readings? and To what extent is a poem open to interpretations? The major
objective is, therefore, not to offer new and interesting readings, but to
locate poetic elements that have contributed to the openness of a poem.
Chapter 8 deals with linguistic openness in poetic creation. Since interpretation is understanding, and all understanding is linguistic, special
attention is paid to the conscious and unconscious structuring function of
poetic Chinese in the formation of open space through the mechanisms of
signification and representation. After examining open textual elements,
syntactic ambiguity, and inherently open qualities of poetic Chinese, I
connect the openness of Chinese poetry with oneiric language and the linguistic model of the unconscious, and suggest that a major source of literary openness in traditional Chinese poetry comes from what I call
"linguistic suture," a complex procedure through which the hermeneutic
space of a poem is made open. Linguistic suture is at the core of what I
would call the "poetic unconscious" and a conscious open poetics.

The epilogue engages in a general inquiry into the positive and negative aspects of open poetics in reading and writing. It first examines some
cases of literary inquisitions in Chinese history in relation to controversies
in hermeneutic openness and seeks to clarify some hitherto vague and controversial issues in the postmodern inquiry into the nature, function, and
value of hermeneutic openness. Second, it analyzes a few famous cases of
poetic composition in Chinese history and argues that hermeneutic openness is a positive thing in both reading and writing. It concludes the study
by calling attention to the benefits that may be derived from a self-
conscious awareness of hermeneutic openness and open poetics.

Assumptions and Orientations

In contemporary thought, hermeneutics consists of three related
strands: (1) hermeneutic theory; (2) hermeneutic philosophy; (3) and critical hermeneutics.[30] My study is not concerned with hermeneutics as a
general theory of interpretation, or as a philosophy of life, or as a tool of
critique. Because of my preoccupation with some major hermeneutic practices in the Chinese tradition, it seeks to explore the interaction between
the politico-moralistic mainstream and the metaphysico-aesthetical undercurrent and its impact upon the perception of the nature of the text,
author, reader, and exegesis with an emphasis on the open trend in reading
and interpretation. In dealing with literary hermeneutics, I have blurred
the subtle distinction between "theory of literature" and "literary theory,"
advanced by James J. Y. Liu: "the former being concerned with the basic

nature and functions of literature, the latter with aspects of literature, such as form, genre, style, and technique."[31] In my study, "open poetics" certainly refers to "literary theory," but "literary openness" is inescapably tangled in "theory of literature." Whereas openness is defined in terms of the idea of unlimited possibilities in interpretation, open poetics refers to how openness is conceived and made in writing practice.

My first assumption is that hermeneutic openness is a cross-cultural phenomenon, and the impulse for artistic openness in literature has deep roots in the Chinese and Western traditions. As history advanced, it eventually blossomed into a major concern in literary thought, East and West. Ironically, insights of openness generally took the form of blindness in Paul de Man's conception, especially in the Chinese tradition. For over two millennia, China has produced a staggering amount of exegesis filled with insights of openness. These insights, however, are paradoxical in nature. Many theorists, commentators, and exegetes have proclaimed the endless meaning of a text to be a supreme goal for a literary work, but more have insisted that the aim of interpretation is to seek out the original intention of the author. Few have been willing to acknowledge the openness of a text, still less to recognize the profound implications of their theories, commentaries, and exegeses for a conception of openness and open poetics. By examining selected materials central to the Chinese hermeneutic tradition, *Yijing* and *Shijing* hermeneutics, traditional poetics and literary thought, and commentaries on classical poetry, this study hopes, with the aid of contemporary theories on linguistics, semiotics, psychoanalysis, and representation, to tease out enough insights of openness to construct a Chinese open poetics.

My second assumption is that the Chinese hermeneutic tradition has traversed a road of development from exegetic closure to interpretive openness similar to that of the Western tradition. But I suggest that the Chinese tradition arrives at that destination through a quite different route. This study is therefore also an attempt to explore hermeneutic openness from a comparative and cross-cultural perspective. Theory-driven, it is not a study of critical practice but one of poetics, for even in the discussion of individual works, the primary attention will be directed to how a text generates its meanings, and the final goal for critical analysis is not so much to enrich our understanding of a particular text as to tease out insights of openness and to advance open strategies of reading and writing. From a purely theoretical perspective, this study will explore not only the essential factors in theories of reading and writing, such as author, reader, text, context, and meaning, but also these central issues: what constitutes openness in reading and interpretation, how openness is manifested in a particular work, to what extent a conscious use of language and writing strategies may give rise to different degrees of openness, and how significant an open poetics is for the making of verbal art. Although its immediate aim seems to be one of identifying elements of openness and mechanisms of openness in the selected materials and formulating a hermeneutics of openness in the Chinese tradition, the larger aim is to find new ways of conceptualizing reading and writing and to work toward a cross-cultural open poetics.

Part I

Conceptual Inquiries into Reading and Openness

Chapter 1

Theories of Reading and Writing in
Intellectual Thought

Reading in a Comparative Context

In contemporary literary thought, theories of reading have constituted an international subject of inquiry. They saw their heyday in the last quarter of the twentieth century. Many international theorists, literary or otherwise, have engaged in this subject at some time and to some extent. The direct reason for the popular interest in the subject may have been what can be called the "theoretical turn" in literary studies, driven by the advancement in hermeneutics, psychoanalysis, linguistics, semiotics, representation, mass communication, and so on. The fundamental reason for its popularity, however, seems to lie in the basic question people from different cultures and traditions have been asking themselves throughout the ages: How can one read a text adequately? All the essential factors in theories of reading, such as author, reader, text, context, and meaning, center on this core question.

Whether in the East or West, conceptual inquiries into reading grew out of the practical need to interpret canonical texts. In the West, the rise of theories of reading as a category of inquiry may be said to be concurrent with the rise of classical hermeneutics in the eighteenth century, though sporadic inquires into the topic appeared much earlier. In China, the beginning of conceptual inquires into reading may be traced to the fourth century BC. Very early in China, reading constituted an integral part of cultured life and an essential procedure for scholarship. Conceptual notions of reading began to emerge in high antiquity, as Chinese thinkers engaged themselves in interpretations of classics, history, poetry, arts, and metaphysics. Aware of the gap between language and thought, or *yan* (words) and *zhi* (ideas) in Chinese terminology, they became concerned with the question of how to read a text adequately. Since then, theories of reading have formed a significant part of traditional Chinese hermeneutic thought. Scholars who have pondered on reading are numerous, but their insights are scattered in philosophical treatises, commentaries, prefaces, postfaces, personal letters, and random reading notes on the margins of a text, and even in literary texts themselves.

In this first chapter, I will bring Chinese conceptual notions of reading by some early thinkers into a meaningful dialogue with similar notions by modern theorists of hermeneutics in the West. In so doing, I attempt to reconsider the foundational ideas of reading and interpretation in the Chinese tradition and hope to reconceptualize scattered conceptual ideas into a model of reading. Among early Chinese thinkers, Mencius 孟子 (c. 372–289 BC) and Zhuangzi 莊子 (c. 369–286 BC) are the pioneers in the conceptual inquiries into reading. Although Mencius and Zhuangzi are separated from contemporary Western theorists by time, space, and tradition, their ideas of reading are amazingly similar to those of contemporary theorists. With a comparative move that seeks to break the barriers of time, space, and culture, I wish to explore whether people's conceptions of the nature, rationale, and epistemology of reading share similarities across historical periods and cultural backgrounds, what insights the ancient Chinese ideas may offer into theories and practice of reading, and to what extent we can bring traditional Chinese ideas into a meaningful dialogue with contemporary Western theories.

Mencius' Positive Thesis of Reading

In traditional literary thought, Mencius and Zhuangzi started their inquiries into the problematics of reading in approximately the same historical period. Mencius (c. 372–289 BC), an older contemporary of Zhuangzi (c. 369–286 BC), inaugurated the inquiry into reading with his famous notion "*yiyi nizhi, shiwei dezhi* 以意逆志，是為得之"[1] (to use one's understanding to trace it back to what was on the mind of the author—this is how one grasps the meaning of a text). As this idea shows his optimistic belief that reading can get what is meant in a text, his view may be called a positive statement. Mencius' positive view of reading came from his answer to the inquiry of one of his students with regard to the understanding of poetic lines in a poem from the *Shijing* (the *Book of Songs*).

Xianqiu Meng, one of his students, accepted Mencius' claim that when the sage king Yao was old and abdicated the throne to Shun, Shun did not regard himself as the ruler to whom Yao was a subject, but quoting from a poem in the *Shijing*—"Of all that is under Heaven,/No place is not the king's land;/And to the farthest shores of all the land,/No man is not the king's subject"[2]—he questioned whether it was appropriate not to regard Shun's blind old father as subject after Shun became the king.[3] To this questioning, Mencius made the following statement concerning the reading of the poem:

> This is indeed from the *Book of Songs*, but it is not what you have said. The poem dwells on the poet's inability to care for his parents when he is laboring in royal service. It says, "Isn't it the royal business? Why should I labor diligently alone?" Therefore, a commentator of the *Shijing* should not allow literary ornaments to harm the wording, nor allow the wording to harm the intent of the poet. To trace the intention of the poet with the understanding of a reader—only this can be said to have grasped what is expressed in a poem. The poem "Yunhan" says: "Of the remaining multitudes of the Zhou, not a single person survived." If these words were to be taken literally, then this means that there was not any person left in the Zhou.[4]

Mencius' statement is a refutation of a distorted reading that resulted from contextualizing a poem by supplying a different context. He argued for the restoration of the original context so as to get the original meaning. His reply not only advances a practical method of reading but also implies an inchoate theory of reading. As a practical method, his idea opposes far-fetched readings that result from splitting the text, ignoring the context, and doggedly sticking to the wording of a text. As a theory of reading, Mencius may be the first Chinese thinker to view reading as part of a communication process and an act of decoding within a context.

Mencius' statement involves a number of central issues on reading: textual meaning, authorial intention, context, contextualization, and the reader's approach to a text. Mencius touched upon several issues in a conceptual inquiry into reading. First, he proposed that the meaning of a text should be decided in its own context, not on a few separate elements. Xianqiu Meng's reading was problematic and wrong simply because he committed the common error in reading: to pick a strand of meaning by separating a discourse block from its context. Second, Mencius emphasized the importance of proper contextualization in the reading of a text. He argued against contextualizing a poem by supplying a different context but in favor of restoring the original context of the poem so as to get the original meaning. Third, he argued against understanding words literally and allowing literary embellishment to hurt the intention of the author. Fourth, he believed that a poet's original intention could be recovered through adequate and sensible reading. His proposed method: "one uses one's own understanding to trace it back to what was originally in the writer's mind" constituted the core of his positive thesis on reading.

Mencius' thesis, when schematized, forms a model that is in essence comparable to the hermeneutic model based on Roman Jakobson's model of verbal communication: "The ADDRESSER sends a MESSAGE to the ADDRESSEE. To be operative the message requires a CONTEXT referred to ("referent" in another, somewhat ambiguous, nomenclature), seizable by the addressee, and either verbal or capable of being verbalized; a CODE fully, or at least partially, common to the addresser and addressee (or in other words, to the encoder and decoder of the message); and, finally, a CONTACT, a physical channel and psychological connection between the addresser and the addressee, enabling both of them to enter and stay in communication."[5] Although Mencius did not use specific terms like addresser, addressee, context, message, contact and code, almost all of Jakobson's terms are implicitly covered by Mencius' statement. The poet is the addresser. Mencius and his student are the addressees. The poem in its textual form is a point of contact, and *wen* and *ci* are the code; the poet's intent *zhi* is the encoded message; his explanation about the poem's origin forms the context. Mencius' and Xianqiu Meng's acts of reading the poem constitute decoding.

Reading is different from verbal communication in that the addresser is only implied. But despite the addresser's absence, Mencius believed that the process of communication is intact and the communication channel is unblocked because the reader can use *wen* and *ci* (language) as a sure tool to generate his *yi* or understanding and then trace it back to what was originally on the mind of the author. In Mencius' opinion, the encoded message from the author could be decoded by the reader so long as the reader places his act of decoding in a sensible context. The decoded message could, at least in principle, match the encoded message. It is in this sense, that his optimistic belief in verbal communication and decoding may be labeled a positive thesis on reading in Chinese tradition.

Mencius' positive view of reading is based on a positive belief in language as an adequate means of communicating the author's intention. His conviction in language's communicative adequacy is reflected in his famous saying, *zhiyan* (knowing language). Gongsun Chou, another of Mencius' students, asked in what Mencius excelled. The latter replied: "I understand [through] language."[6] When Gongsun Chou asked, *"He wei zhiyan* (What is meant by *zhiyan*)?"[7] Mencius explained: "If someone's words are one-sided, I know what has clouded his mind. If someone's words are excessive, I know in what he has indulged himself. If someone's words are warped, I know how he has strayed from the right path. When someone's words are evasive, I know where he is at his wit's end."[8] Stephen Owen rightly points out: "Mencius' 'understanding language' is not simply an understanding of the meaning of words and certainly not an understanding that merely reflects or reproduces what the speaker thinks the words say. Mencius' knowledge of language is a knowledge of what the words reveal about the speaker, what they make manifest."[9]

Mencius' idea of "knowing language" seems to have evolved out of a saying in the *Zuozhuan* 左傳, attributed to Confucius. Confucius was quoted as saying: "The record has it that language adequately conveys one's intent, and literary embellishment makes one's language adequate. If one does not speak, who will know what is on his mind? If his language lacks embellishment, it will not go far."[10] Thus, it is not inappropriate to say that Mencius' idea of "knowing a person through his language" represents a thesis in the Confucian school of thought.

Mencius viewed writing and reading as a connected process of communication between the writer and the reader. The writer's *yi* or thought is the source of a text. It is transmitted through the text to the reader, who receives it through his own *yi* or thought. Conceptualized as such, the text is like a conveyance belt, which can transmit its content from the writer to the reader. In reading, so long as the reader is adequately trained and uses contextualization sensibly, he will be able to get what the writer intended through the text. Clearly, Mencius regarded meaning as thought willed by the author (*zhi*), permanently recorded in a series of words (*ci*), and retrievable by the reader's understanding (*yi*). In this sense, his idea comes close to E. D. Hirsch's intentionalist theory. Like Mencius, Hirsch is concerned with whether an interpretation is the correct meaning of the text. He wants to locate a criterion for validating interpretations that does not depend totally on the reader's subjective reading. The criterion that he proposes is the authorial intention that produced the text. The goal of interpretation is, at least in principle, to reconstruct that authorial intention. Hirsch's theory is based on Edmund Husserl's view of meaning as an "intentional object."[11] The Husserlian view conceives of meaning as a wordless act willed by the author, which is fixed in a series of codes for all time and may be understood through the same system of codes. We can see a basic similarity in Mencius' and Hirsch' theories of reading. Both conceive of writing as an intentional act willed by the author and fixed in a series of words, the original intention of which may be retrieved by decoding the words.[12] For this reason, I may call Mencius a premodern Husserlian, and his idea of reading is, as James J. Y. Liu calls it,[13] an intentionalist theory.

Zhuangzi's Counterstatement

Zhuangzi, who was slightly younger than Mencius, unwittingly entangled Mencius in an argument though they might never have even heard of each other. Unlike Mencius, Zhuangzi was keenly aware of the problematic relationship between the author and his writing and adopted a negative view of reading. He totally rejected the idea of reading as a reliable process of communication and mistrusted language as a tool for recovering the author's intention. In terms of Mencius' positive view of reading, Zhuangzi's view, as Stephen Owen aptly puts it,[14] may be viewed as a counterstatement. His negative thesis was presented in the famous parable of "Wheelwright Bian":

> Duke Huan was reading in his hall. Wheelwright Pien, who was cutting a wheel just outside the hall, put aside his hammer and chisel and went in. There he asked Duke Huan, "What do those books you are reading say?" The duke answered, "These are the words of the Sages." The wheelwright said, "Are the Sages still around?" And the duke answered, "They're dead." Then the wheelwright said, "Well, what you're reading then is no more than the dregs of the ancients."
>
> The duke became very angry with the wheelwright and threatened to put him to death if the latter failed to offer a reasonable explanation for his claim. The wheelwright explained his claim in terms of his own profession and told the duke why it was impossible to pass on something to another person through transmission. His conclusion was: "The ancients have died and, along with them, that which cannot be transmitted. Therefore what you are reading is nothing more than the dregs of the ancients."[15]

As far as reading is concerned, Zhuangzi's parable offers these conceptual insights. First, long before the postmodern age, Zhuangzi proclaimed one of the postmodern tenets in reading and writing: the author is dead. A casual comparison tells us that the essential spirit Zhuangzi expressed in this parable is exactly what Barthes means by his famous saying, "the death of the author." Second, contrary to Mencius' positive conviction, Zhuangzi dismissed any text as capable of transmitting the writer's ideas and thoughts to the reader. This total skepticism was reiterated in another statement:

> Writing is that by which people of the world treasure the Dao. Writing is no more than words. Words have something valuable. What make words valuable are ideas. Ideas follow certain things. What is followed by ideas cannot be transmitted by words, but people of the world transmit writing

because they cherish words. Although people of the world cherish words, still I don't think words are worth cherishing because what people treasure is not that which deserves cherishing.[16]

Zhuangzi expressed an idea about language and writing similar to the reputed Confucian saying in the *Xicizhuan* [*Appendixes to the Book of Changes*]: "*Shu bu jin yan, yan bu jin yi* (Writing cannot fully express words; words cannot fully express ideas)."[17] Clearly, Zhuangzi did not agree with Mencius on the capacity of language to convey ideas and feelings. In the context of modern hermeneutics, his view represents perhaps the earliest rejection in the world of Husserl's intentionalist theory, which views meaning as a wordless act willed by the author, fixed in a series of codes and may be transmitted to posterity. Zhuangzi continued to tell us why an intentionalist theory does not work:

> Those which can be seen when one looks are shapes and colors; those which can be heard when one listens are epithets and sounds. What a great pity that people in the world consider shapes and colors, epithets and sounds as adequate means to obtain another person's inner feelings. If indeed shapes and colors, epithets and sounds are not adequate means to obtain another person's inner feelings, then "a wise person will not speak; he who speaks is not wise." But how can worldly persons understand this?[18]

Step by step, Zhuangzi dismantled Mencius' communicative model of writing and reading and vehemently argued that writing cannot transmit the Dao; words cannot transmit ideas; language cannot transmit subtle thoughts. Because of the inadequacy of speech and language as a means of communication, Zhuangzi dismissed writings in general. Perhaps, this may have inspired later Chan Buddhists' dismissal of language and books as instruments for transmitting the truth. In a way, his idea about the transmission of the Dao comes close to the Hermetic thought regarding the truth of the world. According to Umberto Eco's study, Hermeticism maintains: "Truth is secret and any questioning of the symbols and enigmas will never reveal ultimate truth but displaces the secret elsewhere."[19] The epistemological basis of Hermeticism is "the gnostic conviction that human salvation depends on revealed knowledge of God and of human and natural creations."[20] Hermetic thought turns the whole world into a linguistic phenomenon and yet like Zhuangzi, Hermetic believers cherish profound mistrust for language's power of communication. Language cannot communicate truth; truth can only be personally experienced through moments of revelation. Interestingly, Zhuangzi upheld similar ideas, especially with regard to the Dao and language:

Speaking is not a puff of breath. A Speaker has words, but what he says cannot be determined by any special means. . . . What beclouds the Dao to such an extent that truth and falsehood appear? What beclouds language to such a degree that right and wrong appear? To what extent has the Dao reached so that it does not exist? To what extent has speech existed so that it becomes inappropriate? The Dao was beclouded by small achievement. Speech was beclouded by florid words. Hence, there arose the debate between the Confucianists and Moists over right and wrong.[21]

In Zhuangzi's opinion, limited knowledge will only hinder people from accessing the Dao; a plethora of words will only harm language's function as a tool of communication. The debate between the Confucianists and Moists only makes right and wrong more confounded. While attributing the difficulty of accessing the Dao and language to limited knowledge and plethora of words, Zhuangzi also identified the slippery nature of language as part of the difficulty: "A speaker has words, but what he says can not be determinate by any particular means." Like a modern theorist of language, Zhuangzi further attributed the difficulty to the slippage of meaning in language representation: "There is no object which is not 'that'; nor is there any object which is not 'this.' From the position of 'that,' the position of 'this' will not show itself. But from the position of 'this,' the speaker knows it is 'this.' Hence it is said that 'that' grows out of 'this'; 'this' also depends on 'that.' . . . 'This' is also 'that.' 'That' is also 'This.'"[22]

Zhuangzi noticed the slippage of meaning due to subjective positions in representation and understanding. In *Problems in General Linguistics*, Emile Benveniste arrived at a similar understanding: "There is no concept 'I' that incorporates all the *I*'s that are uttered at every moment in the mouths of all speakers, in the sense that there is a concept 'tree' to which all the individual uses of *tree* refer. . . . Then, what does *I* refer to? To something very peculiar which is exclusively linguistic: *I* refers to the act of individual discourse in which it is pronounced, and by this it designates the speaker."[23]

While Zhuangzi viewed "this" and "that" as reversible categories because of subjective positions, Benveniste describes the pronounced "I" and "you" as signifiers, which are only able to signify their meanings in concrete discursive situations. Except for the different usage of pronouns, both Zhuangzi and Benveniste arrived at the same understanding: these pronouns always imply a speaker and a listener in dialogue. The roles of the speaker and listener are endlessly reversible as the pronouns that depend upon them. The speaker acts as a speaker for one moment and will become a listener for another moment. The pronouns possess only a periodic meaning and have no standardized and permanent significance. There is no doubt that Zhuangzi's idea anticipated Benveniste's more abstract view. Because of the indeterminate nature of language, Zhuangzi viewed meaning as unstable and slippery and the intention of the author as untransmittable to and unattainable by the reader. In a sense, his idea also anticipated the deconstructive view of language and meaning based on Heidegger's language philosophy. The Heideggerians contend that meaning, including authorial meaning, is not as stable and determinate as the Husserlians claim. The reason it is so is because meaning is the product of signs, which have something slippery about them. It is difficult, if not impossible, to know what an intention or meaning is. Moreover, an author's intention is itself a complex text, which may be variously interpreted like any other text.[24] For this reason, we may call Zhuangzi a premodern Heideggerian, and his view of reading a premodern deconstructive theory of reading.

In his theoretical inquiry of interpretation, Eco relates some of the contemporary theory of textual interpretation to the Hermetic legacy in the Western tradition and finds some similarity between Hermetism and Gnosticism on the one hand and many contemporary approaches to texts (especially the Deconstructive school of criticism) on the other. Because those strands of interpretive theories share with Hermetism the similar denial of language's power of communication and the refusal to grant a text its final and attainable meaning, Eco satirically labels those interpretive theories "a Hermetic approach to texts."[25] Without Eco's satirical implication, I wish to call Zhuangzi's ideas concerning reading a Hermetic theory because his ideas share with Hermetism the basic Gnostic principle. In denying language the power to transmit the Dao or communicate meaning and in refusing to read books because they are incapable of conveying the author's meaning, and in advocating an intuitive approach to communication, Zhuangzi's approach to texts may certainly be called a Hermetic approach.

Mencius' Hermeneutic Circle

I have presented Mencius' and Zhuangzi's basic ideas on reading as a positive thesis and a counterstatement. This is the general drift of their thought. However, if we treat their views on reading as two dichotomies that absolutely oppose each other, we would be committing the error of oversimplification with regard to their theories in particular and to the theories of reading in general. Both of them were aware of the complexity of reading due to the nature of language and representation; and both of them attempted to supplement their major ideas with modifications and further elaborations. Their further elaborations on reading seemed as though they were carrying on a dialogue, each trying to answer the other's interlocutions.

Mencius seemed to have been aware of the problematic aspect of his main thesis, which may be boiled down to one question: If you believe that one can form an understanding of a text and match it with what was intended by the author through the text, how can you verify that what you have grasped is the original intention of the author now that he is long gone? As though in response to Zhuangzi's declaration that the author is dead, he supplemented his main thesis with another idea: *zhiren lunshi* (to know the writer and his world):

> A good scholar of a community will make friends with other good schol-
> ars of the community. A good scholar in a state will make friends with other
> good scholars of the state. A good scholar under heaven will make friends
> with other good scholars under heaven. Because it is not enough to make
> friends with other good scholars under heaven, a good scholar will also go
> back in time to discuss people of the ancient past. Is it acceptable to sing
> an ancient person's poetry and read his books without knowing about this
> person? For this reason, one [needs] to discuss the time in which the
> ancients lived. This is how to make friends with the ancients.[26]

Mencius meant to say: a good scholar should befriend not only other scholars in his community, his state, and under heaven but also ancient scholars in the past. When people today want to make friends with people of the past, it is impossible for them to communicate directly; they can only indirectly communicate through the writings left behind by the ancient people. But to correctly understand the writings of ancient people, we must have knowledge of the persons who wrote those books and of the times they lived in. By knowing the person and discussing his time (*zhi qiren, lun qishi*), we may be able to contextualize his writings and fully understand them. Mencius' statement was originally not concerned with reading per se but with how to make friends with ancient people. However, because making friends with ancient people has to be done through reading ancient people's books, his remark directly concerns reading as well. Likewise, although the central idea in the statement "to know a person by discussing his time" was not directly related to his central thesis on reading, "to use one's understanding to trace it back to the author's intention," in the large context of his thought and in view of the fact that both statements are concerned with reading, the two ideas are implicitly linked together.

Later scholars noticed the relevance of the two ideas and joined them into a connected thesis. Gu Zhen 顧鎮, a scholar of the Qing dynasty, made an apt comment on the inner relationship of Mencius' separate ideas in his poetic criticism: "It is impossible to know about someone without considering his time. Likewise, it is impossible to trace back to what was on the writer's mind without knowing about the person. . . . Therefore, one must discuss a writer's time and learn about his person. Only after this can one adopt Mencius' idea of tracing one's understanding to the intention of the writer."[27] Gu Zheng made explicit what was implicit in Mencius' original statements: without "knowing the writer and his time," "to use one's understanding to trace it back to what was on the mind of the author" is not entirely possible, because there is no way to verify whether the reader's *yi* (understanding) could match the author's *zhi* (intention). With adequate knowledge about the author and his time, the subjectiveness of the reader's understanding can be minimized. When the two ideas are combined, they complement each other and make a reader's reading substantially objective.

Wang Guowei 王國維 (1877–1927), the last traditional Chinese literary theorist, also came to the realization that the two ideas about reading expressed in separate places in the *Mencius* should be viewed as a connected argument. In his comment on Mencius' ideas of reading, Wang states:

> Mencius' view of reading poetry is superb: "A commentator of the *Shijing* should not allow literary ornaments to harm the wording, nor allow the wording to harm the intent of the poet. To trace the intention of the poet with the understanding of a reader—only this can be said to have grasped what is expressed in a poem." It is up to me to trace the idea to its origin, but what is intently on the mind belongs to the ancient writer. What can I do to make my grasp of meanings retain the intention of the ancient writer? In talking about this technique of reading, Mencius said: "Is it acceptable to chant a person's poetry and read his books without knowing about this person? Because of this, one must discuss the time of the writer." Thus, one can know about the writer through his time and trace his intention through the knowledge about him. In this way there will be few ancient poems that cannot be understood.[28]

The joining together of the two ideas in separate statements filled the gap left by the death of the author and made the communication model expressed in *yiyi nizhi* theoretically sound. In his original model imparted in Mencius' main thesis, there are these elements: the reader (*shuoshiren* or poetry commentator), code (*wen* and *ci*), text (*shi* or poetry), local context (the context of the writing), and an interpretative strategy (to use one's understanding to trace it back to the author). Now it adds some other essential elements: author (ancient writers) and historical context (writer's time). With the added elements, Mencius' model of reading is complete.

If we examine the complete model, however, we will notice that Mencius' advocated theory of reading is somewhat tautological or circular. If I may synthesize Mencius' ideas, the circular pattern of reading is clearer. *Yiyi nizhi* (to use one's understanding to trace it back to what was on the mind of the author) is the act of reading. Reading is done through language. Through language, the reader may learn about the author's intention. But words alone are not the key for latecomers to unlock the mystery of the author's intent. The reader needs to go back in time to learn about the author. But how can one know about the author? To know about the author, the reader needs to know about his time. How can the reader know about the author's time? The answer returns to where it starts: to read his poetry and books. In a nutshell, one needs to read a writer's books to know the writer and his time and to know his person and time in order to better understand his books.

The circularity of Mencius' model is not problematic but insightful. In a way, Mencius' model of reading reminds us of Schleiermacher's discovery of the hermeneutic law: every idea of the author is invariably related to the unity of an organically structured subject, and of his famous "hermeneutic circle": interpretation is circular in nature. The circularity of interpretation concerns the relation of parts to the whole. The interpretation of each part is dependent on the interpretation of the whole, which is also dependent on the interpretation of each part. It is in the constant interaction between the part and whole that adequate interpretation is achieved.[29] Of course, in Mencius' model, the whole consists of not only a writer's complete works but also his historical time. In dwelling on the importance of knowing the person and his time, Mencius seemed to have come up with a theory of interpretation that comes close to the central idea of hermeneutics in contemporary theory. The central problem of hermeneutics is one of overcoming alienating distanciation: With the death of the author and the elapse of time, how can a work cut off from its original historical circumstances communicate with or be understood by the reader of a different culture and time? Hermeneutic understanding results from an authentic dialogue between the past and the present, which occurs when there is a "fusion of horizons" between the text and reader in Hans-Georg Gadamer's conception of interpretation.[30]

Gadamer's view is quite complicated. Briefly, it proposes a dialogic relationship between the reader and the author. On the one hand, a text is a historical product produced by an author using a specific system of codes at a given historical time. Its historicity is therefore essential to the consideration of its meanings. On the other hand, the reader who interprets the text is grounded in his own historicity, which is also essential to the process of interpretation. At the beginning of interpretation, because of the difference and distance between the two historicities, the text resists the reader's efforts to turn it into something amenable to his perspective. However, when the two historicities merge into one experience as a result of the fusion of the two different viewpoints, a breakthrough in interpretation appears. The text as a meaningful human product has its intentionality. The reader has his own intentionality in approaching the text. When the two kinds of intentionality meet in the encounter of reading, and when the two kinds of historicities are adequately taken note of, there can be a fusion of the author's and reader's horizons, which gives rise to meaning.[31]

Mencius' notion on reading makes a similar proposal. Faced with a text produced in the past, he advised the reader first to form an understanding of his own (*yi*). This is the reader's intentionality. Then, the reader should use his own understanding to trace it back in history to the author's intentionality (*zhi*). When the reader's intentionality (*yi*) matches with the author's intentionality (*zhi*), there is a proper grasp of the meaning of the text. Mencius was keenly aware of the difficulty of matching the reader's intentionality with the author's intentionality, a difficulty made doubly difficult by the gap between the past and present, the author's and reader's historicities, and by the reader's subjective judgment. But he did not abandon the hope for a reading model that views reading as a verifiable reenactment of the subjective experiences. I have mentioned that his idea of tracing back to the author's original intention resembles Hirsch's intentionalist theory, but in his supplementary idea about historical circumstances, one's own understanding, and imagined dialogues between the author and reader, we may find insights of similarity shared by Heidegger's existentialist hermeneutics.

In his *Being and Time*, Heidegger proclaims a hermeneutics that stresses human beings' locatedness in both history and language. In tackling the problem of understanding, Heideggerian hermeneutics rejects a disinterested inquiry into another person's mind. In its place, it emphasizes one's embeddedness in a temporal world the meaning of which precedes him but of which he has a tacit understanding. We exist understandingly, and the aim of interpretation is to make explicit this preunderstanding that we already have of our being-in-the-world.[32] In Mencius' central thesis, the reader's understanding (*yi*) is precisely a preunderstanding generated by the reader's mental activity and shaped by his temporal situation. Heidegger's existential model also suggests that literature is less the expression of an individual's thoughts or intentions than the raising to consciousness of a historical sense and a world. Through reading, we experience in literature a world portrayed by the author rather than particular and idiosyncratic mental states or intentions. In the following, I will demonstrate that Mencius' ideas of "using the reader's understanding to trace it back to the author's intentionality" and "knowing the writer and his time" are endowed with similar insights into reading.

According to Heidegger, all human inquiries are circular. In fact, the very notion of inquiry presupposes circularity and foreknowledge, because a lack of prior knowledge of what one seeks would practically prevent any possibility of questioning. Heidegger presents this idea at the very opening of his *Being and Time* as "a knowing search."[33] He further asserts: "Inquiry, as a kind of seeking, must be guided beforehand by what is sought. So the meaning of Being must already be available to us in some way."[34] Heidegger's existential-ontological hermeneutics explicitly and implicitly suggests that the exploration of Being and the interpretation of a text are essentially one and the same matter in the sense that just as being is somewhat already known in advance by the explorer, so the being (or form) of a text that can be repeatedly read must already be known somewhat by the reader. Interestingly, Mencius came to an understanding of reading that displays similar insight. Mencius' idea, "to use one's understanding to trace it back to what was on the mind of the author," suggests that a reading is invariably a kind of knowing search, for, as the word *yi* (reader's idea or understanding) indicates, the reader has already formulated a kind of understanding, and what needs to be done is to verify its relatedness to the author's intentionality. Heidegger's claim, "Any interpretation which is to contribute understanding, must already have understood what is to be interpreted,"[35] should serve as a most apt footnote to Mencius' central thesis of reading. To some, Mencius' central idea may smack of subjective presuppositions. Again, Heidegger's existential hermeneutics comes to its defense: "An interpretation is never [despite those committed to objectivity, including Husserl] a presuppositionless apprehending of something presented to us."[36]

In terms of Heidegger's existential hermeneutics, Mencius' hermeneutic circle is not a vicious one, for it emphasizes the author's and reader's locatedness in history, and the foreknowledge or foreconception formulated at the outset of reading keeps being enriched by circular readings. Mencius' idea of "knowing the writer and his time" is an effective means to overcome alienating distanciation, enabling the reader to enter the world created by the author in his writing. As a whole, Mencius' theory of reading, especially the complete model that combines the central ideas in his statements and reading practice, touches upon both the Husserlian and Heideggerian hermeneutics for adequate reading.

In spite of his interest in the author, Mencius is a text-oriented theorist of reading. He believed in the text as a medium that inscribes the author's totality: his personality and social context. This belief anticipated Edward Said's alternative to Foucault's conception of the author as a discursive function, which is "to take the author's career as wholly oriented towards and synonymous with the production of a text." Said's suggestion that we should view an author's career as a course "whose record is his work and whose goal is the integral text that adequately represents the efforts expended on its behalf" would serve as a most apt elucidation of Mencius' idea, "*zhiren lunshi* (to know a person through his time)," and of his rhetorical question, "Is it acceptable to chant a person's poetry and read his books without knowing about this person?" Mencius' emphasis on the relationship between the text and its author also anticipated Said's understanding: ". . . the text is a multidimensional structure extending from the beginning to the end of the writer's career. A text is the source and the aim of a man's desire to be an author, it is the form of his attempts, it contains the elements of his coherence, and in a whole range of complex and differing ways it incarnates the pressures upon the writer of his psychology, his time, his society."[37]

By emphasizing *zhi* (intent or intention), Mencius considered writing as an intentional act. Nowadays, it is suspect to talk about intentions in literary studies due to the "intentional fallacy." Mencius' idea of *yiyi nizhi* (to use one's own understanding to trace it back to the original intention of the writer) coupled with the idea of *zhiren lun shi* (to know the writer and his time through his writing) does not smack of intentional fallacy (the author's pretextual or retrospective purpose), but may restore part of authorial intention to its rightful place in the domains of literary studies. His idea amounts to an inclusive totality of the relationship between the writer and the reader and anticipates Said's idea of "beginning intention." Like most modern theorists, Said dismisses a simplistic view of intention, which regards meaning as merely what the author intends to convey in a text, and proposes notion of created inclusiveness that develops out of the totality of a relationship between the text and its author.[38]

An overview of Mencius' complete statement on reading reveals that he firmly believed in the effectiveness of language to convey one's inner thoughts, and even involuntarily to reveal a person's personality, predilection, and behavior. It also reveals that Mencius viewed writing as constituting outer and inner spaces. Its inner space inscribes the writer's conscious meaning (*yi*), willed intention (*zhi*), and personality structure (*qi*). Its outer space covers the wording (*yan*), literary embellishment (*wen*), and text (*wenzhang*). Language is the ultimate form of mediation that connects the inner and outer spaces. It imparts most perfectly and yet problematically the correspondence between the inner and outer spaces. Through language, one can perceive the totality of a writer by tracing from *wen* (literary embellishment) and *yan* (wording) to *yi* (thought), *zhi* (intention), and *qi* (personality). Mencius' theory of reading is optimistically positive—reading can objectively reflect the original intention of the author and the conditions of his time—but it did not directly address the linguistic skepticism raised by Zhuangzi and the *Xicizhuan*. His theory did not deal directly with the anxiety that can be constantly troubling to a writer, an anxiety expressed by many thinkers and writers. It was succinctly summarized by Lu Ji 陸機 (261–303): "I am constantly troubled by the anxiety that my ideas are inadequate for objects of the world and my writings incapable of capturing my ideas."[39]

Zhuangzi's Wordless Communication

In terms of Mencius' positive theory of reading, Zhuangzi's negative thesis can be said to be one of agnosticism bordering on nihilism. I have mentioned that Zhuangzi's negative view of reading is derived from a language philosophy that views language as an inadequate means of communication. He was not the only one who held this view. His idea was echoed in the *Xicizhuan*, where Confucius was quoted as saying: "Writing cannot fully express speech; speech cannot fully express ideas 書不盡言，言不盡意."[40] But having voiced an opinion about the inadequacy of language and writing as a means of communication of ideas, Confucius hastily added a remark to qualify his negative view of language and representation: "The sages established images to fully express their thought, designed hexagrams to fully express the true and false conditions of affairs, and attached verbalizations to fully express what they wanted to say."[41] Thus, the *Xicizhuan* adopted a dialectical view of the relationship between language and thought. If we continue the imagined dialogue between Mencius and Zhuangzi, we could hear the former asking the latter, How can you tackle the same question raised to Confucius? "If writing cannot fully express speech; speech cannot fully express ideas, then does it mean that the sages' ideas cannot be shown (seen)?"[42] As though in response to this question, Zhuangzi supplemented his main thesis with a distinction: "That which can be talked about in words is the general aspect of things. That which can be communicated through ideas is the refined aspect of things. That which cannot be talked about in language or observed and communicated through ideas cannot be described in terms of the general and refined conditions."[43] Zhuangzi was practically saying, "I do not mean that language is totally useless, nor that representation by language is completely impossible." There is a distinction that is the tricky part of the matter. Language can describe the general conditions of things; but it cannot describe the subtle aspect of things, which only the mind can intuitively grasp. Things in the world are tangible objects (*xing'erxia*), but metaphysical objects like the Dao cannot be described by language or understood by the mind.

Thus, while recongnizing the slippery nature of language, Zhuangzi divided objects of representation into three categories: (1) that which can be represented by language, (2) that which can only be understood in nondiscursive ways, (3) that which cannot be grasped by whatever means. The category that can be understood only by intuition and contemplation embraces the unnamable and indescribable feelings and transcendental principles. Metaphysical categories like the Dao cannot be perceived through language or understanding. But other categories can be understood either through language or through contemplation. Liu Xie explicated this idea in clear terms:

> That which rises above tangible shapes is called the Dao; that which exists in tangible shapes is called object. The divine Dao is difficult to imitate, for even the most refined language cannot capture its ultimate form. Tangible objects are easy to depict, for robust words are capable of representing their real conditions.[44]

Did Zhuangzi mean to say that the metaphysical principles like the Dao are totally beyond language and understanding? Not exactly. In a later chapter, Zhuangzi reiterated the boundlessness and indescribable nature of the Dao, but gave his idea a twist: "The name of the Dao can function only when it relies on something." He further stated: "If language is adequate, a whole day's talk will be able to exhaustively transmit the Dao; if language is inadequate, a whole day's talk can only exhaustively describe the appearances of things. The Dao is the ultimate principle of things and cannot be conveyed by speaking or silence. [A mode of representation] between speaking and silence may discuss its ultimate principle."[45] Thus, Zhuangzi did not completely reject language or representation. In a subtle way, Zhuangzi admitted to the function of language as a necessary tool for verbal communication:

> The fish-trap is a tool to catch fish. Once the fish is caught, the fish-trap is forgotten. A rabbit-snare is a tool to catch rabbits. Once the rabbit is

> caught, the snare is forgotten. Language is a tool to hold ideas. Once ideas
> are conveyed, language is forgotten. Where on earth could I find a person
> who has forgotten words to have a word with him?[46]

Here, "rabbit-snare" and "fish-trap" are obviously metaphors for words, which stand for language. By the same token "rabbit" and "fish" refer to ideas or thought. By saying that snares and traps can catch rabbits and fish, Zhuangzi was using figurative language to underscore his idea that language can perform the function of conveying ideas or thought. But the last sentence in the above passage gives his idea a subtle twist. It suggests that though Zhuangzi recognized the communicative power of language, he still considered it a second-best tool that is incapable of communicating the subtle and delicate. The last sentence of Zhuangzi's statement is a rhetorical question. It implies that Zhuangzi pined for a person with whom he can communicate without the aid of language. Thus, in the final analysis, he still preferred wordless communion as the most ideal mode of communication. Moreover, in using metaphors, Zhuangzi was aware of the metaphorical nature of language (the gap between language and thought), and mistrusted the function of language. He therefore advocated abandoning language as a communicative tool and posited a mode of communication that does not use language. The condition in which one can communicate with another person without language represents, for Zhuangzi, the highest status of communication. This is another way of conveying his understanding that some subtle things like the meaning of the Dao cannot be communicated to another person by the use of language.

The contradictory stance in his statement indicates that Zhuangzi was aware of the paradoxical nature of language as a tool of communication. On the one hand, he seemed to have suggested that language is a tool for communication and it is an illusion to think that one can get ideas (fish and rabbits) without words (snares and traps). But on the other hand, his rhetorical question implies that there should be persons who can communicate without the use of language. Although Zhuangzi did not categorically say language and thought are inseparable, his question suggests it: ordinarily, people conceive of language as a tool in the way one uses a fish-trap or a rabbit-snare. This conception is a specious illusion. One cannot retain *yi* (ideas) without *yan* (words). Once one gets hold of *yi*, *yan* will stick to the *yi* whether he likes it or not; or to put it in another more appropriate way, whether he is aware of it or not. Heiddeger, in his metameditation on the nature of language, touches on a phenomenon in language communication similar to the situation in Zhuangzi's argument. He points out that human beings' "relation to language is vague, obscure, almost speechless." In our everyday life, we have a paradoxical relation with language. Though we are so close to language and speak it every day, we scarcely notice the existence of language. We become conscious of the existence of language only when we "cannot find the right word for something that concerns us, carries us away, oppresses or encourages us."[47] Zhuangzi made a similar point. Ordinarily, people do not become conscious of the use of language. Once they express their ideas or understand the idea imparted by others, they seldom think about the language that transmits the ideas. This is like abandoning a tool after using it. But this is an illusion, which results from the conventional view of language as a container that holds meaning. According to this container theory, the process of signification is like this: an addresser has an idea, which is a message. He encodes it and puts it in language, which is the carrier. An addressee comes along, gets the container (language), and decodes the message in the container. Once he gets the message, the container (language) is cast away. The idea imparted by the rhetorical question may be viewed as an argument against the illusion and the conventional view. It seems to imply that it is impossible to communicate with a person who has forgotten language.

Thus, Zhuangzi revealed the paradoxical relationship between language and ideas. Language and thought are compatible and conflict with one another. The former can represent the latter but only to a certain extent. This is because although language is the direct realization of ideas, language is not equivalent to ideas. Language can only express general ideas, but what is on the mind of a writer/speaker is something particular. Therefore, it cannot express the individual thought of an individual writer. From the writer's point of view, Zhuangzi suggested that because *yanbu jinyi* (language cannot fully express ideas), a writer should go beyond the confines of language and make full use of the suggestiveness of language to capture thought. But what should a reader do given the fact that language is a second-best tool? Zhuangzi's advice is: give up reading altogether. Do not read books for the truth of the Dao, but rely on direct experience. But since wordless communication is rare and communication through words, verbal and written, is an everyday occurrence, how can one deal adequately with the paradox of language communication? Zhuangzi did not elaborate on this point. He left a huge puzzle for later thinkers, Chinese and Western, to unravel.

Views of Reading after Mencius and Zhuangzi

Scholars after Mencius and Zhuangzi felt the power of their arguments and were at the same time disturbed by their conflicting implications. A casual look at the ideas of reading after the Warring States period seems to suggest that scholars were divided into two opposing camps. While one camp sided with Mencius' positive view of language and reading, the other sided with Zhuangzi's negative view. Although there certainly existed a division among scholars, I venture to suggest that because all of them were engaged in an effort to get to the bottom of language representation, there was also a trend that aimed at reconciling the conflicting views on language and reading. Yang Xiong 楊雄 (53–18 BC) may be the first to notice the contradictory stance in Mencius' and Zhuangzi's positions and to make an effort to reconcile the opposite views:

> Speech cannot express the heart; writing cannot express one's thought. Indeed, it is difficult! Only sages can obtain the meaning of speech and the essence of writing. . . . Nothing excels speech in expressing the desires at heart and in understanding the complex feelings of people. Nothing excels writing in comprehensively covering things under heaven, recording bygone eras, clarifying the distant past, illuminating the murkiness of ancient times, and transmitting what happened afar. Therefore, it is said that speech is the voice of one's heart; writing is the picture of the heart. When speech describes the shapes and forms, superior and inferior men will be distinguished. What the speech pictures is that which moves the hearts of gentlemen and inferior men alike.[48]

This passage contains a contradiction and a solution for it. The contradiction seems to center on the discrepancy between language and thought, but if we place Yang Xiong's statement in the large context of Chinese views of reading and writing, the contradiction is really a conflict between Mencius' and Zhaungzi's positions on language and representation. Yang Xiong started with the idea that traces its origin to the "Appended Verbalizations" and Zhuangzi: speech cannot express the heart; writing cannot express thought. He seemed to side with Zhuangzi. But he ended his argument with a conflicting idea: speech adequately expresses one's inner thoughts; writing adequately expresses desires. He shifted his position and sided with Mencius. He himself must have been aware of the contradictory stance in his statement. So, he made a move to reconcile the contradictory positions by relying on the sagacity of sages. For ordinary people, speech cannot express the heart; nor can writing convey adequately one's inner thoughts. But sages are persons of a different caliber. In the hands of sages, speech and writing are adequate means of communication. Yang Xiong's reconciliatory effort offers a solution to the conflicting views in Mencius and Zhuangzi.

His solution was in a way indebted to the passage in the "Appended Verbalizations" that quotes Confucius as saying, "Writing cannot fully express speech; speech cannot fully express thought." Then an interlocutor raises a question: "If this is so, then does it mean that the ideas in the mind of sages cannot be perceived?" Confucius is quoted as replying: "The sages established images to fully express their thought, designed hexagrams to fully express the true and false conditions of affairs, and attached verbalizations to fully express what they wanted to say."[49] In an ingenious move, the writer of the "Appended Verbalizations" combined the opposite ideas of *yan bu jin yi* (words cannot exhaustively express ideas) and *yan yi zu zhi* (words can adequately convey intention) into a whole statement and smoothed out their conflicting views. Thus, long before Yang Xiong, Confucius was believed to have already relied on the sages in an attempt to bridge the gap between thought and language and to reconcile the opposite views on language representation. The difference lies in that while Confucius discussed how the sages solved the contradiction in sign representation through a triadic structure of *yi* (idea), *xiang* (image), *yan* (language), Yang Xiong was purely concerned with the problems in language representation. Yang Xiong's attempt at reconciliation shifted the focus from sign representation to language representation, and made the focus more directly related to writing and the reading of texts.

Yang Xiong's solution did not lay to rest the differences in language and representation arising from the opposite views of Mencius and Zhuangzi. The dispute came to a head in the famous debate that took place during the Wei-Jin period. The debate centered on a positive thesis and a counterargument. The positive thesis is: "Language can exhaustively express thought 言可盡意." The counterstatement is: "Language cannot exhaustively express thought 言不盡意." The debate, encouraged by the self-consciously inquisitive spirit of the Wei-Jin period, challenged the so-called Confucian saying from opposite directions. From one direction, some scholars questioned the authority of sages. The unknown writer of the "Appended Verbalizations" invoked the authority of sages to smooth out the discrepancies in the opposite views on language representation. But when it came to the Wei-Jin period, scholars were no longer willing to take sages' authority for granted. Xun Can 荀粲 followed Zhuangzi's line of thinking in the parable of the wheelwright and said: "I often ponder on Zigong's remark that the implications of Confucius's talk on human nature and the heavenly way cannot be comprehended. If so, then, even though the six kinds of classics exist, they are essentially the chaff (worthless stuff) left behind by sages." His brother quoted the reputed Confucian saying to argue with him: "The *Zhouyi* states, 'The sages established images to fully express their thought and attached verbalizations to fully express what they wanted to say.' Why on earth can't subtle language be conveyed and comprehended?" To this he replied:

> The subtlety of a rationale is not embodied in objects and images. Now the *Xicizhuan* says, "the sages established images to exhaustively express ideas." This is not connected to that which is outside ideas. The *Xicizhuan* also says: "[The sages] attached verbalizations to fully express what they wanted to say." This is not expressing words which lie beneath the surface. Ideas beyond images and words beneath the surface are deeply hidden and remain latent.[50]

In his opinion, metaphysical subtlety cannot be conveyed by images and words. His idea further refined Zhuangzi's linguistic skepticism and paved the way for the later notions of *bu jin zhi yi* (endless meanings) and *hanxu* (subtle reserve). In the debate on the relationship between words and ideas, Wang Bi was the first to conduct a systematic inquiry into language representation, but as I will examine his treatise in one of the following chapters, I will not discuss his ideas here. Due to the ethos of the age, the counterstatement seemed to have had the upper hand. This state of affairs provoked a challenge from the opposite direction. Ouyang Jian 歐陽建 (?–300) questioned linguistic skepticism in the "Appended Verbalizations" and defended the positive thesis. He wrote a treatise titled "*Yan jin yi lun* (Words Can Exhaustively Express Ideas)" to counter the negative thesis:

> If one traces the origin of things and seeks the root cause of events, [he will see that] it is not that an object is endowed with a natural name, nor does a rationale have its inevitable name. If one wants to express his intention, he will establish a name. The name changes with objects; words change with principles. This is the same as the fact that an echo follows a sound and a shadow attaches to the shape. They cannot be separated from each other. If they are inseparable, then, nothing like endless meaning exists. Therefore I think words can exhaust meaning.[51]

He touched upon something that borders on the performative function of language. But he failed to take into account situations in which it is often impossible to adequately perform the language function. Under certain circumstances, words really fail to express the fullness of ideas in the mind. Hence the common expressions like "indescribable," "unnamable," and "speechless." Ouyang Jian's defense left a gap.

The debate on the relationship between language and ideas sharpened later scholars' perception of the slippery nature of language and the unreliability of language representation. But the Mencian view of language representation seems to have regained its dominant position in later times. In the Song dynasty, for example, Ouyang Xiu 歐陽修 (1007–72) reexamined the dictum in the "Appended Verbalizations" and criticized a blind advocacy of linguistic skepticism in language representation:

"Writing cannot adequately express words; words cannot adequately express ideas." But aren't the ideas of ancient sages that have been sought out through extrapolation since high antiquity transmitted by words? Aren't books the means by which the ideas of the sages were able to survive? If so, then writing cannot exhaustively convey the plethora of words but can adequately express their generalities; words cannot exhaustively convey the subtlety of ideas but can adequately convey their principles. Those who uphold writing's inadequacy of expressing words and language's inadequacy of expressing ideas do not hold profound and clear views.[52]

Yang Wanli 楊萬里 (1127–1206) of the Southern Song dynasty offers an innovative understanding of the dictum in the *Xicizhuan*:

It is not that the sages' words cannot exhaustively convey their ideas. The sages can adequately express their ideas but simply do not thoroughly express them. It is not that the sages' books cannot exhaustively convey the meanings of their words. They can adequately express the meanings of their words but simply do not thoroughly express them. Why don't they want to seek thoroughness in expressions? Because they do not dare to pursue this end. The *Golden Mean* states: "Leave room and never seek exhaustiveness." This is the subtle brilliance of the *Book of Changes* and the *Golden Mean*. But why didn't the sages dare to seek thoroughness in expression? Because they fear that thorough expression may lead to people's mental retardation.[53]

In his opinion, the sages adopted a heuristic method in teaching their ideas. They deliberately left some blank space in their teachings for people to generate doubts, to fill up the gaps, and to create new ideas out of existent ideas. He further cited the ambiguity of the *Book of Changes* to expound his understanding: "The profound implications of the *Book of Changes* are what plunges people of the world into doubts and makes them think." Clearly, he was aware that writing could be suggestive on the part of the author and open to the reader's understanding. Ge Zhaoguang, a contemporary historian of Chinese thought, considers this kind of consciously or unconsciously left gaps to be the fertile intellectual space in which later thinkers constantly exercise their imagination and open up new avenues to intellectual thought.[54]

The debate on language representation sensitized scholars' views on reading and writing. In the Wei-Jin period, Lu Ji 陸機 (261–303) who wrote *Wenfu* 文賦 (the Rhyming Prose on Literature) transposed the debate on language and meaning into literary study and related it to reading and writing. In his discourse on literature, he stated in the preface:

> Whenever I read the writings by talented writers, I secretly nurse the idea that I have been able to grasp their intentions. Although they displayed colorful mutations in their verbal expressions, we can still grasp their descriptions of the beautiful, the ugly, the good and the bad, and talk about them. Each time I compose my own writing, I become more keenly aware of their state of mind. I constantly worry lest my ideas are inadequate for objects and my writing inadequate for my ideas. It is not so much that knowing is hard as that performance is hard.[55]

Lu Ji discussed language representation from both the writer's and reader's points of view. From the reader's perspective, he believed that the reader could have access to the writer's mind through his writings despite the dazzling mutations in ways of representation. But from the writer's perspective, it is a difficult endeavor to perform adequately the function of language in representation, although it is by no means impossible to perform it well. It is not difficult to conceptualize things in representation. What is difficult is how to find adequate means for representation. He seemed to have held the belief that so long as the writer finds adequate means for representation in his writing, the reader would be able to grasp fully what is represented. In his contemplation of literary creation, he viewed reading and writing as a connected process of verbal communication and broadened the scope of language representation beyond the *Xicizhuan*'s triadic relationship among thought, image, and words. In other words, he brought the object of representation into consideration.

In "Writing cannot fully express speech; speech cannot fully express thought," the triadic relationship covers thought, speech, and writing. This triadic structure is like the Western model of language representation: thought is located in the mind; speech is close to thought as it is a transcription of ideas; writing is once removed from the mind because it is a transcription of speech. But the *Xicizhuan* model leaves out objects, or the world, to be represented. Lu Ji's reconceptualization resulted in a model of language representation that covers the three essential elements in language representation: the world, thinking, and writing. In Chinese language, they are respectively *wu* (objects), *yi* (thought or meaning), *wen* (writing). More importantly, he seemed to have offered a clue as to how language can adequately represent ideas. First, clear thinking is a prerequisite for representation. To put it another way, to judge whether writing can adequately express thought, one must see whether one's ideas are fit for the observation of objects. Second, language representation is an intricate skill: "It is not so much that knowing is difficult as that performance is difficult." Here, he filled the gap left behind by Ouyang Jian. Lu Ji's contemplation yields an inchoate model of language representation in reading and writing. It comes quite close to Peirce's triadic model of sign representation, which covers object, thought, and sign.

In *The Literary Mind and the Carving of Dragons*, Liu Xie 劉勰 (465–522) extensively discussed language representation. His views are indebted to both Mencius and Zhuangzi. In chapter 26, he stated:

> The subtle meanings beyond our thought and the profound inner workings of the heart inexpressible in words are not to be reached by language; here one should know enough to halt his brush. Only the most subtle pen can transmit their secret, and only the most intricate mind can comprehend the methods of writing. The master chef Yi Zhi was unable to impart to people the knack of cooking, and Wheelwright Bian could not talk to people about how he wielded his ax. The art of writing is indeed subtle.[56]

By citing the parable of Wheelwright Bian in the *Zhuangzi*, Liu Xie was evidently in agreement with Zhuangzi and approved of his linguistic skepticism and wordless communication. But immediately after the above statement, he shifted his position in the next chapter. In chapter 27, he stated in a fairly technical way Mencius' positive conviction in language's capacity of conveying ideas: "When a writer's emotions are stirred, they will take form in words; and if a rationale is to be expressed, it manifests itself in writing. This is because a writer's thought moves from what is latent in the mind to what is manifest on the page. What is within corresponds with what lies without."[57] His view is another way of stating Husserl's view of meaning as an "intentional object"[58] and paves the way for his positive belief in the possibility of retracing the intention of the author through reading in chapter 48, "Zhiyin 知音 (An Understanding Critic)." The chapter is a treatise on the nature, rationale, characteristics, and methodology of literary criticism and evaluation. As both criticism and evaluation depend on reading, it also touches upon the nature and rationale of reading and writing. Following Mencius' positive thesis, Liu Xie believed that just as writing is capable of expressing what is intently on the author's mind, a reader may be able to recover the author's intention through adequate reading. Citing the famous legend in which a sympathetic music connoisseur correctly revealed what is expressed by a lute player, he reiterated Mencius' positive belief in writing's capability of expressing an author's inner feelings:

> If it is possible for a man's impressions of mountains and rivers to find expression in his lute playing, how much easier it must be to depict physically tangible forms with a brush, from which no inner feeling or idea can be successfully hidden. Our mind reflects reason just as our eyes perceive

physical forms; as long as our eyes are keen, there are no physical forms which cannot be distinguished, and as long as our mind is alert, there are no feelings or idea which cannot be conveyed.[59]

Of course, Liu Xie admitted that it is very difficult to read an author's writing adequately and even more difficult to give adequate evaluation. But basing himself on the positive belief, he voiced a method of reading similar to that of Mencius:

> Moved by his inner feelings, a writer expresses his thoughts in words. A reader peruses the writing so as to enter the writer's inner feelings. If the latter can trace the waves back to their sources, there will be nothing, however deeply hidden, that will not reveal itself. Although the reader is unable to meet the writer because they are separated from each other by distant eras, he may succeed in grasping the inner thoughts of the writer through the reading of his writing.[60]

In this statement, Liu Xie, like Mencius, viewed reading and writing as a process of communication through language codes. His view is more nuanced and refined than that of Mencius and further enriches Lu Ji's conception of reading and writing as a connected process of communication and representation.

Through the debate on *yan* (words) and *yi* (ideas), scholars became clearly aware of the capacity of language and its paradoxical nature in its function of thinking and communication: language has both its strengths and limitations. Its strengths lie in that it can adequately represent objects and convey some ideas. Its limitations exist in the fact that it cannot adequately represent the subtle, delicate aspects of complex feelings, rich imagination, and metaphysical principles. The two sides of the paradox are adequately conveyed by the two expressions: "language is capable of conveying intention 言以足志," and "language is incapable of exhaustively expressing ideas 言不盡意." How can we break through the limitations of language and solve the contradiction between *yan* and *yi* in reading and writing? Synthesizing Mencius' positive view of language and Zhuangzi's skeptical view of language, later scholars proposed a syncretic view. Guo Xiang 郭象, for example, proposed a view in his comment on Zhuangzi's ideas: "Words and ideas are being, but that which is spoken of and conceived of is non-being. One should seek [meaning] from the surface of words and ideas but enters the realm of no words and no ideas. Only then can one reach there."[61]

Guo Xiang's proposal synthesizes Mencius' hermeneutic circle and Zhaungzi's wordless communication. It maximizes the strength of language: "language can be adequate in conveying one's intent," but minimizes its shortcoming: "language cannot exhaustively express ideas." In writing, because "language cannot fully express ideas," a writer should find a method of expression that makes a full use of language's function to convey ideas and at the same time takes advantage of metaphor, suggestion, symbolism, and other suggestive ways to set in motion the reader's imagination and association so as to convey implications beyond the expressed words. In reading, a reader should not be restricted by what has been expressed in the words on the page, but instead tries to imagine along the path of thought strewn with metaphor, symbol, and suggestive details to seek the implications beyond the words on the page. In this way, the negative thesis, "language is incapable of adequately expressing ideas," will stand on its own head and give rise to the supreme condition in Chinese literary art: "meanings beyond words 言外之意" and "endless meanings 不盡之意." In Liu Xie's opinion, under these circumstances, the writer and the reader may be connected in a rapport, conducive to a perfect understanding: "When the description of physical things in a writing comes to an end but the feelings aroused in the reader are more than plenty, the reader's understanding dovetails perfectly with what the author wants to impart."[62]

A Chinese Model of Reading and Writing

Mencius and Zhuangzi are pioneers in the exploration of reading and writing in the Chinese tradition. Later thinkers and scholars have basically followed their pioneering efforts and conducted their conceptual discussions of reading and writing along the pioneers' lines of thought. In terms of contemporary theories of language, communication, and representation, I may schematize the foundational ideas of reading in Chinese intellectual thought into a model of reading and writing:

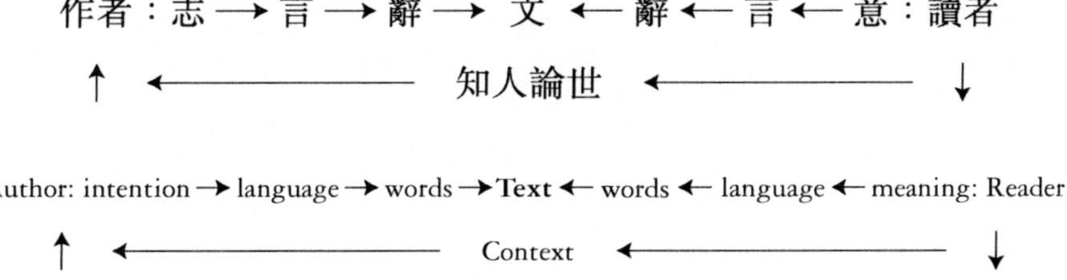

From one direction, the writer conceptualizes his ideas in his mind, uses a language system to dispense his ideas in language codes, and creates a text. From the opposite direction, the reader formulates an initial understanding of the text, traces its meanings back to the author's ideas through language codes, and refines his meanings by situating his reading within the context of the writer and his time.

With the aid of the formulated model, the differences in Mencius' and Zhuangzi's ideas of reading can be better understood. In Mencius' conception, with the text as the center, the communication channel between the writer and the reader is not blocked if one adopts a right approach to the text. What the writer intends the reader can grasp through sensitive and sensible reading. For this reason, we may regard him as a premodern Husserlian. But Mencius was not unaware of the problematics of communication. He, therefore, supplemented his positive conviction with extra-textual and supralinguistic considerations, making his idea of reading close to those of existentialist hermeneutics propounded by Dilthey, Heidegger, and Gadamer. To Zhuangzi, the communication channel is not always through because language cannot exhaustively express the writer's intention, nor can it exhaustively recover the writer's intention for the reader. As a result, what the reader understands may not always be what the writer has intended. In this sense, he may be considered a premodern deconstructionist. Their concerns are basically the same as those with which contemporary theorists of reading are preoccupied. As they lived in high antiquity, their precious insights may be said to have anticipated the contemporary inquiries into the complex relations among language, thought, representation, and hermeneutics. The fact that Mencius and Zhuangzi can be brought into a meaningful dialogue with contemporary theorists of hermeneutics suggests that reading is truly a subject of inquiry across time, space, and culture. Mencius' view of reading as a process of making friends with authors not only anticipates Gadamer's "fusion of horizons," but also suggests that reading is a human endeavor that requires sympathetic understanding, constant modification of one's preconceptions, and relentless overcoming of prejudices and biases. By contrast, Zhuangzi's view of reading based on linguistic skepticism produces a liberating effect that sanctions conceptual inquiries into openness by later thinkers and encourages explorations of interpretive and creative openness by traditional commentators, critics, and writers.

Chapter 2

Hermeneutic Openness in Aesthetic Thought

Since I have suggested in the introduction that the Chinese tradition had an early start in the inquiry into concerns of hermeneutic openness, the reader will naturally ask, Are there such concepts as "openness," "open work," and "open poetics" in traditional Chinese literary thought? To this question, my answer is an unequivocal no. If, however, he/she rephrases the question and asks, Are there any concepts with similar implications? my introduction has already provided a preliminary answer. The first objective of this chapter is to prove beyond doubt: though hermeneutic openness and open poetics are modern ideas, the concern with textual openness has existed as a major current in the Chinese tradition from antiquity and is filled with intriguing insights. In many ways, the insights anticipated modern concerns with openness and open poetics. As I will discuss *Zhouyi* hermeneutics and *Shijing* hermeneutics in later chapters, this chapter will concentrate on concerns with openness in Chinese aesthetic thought exclusive of the two hermeneutic traditions.

It is almost a scholarly consensus that Chinese aesthetic thought is fragmentary, impressionistic, and unsystematic. The same may be said of Chinese insights of hermeneutic openness. I, however, believe that Chinese aesthetic thought has inherent systems and definable concepts in its sheer voluminosity. The question is how to make an implicit system explicit and how to construct the hidden insights. Thus, another major aim of this chapter is to explore whether traditional concerns with the conditions of literary texts have already constituted a system, whether the insights have gone beyond suggestiveness to embrace the modern idea of openness, and what impact Chinese history, culture, and philosophical thought have exerted upon those concerns and insights. Another often lodged complaint in studies of Chinese poetics is that Chinese literary thought is expressed in concepts and terms that are opaque, unstable, and undefinable. Scholars in China and the West have gone to some length to tackle this problem. Stephen Owen's *Readings in Chinese Literary Thought* has achieved impressive success in this direction.[1] I will make similar efforts to redefine vague terms and to reconceptualize intuitive notions in terms of conceptual categories.

Suggestiveness as an Aesthetic Category

One of the closest Chinese notions to openness is suggestiveness. It is a major theoretical category in Chinese art—verbal, visual, and auditory. Fung Yu-lan, the renowned historian of Chinese philosophy, states: "Suggestiveness, not articulateness, is the ideal of all Chinese art, whether it be poetry, painting, or anything else."[2] Fung Yu-lan also points out: "Such is the ideal of Chinese art, and this ideal is reflected in the way in which Chinese philosophers have expressed themselves." If aesthetic suggestiveness has influenced formal presentations of philosophy, the impact in the reverse direction is even more profound. Aesthetic suggestiveness is certainly a category to be found in discussions of arts, but in many ways, one may almost say that it grew out of philosophical discourses and treatises and had its philosophical foundation firmly laid in Chinese thought. Since at the outset of the Chinese tradition, there was little formal differentiation between philosophical and literary thought, the question of which had given rise to which is one as difficult to answer as the question of which came into the world first, the chicken or the egg. Perhaps, a reasonable view seems to be that philosophical discourse and literary thought initially experienced a symbiotic growth, and then, the latter borrowed a great deal from the former in the development of Chinese aesthetics. Within the broader context of Chinese tradition, the Chinese concept of suggestiveness is a product of the interpenetration of and exchanges between philosophical and artistic discourses. It is a symphony performed by metaphysics and aesthetics in harmonious accord.

Suggestiveness has been widely explored in studies of Chinese literary thought,[3] but it has only been examined diffusely in relation to other aesthetic ideas. Few scholars have examined it as an aesthetic category in its own right, still less have explored its implications in relation to contemporary Western theories. I will reexamine suggestiveness and its seminal ideas and concepts as an aesthetic category in Chinese tradition, exploring their relations to philosophical thought, and reconceptualizing their implications in terms of contemporary theories. I also intend to inquire whether the insights of this Chinese aesthetic, often characterized as gems of "Oriental mysticism," can be understood through reflective analysis and have a meaningful dialogue with contemporary Western literary thought.

In everyday discourse, suggestiveness in Chinese is called *anshi* 暗示 (suggestion). Literally, it means "to show something by indirectly hinting at it." In artistic discourse, it is often coupled with the word "aesthetic" and so becomes an aesthetic principle. It generally refers to a desirable artistic quality highly valued in different forms of art, especially in poetry. Shen Deqian 沈德潛 (1673–1769), a poet-scholar of the Qing dynasty, makes this statement: "Poetry is valued for its surplus meanings. While words refer to this, meanings reach out to that."[4] Fung Yu-lan identifies it as a poetic technique: "In poetry, what the poet intends to communicate is often not what is directly said in the poetry, but what is not said in it." He also considers it an artistic effect: "According to Chinese literary tradition, in good poetry 'the number of words is limited, but the ideas it suggests are limitless.' So an intelligent reader of poetry reads what is outside the poem; and a good reader of books reads 'what is between the lines.'"[5] Fung Yu-lan is quoting Yan Yu's 嚴羽 (*fl.* 1180–1235) famous dictum,[6] which evolved out of Zhong Rong's 鐘嶸 (465–518) similar notion: "The text may come to an end, but the implications are more than plenty."[7] In traditional Chinese literary thought, there are quite a few expressions that voice similar ideas in the making of poetic art: *yanwai zhi yi* (meanings beyond the expressed words), *xianwai zhi yin* (sound off the string), *xiangwai zhi xiang* (images beyond the image), *weiwai zhi zhi* (flavors beyond the flavor), and *hanxu* (subtle reserve). All these expressions advocate unlimited suggestiveness, which comes very close to the postmodern conceptions of unlimited semiosis and "openness." Both in theory and practice, the Chinese conception of suggestiveness is compatible with unlimited semeosis or openness.

Being an art of making art, suggestiveness epitomizes a poetic technique identified by Liu Xie 劉勰 (465–522): "*yishao zongduo, qingmao wuyi* (to use limited words to represent innumerable phenomena, leaving nothing in one's feelings or in the appearance of objects undescribed)."[8] As such it seems to have grown out of the dilemmas confronted by the artist: the infinite varieties of life and the limitations of artistic media; boundlessness of thought and the inadequacy of language. In their efforts to make art adequately represent observed reality and imaginative thought, Chinese artists found in suggestiveness an effective way to represent unlimited life with limited artistic means. This discovery set

Chinese thinkers on a journey of inquiry into the rationale and techniques of suggestiveness all the way from high antiquity up to modern times. As early as the Warring States period, Mencius (390–305 BC) designated suggestiveness as a feature of superior oratorical skill: "He is a good speaker whose words refer to things nearby, but allude to things afar."[9] In the same period, the anonymous writer(s) who composed the *Xicizhuan* [the appendixes to the *Book of Changes*] noticed the use of suggestiveness in hexagram statements and discussed its significance for imagistic and verbal representation:

> The *Yi* [*Book of Changes*] is to make manifest the past events and to observe future events so that the subtle may be shown and the profound may come to light. Its creators started by giving the hexagram images proper names so as to distinguish objects, and appending proper hexagram statements so that the language for judgment is ready at hand. The names for hexagram images and lines are insignificant, but their symbolized categories are great. Its thought is profound; its rhetoric is colorfully patterned; its language is tortuous but accurate; its allusions are blatant but their implications are concealed.[10]

This passage is an evaluation of the hexagram names and statements. Since names and statements are words and verbal texts, this passage is relevant not only to imagistic representation but also to literary representation. It touches upon several facets of aesthetic suggestiveness. First, it points out the representational law of using limited media for unlimited representation. The hexagram statements were so aptly worded that they could reflect the changes in the past and illuminate affairs in the future, show the signs of events in their beginning stages and elucidate profound principles and their rationale. Second, it brings out the technique of suggestive representation. The openness of a statement largely depends on the apt choice of words, epithets, and allusions which, though small and insignificant, may suggest large, broad, and significant categories of affairs under heaven. The *Xicizhuan* has always been considered a philosophical text. I suggest that what this passage says concerns more than philosophy, for it touches on a theory of artistic representation with incredible potential for openness. Aristotle makes a radical distinction between history and poetry: "The true difference is that one relates what has happened, the other what may happen. Poetry, therefore, is more philosophical and a higher thing than history: for poetry tends to express the universal, history the particular."[11] In claiming that "The *Yi* [*Book of Changes*] is to make manifest the past events and to observe future events so that the subtle may be shown and the profound may come to light," the *Xicizhuan* seems to say that the *Book of Changes* as a system of representation is capable of representing not

only what may happen, but also what has happened; the universal as well
as the particular. Indeed, the book has been treated as such over history.
Certain hexagram statements have been explained as records of certain historical events, but at the same time these particularized explanations have
not prevented people from using those statements to predict what may
happen.

Following the lead of the *Xicizhuan*, a number of scholars in ancient
China voiced similar opinions in their assessment of the literary achievement of a writer and in their evaluation of a literary work. Commenting
on Qu Yuan's 屈原 (c. 340–278 BC) literary writings, Sima Qian 司馬遷
(c. 145–c. 85 BC) said: "Qu Yuan's language is concise, his diction incon-
spicuous, his aspiration lofty, and his conduct honest. His language for
representing things may be small, but its implications are extremely great;
its cited categories may be near at hand, but its implied meanings reach
into the distance."[12] In this statement, the essential point is that literary
representation must have the potential of leading the imagination to go
from small to large, from things near at hand to things afar, from con-
ciseness to complexity, from limited categories to unlimited implications.

Yiyin (Lingering Sound) and *Yiwei* (Lingering Taste)

Starting from the Wei and Jin period, as Chinese literary creation
entered a self-conscious era, the discussion of literary suggestiveness and
openness experienced a process of broadening and deepening. Lu Ji 陸機
(261–303), in his "Discourse on Literature," led the way in exploring the
philosophical rationale of literary suggestiveness:

Suppose one cultivates pure emptiness and graceful restraint,	或清虛以婉約，
Always cutting away all trimmings and excessive ornaments.	每除繁而去濫。
His writing may lack the lasting taste of the sacrificial broth;	闕大羹之遺味；
But it shares the twang of pure breath off wrought silk strings.	同朱弦之清汜。
Despite endless resonance to one plucked string,	雖一唱而三歎，
Essentially, it has all the graces but no allure.[13]	固既雅而不艷。

Here, Lu Ji attempts to consider literary suggestiveness in terms of culi-
nary taste and musical acoustics. His inspiration came from a passage in
"Yueji 樂記": "The *se* zither of the Purity Temple has red strings and far-
apart vibration holes. One string is plucked and three other strings will

reverberate in murmurs so that there is a lingering sound. The etiquette of the great sacrificial feast sets great store by the use of original [or mysterious] wine [i.e., pure water] and the display of uncooked fish and meat. The great broth is not blended [with the five tastes], so it has a lasting flavor."[14] In this passage, *yiyin* "lingering tone" and *yiwei* "lingering flavor" are not literal but metaphysical in nature because both refer to something that is materially absent but potentially present and profuse.

According to Kong Yingda's 孔穎達 (574–648) annotation, in the Purity Temple where music was made, the *se* zither was designed with vibration holes wide apart and fitted with strings of wrought silk so that a lingering sound came from the instrument. As for the food for the sacrificial feast, fresh meat and fish were not cooked and the great broth was not seasoned with any salt or mixed with any vegetables.[15] Also, the "original/mysterious wine" was really pure water. There is metaphysical and ironic wit in calling pure water "original/mysterious wine." Because the offerings retained their primal taste, they could be associated with any flavors. The ideas of *yiyin* (lingering sound) and *yiwei* (lingering taste) seem to share the metaphysical conception of similar ideas in Lao Zi's Daoist system. Lao Zi expressed the paradoxical notion *Dayin xisheng*[16] (The great note is rarefied in sound).[17] Wang Bi's annotation to this notion reads: "When one listens but does not hear the sound, this is called *xi*, which refers to a sound that cannot be heard. From sound comes distinctive notes. The notes are either the *gong* note or *shang* note. A distinctive note cannot represent all notes. Therefore, an audible sound is not the supreme sound."[18] Here, we see the metaphysical rationale of the Swiss proverb *Sprechen ist silbern, Schweigen ist golden* (Speech is silvern, Silence is golden). In his meditation on the values of speech and silence, Thomas Carlyle adapted the Swiss proverb and obtained an understanding that helps us better understand Lao Zi's idea: "Speech is of Time, Silence is of Eternity."[19]

Lao Zi's idea was put to concrete poetic practice by some poets. The most brilliant and magnificent example is found in Bai Juyi's 白居易 (772–846) famous "Pipa xing" (Song of the Pipa), a poem that describes the music performance and sad life of a female entertainer, whom he met during his exile. The poet describes with vivid language how her music conveyed her sorrow-ridden life story. In the middle of her performance, she suddenly stopped playing the instrument. The sudden silence following the sound of pipa produced an endless effect that was adequately summed up by the poet in one poetic line: "The silence at that time was louder than any sound."[20] This line, equivalent to "thunderous silence," is a triumphant achievement in making language represent sonic absence and endless affective associations. It also reminds us of John Keats's poetic lines in "Ode on a Grecian Urn": "Heard melodies are sweet, but those unheard/ Are sweeter; therefore, ye soft pipes, play on; / Not to the sensual ear, but, more endear'd, / Pipe to the spirit ditties of no tone."[21]

Zhuangzi went a step further in turning Lao Zi's *xisheng* (rarefied note) into an idea of *wusheng* (no sound): "When one looks, he sees indistinction; when he listens, he hears no sound. Only in the midst of indistinction does he see brightness; only in the midst of no sound does he hear harmonious sound."[22] Zhuangzi has a visual dimension that interconnects with Lao Zi's idea of *daxiang* (great image). Zhuangzi's remark touches upon both the visual and acoustic images in the composition of a symbol. Moreover, it attributes the source of endless associations to the simultaneous presence of concealment and revelation, silence and sound, finite and infinite, visible and invisible. Here, I would like to quote Carlyle's view of symbol as an elucidation of my understanding: "In a Symbol there is concealment and yet revelation: here, therefore, by Silence and by Speech acting together, comes a doubled significance. And if both the Speech be itself high, and the Silence fit and noble, how expressive will their union be!" He went on to say: "In the Symbol proper, what we can call a Symbol, there is ever, more or less distinctly and directly, some embodiment and revelation of the Infinite; the Infinite is made to blend itself with the Finite, to stand visible, and as it were attainable, there."[23]

Similarly, the paradoxical connotations of *yiwei* (lingering taste) are compatible with Lao Zi's explication of the Dao in terms of *wuwei* (no taste) and *weiwai wei* (flavor beyond flavor).[24] In chapter 35, Lao Zi describes the Dao thus: "The way (Dao) in its passage through the mouth is without flavor. / It cannot be seen, / It cannot be heard, / Yet it cannot be exhausted by use."[25] The Dao is a universal quality existing in everything under heaven, but it is not any of the tangible things. It therefore does not confine itself to the qualities of any material thing. The quality of the Dao is like the tastelessness of all tastes. Because it is tasteless, it can embody all the tastes. Here we find the genius of negative metaphysics that is completely opposite of Platonic ontology. The "Yueji" itself echoes Lao Zi's and Zhuangzi's ideas. Right before the "Qingmiao" passage, the "Yueji" states: "The grandeur of music does not reside in the extremity of sounds; the protocol of the sacrificial feast does not rest on the greatest flavors."[26]

Previous scholars have all read Lu Ji's passage as describing one of the five faults in literary creations,[27] the other four being: "A weak string plucked alone, / Without resonance, its sound into thin air vanishes," "'Tis as if pipers down the hall pipe hurried notes at random, / Resonant but out of tune, that only throw the hymn into discord," "'Tis like a zither, too high-strung and hard pressed by rapid fingers; / Although the melody is played in tune, it fails to move with pathos," and "Beware of resemblance to the 'Dew Shelter' and 'Mulberry Grove,' / Which, though full of pathos, are an offense to grace."[28] A look at the five couplets tells us that they all appear at the end of a passage, serving as a value judgment on what has been presented. A careful reading of the five passages reveals that all of them are discussions of five styles of composition in terms of musical performance. Each of the first four passages indeed points out a kind of shortcoming that is likely to appear in literary writings. But the last passage is ambivalent in tone and theme. "Pure emptiness" and "subtle restraint" are positive qualities for a literary work. "Cutting away all trimmings and excessive ornaments" is also a positive way of writing. If a writer cuts away all trimmings and excessive ornaments, his writing should attain the condition expressed by the "lingering taste of the sacrificial broth."

Why, then, did Lu Ji say that this kind of writing lacks the lingering taste of the sacrificial broth? What is more puzzling is that according to the "Yueji" and Lao Zi's and Zhuangzi's conception, both *yiyin* and *yiwei* are compatible philosophical ideas. Why, then, did Lu Ji say the fifth style of writing lacks one quality but has the other? The couplet representing the value judgment is particularly ambivalent: "Despite endless resonance to one plucked string, / Essentially, it has all the graces but no allure." A possible explanation of Lu Ji's ambivalent stance may be this: he seemed to argue that all the four styles of writing are less desirable than they should be because they have shortcomings emanating from a lopsidedness in either form or content: "weak string, without resonance, hurried notes, resonant but out of tune, hard pressed by rapid fingers, harmonious but without pathos, full of pathos but without grace." The fifth style of writing seems to have lopsidedness of another kind; that is, too much substance and too little ornament. But it is compensated by its metaphysical profundity. Another possible explanation is that the last passage offers an alternative situation. When one reveres pure emptiness to the point of subtle restraint, gets rid of all excessive ornamentations, even though his writing may not attain the supreme condition suggested by Lao Zi's and Zhuangzi's idea of "lingering taste," it will produce effects and affects comparable to the result of zither playing in the Purity Temple.

Whether the fifth style of writing is a faulty form is open to further exploration. In spite of the ambivalence in Lu Ji's argument, he was the first scholar to theorize on profound textual effects in terms of "lingering taste and lingering sound." His idea also anticipated some similar ideas by later scholars such as "flavor beyond flavor" and "sound beyond the string." For my inquiry into theories of openness, it is sufficient that Lu Ji valued the literary effect characterized by "the lingering taste of the sacrificial broth" and "the endless resonance to the plucking of a single string." Previous scholars have annotated *yichang er santan* as "one sings and three join in sighs." This may be a likely interpretation. But another reading is also possible. It may not refer to a person who sings but to a string which is plucked. Because of vibration and the acoustic design of the instrument, other strings on the same zither resonate. These reverberations may be the basis for the philosophical idea of "lingering sound." Insofar as literary compositions are concerned, these reverberations are apt acoustic images for literary effects and affects. On the one hand, they are a sort of faint sound; on the other they are not the original sound. It is a sound generated by another sound through acoustic vibration and borders on no sound. As a borderline sound, it comes close to Zhuangzi's philosophical idea of *wusheng* (literally, no sound). Since it is suggestive of endless resonance, those reverberations may be comparable to the intro-textual relations of and extratextual responses to a profound writing: the words of a text have come to an end, but the implications do not. This textual condition analogized by the zither playing was picked up by a number of later scholars. (I will deal with this in detail.) In many ways, Lu Ji's innovative adaptation of the passage from the "Yueji" (Records of Music) paved the way for Zhong Rong's 鐘嶸 (465–518) famous saying: "Words may come to an end but the meanings are endless." Overall, in the fifth passage, Lu Ji valued a textual condition that opens the text beyond itself with limitless implications.

In Lao Zi's *Daode jing*, there is another saying parallel to the idea of *wusheng* (no sound): "A great note is a rarefied sound." It is "A great image is rarefied in shape 大象無形."[29] Wang Bi explains this saying: "Once an object has shapes, it can be distinguished. That which can be distinguished is either warm or cool, either hot or cold. Therefore, an image with tangible shapes is not a great image."[30] By this statement, Wang Bi means to say that an image with a tangible shape is limited in perception; only an image with no tangible shape is capable of arousing unlimited perceptions of itself. Evidently, the image in Lao Zi's and Wang Bi's conception does not refer to any concrete object; it is a mental representation of certain idea that transcends the limitations of senses. In philosophical Daoism, the transcendental idea represented in verbal terms is the Dao. But in reality, what sort of images can be counted as images without tangible shapes? Wang Bi does not give us any example. From the literary perspective, I may supply a new annotation to Lao Zi's saying. In my opinion, literary images can be considered "great images" because a literary image, generated by a series of words, has no tangible shapes and is a verbal representation of perceptions. For example, poem 57 of the *Shijing* describes in vivid details a beautiful girl. Despite the minute description, the image can still evoke unlimited impressions in the reader's imagination. The same is true of all characters in literary works. We often hear that adaptations of literary masterpieces into films fail to convey the artistic achievement of the original works. The failure is partly determined by the lack of metaphysical suggestiveness. In adapting a literary work for the theater or cinema or other visual media, one inadvertently deprives the work of its status as having many "great images." For the adapted version in visual forms will inevitably curtail the signifying flux of a verbal image. In this respect, Lu Xun's observation of literary imagery may serve as a footnote to Lao Zi's "great image." He was opposed to the idea and practice of adapting his masterpiece the *True Story of Ah Q* for the theater and cinema on the grounds that the work would be reduced to its comic effects on the stage.[31] After some dramatist went ahead with the adaptation, Lu Xun requested that "the best thing is not to make the play too particularized but capable of rather free adaptation."[32] Obviously, he was aware of the loss of hermeneutic potential due to visual adaptation, as can be seen from his comment on the visualized image of literary characters: "[I]f we read *A Dream of Red Mansions* and want to form a picture from the text of Lin Daiyu, we must first erase the impression made on us by the photograph of Dr. Mei Lanfang in the opera, *Lin Daiyu Buries the Flowers*. If we then imagine another Lin Daiyu, she will probably be a slim and solitary modern young woman with bobbed hair and a gown of Indian silk, or some other type—I cannot determine which. But she is bound to be quite different from the pictures published between thirty and forty years ago."[33]

Bujin zhiyi (Endless Meaning): Multivalence and Polysemy

Multivalence and polysemy are two frequently used terms in contemporary theoretical discourse. In traditional Chinese literary thought, there are some terms that match the denotation and connotation of the two English terms so neatly that we can almost translate one term from Chinese into English or vice versa without substantial loss of the original implications. In Liu Xie's *Wenxin diaolong*, we can find some equivalents of these two terms. What's more, Liu Xie systematically discussed the nature, function, and technique of a dual concept called *yinxiu* 隱秀 (concealed and conspicuous beauty), which comes even closer to the modern idea of literary openness. In chapter 40 he states:

> The movement of our thought reaches remote distances, and literary feeling develops from deeply buried sources. A source which is profound permits growth in many directions, and vigorous roots foster conspicuous branches. In the case of the beauty of a literary composition, there are both visible and hidden beauties. The hidden beauties are the multivalent [or important] ideas beyond the text, and the visible the excellent features that stand

out in the text. The artistry of the hidden beauty lies in its polysemy, and that of the visible in its unsurpassed preeminence. These are the exquisite qualities of the ancient literature, and form the happy conjunction of talent and feeling. The hidden beauty, as form, focuses on ideas which are beyond the text, and are comprehended indirectly through secret overtones, which unobtrusively reveal hidden brilliance. The generation of new significance may be compared to the practice of forming a new hexagram using the technique of internal trigrams, or to the appearance of square or round ripples on the surface of rivers due to submerged pearls and jade. The changes of a hexagram through internal trigrams and line changes give birth to the "four images," and the pearls and jade in the depth of the water cause the formation of square and round waves. A reader of this kind of literature begins with a normal response but ends with a recognition of its unusual beauty. Its internal brilliance and external mellowness are such that common readers will have unlimited responses, and connoisseurs will never grow tired of it.[34]

This is perhaps the most concentrated discussion of concealed implications in traditional Chinese literary thought. There are a number of points that coincide with the modern conception of literary openness. Indeed, some terms like *chongzhi* 重旨 (literally "double intentions") and *fuyi* 復義 (literally "multiple meanings") are respectively equivalents of the critical concepts "multivalence" and "polysemy," frequently used in contemporary critical discourse. First, Liu Xie defines *yin* (concealed beauty) in literature as "rich implications beyond the text 文外之重旨." It echoes a similar idea in another chapter: "思表纖旨，文外曲致 minute intentions beneath thinking and subtle connotations beyond the text."[35] Fan Wenlan 範文瀾, a modern scholar of the *Wenxin diaolong*, annotates *chongzhi* as "the use of diction is simple but the meanings are abundant; the implications are unlimited."[36] Second, Liu Xie considers multivalence as the prerequisite for *yin*: "the artistry of the hidden lies in its polysemy." Third, Liu Xie regards opening the text beyond itself as of ontological importance and stresses hidden polysemy: "The hidden, as form, focuses on ideas which are beyond the text, and are comprehended indirectly through secret overtones, which unobtrusively reveal hidden brilliance." Fourth, he views a literary text with openness as a semiotically self-generating entity like a hexagram image in the *Zhouyi*: "The generation of new significance may be compared to the practice of forming a new hexagram using the technique of internal trigrams, or to the appearance of square or round ripples on the surface of rivers due to submerged pearls and jade." Just as a hexagram image can mutate into different hexagrams through various techniques, so a literary text can generate different meanings. Fifth, he foresees the profound effect a text with *yin* may have on readers and the unlimited affect it may produce. The five points I have identified in Liu Xie's discourse suggest that though Liu Xie never used the term "literary openness," his theoretical inquiry covers a gamut of its meanings.

Jiaoran 皎然 (730–799) proposed some terms that are variations of Liu Xie's *chongzhi* and *fuyi*: *erchongyi* (twofold meaning), *sanchongyi* (three-fold meaning), and *sichongyi* (fourfold meaning). He also provided some poetic examples to illustrate what he meant by these terms.[37] James Liu analyzes how some of the examples produce multiple meanings, but he admits that he could not tell how some other examples may generate multiple interpretations.[38] Jiaoran's terms, despite their specificity, come even closer to the modern concept of deliberate openness, as can be seen from his remark: "All poems with twofold or more meanings impart intention beyond words." In Liu Xie's term *fuyi* (double meaning), the *yi* may be translated as "significance" whereas in Jiaoran's terms, the *yi* refers to the poet's intended meanings. Although, as is characteristic of ancient Chinese critics, Jiaoran did not tell us how a poet could make his poems express multiple levels of meanings, his ideas definitely anticipated the modern consciousness of deliberate openness. As Liu puts it, "He may therefore be said to have anticipated not only later Chinese critics but also some Western ones who emphasized 'ambiguity' or 'plurisignation.'"[39]

Jiaoran's "*wenwai zhi zhi* (intention beyond words)" is indebted to his predecessors. Liu Xie ends his chapter with the notion of "surplus flavor": "Profound literature hides profuse meanings; its lingering flavor is indirectly wrapped. Its language gives birth to new meanings in the way line changes in a hexagram produce a new hexagram."[40] In chapter 46, "Wuse 物色," Liu Xie raises a related proposition which was to have great repercussions for later literary thinkers; "The description of objects and their colors may come to an end, but the inspired emotions are more than plenty 物色盡而情有餘." This was anticipated by Zhang Hua 張華 (232–300) of the Jin who praised Zuo Si's 左思 (c. 253–c. 307) literary works—"[Zuo Si's writings] enable readers to have surplus meanings at the end of a reading, and to find them changed and renewed in meanings after a long time has elapsed"[41]—and became a seminal idea which culminated in Zhong Rong's famous notion: "The text may come to an end but the implications are more than plenty 文已盡而意有餘."[42]

We can hardly overestimate the significance of Zhong Rong's idea. In practice, it has been frequently used by writers as the last resort to express emotions about a situation beyond language. Han Yu 韓愈 (768–824), for example, used a similar saying when he was overwhelmed by an endless sorrow in his elegiac address to his dead nephew: "Alas! Words may come to an end but my emotions cannot come to an end. Do you know this? Or don't you know this?"[43] In theoretical discourse, Zhong Rong's idea became central to traditional literary thought. It was originally intended as a definition of a key idea of Chinese literary thought in particular relations to the criticism of the *Shijing* or *Book of Songs*: *xing* 興. In his "Shipin or Gradations of Poetry," Zhong defines *xing*: "That the words come to an end but the implications are more than plenty is called *xing*."[44] Since its first appearance in the *Zhouli* (*Rites and Rituals of the Zhou Dynasty*), *xing* has remained an elusive concept in Chinese literary thought. Zhong Rong's definition not only gave this hazy concept a viable definition but also enlarged the scope of this concept. Before Zhong Rong's time, *xing* was viewed as a formula to start a poem or a form of allegory. Liu Xie summed up the views before Zhong Rong: "*Xing* is to arouse. . . . To arouse emotions depends upon responses to subtle stimuli. When emotions are aroused, the *xing* as a form is established. . . . *xing* is to lodge indirect criticism through the use of indirect allegories."[45] After Zhong Rong's definition, *xing* became a concept that concerns not only literary representation but also reader's response to a representation. Moreover, by saying that *xing* is a concept about unlimited connotations and interpretations, Zhong Rong was practically promoting a concept of openness.

Zhong Rong's idea became widely accepted after it was circulated in the Song period and promoted by scholar-poets like Mei Yaochen 梅堯臣 (1002–60), Ouyang Xiu 歐陽修 (1007–72), Sima Guang 司馬光 (1019–86), Su Shi 蘇軾, Jiang Kui 姜夔 (c. 1155–1221), Wei Tai 魏泰 (c. 1050–1110), Ge Lifang 葛立方 (d. 1164), Yang Wanli 楊萬里 (1127–1206), Yan Yu 嚴羽 (thirteenth century), Yang Zai 楊載 (1271–1323), and others. Ouyang Xiu attributed the idea of "endless meaning" to his contemporary, Mei Yaochen: "Mei Shengyu once told me: 'Though a poet may command his ideas, yet, the creation of a specific language is still difficult. . . . [A poem] must be able to depict difficult-to-describe scenes as though they appeared before one's eyes. His writing must contain unlimited implications which appear outside the text. Only then can a poem be considered superb.' "[46]

Sima Guang, a little younger than Ouyang Xiu, raised the key concept of *yi zai yanwai* (meanings lie outside the text): "When ancient poets composed poetry, they valued the ways in which intended meanings go beyond words and readers are made to understand them after thinking."[47] Wei Tai emphasized the value of endless connotations by citing both positive and negative examples: "A few years ago, when I was commenting on poetry with Wang Anshi, I said: 'Whenever one composes poetry, he ought to make it such that its source would not be exhausted when scooped up, and its flavor would become long lasting when chewed over. As for Ouyang Yongshu's poetry, his talent is quick and strength

superior; his poetic lines are also clear and robust. I, however, feel dissatisfied with its lack of lingering flavor.' "[48] Ge Lifang in his poetic criticism
reiterated Mei Yaochen's idea: "Mei Shengyu said, 'To write poetry, one
must be able to depict difficult-to-describe scenes before one's eyes; his
poetry must contain unlimited implications outside the text.' What a true
maxim."[49] Jiang Kui expressed Su Shi's as well as his own approval of
Zhong Rong's conception:

> What is valued in poetic diction is subtle reserve. Su Dongpo once said:
> "That words may end but implications are endless is a supreme adage under
> heaven." Huang Shangu was especially good at this. On the *se* zither of the
> Purity Temple, one string is plucked and three others will echo in sighs
> which spread far into the disxtance! Can later scholars refuse to strive for
> this effect in their writings? If a writer's sentences contain no words of lin-
> gering meanings, and his literary compositions feature no long-lasting lines,
> he cannot be considered a good poet among the best. Only when his sen-
> tences contain surplus flavor and his compositions have surplus meanings
> can he be viewed as the best poet among good ones.[50]

Zhong Rong's open conception of poetry is a major theme in Yang
Wanli's "Chengzhai shihua 誠齋詩話." This poetic discourse is full of
theoretical considerations of literary openness and critical analysis of open
poems. For example, he remarked: "The Golden Needle method states: 'In
an eight-line poem of the regulated style, once a line is set, it ought to
resemble a stone rolling down a high mountain, never to return.' I disagree with this view. When a poem has come to its end but its flavor is
long lasting, it is the best among the best."[51] Zhang Jie 張戒, in his poetic
criticism, attributed the merits and demerits of some poets to whether
their poetry contains suggestiveness or not. He cited some poetic lines
from the *Shijing* and considered them superb because "their wording is
intricate, their meaning profound, and it is neither obvious nor shallow.
It is precisely this quality that is valuable." He cited some other poetic
lines and viewed them as less desirable, not because their ideas are not
good but because "their wording makes meanings shallow and obvious and
conceals little surplus implications." He regarded lack of endless meaning
as a shortcoming in some of the best poets in the Tang dynasty: "The shortcoming in Yuan Cheng's, Bai Juyi's and Zhang Ji's poetry is precisely this:
they only know how to capture thoughts in one's heart but do not know
that an expression too close to the thoughts leaves a poem shallow and
plain."[52]

During and after the Song dynasty, Zhong Rong's new conception
of *xing* became a widely accepted literary conception and a critical stan-

dard. But it was Yan Yu who promoted the idea to its apotheosis: "Poetry is what sings of one's emotion and nature. The poets of the High T'ang [eighth century] relied only on inspired feeling [*hsing-ch'u*], like the antelope that hangs by its horns, leaving no traces to be found. Therefore, the miraculousness of their poetry lies in its transparent luminosity, which cannot be pieced together; it is like sound in the air, color in appearances, the moon in water, or an image in the mirror; it has limited words but unlimited meanings."[53] After Yan Yu's new interpretation, the idea of *xing* and its definition were no longer a restricted concept of *hanxu* (reserve), but a concept of openness. The sound in the air, the color of the face, the moon in the water, the image in a mirror, and to crown it all, "words end but the implications are limitless"—all refer to the nonclosure of a literary text and suggest a conception of signification beyond the surface text. Since the Northern and Southern dynasties, Zhong Rong's new conception of *xing* has become a supreme objective in artistic pursuit which is not confined to poetry alone. In the Tang, the historian Liu Zhiji 劉知幾 (661–721), applied Zhong Rong's new conception to historical narratives: "Words may seem near but the theme is far; the diction may be shallow but the meaning is profound. Though utterances have come to an end, the implied meanings are endless. If it is so, the reader will know the inner substance by looking at the outer markings, and recognize the conditions of the bones by feeling the hair [on the skin]. While he sees one thing in the lines, he will revert instead to three meanings outside the text."[54] He unequivocally declared: "Where language is economical but meanings are profuse, there lies the extraordinary beauty of narrative compositions."[55] Echoing Liu Xie's dual concepts *yinxiu*, he proposed a pair of similar concepts *xian-hui* 顯晦 for narratives: "The language of compositions is sometimes manifest and sometimes latent. Where language is manifest, elaborate words and detailed views are used with the result that the principle is exhaustively expressed in the composition. Where language is latent, words are economical but the implications of the composition overflow outside sentences."[56]

After the Song, Zhong Rong's idea became a theoretical truism and was repeated and adapted by many scholar-poets. Yang Zai 楊載 (1271–1323) of the Yuan regarded "reserve" and "endless implications" as the hallmark of superb poetic language: "What is valued in language is subtle reserve. That words may end but implications are endless is a supreme adage under heaven. On the *se* zither of the Purity Temple, one string is plucked and three others will echo in sighs, thereby producing lingering notes."[57] He also remarked: "Poetry consists of inner and outer meanings. The inner meaning is meant to exhaustively express the principle while the outer meaning is intended to exhaustively represent the images. A poem attains subtle perfection when both inner and outer meanings are suggestive of reserve."

A number of prominent scholar-poets of the Qing, who made some important contributions to Chinese literary thought, reiterated and further developed Zhong Rong's idea in one form or another. Liu Xizai 劉熙載 (1813–81) employed Zhong Rong's idea to explore the nature of *ci*-style poetry. By tracing the origin of the character *ci* and its relations to music, he views it as a literary form which signifies beyond words and sounds: "*Shuowen* annotates the character *ci* as: 'It is inside one's thought but outside words.' Xu Kai's (920–74) *Tonglun* states: 'It is inside sound but outside words. It resides in sounds but signifies beyond words. From these I came to know that *ci* is a form of poetry in which words may come to an end, but resonance and meanings are endless."[58] Shen Deqian 沈德潛 (1673–1769) voices a similar opinion related to *shi*-poetry: "*Shi*-poetry is valued for its surplus meanings. While words refer to this, meanings reach out to that"[59] In his comment on the desirable conditions of quatrains, he expresses an opinion that has been at the center of poetic suggestiveness first expounded by Sikong Tu: "The seven-character line quatrain should be dominated by this feature: language is near but feelings are far; there is no clear indication of what is held up and what is expressed. That which is described is only the scene before the eye and that which is expressed is only the words uttered by the mouth. But there should be sound off the string, flavor beyond the flavor, and it should make people's spirit wander far away. Li Taibei's poetry has all these characteristic features."[60]

Yuan Mei 袁枚 (1716–98) regarded the idea of endless implications beyond words as a critical standard: "If a poem has no meanings outside its utterances, it would taste like wax."[61] In his poetic commentaries, he explained why Su Shi's regulated style poetry was not as good as his *ci* poetry: "Su Dongpo's modern style poetry lacks the arduous efforts of brewing and distilling, cooking and smelting. Therefore, when its words come to an end, its meanings also end, having no tunes beyond the string or flavor beyond the flavor. Wang Shizhen (1634–1711) did not consider it Su Shi's forte nor a model for later generations. This is a right judgment."[62] Ye Xie 葉燮 (1627–1703) expressed a more systematic view of suggestiveness: "Where poetry is at its best, the subtle perfection lies in boundless reserve and limitless implications, and in poetic imagination reaching what is minute and opaque. What is expressed in poetry borders on the expressible and inexpressible. Its referents and source reside at the juncture of the comprehensible and incomprehensible. Its words may say something, but its meanings refer to something else. It abolishes any points of reference and transcends shapes and images; it rejects all arguments and discussions while it stretches the thinking process to its limit and leads one into a realm of a profound trance and hallucination. This is how poetry attains its perfection."[63]

Most traditional scholars primarily engaged in sweeping generalizations about literary openness, or liked to illustrate it with poetic examples. If they touched upon linguistic and formal aspects of openness, their discussion tended to be very cursory. Jiang Kui, for example, wrote: "Where words come to an end but meanings do not end, it is not that some meanings are left unsaid but that some implications seem to be discernible in the expressed utterances."[64] Ye Xie was one of a few traditional theorists who extensively discussed the psychological, linguistic, and semiotic mechanisms of how poetic openness is achieved. He selected a few poetic lines from Du Fu's poetry and engaged in a word-for-word close analysis of their signifying mechanisms to show how the apt choice and arrangement of words leave the poems full of implications. One of the lines is from Du Fu's 杜甫 (712–70) "Xuanyuan huangdi miao" (The Temple of the Primal Mysterious Emperor): "Blue tiles exposed to the early chill without 碧瓦初寒外." Ye Xie's reading is so perceptively conducted that I am amazed at the modernity of his close reading. He suggests that the poetic line was so suggestively worded that it refers to conditions and situations quite beyond itself. For example, the word *wai* (or outside) suggests *nei* (or inside) because "blue tiles" as a synecdoche for the temple serves as a demarcation line between the inside and outside of the temple. Overall, this single line yields a series of what scholars in the West could term binary oppositions: inside and outside, presence and absence, empty and solid, far and near, early and later, microcosm and macrocosm. But in the Chinese tradition, these opposite terms form a series of complementary bipolarities. He exclaimed:

I do not know whether it describes blue tiles or early winter, nearness or distance. If one insists on understanding it in terms of reason and solid event, I am afraid that even though he might command the eloquently argued discourses on heaven by the Ji Xia scholars, he would feel his ability taxed to its limit by this. However, were he to put himself in the mood and situation of that occasion, he would feel that the scene created by the five characters looks as though it were created by heaven and arranged by earth. It was shown as an image, perceived by the eye, and understood by the heart. It is an idea in one's consciousness but it cannot be expressed in words; when it is expressed in words, its significance would defy comprehension. With distinctive description it shows me that which lies beyond silent understanding and vivid image in the mind. It seems as though it had an inside and an outside, a cold and an early cold—all were especially entrusted to the solid image of blue tiles. There are a center and peripheral borders; the real and unreal complement each other; presence and absence are mutually established. It was taken from an immediate scene which begets itself. Its principle is as clear as light; its event as solid as can be."[65]

Since the Song, the open conception of *xing* has become intertwined with some other key concepts like *shenyun* 神韻 (divine rhythm), *wenqi* 文氣 (literary pneuma), and *yijing* 意境 (idea-realm). The last concept has been considered by many scholars to be the supreme aesthetic principle of Chinese literary thought. Zhu Chengjue 朱承爵 (fl. early sixteenth century) of the Ming expressed this belief: "The full artistry of poetry lies in the thorough mastery of *yijing* [idea-scene]. It transcends sound and tones in order to achieve the true flavor."[66] Wang Guowei 王國維 (1877–1927), the last giant of traditional literary thinkers, pushed *yijing* (idea-scene) to its apotheosis. He reiterated in his poetical discourse that if one does not understand *yijing*, he is unqualified to engage in literary criticism, and if a writer does not make arduous efforts to create *yijing* in his writings, he cannot become a first-rate writer. The major theme of his *Renjian cihua* [*Poetic Talk of the Human World*] is on *yijing*, which he defined in terms of Zhong Rong's conception of *xing* and Yan Yu's 嚴羽 (fl. 1180–1235) conception of *xingqu*: "No other *ci*-style poet, ancient or modern, has reached as high a stylistic form as Jiang Kui. It is a pity that he did not make arduous efforts in studying *yijing*. One, therefore, feels that his *ci* poetry lacks flavor beyond words, sound beyond the string, and cannot but be relegated to the second best. He had plenty of clear and lofty aspirations, but had little profound and far-reaching taste."[67]

My study of traditional literary concepts related to literary openness is far from exhaustive. Nevertheless, it is sufficient to show that discussions of these concepts formed a major current in the mainstream of traditional literary thought especially with respect to poetic criticism. My analysis of some scholars' ideas confirms beyond doubt that the conception of *xing* in terms of unlimited writerly connotations and readerly associations is comparable to the modern conception of a literary text as an open space of connotations and hermeneutics. The insight reaped from the discussions is not just modern; some may be said to be incredibly postmodern. For example, Liu Xie's idea of *yinxiu* (concealed grace) was picked up by a scholar who developed it to the level of insight into literary creativity that goes beyond the New Critical "intentional fallacy" and echoes "intertexuality." Tan Xian 譚獻 (1830–1901) of the Qing remarked in his poetic criticism: "Again, its form does not have to be the central thesis. It puts forth its words from the rear and from sideways, makes sidewise connections with the emotions. It starts by touching similar stimuli, and ends by exhausting the category. It is even possible that the writer may not have had the implications on his mind, but there is no reason to say that the reader should not have the implications in his mind."[68] Tan Xian's assertion blatantly declares that the reader's construal need not coincide with authorial intention. The boldness of his vision in this passage is truly modern. We can appreciate its full impact when we compare it with a similar idea expressed by T. S. Eliot: "A poem may appear to mean very different things to different readers, and all of these meanings may be different from what the author thought he meant. . . . The reader's interpretation may differ from the author's and be equally valid—it may even be better. There may be much more in a poem than the author was aware of."[69] Tan Xian's insight into creativity has reached the deep recess of the author's unconscious and anticipated Eliot's idea that "the poet is occupied with frontiers of consciousness beyond which words fail, though meanings still exist" and Kristeva's "semiotic chora," the nonexpressive totality which is a prelinguistic and extralinguistic dimension of signifying practice.[70] It certainly is compatible with what I wish to call "unconscious openness," the implications of which the author is not conscious until the reader brings them forth through textual analysis.

Hanxu (Subtle Reserve): Unlimited Semiosis

In the development of Chinese theories on literary openness, Sikong Tu 司空圖 (837–908) made an extraordinary contribution that was many sided. In my opinion, however, the most important facet of it lies in his advancing the idea of *hanxu* (subtle reserve) and its accompanying thesis, "Without attaching a single word,/[the poem may] Fully capture the wind and flow." Here, he treats signifying practice in such a way that it may be viewed as a burgeoning form of unlimited semiosis. In his "Yu Li sheng lun shishu 與李生論詩書," he carried on the gustatory metaphor for the endless implications of meaning in Lao Zi's and Zhuangzi's idea of *wuwei* 無味 and Zhong Rong's "lingering flavor 遺味," and started a tradition that went all the way to Yuan Mei, Wang Guowei, and beyond: "The difficulty of writing prose is great, but the difficulty of writing poetry is even greater than that of writing prose. There are innumerable metaphors, ancient and modern, to describe this difficult situation. I, however, believe that one must be able to make distinction among flavors before he can talk about poetry."[71] By comparing literary taste to the tastes of food, he disapproved of a literary work imparting a single flavor. Instead, he advanced the famous dictum that poetry should be capable of conveying flavors beyond flavor: "It is nearby but does not float; it is distant but not exhausted—only after these conditions are met can one speak of reaching beyond the rhyme. . . . If one complements it with full beauty as artistry, he would know what the meaning beyond flavor is." In another letter, "Yu Jifu shu 與極甫書," he advocated "images beyond the image and scenes beyond the scene."[72] As his advocacy touches upon the visual, auditory, and gustatory senses, he seemed to have conceived of a good poem as a multimedia art product with multiple levels of implications capable of appealing to the reader's five senses. Moreover, he advocated that a good poem should have connotations beyond these perceptible sensations. In so doing he paved the way for the emergence of the highest aesthetic principle in Chinese poetry, *rushen* 入神 (entering the divine), proposed by Yan Yu: "There is only one ultimate achievement in poetry: it is called 'to enter the divine.' When poetry enters the domain of the divine, it has reached its perfection and limit. Nothing can be added to it."[73] *Shen* (divinity) is a vague term in Chinese poetics. One of its hallmarks is whether a poem has meanings beyond words. Li Chonghua 李重華, a poetic critic of the Qing, identified this quality after examining some first-rate poetry in terms of Sikong Tu's dictum: "set the divine in motion as through the void, / set the pneuma in motion like a rainbow." He declared: "The reason poetry especially values divinity is precisely because a poem that has achieved divinity evokes meanings beyond its words."[74]

As for how a poem can reach a supreme state of excellence, Sikong Tu proposed the key concept *hanxu* 含蓄 in one of the most important treatises on traditional literary theory, the *Ershisi shipin* (*Twenty-Four Forms of Poetry*), Yang Tingzhi 楊廷之 (fl. 1821), a scholar of the Qing, provides a useful gloss of this concept: "*Han* means 'hold in the mouth.' *Xu* means 'store up.' [The concept means] holding within the unsubstantiated and storing up the substantiated."[75] The open-endedness of this concept can be partially seen from the diverse English translations: "conservation" by H. A. Giles,[76] "the pregnant mode" by Yang Hsien-yi and Gladys Yang,[77] "reserve" by Wai-lim Yip,[78] and "potentiality" by Pauline Yu.[79] James Liu considers "reserve" to be the best translation because "it means both 'holding back' (*han*) and 'storing up' (*xu*)—by being 'reserved' in words, one can build up a 'reserve' of meaning."[80] To discuss the full implications of this concept, I need to quote in full the passage that explains it:

Without attaching a single word,	不著一字，
Fully captures the wind and flow.	盡得風流。
Words may not involve the poet's self,	語不涉己，
Yet they seem unable to bear such grief.	若不勘憂。
Something is truly in control of all this,	是有真宰，
With which one should sink and swim.	與之沈浮。
'Tis like straining wine from a full container,	如淥滿酒，

Or a blooming season reverting to autumn.　　　花時反秋。
Dust in the sky roams to and fro;　　　　　　　悠悠空塵；
Foam in the sea comes and goes;　　　　　　　忽忽海漚；
Shallow or deep, gathering or dispersing:　　　　淺深聚散，
Of myriad things seen, only one is taken.　　　　萬取一收。[81]

This is one of the twenty-four passages in the *Ershisi shipin*. There have been different interpretations. Because of the character *pin* in the title, Sikong's work has often been viewed as a critical work on different kinds of poetic styles. Accordingly, the title has been translated variously as "twenty-four modes of poetry," "twenty-four categories of poetry," "twenty-four orders of poetry," and "twenty-four moods of poetry." This restricted sense in a way hinders our understanding of the work as a whole and of *hanxu* in particular. Instead of viewing the work as only a study of poetic styles, we ought to consider it as metacriticism or philosophy of poetry. My idea is not entirely new. In fact, Zhu Dongrun 朱東潤, in his study of ancient Chinese literary criticism, advanced this idea as early as the 1930s. In his comment on the *Ershisi shipin*, Zhu Dongrun states: "The *Shipin* can be said to be a philosophical treatise on poetry. It discusses in detail the life outlook of a poet, methods of poetic composition, and the classification of poetic subjects."[82] Zhu regroups the twenty-four categories into five big divisions and classifies "Hanxu" into the division of compositional methods. Zhu's opinion is fairly sound and may help us better understand the category in question.

The "Hanxu" category is perhaps the most important section in the *Ershisi shipin*. One scholar regards it as the central theme of the whole book.[83] Of course, it may be the most difficult to understand. It poses difficulties for several reasons. First, it is full of indeterminate or ambiguous words. Second, some wording occurs in variant forms. For example, the third and fourth lines in the common edition become "語不涉己，已不勘憂" or "語不涉難，已不勘憂" in other versions. Similarly, a variant of "如淥滿酒" reads as "如滿淥酒." Third, it is dominated by metaphysical thinking heavily indebted to philosophical Daoism. Last and most importantly, its own poetic language is characterized by an interpenetration of logical thinking and imagistic thinking. The last difficulty is perhaps the principal barrier and also the key to an adequate understanding of the meanings of the passage. Previous scholars have noticed all the stated difficulties. And some of them have also argued that this passage was meant by Sikong Tu to convey his idea of "themes beyond flavor 味外之旨," "meanings beyond the rhythm 韻外之致," "images beyond the image and scenes beyond the scene 象外之象，景外之景." Still others have pointed out that the difficulty arises from the fact that it was written in imagistic language rather than expository language. No one, however, seems to have paid much attention to the conception of using formal presentation as a supplement to the theme of the work.

In a curious way, this mode of using form as content can be compared with Jacques Lacan's explications of Freud's theory of dreams and the unconscious. In the *Interpretation of Dreams*, Freud describes the dream as a rebus, an enigmatic puzzle. In his elucidation of Freud's insight into dreams, one scholar points out: "Lacan's own message is locked up in an expression so obscure and enigmatic that for the uninitiated it constitutes a kind of rebus in itself."[84] The reason Lacan's elucidation becomes a sort of rebus is because of his writing style that mimics the subject matter. Indeed, Lacan's theoretical discourse on the unconscious is notoriously difficult to understand because of its convoluted sentence structure and obscure line of thinking. When people ask why Lacan writes in such a difficult-to-understand style, one answer is that he thinks that only by writing in this way can he fully capture the mechanisms of dreams and the unconscious. I venture to suggest that Sikong Tu was writing in the same way in which Lacan tries to replicate the workings of the unconscious. Sikong's paramount aim was to expound the idea of "meanings beyond words" in poetry. He employed a number of analogies to present his idea. Perhaps he might have thought that, since he was expounding the unlimited implications of poetry, the best way was to present his idea in a language that by itself somehow constitutes the source of unlimited implications. Su Shi, after repeated study of Sikong Tu's poetic language, came to a similar understanding: "He consciously inscribed what he obtained from the surface of language in his twenty-four poems. It was a pity that I did not understand its trick in the past. I lamented my lack of understanding after I went over his wording many times."[85]

That literary theories were expounded in poetic language is not an isolated phenomenon. After all, Lu Ji's "Discourse on Writing" and Liu Xie's *Literary Mind and the Carving of Dragons* were written in a poetic form, too. But there is a difference between Sikong Tu's use of poetic form and that of his predecessors, at least in the "Hanxu" passage. His predecessors' use of poetic language is mainly a formal issue; their primary aim was to illuminate their ideas in as easy-to-understand a way as the poetic form allowed. The use of poetic form was only a means to an end. In Sikong Tu's case, the use of poetic language is both a means to an end and an end in itself. In other words, I would argue, the use of highly poetic language was a deliberate move to replicate the process of open signification and representation, a way both to expound the idea of *hanxu* (or reserve) and to show how the idea is conveyed. By compelling the reader to ponder the poetic language as well as the message conveyed through the language, Sikong Tu dealt with not only a metalanguage but also a metatheory of poetry making. What I mean is that his move seems to suggest that he was (un)consciously brooding over what Jacobson calls the "poetic function." In his study of verbal communication, Jacobson brings out a set of six factors: addresser, addressee, context, message, contact, and code. According to his theory, if the set of factors focuses on the message for its own sake, what results from this self-focusing effort is the poetic function of language.[86] Sikong Tu wanted to put across a theory of unlimited implications in poetry. The self-focusing message exemplifies a theory of poetic openness precisely through the openness of the poetic form.

From this point of view, it is perhaps an illusion for anyone to presume that he can somehow get a correct reading of "Hanxu" in particular and of the *Ershisi shipin* as a whole. In contrast to the accepted elucidations, I wish to argue that Sikong's concept of *hanxu* has exceeded the traditional conception of metaphysical suggestiveness and gestures toward the modern concept of openness through unlimited semiosis. For my argument, I will conduct a detailed analysis of the category. The passage as a whole is structured like a minitreatise with a title that is the central idea and guiding principle for the whole discourse, and with vivid details that serve as evidence to support the central argument. The opening couplet expresses the thesis of the minitreatise: "Without attaching a single word / [the poem] Fully captures the wind and flow." There have been several interpretations. First, it conveys the metaphysical suggestiveness of "saying nothing and therefore saying everything." Weng Fanggang 翁方綱 (1733–1818) provided such an explanation: "'Not to attach a single word' is precisely to say that this way can embrace myriads of existent things."[87] Second, it means that a certain theme is implicitly presented not by directly touching the subject but through antithesis, contrast, and the creation of an ethos. Third, it tries to convey profound emotions and evoke unlimited responses through limited, concrete but evocative images and scenes.

The second couplet elaborates the thesis expressed in the first couplet: "Words may not involve the poet's self; / Yet they seem unable to bear such grief." Different versions may lead to different readings. Here, I will adhere to the standard version but will try to bring out the ambiguities. *Ji* 己 (self) is an ambiguous word. It may refer to the poet; it may refer to the theme of a poem; it may even refer to the creative self. Similarly, *ruo* 若 may be either a connective meaning "as if" or an indefinite pronoun referring to an indefinite person. As a connective, the couplet may mean that a poem does not touch a subject and therefore it should not arouse strong feelings, but the total effect of it amounts to a powerful response.[88] As a pronoun, it may refer to the reader, to the reader's response, and to an "other." Accordingly, the couplet may mean: words may not touch directly the theme of a poem but the full significance is already adequately conveyed; or words do not seem to involve the poet or his self, but the poem produces a powerful affect in the reader; or words may not touch one subject, but they implicitly impart its full impact.

The third couplet works on the rationale behind the central thesis: "Something is truly in control of all this, / With which one should sink and swim." Many scholars accept the interpretation that the "something truly in control" is the "master of the universe" or the Dao. They have cited as support Lao Zi' words: "There is a real master that controls the myriads of things" and Zuang Zi's words: "There seems to be a real master, but one just cannot see signs of it."[89] James Liu offers a slightly different view: "Sikong Tu is speaking of capturing the dynamic force of nature through intuition."[90] Still another scholar argues that the "real master" is the major theme of a composition, which is its soul.[91] Since Sikong Tu was presenting his theory of poetry, I may also argue that the "real master" may be the force of poetic creativity that controls composition. Due to different readings, the word *shi* 是 may mean the real universe, the universe reflected in poetry, the idea of "reserve," and the way of poetic composition. All are possible, but for my semiotic reading, I prefer to settle on the creation of "subtle reserve."

The fourth couplet resorts to analogies: " 'Tis like straining wine from a full container, / Or a blooming season reverting to autumn." Scholars all agree that this couplet employs the analogy of straining wine and the budding state of a flower to illustrate the idea of "reserve." The only disagreement centers on how wine is related to the idea of reserve. Guo Shaoyu is of the opinion that in straining out wine, even when the cup is full, one still leaves something behind in the strainer.[92] Another interpretation argues that just as in the brewing process, when the wine yeast is fermenting, wine will ceaselessly ooze out of the brewing container, so a poem with reserve will radiate out endless implications from the text.[93] The second analogy compares poetic suggestiveness to the withholding of the full bloom of a flower at the return of cold weather. The last four lines further illuminate the central idea and nicely wrap it up.

The last four lines have very different interpretations. Scholars generally believe that dust in the sky and foams on the sea are two more analogies for the conditions of reserve or the different ways of achieving reserve. Flying dust will roam freely in the infinite sky and foam on the sea will appear and disappear endlessly—both are apt metaphors for the complex and indescribable process of poetic creation that has no definite closure and adheres to no definite ways of composition. But despite the fact that poetic creation is as indefinite and profound as the magnitude of the sky and the depth of the sea, one piece of general advice is sound: poetic creation must try to achieve *hanxu* (reserve). The practical measure is to "take one [apt image] out of ten thousand things observed." This is an understanding from the poet's point of view. For the poet, he may observe different phenomena but he cannot write down all he has observed. So he must incorporate the different phenomena in a single mode of reserve. From the reader's point of view, the implications of a poem resemble the dust in the sky that flies freely or the foam in the sea that appears and disappears endlessly and unexpectedly. The implications may reach in all directions and cover different levels or dimensions. The readers' response may be thousandfold but the different responses all emanate from the evocativeness of reserve.

I have stated earlier that Sikong's idea of reserve may have gone beyond suggestiveness and touched upon the modern idea of unlimited semiosis. From this perspective, I may offer another psycholinguistic reading: the analogy of dust and foam may be viewed as the free play of signification, endlessly generating new meanings and implications. Psychologically, the analogy of dust and foam is like memory trace in the psychic apparatus, particularly in relation to the unconscious, which cannot be perceived by its presence but can be apprehended by its effect. Writing about the human capacity for retaining or reviving the experience of things past, Freud uses the term "memory trace" to refer to the ways in which the perceptual apparatus of the mind is always already inhabited by incidents inscribed upon the memory. In terms of literary creation, the analogy may be viewed as an intuitive grasp of what Derrida calls "trace," a theoretical term associated with other terms like arche-writing, spacing, and especially différance. Derrida agrees with Saussure's theory of language as a system based on differentiation, but extends the latter's idea further by arguing that meaning is never present in words themselves. For example, "cat" has meaning only because it differs from "bat," "vat," "cap," and so on. Therefore, the meaning of a word is always dependent on everything that is not the word. In other words, meaning is constantly deferred and generated in a relationship among other words, a potential space which he calls "différance." The basic meaning of différance is derived from the coincidence of meanings in the verb *différer*: to differ (in space) and to defer (to put off in time, to postpone presence). The word does not function simply either as *différence* (difference) or as *différance* in the usual sense (deferral), but plays on both meanings at the same time.[94] This theory may offer a new way of understanding Sikong's idea of *hanxu* and its theoretical potential. The act of *han* (holding back) and *xu* (storing up) is not simply a way of representation but moreover a psycholinguistic process of signification. What supports my reading is that the idea of *hanxu* coincides exactly with Derrida's notion of *différance* in some concrete terms: "The two apparently different values of *différance* are tied together in Freudian theory: to differ as discernibility, distinction, separation, diastem, *spacing*; and to defer as detour, relay, reserve, *temporization*."[95] We need to pay attention to the series of terms in Derrida's statement, especially to such terms as "distinction," "separation," "diastem," "detour," "relay," and "reserve."

Just as "trace" in Derrida's theory serves as a provisional analogy for the production of meaning in language, so the analogy of dust in the sky and foam in the sea may be an intuitive understanding of the endless differing and deferring of meaning in language signification. In the "Hanxu" passage, the first two couplets mention *zi* 字 and *yu* 語, both of which mean "words" in spoken and written forms. In the rest of the passage, most of the concrete images may be considered to be metaphorical references to the implications generated by "words," for example, meaning or poetic effect. In the light of this understanding, I argue that the image of dust and foam are not mere analogies for myriad things in the universe; they may be viewed as symbolic representations of the trace or free play in language signification. "Foam in the sea comes and goes 忽忽海漚" may refer to the spatialization of signification, the spatial deferring of meaning, as is suggested by *qianshen* 淺深 (shallowness and depth) and the sudden appearance and disappearance in *huhu* 忽忽. "Dust in the sky roams to and fro" may refer to the temporalization of signification, the spatial difference of relations as is suggested by gathering and dispersing (*jusan* 聚散) and the temporal sense in "to and fro" (*youyou* 悠悠). The two analogies imaginatively capture the vertical and horizontal movements in the production of discourse, thereby coinciding with the poetic function working on the two axes of selection and combination in Jacobson's theory of poetic language.[96] "Shallow or deep" may refer to the act of choosing words on the axis of selection while "gathering and dispersing" may refer to the act of arranging words on the axis of combination. Such a reading, let me point out, finds support in a traditional reading, too. Sun Liankui 孫聯奎 (fl. 1821) wrote in his commentary: "'Shallow and deep' refers to the vertical way of saying; 'gather and disperse' refers to the horizontal way of saying."[97] But the spatial and the temporal senses in the two analogies are not clearly cut. "Shallow and deep" is used to describe foam which pops up in the sea, but "gathering and dispersing" is also fit to describe the movement of foam. Conversely, "shallow and deep" may also be used to describe the movement of dust because "shallow and deep" may be transformed spatially into "high and low." In other words, the two analogies display an equivalence further strengthened by their insignificant quality.

The two analogies may therefore be regarded as an imagistic representation of Jacobson's famous saying: *"The poetic function projects the principle of equivalence from the axis of selection into the axis of combination."*[98]

Sun Liankui further added: "shallow and deep, gathering and dispersing—all refer to things outside of the subject. The four characters embrace all images which are referred to as *wan* or ten thousand in the next line."[99] Since myriad images all lie outside of the subject, how can they be inscribed in the text or implied by the text? Although traditional scholars have never elaborated on this, their reasoning comes close to an intuitive understanding of unlimited semiosis, the interaction of the sign. In an evocative interpretation, Yang Tingzhi touches upon the mechanism of semiosis: "This has a real master which controls its inner mechanism. Sinking and swimming with it, a poem can exit from the shallow but enter the deep with layers upon layers of waves and ripples that embrace unlimited implications. This shows not only what it withholds through the real master but also what it stores up through sinking and swimming with it. When Sikong says 'this has a real master,' he means that what the poem withholds is not without substance. When he says 'sink and swim with it,' he means that what it stores up comes from inside."[100]

In the main conceptual discourses, semiosis is viewed as a mental process that underlies the very structure of the mind. In semiosis, there are three primary components: the sign (a representative image or a word), the object referred to (which can be either concrete or abstract), and the meaning that results from the connection between the sign and object through association. Meaning can be unlimited because it results from successive production of interpretants. An interpretant is C. S. Peirce's notion of the individual's particular interpretation of the triadic relationship that inheres in semiosis.[101] As the mental effect or thought generated by the relationship between the sign and objet, the interpretant produces a further interpretant through the process of understanding and interpretation. Peirce calls this successive and perpetual production of new interpretants "unlimited semiosis." I consider it to be at the core of Sikong Tu's conception of *hanxu*.

In terms of psycholinguistic theories, Sikong Tu's concept of *hanxu* and its poetic explication may be viewed as an intuitive grasp of the signifying mechanism of not only poetic language but also literary openness. In this connection, the "real master" in the passage may be the poetic unconscious responsible for the act of "picking one [apt image] out of ten thousand things," and for the artistry of achieving "reserve." In the same vein, *fengliu*, which literally means "wind and flow," may be construed to mean a dynamic and endless process of signification. James Liu, dissatisfied with previous scholars' interpretation of the term, argues for defining *fengliu* as the "dynamic force" or "life-rhythm of nature" on the ground that the *Cihai* 辭海 defines the term as "the quintessential spirit, the tone or flavor, which cannot be sought from traces or appearances."[102] The definition in the *Cihai* supports my semiotic interpretation of the term equally well. And the thesis statement, "Without attaching a single word,/Fully captures the flowing wind," may be said to have captured the essence of semiosis: unlimited meanings are not to be found in the words on the page, but to be generated by the differential relations among signifiers. The condition of *fengliu* is the endlessly deferred and delayed dynamics of signification in the differential network of signs. Meaning is not produced as a result of the sequence of already existing words but exists in the gaps between already existent words. It is in this sense that we may say that without putting down additional words, a poem may exhaustively represent a multitude of meanings, thereby becoming a space without closure. In the final analysis, Sikong Tu's concept of *hanxu* is an intuitive way of conceptualizing literary openness and poetics of openness in a psycholinguistic sense. The unlimited meanings beyond words are not withheld (*han*) or stored (*xiu*) in the textual content but are generated in the gap between signifier and signified and in the space between words. My semiotic analysis of Sikong Tu's idea of *hanxu* may serve to open the hitherto unrecognized possibility of envisioning the Chinese idea of "meanings beyond words" as a psycholinguistic concept built on the free play of signification, in addition to metaphysical suggestiveness.

Wu (Ontological Non-Being): Self-Generative Suggestiveness

In contemporary literary thought, literary openness is predicated on the ontological conception of a literary text as an empty structure constructed of words which are empty signifiers. In metaphorical ways, some contemporary theorists have employed the analogies of "empty basket" and "empty shelf" to characterize the openness of a text. These are the Western ways of representing the ontological basis of literary openness. In traditional Chinese literary thought, the openness of a text is given a philosophical basis of ontological void similar to the empty Dao or Taiji [the Great Ultimate] or Wuji [the Non-ultimate]. The essence of this ontological void is *wu* (nothingness or non-being). Centering around *wu* are a series of ideas related to aesthetic suggestiveness: *wusheng* (no sound), *wuxing* (no shape), *wuwei* (no taste), *wuzhuang* (no condition), *wuming* (no name), *wuwu* (no substance), and so on. That these ideas originated from *wu* (or nothingness) finds a concentrated expression in a passage of the *Lao Zi*:

What cannot be seen is called evanescence; / What cannot be heard is called rarefied; / What cannot be touched is called minute. These three cannot be fathomed / And so they are confused and looked upon as one. / Its upper part is not dazzling; / Its lower part is not obscure. / Dimly visible, it cannot be named / And returns to that which is without substance. / This is called the shape that has no shape, / The image that is without substance / This is called indistinct and shadowy.[103]

In this passage, Lao Zi attempted to give a verbal representation of the Dao in his conception. It is nameless and indescribable, and transcends human senses and experiences. Nevertheless, it is not airy nothing but a natural law that exists in the universe. A sensitive person can feel its existence through his inner eye and inner ear. The Dao or the natural law of the universe and aesthetic suggestiveness belong to two different categories of inquiry, but in the Chinese tradition, the latter is firmly predicated on the epistemological perception of the former. And in some ways, a literary work is conceived of as a verbal entity comparable to the Dao.

This conception of literature as a Dao-like entity was not explicitly expressed in the mainstream of literary thought, where a literary text was conceived ontologically as a manifestation (*wen* or patterns) of the Dao which is both its source and substance. In his "Yuandao" chapter of the *Wenxin diaolong*, Liu Xie posited the concept *dao zhi wen* (patterns of the Dao). This concept has two aspects of meaning. One aspect refers to the natural patterns of the universe: *tianxiang* (celestial phenomena), *dixing* (terrestrial topography), *dongzhi zhi wen* (shapes and colors of flora and fauna), and so on. Another aspect refers to *renwen* 人文 (human culture) and *wenci* (literally, patterned words/phrases). Like all patterns, *wenci* is a manifested form of the Dao: "The reason *ci* is capable of stimulating all under heaven is because it is the *wen* of the Dao."[104] Given that *wenci* refers to literary writing, this conception implies that a literary text is ontologically an empty structure which derives its meanings from the omnipresent Dao. In a different but related line of thinking, a literary text was conceived of not only as an empty structure but also as a self-generative entity like the Dao or *Taiji* (the Great Ultimate). This conception was implicitly stated in a variety of poetic discourses. An explicit expression is found in the Qing dynasty literary theorist Huang Ziyun's 黃子雲 (1691–1754) poetic criticism:

Poetry is none other than a Great Ultimate where the *yin* and *yang* were born and myriad things attained their life, and where there are infinite changes. Therefore, a topic has one theme, a chapter one formal style, a sentence a [syntactic] method. Though there is one, that one gives rise to tens; the tens in turn give rise to hundreds and thousands. None follows conventions; none duplicates. It is like heaven giving birth to human beings. Millions of people have ears, eyes, mouths, and noses, yet within the tiny space of these organs, there is not the least trace of duplicated sameness. If we want to know why, the rationale originates from the Great Ultimate.[105]

This passage represents a daring reconception of literary composition in terms of some of the most venerable categories in the Chinese tradition. The originality of it can be seen from a comparison with Liu Xie's classic conception: "Human culture originated in the Great Ultimate. . . . From Fu Xi, the mysterious sage who created the *Classic of Changes*, to Confucius, the 'king without Crown,' who transmitted the teachings—none of the sages did not follow the principle of the Dao in their writings; all of them transmitted their teachings by studying the divine principle. The Dao hands down writing through the sages; the sages make the Dao manifest through their writing."[106] While Liu Xie and most scholars conceived of literary composition as a manifestation of the Great Ultimate or Dao, Huang Ziyun compared it to a miniature *Taiji* having the same self-generating mechanism as the Dao.

In his "Taiji tushuo 太極圖說" (A View of the Taiji Diagram), Zhou Dunyi 周敦頤 (1017–73) of the early Song opens his treatise with this statement: "*Wuji er Taiji* The Non-ultimate! And also the Great Ultimate (*T'ai-chi*) 無極而太極."[107] Zhu Xi 朱熹 (1130–1200), in his "Taijitu shuo jie" (Explanation of the View of the Taiji Diagram), explains: "The content of the upper heaven has no sound or smell, but it is actually the pivot of Nature and the root of all kinds of things. It is therefore said that 'the Non-ultimate is also the Great Ultimate.'"[108] There is little doubt that this explanation comes from Daoism. In philosophical Daoism, the Great Ultimate converges with the Dao. The philosophical discourse that attempted to merge the Taiji and the Dao started with the *Xicizhuan*, and by the time of the Song dynasty, the Taiji became completely merged with the Dao. Shao Yong 邵雍 (1011–77), an philosopher of the Song, viewed the Taiji as the exact equivalent of the Dao. He unequivocally declared that "*Dao wei Taiji* (The Dao is the Taiji)."[109] He further clarified their relationship: "Taiji Dao zhi ji ye (The Taiji is the ultimate of the Dao)."[110] Lu Xiangshan 陸象山 (1139–93) also expressed the same opinion. Since the Song, the convergence of the two concepts has been widely accepted. Zhu Bokun, a leading modern scholar on the *Book of Changes*, compares the concept of the Dao with the ideas conveyed by the Taiji Diagram in the *Daozang* 道藏 (*The Treasure of Daoism*) and comes to the conclusion that the Great Ultimate is precisely the Dao in the *Laozi*.[111] Fung Yu-lan draws the same conclusion, though he views the Taiji and Wuji as collectively constituting the Dao.[112]

In his comment on the nature of the Dao, Wang Bi, like all Daoist scholars, considers *wu* 無 ("nothing") to be the origin of the universe: "Myriad things and shapes share their home in One. Through what do they lead to One? Through *Wu* (nothing)."[113] Whether it is the Non-ultimate or the Great Ultimate or the Dao, the origin and foundation of the universe is believed to be *wu*, a concept which covers a gamut of meanings like "absence," "emptiness," "nothingness," "unperceived presence," or "non-being."[114] Daoism holds that the Dao is the emptiness or nothingness that gives birth to all things. In the *Daode jing* 道德經, the unnamable and indescribable Dao is compared to an "empty bowl." In Lao Zi's conception, "nothing" is the ontology of the Dao while "something" is its function.[115] Though both "nothing" and "something" are the two aspects of binary opposition in the Dao, "nothing" predates "something," for the *Daode jing* states in a later chapter (chap. 41), "The myriad creatures in the world are born from Something, and Something from Nothing."[116] Zhuangzi also views "nothing" as the origin of "something": "In the beginning, there was *wu* or nothingness; the nameless *wu* is the origin of one." In another chapter (chap. 42), Lao Zi describes the generative principle of the Dao: "The Way [Tao] begets one; one begets two; two begets three; the three begets the myriad creatures."[117]

Within the large context of Chinese philosophical thought and literary criticism, we may see that Huang Ziyun's statement about the ontological basis of poetry (literature) is not just an apt analogy; it is an apt extension of similar views implicitly held by some scholars. For example, Confucius expressed a similar view, though in a less discernable language. In the *Hanshi waizhuan* 韓詩外傳 there is a passage concerning the greatness of the "Guanju." Zi Xia 子夏, a disciple of Confucius, asked his master why the poem came to be the first of the anthology. Confucius answered: "The person who composed 'Guanju,' looking up, modeled [it] after the heaven, and looking down, modeled [it] after the earth. Mysterious and profound, it is where virtue resides. Multifarious and bubbling, it is where the Way is practiced. [The poem] is like a divine dragon which constantly changes, and a piece of patterned composition full of dazzling charm. Great indeed is the Way of 'Guanju,' to which the myriad things attach and on which the life of all living beings depends."[118] A reader familiar with the legend of how Fu Xi created the eight trigrams will notice the similar wording and tone with which Confucius is believed to have described the importance of "Guanju." The allusion to the creation of trigrams and the explicit equation of the poem's multiplicity of meanings with the self-generating principle of the Dao seem to suggest that the poem is a self-generative entity like the Dao or Taiji constructed on a principle of metaphysical emptiness or ontological openness. The difference between Confucius's view and Huang's idea is superficial. While the former referred to a specific poem, the latter addressed poetry in general. Even this superficial difference is negligible when we take note of the way in which Confucius expounded on the implications of the poem. In Confucius's conception, "Guanju" as the first poem of the *Shijing* stands for the poetic collection as a whole through a synecdochic representation and was perhaps meant to represent poetry in general.

As my exploration unfolds, we will see that Huang Ziyun's reconceptualization of Confucius's similar idea is the philosophical basis of aesthetic suggestiveness and literary openness in the Chinese tradition. The ontological status of literature in a cultural tradition cannot be separated from its philosophical tradition. Huang Ziyun's reconception was based on the self-generating principle of *wu* in Daoism and of the *Taiji* in the *Book of Changes*. For an inquiry into literary openness, Huang Ziyun's conception can be further extended to form the philosophical basis of literary openness in the Chinese tradition and to serve as a bridge between Chinese and Western conceptions of openness and open poetics. The Great Ultimate or the Non-ultimate is not simply the ontological basis of Chinese aesthetic suggestiveness. In Huang Ziyun's reconceptualization, there is an implicit idea that the self-generating principles of *yin* and *yang* are linguistic principles pertaining to signification and representation in reading and writing. Huang admits that "a topic has one theme, a chapter one formal style, a sentence a [syntactic] method." But he suggests that that "one" (theme, form, and method) has the potential of multiplying itself into tens, hundreds, and thousands. Although Huang does not tell how multiplicity comes about, we may relate his view of *yin* and *yang* as self-generating principles for writing to the principles of selection and combination in language discourse and to the projection of the poetic function from the axis of selection to the axis of combination in reading/writing poetry. In this linguistic reconceptualization, the metaphysical basis of Chinese aesthetic suggestiveness has been transformed into a poetic and linguistic basis that shares with the contemporary conception of literary openness the same rationale.

Beyond Aesthetic Suggestiveness

Having explored traditional Chinese literary thought so far, I am in a better position to say that though we cannot find exact concepts or terms like "openness," "open work," or "open poetics," the Chinese tradition does not lack critical views that express equivalent ideas without actually using the modern terms. In Xue Xue's 薛雪 (1681–1763) poetic criticism, his appraisal of Du Fu's poetry practically expresses all the implicit and explicit meanings of "open work" but stops short of using the term "openness": "Du Fu's poetry can only be read but cannot be interpreted. Why so? Because his poetry is like the Ming Sea and Bo Sea that do not reject any stream; it is like the sun and moon that do not refuse to shine on any dark places; it is like a big round mirror that will reflect any objects. How can one interpret his poetry? To speak on a smaller scale, it is like the *Yinfu* and the *Daode jing*. Military strategists will read it as writings on military strategy; the Daoist will read it as writings on Daoism; those who govern the state will read it as writings for ways of government. All the readings are possible."[119]

My study only concentrates on a few seminal ideas in Chinese thought. There are more literary terms, concepts, and notions which address the same issues as ideas of "open work" and "open poetics." Apart from the already discussed categories, I can supply more terms and expressions that contain the implications of literary openness: *biequ* (interests other than stated), *xingqu* (inspired or aroused interests), *yuwei* (surplus flavor), *shenyun* (spiritual resonance), *miaowu* (subtle epiphany), *yijing* (idea-scene), *kongling* (empty deftness), *rushen* (entering the divine), *wenyue yiguang* (words are concise but meanings are broad), *shen you xiangwai* (the spirit roves outside the image), *chao yi xiangwai* (to rise above the image), *shen yu yanwai* (the spirit lingers beyond words),[120] *yanwai zhi yi* (meanings beyond the expressed words), *yi zai yanwai* (what is intended should go beyond words), *wenwai zhi zhi* (themes beyond the text), *xing zai xiangwai* (the interests are located beyond images), *jingwai zhi jing* (scenes beyond the represented scene), *jing sheng xiangwai* (scenes rise beyond images), *shu bu jinyan, yan bu jinyi* (writing cannot exhaust words, words cannot exhaust meaning), and another of Zhong Rong's famous sayings, *yan zai ermu zhi nei, qing ji bahuang zhi biao*[121] (Words are perceived by ears and eyes, but aroused feelings reach remote places in all directions).

As the two notions: *chao yi xiangwai* (to rise above the image) and *yi zai yanwai* (what is intended should go beyond words) are considered by many Chinese critics as the highest aesthetic condition a traditional artist aspires after, it is appropriate to say that one of the most important pre-occupations of traditional Chinese creative artists is how to achieve artistic openness in their created works. Predicated on the pivotal notion of suggestiveness, the large number of similar terms, concepts, notions, and categories have constituted an implicit system of aesthetic suggestiveness, the implications of which have gone beyond suggestiveness to be right-fully called a theory of openness. What is fascinating to us modern readers is that traditional literary thinkers have already made a distinction between conscious openness intended by the author and textual openness perceived by the reader. The two expressions: *yi zai yanwai* (what is intended should go beyond words) and *yanwai zhi yi* (meanings beyond the expressed words) are not simply variations of the same idea. The former is a lofty goal set for the author and embodies a desirable condition of a created literary text. It advises the author to make a text open. The latter views the open conditions of a text from the reader's perspective and calls attention to its intended and unintended openness.

Suggestiveness in writing and suggestiveness in reading are closely related in Chinese tradition and form a dialogic relationship between the writer and reader, the past and present. My reconceptualization of aesthetic suggestiveness has made it possible for us to organize those insights in Chinese thought into a systematic theory of literary openness. In conclusion, I wish to say that this system has metaphysical emptiness as its ontological basis, aesthetic suggestiveness as its epistemological principle, *hanxu* (reserve) as the desired condition of a literary work, *yiyin* and *yiwei* (lingering sound/taste) as unlimited affects and effects, and *bujin zhiyi* (endless meaning) as the lofty goal of artistic creation. In addition, there is *tuiqiao* (self-reflective making) as the practical means to multivalence and polysemy. (I will discuss this last point in the conclusion.) This Chinese system of literary openness is deeply rooted in Chinese history, culture, religion, and philosophy with characteristic emphasis on poetic, metaphysical, and aesthetic suggestiveness.

Part II

Zhouyi Hermeneutics

Chapter 3

The *Zhouyi* and Open Representation

The first Chinese hermeneutic system is *Zhouyi* hermeneutics, which centers on exegeses of China's first classic, the *I Ching* 易經 (*The Book of Changes*). As early as the Western Han, the *Zhouyi* was already accepted as the first of all Chinese classics. Yang Xiong 揚雄 (53 BC–18 AD), a leading scholar of the time, proclaimed: "Of the six classics, no other classic is greater than the *Zhouyi*." Ban Gu 班固 (32–92) followed his lead in praising it as "the source of the Great Dao."[1] Their evaluation set the tone for later exaltations and has never been challenged. The study of the *Zhouyi* has, since the seventeenth century, aroused continuous interest from scholars outside China and the Far East and become an international subject of inquiry. Western thinkers and scholars from G. W. Leibniz and J. T. Haupt to C. G. Jung and Richard Wilhelm have time and again reconfirmed the intellectual value and extraordinary fascination of this book. "Whoever has realized what the Book has to offer," says Hellmut Wilhelm, "be he a philosopher, a social reformer, or a pragmatic statesman, even an empire builder, will not be able to let it go again."[2] For nearly three thousand years, numerous Chinese intellectuals have devoted their best intelligence to the study of this classic and turned out literally cartloads and boatloads of exegeses and studies. According to a commonly accepted estimate, the *Zhouyi* literature produced in ancient China counts more than three thousand items.[3] As for the exact nature of the book, traditional scholars differed widely and came up with divergent views. The *Siku quanshu zongmu* provides an apt summary: "The Way of the *Yi* is so comprehensive that it leaves nothing uncovered in its domain. It, among other things, encompasses astronomy, geography, musicology, art of war, phonetics, mathematics, and even the practice of alchemy, which lies beyond proper categories of learning, etc. All these branches of learning can employ the *Yi* to elucidate their rationale."[4]

What makes the complexity of *Zhouyi* scholarship even more complex is that the multiple views on the book are often diametrically opposed to each other. Take the view of the book as a divination manual for example. Is *Zhouyi* prognostication scientific? This should be an easy question to answer, but authoritative scholars uphold entirely different views.[5] The multiplicity of different views has caused many scholars to throw up their hands in the air and despair of ever coming to a sensible view of the nature of the book. In my opinion, however, the multiplicity of opinions should not be viewed merely as a problem. Hidden in the multiple views may lie the clues to the true nature of the classic. I argue that the *Zhouyi* was able to retain its exalted status as the primary classic in history and has attracted the attention of scholars all over the world largely because it is an open book amenable to appropriations and manipulations by people of any political doctrines, religious beliefs, and moral values, and its openness comes from its being a semiotic system whose principle of composition warrants unlimited interpretations. During the last two millennia the *Zhouyi* has been appropriated by all major religions of China and by practically all schools of thought for their political, social, ethical, and aesthetic agendas. Most schools of thought have adopted the text wholly or partially. In the West, Leibniz's use of the eight trigrams for the advancement of his mathematical theory of binary system is perhaps the most famous and most brilliant case of appropriation in the international *Zhouyi* scholarship.[6]

My brief survey supports the suggestion that the *Zhouyi* is an open book. In this chapter, I attempt to argue that the *Zhouyi* is first and foremost a system of representation for the transmission of knowledge and because of the idiosyncratic principle and elements of representation that have constituted its structure, the system forms an open interpretive space with a principle of multiplicity. As the first open book in Chinese culture, it marked the beginning of the Chinese tradition of openness in reading and writing. *Zhouyi* hermeneutics, the collective system of elucidations of and commentaries on the first classic, inaugurated the three-thousand-year-long inquiry into openness of representation and ways of open representation.

The *Zhouyi* as a System of Representation

Nowadays, the general consensus on the nature of the *Zhouyi* is that it was originally a manual for divination. My suggested view of the *Zhouyi* as a system of representation, different as it is, does not directly conflict with this accepted view; in a way, it complements it if we change our perspectives. In terms of its intrinsic nature, the *Zhouyi* was first and foremost a system of representation, and divination is but one of the many practical uses it has been put to over history. Since the Han dynasty, the *Zhouyi* has been regarded as a book that serves to transmit the wisdom of the sages. The *Xicizhuan* states: "The sages were able to display (discover) the complex rationale behind the phenomena under the sky and represented it in images and shapes used to symbolize the meanings appropriate to a particular object. This was how hexagram images came to be designated."[7] After they had discovered the knowledge of the universe, the sages wanted to pass it on to others and future generations. For the purpose of transmission, they devised a set of representational signs, which were hexagram images and statements. Therefore, the *Xicizhuan* further states: "The sages established images to fully express their thought, designed hexagrams to fully express the true and false conditions of affairs, and attached verbalizations to fully express what they wanted to say."[8]

In the remotest past, ancient people, in their struggle for self-preservation and reproduction, acquired skills, experience, techniques, and insights into the workings of the universe, which would prove to be of great importance for the survival and development of the race. The accumulated knowledge was at first passed on from one generation to another by mouth. This way of transmission was understandably difficult and unreliable. There appeared the need for a recording system that does not depend on unreliable memory. The invention of a writing system marked a leap forward in the history of human development. It was not by accident that many sages in Chinese antiquity were believed to have contributed in one way or another to the invention of various systems for the transmission of knowledge. Fu Xi was believed to have invented the eight trigrams. Shen Nong and Xia Yu were believed to have doubled the trigrams to give added power for representation. King Wen and the Duke of Zhou were believed to be the writers of the hexagram statements and line statements. Cang Jie was accredited with having invented Chinese writing, which was even more conducive to the transmission of knowledge. Confucius was reputed to have written the appended verbalizations to the *Zhouyi*. It is for this reason that I claim that the *Zhouyi* has been upheld as the first of all Chinese classics because it was the first viable system for the transmission of knowledge.

The Eight Trigrams as an Open System of Representation

As early as the seventeenth century, the French Jesuit missionary Joachim Bouvet (1656–1730) posited a view of the *Zhouyi* that is similar to mine. He believed that in the remotest past Fu Xi invented the eight trigrams as a system of notation for scientific observation and experiment. To prove the validity of his view, he correlated the eight trigrams with Leibniz's binary arithmetic, identifying the broken line with zero and the solid line with one. He suggested that as time went by, the mathematical and scientific significance of the eight trigrams became lost to later Chinese and the trigrams and the doubled form, hexagrams, came to be used simply as part of a system of divination.[9] I differ from Bouvet only in that I view the *Zhouyi* more broadly as a system of representation for the transmission of knowledge, which incorporates the function of notation suggested by him.

If my above discussion provides only external or circumstantial evidence to argue for the *Zhouyi* as a system of representation, a brief examination of the internal signifying mechanism of the eight trigrams will provide an intrinsic proof to support my proposition. Nowadays, the hexagrams are commonly viewed as a divination system by the ancient people, but there are a few scholars who follow Xu Shen's (30–124) cue and believe that they were originally used as a writing system. These scholars include Zhang Binglin 章炳麟 (1868–1936),[10] August Conrady,[11] Ma Xulun 馬敘倫 (1884–1970),[12] Chen Weizhan 陳煒湛, and Tang Yuming 湯鈺明.[13] They, however, do not provide much evidence. Ma Xulun goes into some length to speculate: "I believe that Bao Xi first invented the eight trigrams, not for the purpose of using them as tools for divination. Most likely, before the writing signs that we use today were created, the hexagrams were meant to be a substitutive tool for written language."[14] Zhang Binling also briefly mentions: "The eight trigrams were ancient writing symbols before they developed into full forms."[15] People would ask: In what way can the eight trigrams be viewed as a writing system? A semiotic analysis may help us:

Trigram Name:	Qian	Kun	Zhen	Xun	Kan	Li	Gen	Dui
Trigram Image:	☰	☷	☳	☴	☵	☲	☶	☱
Symbolic Meaning:	heaven	earth	thunder	wind	water	fire	mountain	valley

The most fundamental elements of a trigram are two kinds of lines, the broken line for *yin* and the unbroken line for *yang*. They may be viewed as the rudiments of alphabets since each trigram is composed of three of these lines. The alternation of broken and unbroken lines enables the eight trigrams to be differentiated from one another. The eight trigrams stand respectively for heaven, earth, thunder, wind, water, fire, mountain, and valley—the commonest phenomena that were directly related to the life of the primitive people. From this point of view, the eight trigrams already form a system of writing symbols. Essentially, they constitute a semiotic system because they conform to the cardinal semiotic principle discovered by Saussure: the negatively differentiated relations of a sign system. The trigram of *qian* stands for heaven, *kun* for earth, *zhen* for thunder, and so on—not because they contain within themselves any positively identifiable qualities of heaven, earth, thunder, and so on, nor even because they have any inherent correlations with the named categories, but because they are artificially designated as relating the symbols to the concepts. The fundamental characteristic that entitles the eight trigrams to be regarded as a semiotic system is that among these trigrams there are no positively defined qualities but only negatively differentiated relations. Among the eight trigrams, *qian* stands for heaven precisely because it does not stand for earth, thunder, wind, and so on. The same is true of the other seven categories. One may object to my suggestion by pointing out that the eight trigrams were not entirely arbitrarily designated. For example, the trigram *li*, which stands for a net, does resemble the image of a net. The trigram *kan* that stands for water also resembles the stylized image of flowing water. Still, to a lesser extent, the trigram *qian,* which has three solid lines, faintly recalls skylines, and the trigram *kun*, which has three broken lines, simulates the land with water. Although one may view these cases as exceptions to the rule, they would cast doubt on the arbitrariness of the sign, especially the written sign. At least, they seem to suggest that the difference between symbol and image is a borderline case rather than a clear-cut demarcation.

According to Xu Shen's 許慎 (30–124) postface to the *Shuowen*, the eight trigrams were invented by Bao Shi (Fu Xi) who "looking up, contemplated the images (*xiang*) in the sky, and looking down, the markings (*fa*) on the earth. He observed the patterns (*wen*) on birds and animals and their adaptations to the earth. From nearby, he took hints from his own body, and elsewhere from other things. Then he began to make the 'eight trigrams' of the *Book of Changes*, to pass on the model symbols (*xianxiang*) to later times."[16] In this passage, *xiang* (images), *fa* (markings), and *wen* (patterns) refer to more or less the same thing—that is, the visually perceived patterns and images. Hence, they belong to the large category of *wen*. Since the eight trigrams were called *xianxiang* (model images), they are but visual configurations modeled after natural markings and patterns for human purposes. As model images, it is implied, they could proliferate into more images within a generative system. Thus, the model image or *wen*, when it first appears as the eight trigrams, already formed a representational system.

As a semiotic system, the eight trigrams are complete and self-contained in themselves with the basic component parts, the *yin* and *yang* lines, serving as differentiating symbols. But this semiotic system has a limitation that disqualifies it for a language system. There are more than eight phenomena people of high antiquity wanted to represent. To overcome the representational limitation, the eight trigrams assume double, triple, and quadruple roles. According to "Shuogua 説卦," they also represent family members: father, mother, elder brother, younger brother, elder sister, younger sister; animals: sheep, goat, horse, cow, dog, mouse, tortoise; body parts: stomach, tongue, mouth; qualities: strength, compliance, coldness; ideas: movement, progress, profit, pattern; symptoms: worry, heart trouble, earache; objects: gold, jade, cloth, pot, bamboo, wood, wheel, cart, and so on.[17] Previously, scholars have puzzled over why the eight trigrams stand for so many things, but no one has found a plausible answer. If we regard the eight trigrams as a primitive semiotic system, the answer may already be in view. An examination of the "Shuogua" informs us that all the listed items represented by the eight trigrams form a core vocabulary big enough to meet the needs of a primitive life.

My conception of the eight trigrams as a system of representation will prove useful in several ways. First and foremost, it will help answer the question that I have just raised: How did the eight trigrams come to stand for so many things? By the time the eight trigrams appeared, the ancient Chinese seemed to have already possessed the abstract mental power to classify myriad things in the universe into large categories. This can be seen from the fact that each of the trigram images is associated with a cluster of objects or phenomena in the world. But the associations are in a way open-ended. Each of the eight trigrams was assigned a base symbolism: heaven, earth, thunder, wind, water, fire, mountain, valley, and so on, and a series of other symbolic associations. According to "Shuoga 説卦," *qian* symbolizes heaven, ring, king, father, jade, gold, cold, ice, scarlet color, thoroughbred horse, old horse, lean horse, motley-colored horse, trees, and fruits; *kun* symbolizes earth, mare, money, wok, parsimony, evenness, calf, cow, big cart, colored patterns, abundance, handle of an ax, and black-colored soil of the earth; *zhen* symbolizes thunder, dragon, mixture of indigo and yellow colors, flower, road, eldest son, and so on. I can continue to quote the list from the "Shuogua," but it would be unnecessary. In a word, each of the trigrams may symbolize several dozen objects, phenomena, qualities, and conditions. Some of the base symbolisms still have associations with objects and are discernible to modern people with some explanation. The rest might have had internal associations in the remote past, but the symbolic associations have been lost, probably never to be recovered. The multiple designation of meanings for a trigram constitutes a key factor for open representation in the *Zhouyi*.

As human life broadened, the designation of multiple roles to a single trigram had an obvious drawback. If one trigram were made to stand for many things, confusion would surely arise. A way out of confusion is to double the trigrams. When two trigrams were combined, hexagrams were born. There are altogether sixty-four hexagrams formed by the doubling of the eight trigrams. Whoever was the first to double the trigrams, the inspiration might have been derived from the necessity to increase the representational capacity of the trigrams. Based on the above analysis, it is not a stretch to postulate that the sixty-four hexagrams constitute a more powerful system of representation than the eight trigrams. Nevertheless, as a system of representation, the hexagrams have both positive and negative features. The hexagrams may form a simple and easy semiotic system, but it falls far short of being an effective system of transmission. The system itself easily gives rise to ambiguity. This might be the reason why hexagram statements and line statements were later added. But from the literary and artistic viewpoint, the hexagrams have a strong point as a system of representation. Because of their versatility, they can be used to represent anything under heaven. For this reason, I will further refine my argument: the fact that the *Zhouyi* has fascinated numerous Chinese scholars for three millennia is not so much because it contains any esoteric knowledge as because it is an open system of representation. The variety of views concerning its nature, origin, and function, and the numerous uses that it has been put to by people over history are an eloquent testimony to its openness.

The Mechanisms of Openness in Hexagram Images

Having said that the *Zhouyi* is a system of representation and an open system, I need to explore in some detail the mechanisms of signification and representation that make it open. To understand the mechanisms of the *Zhouyi*, I need to answer one question: What kind of semiotic system is the *Zhouyi*? The *Zhouyi* consists of two parts: the *jing*, or the text proper, and *zhuan*, or appended commentaries. The text proper of the *Zhouyi* consists of *guaxiang* (the hexagram images) and *guaci* (hexagram and line statements). The hexagram images constitute a system of symbols, while the hexagram and line statements form another system of linguistic signs. They are two different systems, but deal with the same subject. Whether hexagram images or hexagram statements, they are both semiotic systems because both are systems of signs. The *Zhouyi* is a grand semiotic system made up of two different but related subsemiotic systems. The hexagram images form a semiotic system of pure signs; the hexagram statements form a secondary semiotic system of linguistic signs. The two subsemiotic systems are believed by some scholars to serve the same purpose: the recording of the sages' observation, perception, and understanding of the universe. In this section, I will concentrate on the pure sign system of the hexagram images, leaving the linguistic system of line statements to the next section.

The pure signs and linguistic signs are sometimes correlated, sometimes overlapping, and sometimes unrelated. The mediating factor linking the two semiotic systems is the concept of *xiang*, which has a congeries of denotations and connotations. In its narrow sense, it refers to *guaxiang* (hexagram images, the six-line diagram), *yaoxiang* (line images, broken or full line); in its broad sense it refers to *wuxiang* (natural phenomena: heaven, earth, mountain, river, thunder, wind, fire, etc.) and *shixiang* (social phenomena: social institutions, war, famine, marriage, divorce, etc.); in its still broader sense, it may refer to *yixiang* (nerve stimuli, mental picture, the use of language to represent objects, actions, feelings, thoughts, ideas, states of mind, and any sensory or extrasensory experience). On its local level—that is, the elucidation of the *Zhouyi*—both *xiang* and *yan* are believed to be the carriers of the original intentions of the sages. Thus, the sages' original thoughts in creating the hexagrams are immanent in *xiang* (images), the pure sign system, and accessible through *yan* (words), the linguistic system conveying the meanings of images couched in language and covering natural phenomena, social phenomena, and poetic images. As an indispensable link between various aspects of that which is represented, *xiang* occupies an important place in the process of signification and representation.

All the hexagram images can be said to be symbols, but they are not ordinary symbols. Ordinary symbols we know, such as traffic lights, refer to commonly agreed meanings. In other words, they are conventions. The hexagrams share some conventional qualities with common signs, but they have these characteristics which both conform to and go beyond conventional symbols: (1) some were created in imitation of the phenomenal world; (2) they are designated representations of the myriad things in the world; (3) they have inherent meanings; (4) though they were representations of the natural world, we do not see the actual images on the face of the hexagrams. Here lies the borderline nature of the hexagrams: they are at once concrete and abstract; they reflect the images of real objects and at the same time have symbolic meanings.

As time went on, the system acquired multiple symbolic associations, some of which would have made sense in entirely different ways to early thinkers and exegetes. In the previous section, I have, from a functional perspective, provided an answer to the question: How did one trigram come to assume so many symbolic meanings? Now I attempt to answer an even more baffling question from the perspective of signification and representation. One does not need to take much time to examine the listed symbolic associations in the "Shuogua" to be puzzled by one phenomenon: the objects or qualities or conditions that one trigram stands for are often opposite, mutually exclusive, or downright contradictory by common sense. For example, among the list of symbolisms of *qian*, some are in line with the basic principle that the trigram is supposed to represent. The heaven, king, father, thoroughbred horse, old horse, and so on, roughly correspond to the *yang*, or male principle. But the other symbolisms—ring, jade, cold, ice, thin horse, and fruit—seem to represent just the opposite qualities of the *yang* (male principle). A ring by its circular shape would belong to the *yin* (female principle) and should be associated with a female quality; jade in the Chinese tradition has with some exceptions been used to describe a female; cold and ice, because of their opposite qualities to heat and fire, belong to the *yin*; a thin horse is the opposite of a thoroughbred; fruits are associated with fertility and hence are objects of the *yin* category. Obviously the principle of natural correspondence cannot answer the question. However, if we view these associations in terms of representation, a reasonable answer can be found.

Representation is related to natural correspondence, but it differs from the latter in some significant ways. One major difference is that while natural correspondence emphasizes the dual relationship between two objects, representation always stresses a triangular relationship: the object of representation, the object represented, and a person to whom an object is represented for another object. As W. J. T. Mitchell, a theorist of representation, puts it, "representation is always *of* something or someone, *by* something or someone, *to* someone."[18] In fact, Mitchell speaks of four parties, the fourth being the "intender" or "maker" of representation, the person who says to the beholder: Let this object stand for the object to be represented. The second difference is that whereas the relationship in natural correspondence is perceived to be natural, the relationship in representation goes beyond the natural. According to C. S. Peirce's widely accepted theory, representation involves three relationships: the iconic, indexical, and symbolic. The iconic stresses resemblances; the indexical emphasizes cause and effect or existential conditions; the symbolic emphasizes arbitrary stipulation. Natural correspondence seems to stress resemblances. In terms of the three semiotic principles, we may say that the jade symbolizes the *yang* principle in *qian* perhaps because it might have been an ornament worn by a male, a father, or a king. The relationship between the wearer and the object is an indexical one: the object points to its wearer, hence the object stands for the quality its wearer possesses. Here, I am only suggesting a hypothetical explanation. It does not follow that my elucidation is actually the way those objects came to be associated with *qian* in the remote past. For another hypothetical example, people in high antiquity might designate a certain fruit as having the quality of *qian* because the leader of a tribe was also the person who gathered most of the fruit from a tall tree.

Arbitrary stipulation is much more flexible. It allows for willful designation in certain circumstances. Something may stand for something else simply because we agree to view it in that way. Arbitrary stipulation is one of the cardinal principles of representation in languages and in the *Zhouyi* system: "[T]here is no meaning which is not designated."[19] Guo Yong 郭雍 (1091–1187) obviously understood the significance of this principle when he said: "But to say 'Hexagram images are resemblances,' does it mean that the hexagram images are heaven, earth, horse, and cow? Heaven, earth, horse, and cow may be endowed with images of *qian* and *kun*; it is not that the images of *qian* and *kun* are confined to heaven, earth, horse and cow only."[20] Heaven, earth, cattle, and horse cannot by themselves stand to symbolize the abstract hexagram images. It is the hexagram makers who projected abstract qualities like robustness or compliance onto these concrete objects, hence making an act of designation. At the same time, the maker must also negotiate a social agreement with other persons: "Let us agree that A will stand for B." This social agreement endows a system of representation with open possibilities. As Mitchell puts it, "the decision to let A stand for B may (and usually does) open up a whole new realm of possibilities for representation: B becomes a likely candidate to stand for C, and so on."[21]

Since representation is always *of* something or someone, *by* something or someone, *to* someone, by clarifying the order of mimesis, I may provide a theoretical ground to correct an erroneous view with regard to the relationship between the hexagram images and hexagram statements. In the *Xicizhuan,* the legendary story about how ancient sages got their inspirations for creating the basic means of material culture vividly describes the salient nature of this peculiar symbolism. This is the so-called legend of "inventing implements and customs by observing hexagrams." According to this legend, the basic material aspects of ancient civilizations came into being as a result of the sages' observation of the sixty-four hexagrams which, in their turn, came from Fu Xi's observation of the miscellaneous patterns of heaven, earth, the human body, and animals. This legend as a theory about the origin of civilization has been persuasively refuted by Gu Jiegang 顧頡剛 (1893–1980), Hu Shi 胡適 (1891–1962) and other scholars.[22] The fallaciousness of this theory lies in that it commits the error of putting the cart before the horse. If we view the legend in inverse manner, however, it reveals an elaborate system of representation, built on a peculiar symbolism. Take the invention of the boat for example: "The benefit of the boat . . . was derived from the *huan* hexagram."[23] The hexagram image of *huan* ䷺ is composed of two trigrams, ☴ *xun* on top and ☵ *kan* at the bottom. *Xun* stands for wood while *kan* stands for water. According to the legend, when the Yellow Emperor saw the composite image of *huan*, he visualized wood floating on water and got the inspiration for inventing the boat. If we disregard the legend and view the pairing of *xun* and *kan* with their respective symbolic meanings as representing the condition of a boat floating on water, the hexagram stands as an ingenious method of symbolic representation.

The system of representation in the *Zhouyi*, built on the basis of *yixiang* 逸象 (symbolic images), supplemented with various exegetic methods such as *huti* 互體 (internal trigram), *guabian* 卦變 (trigram changes), *yaowei* 爻位 (line positions), and so on, could represent anything under heaven. Of all the strategies, *huti* and *guabian* are the most commonly used. I will employ them to illustrate the mechanism of how a hexagram achieves "openness." The so-called *huti* is an interpretive strategy in which the second, third, and fourth lines, and the third, fourth, and fifth lines could form two internal trigrams. *Guabian* is a practice in which the first and sixth lines of a hexagram are exchanged so that a different hexagram image is formed, but the original hexagram image can still be explained in terms of the newly formed hexagram image. Let us employ these two strategies to reexamine the *huan* hexagram ䷺. *Huan* is made up of *xun* ☴ and *kan* ☵. If we employ the *huti* method, the second, third, and fourth lines form another trigram which is *gen* ☶; the third, fourth, and fifth lines form still another trigram which is *zhen* ☳. The juxtaposition of *gen* and *zhen* will form a new hexagram image. For the same hexagram *huan*, if we use the *guabian* method, exchanging the first and the sixth lines, the hexagram image will be composed of two new trigrams, which are respectively *kan* ☵ and *dui* ☱. Since *gen* and *zhen* have a cluster of symbolisms, the newly formed hexagram image can be construed to represent many things. For example, if we select from the list of symbolisms for *gen* the meaning of "mountain," and for *zhen* the meaning of "thunder," we may interpret the newly formed hexagram as "thunder booming on top of a mountain." If we select the symbolism of "path" for *gen* and the symbolism of "dragon" for *zhen*, we may say that the newly formed hexagram stands for the picture of a dragon crawling on a road. Since, according to "Shuogua," the symbolisms of *gen* and *zhen* can be numbered by the score, the combinations will produce almost limitless interpretations. The same procedures can be easily applied to the new hexagram formed with the method of *guabian* and another series of interpretations will arise from the applications. Of course, in the actual interpretation of a hexagram, the procedure is complicated by the fact that there are hexagram statements and line statements, which serve pragmatically as constraints of interpretations. A convincing interpretation would involve a correlation between the symbolism of the hexagram image and the reading of the attached statements. Nevertheless, what I have demonstrated is the semiotic mechanism of how the eight trigrams may symbolize everything and anything in the world. It is an "open" mechanism that, in turn, renders the *Zhouyi* an open book.

Open Representation in Hexagram and Line Statements

The two parts in the *Zhouyi*—*guaxiang* or the hexagram and line images; *guaci* or hexagram and line statements—constitute an extraordinary case of the interpenetration between image and word, the visual and the verbal. Of the two parts, the verbal part is more directly related to verbal exegeses. The hexagram and line images are visually based. Though they are very simple, they can be construed to represent almost anything under heaven precisely because they simply consist of a solid line and a broken line. They do not seem to be directly related to writing since they are not verbal discourses. The two parts, however, are usually correlated in the process of reading. The hexagram and line statements are words, verbal signs. As such, they come close to verbal discourses. Some hexagram and line statements resemble short poems and brief parables. Hexagram and line statements seem to be pretty limited as the words are finite and definite. Nevertheless, because the verbal statements were so concisely worded and syntactically so vague, they possess the potential to generate different and even conflicting readings.

Philological Openness. In the next section, I am going to analyze a hexagram statement to reveal the linguistic openness of the *Zhouyi* discourse. My analysis has two objectives: (1) to demonstrate how ambiguous syntax and morphology have enabled scholars over history to come up with different readings of a simple hexagram statement; (2) to explore what insights we can draw from their ways of reading for the construction of an open paradigm of reading. The hexagram statement to be examined is the first line in the *Zhouyi*: 乾元亨利貞. There are several ways of punctuating it: (1) *Qian: yuan, heng, li, zhen* 乾：元，亨，利，貞; (2) *Qian: yuan, heng, lizhen* 乾：元，亨，利貞; (3) *Qianyuan: heng, lizhen* 乾元，亨，利貞; (4) *Qian: yuanheng, lizhen* 乾：元亨，利貞. These different readings were actually attempted over history.[24] Li Jingchi, a modern scholar, through grammatical and discourse analysis, argues that the fourth reading is perhaps the most correct reading.[25] Different punctuations signify different syntactical relations and result in different interpretations. The *Zixia yizhuan* reads: "*Yuan* means beginning; *heng* opening; *li* harmony; *zhen* correctness."[26] This reading gave rise to the so-called four virtues which were reiterated in major *Zhouyi* exegeses. Kong Yingda's annotation reads "*Yuan, heng, li,* and *zhen* represent the four virtues of the *qian*."[27] The so-called four virtues seem to have been derived from a passage from the *Zuozhuan* that supplies a detailed explanation of the four virtues: "*Yuan* is the head of the body. *Heng* is the meeting of good things. *Li* is the harmony of righteousness. *Zhen* is the doing of things."[28] "Wenyan 文言" offers a slightly different version: "*Yuan* is the leader of goodness. *Heng* is the meeting of good things. *Li* is the harmony of righteousness. *Zhen* is the doing of things."[29] A comparison of the three ways of glossing tells us that the difference with regard to *yuan* is quite considerable. *Zixia yizhuan* glosses it as "beginning"; the *Zuozhuan* passage glosses it as "head of the body"; "Wenyan" glosses it as "the leader of goodness."

With the same punctuation and within the same ideological frame of mind, scholars came up with different interpretations. Li Dingzuo 李鼎祚 (eighth century) amplified Zixia's idea saying: "The *qian* is endowed with the nature of the pure *yang*, and therefore it was born first of all things. Then myriads of things each got their origin and beginning, opening connections, harmonious nature, proper firmness."[30] Cheng Yi's exegesis departs from the standard interpretation: "*Yuan* is the beginning of myriad things; *heng* represents their increase; *li* embodies their growth; *zhen* signifies their completion."[31] Zhu Xi's exegesis also deviates considerably from the standard reading: "*Yuan* means greatness; *heng* connection; *li* appropriateness, *zhen* correctness and firmness."[32] Thus, even among scholars using the same punctuated reading, there appeared considerable differences in interpretations.

The second way of punctuation puts *li* and *zhen* together, but it still views the four characters after the first one as an explanation of *qian*. The third way of punctuation attaches *yuan* to *qian* and puts *li* and *zhen* together, thereby making the sense group entirely different from the first two readings. "Wenyan," for example, reads the statement in this way:

"*Qianyuan* begins with open connections. *Lizhen* refers to nature and dispositions."[33] The fourth way of punctuation relies on Xu Shen's definition of *zhen*: "*Zhen* is to ask by means of divination"[34] and glosses *lizhen* together as "beneficial for divination." Wu Cheng (1249–1333), who punctuated the phrase in a way different from the standard reading, provided two different strands of *yuan*: (1) "The *yuan* is located on top of the human body; it is the commander of all body parts. Anyone (anything) endowed with great virtue and the superiority of all goodness is called *yuan*." (2) "Some may occupy a great position above people, such as the principal leader in officialdom, or the direct descendent of a clan. They can be entitled *yuan*."[35] As for *heng*, he offered an annotation entirely different from those of other scholars: "The word *heng* is the same as the word *xiang* in the phrase 'xian-xiang.' To get things ready for presentation is called *heng*. *Heng* is the same as partaking of the rites at a gathering of a hundred worthies on a extremely prosperous occasion, when a great variety of beautiful things are prepared." Though he read *li* and *zhen* together, he annotated them separately: "*Li* is conducive to doing things. It is like cutting crops with a knife; one cuts in a suitable and convenient way. *Zhen* is to preside over things. It is like the trunk of a tree; when the trunk is straight, the tree stands secure. Divination is conducive to propriety; it commands affairs." His annotation not only provides an explanation to the annotation in "Wenyan" but also echoes a position adopted by Zheng Xuan 鄭玄 (127–200), who gave a compromised view that attempted to reconcile the two notions of *zhen*: divination 卜問 and propriety 正 . In his annotation to "the Great Diviner," Zheng said: "*Zhen* is to ask. When the state is faced with indecision for a matter of great importance, a divination using milfoil stalks and a tortoise shell is conducted. *Zhen* as 'ask' is to inquire into propriety."[36] Li Jingchi admires Zheng Xuan's ingenuity, but still insists that "zhen" must be read as "to divine."[37]

In the existent Western translations, scholars have followed the Chinese scholarship in one way or another but still demonstrated considerable differences. James Legge renders the *qian* hexagram statement: "*Khien* (represents) what is great and originating, penetrating, advantageous, correct and firm."[38] Richard Wilhelm, the German *Zhouyi* scholar, translates *yuan* as "sublime," *heng* as "success," *li* as "further," *zhen* as "perseverance."[39] Iulian Shchutskii, the Russian *Zhouyi* scholar, translates *yuan* as "impulse," *heng* as "completion" or "development," *li* as "favorable," and *zhen* as "steadiness."[40] He also suggests that the *Qian* hexagram statement should be rendered as "The creative heaven is the great all-penetrating and the proper steadfastness."[41] In a more recent translation, Richard Kunst translates the *qian* hexagram statement as "Grand treat. A favorable determination."[42]

I have made no attempt to provide an exhaustive account of the different readings. It is an amazing phenomenon that there should be so many different interpretations for a short phrase consisting of only four characters. If we take a little time to analyze the above annotations, we will notice that the scholars have followed a semiotic approach to the elucidation of the statement. *Yuan* 元 is a homophone for *yuan* 原 (origin) and *yuan* 源 (source). Both origin and source have the connotations of "beginning." Xu Shen's *Shuowen* defines *yuan* as "beginning."[43] *Yuan* 元 is also a synonym for *shou* 首 (head) since it is "the leader of all body parts." Then, in a metaphorical way, *yuan* refers to a leader of people. In terms of the glossing in "Wenyan," "*Yuan* is the leader of goodness," *yuan* becomes synonymous with *shan* 善 (goodness). For this reason, in some ancient texts, *shanren* 善人 is also called *yuanren* 元人. In terms of still another glossing offered in "Tuan 彖": "Great indeed is *qianyuan* 大哉乾元," *yuan* becomes associated with *da* 大 (great). This might have been the basis for Zhu Xi's annotation. As for *heng*, in the light of "Wenyan" glossing, "*Heng* is the meeting of good things," *heng* becomes a magnificent gathering. *Heng* 亨 is similar to *xiang* 享 not only in shape but also in sound. The two words are cognate. Therefore, *heng* becomes "to partake." *Zhen* is a homophone for *zheng* 正. It is understandable that some scholars should have glossed it as "correct" or "proper."

In further elucidation, "Wenyan" states: "A gentleman who uses benevolence as his moral principle is capable of leading/nurturing people." Here, 長 may have two facets of meanings: leading and growing. It gives rise to the idea of "growth." This might have been the basis of Cheng Yi's annotation. Zheng Xuan's attempt to reconcile the two different meanings of *zhen* is most interesting. Like a literary critic of a literary text, he tried to offer a synthetic reading by smoothing out inconsistencies. Whether the annotations and glosses are predicated on the shape, sound, or sense of the characters, previous scholars have paid a great deal of attention to their materiality (sound and shape) and their intertextual connotations. Their ways of reading conform to the three fundamental principles of *xungu* 訓詁 (philological scholarship): "to seek meaning through the shape of a word," "to seek meanings through the sound of a word," and "mutual interpretation through comparison and contrast."[44] In the final analysis, what is responsible for the generation of different and conflicting readings is the materiality of the Chinese characters, including the textual materiality (punctuation and syntax, etc.).

Contextual Openness. An interpretation always requires a context, and in *Zhouyi* divination the context is unlimited. The colorful interpretations of hexagram statements are further enriched by the act of situating the hexagram statement in an actual situation of divination. The situating efforts may not just produce more varied interpretations; sometimes it may yield an interpretation entirely opposite to the tenor of the statement. The aforementioned *Zuozhuan* passage is taken from the utterances supposedly made by a historical person, Mujiang 穆姜. Mujiang, mother of Duke Cheng 成公, had an illicit relationship. She also plotted to depose Duke Cheng. When the attempt failed, she was confined in the eastern palace until her death. At the beginning of her confinement, she wanted to know whether it might be possible for her to get out of confinement. So she asked a scribe to divine for her. The scribe encountered the hexagram of *gen* 艮 which changed into *sui* 隨. The hexagram statement reads exactly as that of *qian*: "*Sui: yuan, heng, li, zhen*. No harm."[45] The scribe told Mujiang that the divination foretold that she should emerge from the confinement soon. Mujiang, however, viewed the divination result differently. She agreed that the hexagram statement was auspicious and proceeded to offer an annotation of the four characters that I have quoted earlier. Then she went on to read the statement in relation to her own situation and explained why she could not escape unharmed.[46]

The significance of Mujiang's interpretation lies not just in her self-knowledge; it also shows that divination as an open system of representation must be interpreted in relation to a text as well as a context. In the *Yiya* 易雅, Zhao Rumei 趙汝楳 (fl. 1226) listed five principles for divination that are the rationale behind Mujiang's reading: "The fundamental principle Confucians employed in performing divinations originated from sages. The method involves a fivefold concern with the person, position, time, topic, and divination. Whoever orders a divination is the person; where he is located is his position; when he encounters the divination is the time; what he orders the divination for is the topic; auspicious or inauspicious omens are the outcome of divination. Therefore, a skillful diviner, after he obtains a hexagram, will observe the usual behavior of the person, the propriety of his position, the condition of his time, and also consider the propriety of the topic under divination so as to determine the auspicious or inauspicious nature of the divination."[47] Thus, it seems that the correctness or incorrectness of a divination does not depend solely on the hexagram and line statements. An interpretation has a lot to do with the diviner, the interpreter, and the context. In the interpretation of a given hexagram statement or line statement, because of the nature of the *Zhouyi* as an open system of representation, an interpreter always has ample room to come up with an interpretation that fits the immediate situation in the way a competent reader of a literary text is always able to come up with a reading that finds support in the text itself.

Many scholars of the *Zhouyi*, past and present, are seduced by the efficaciousness of *Zhouyi* prognostication. Among those believers, few of them seem willing to consider that the *Zhouyi* is an open system of representation amenable to interpretations suitable for a given situation. Mao Qiling 毛奇齡 (1623–1716) argued enthusiastically for the accuracy of *Zhouyi* divination for anticipating future events. He cited a case of divination in the Han history and provided a case study. Through a detailed analysis of the hexagram and line statements obtained at the time of divination, Mao Qiling argued that the divination accurately predicted the disastrous events in history. Unfortunately, the Han scribe in charge of the divination was unable to read the divination correctly. Hence his interpretation totally fell short of the actual historical events. According to Mao Qiling, the obtained hexagram and its reading in "Shuogua 説卦" were so accurate that they predicted the historical events in their minute details involving the empress's brother and the eunuchs who committed regicide and brought chaos to the state.[48] But as I have already pointed out earlier in my analysis of the compositional mechanisms of the *Zhouyi*, Mao Qiling's positive argument rests on a system of open representation and on his being able to review the divination in terms of history. Li Jingchi, a modern scholar, is perfectly right in ridiculing Mao Qiling for his cleverness in retrospect.[49] My mention of Mao Qiling's case study is meant to show that, for the same divination, people can come up with entirely opposite interpretations. The Han scribe took a reading of the line statement in relation to the current situation. At the time of divination, "auspiciousness" would seem a suitable correlation with the immediate situation. It would be wise for the scribe to ignore the not so auspicious implications in the line statement. Mao Qiling had a reading from the opposite direction. He ignored the auspicious words, correlated the rest with the recorded historical events, and came up with an inauspicious interpretation. Both interpretations were based on readings of the images and statements. The cause of conflicting interpretations lies partly with the interpreters and partly in the potentially conflicting elements in the hexagram images and statements.

Indeterminacy in the *Zhouyi*'s Genesis

The hermeneutic openness of the *Zhouyi* is also related to its genesis and evolution. The *Zhouyi* has an indeterminate origin of composition, and this indeterminacy gives added power to its openness. Basically, there are two theories about its genesis: image-centered genesis and number-centered genesis. The image theory which has been accepted throughout history tells us that both the hexagram images and hexagram statements came from the sages' observation of the universe. The number theory holds that the hexagram images were not the result of observing the universe and imitating it, but that they grew out of the manipulations of numbers. The second theory is as old as the first one and it was proven in recent scholarship. After studying the oldest extant symbols standing for the basic numerals, Zhang Zhenglang, a scholar in Mainland China, has suggested that the hexagram images may have indeed evolved out of the ancient symbols for numerals.[50] I would argue, however, that image-centered genesis and number-centered genesis are in essence one and the same thing, because numerals, especially ancient Chinese numerals, are imagistic ideographs. The number-centered genesis does not in any way contradict the image-centered genesis. The former only serves to provide another subtle distinction between images and numbers. Shao Yong 邵雍 (1011–77) pointed out the interrelatedness of images and numbers: "When there are ideas, there will be utterances; when there are utterances, there will be images; when there are images, there will be numbers. When numbers are established, images will be born. When images are born, utterances become clear and ideas manifest."[51] The ancient scholars classified image-centered theory and number-centered theory into the larger category of *Xiangshu pai* (Image-Number school). Their classification shows that the image-oriented and number-oriented geneses are one and the same thing. Both are subtle distinctions of the same big category that I wish to call "sign-centered genesis." The sign-centered genesis conforms to the reasonable speculation that before the invention of hexagrams there existed a period in which human civilization depended on icons, indexes, tokens, and symbols.[52]

The sign-centered genesis finds support in the content of the *Zhouyi* itself. Indeed, the book is a grand system made up of the different kinds of signs created through three sign-making principles posited by Peirce: iconic, indexical, and symbolic. There is, moreover, a fourth principle that I wish to call "juxtapositional representations." The *Zhouyi* contains all four representations. Some hexagram images are iconic representations. According to Peirce, an iconic representation is a sign that resembles its conceptual object in certain ways. In this sense, the hexagram images of *kan* (for water), *li* (for net), and *ding* (for cauldron) are iconic signs because we can observe in these images faint resemblances of water, net, and cauldron respectively. Some are indexical representations: *jing* for well, *jin* for the rise of the sun, *mingyi* for the setting of the sun, and so on. An indexical representation is easily confused with an iconic representation. For the sake of distinction, Peirce makes these observations: "Indices may be distinguished from other signs, or representations, by three characteristic marks: first, that they have no significant resemblances to their objects; second, that they refer to individuals, single units, single collections of units, or single continua; third, that they direct the attention to their objects by blind compulsion."[53] Some typical indexical signs Peirce cites are a weather vane, a pointing hand, and a symptom. The hexagram image for *jing* is made up of *kan* and *xun*. *Kan* is an iconic image of water; *xun* is a symbol for wood. "Daxiang zhuan 大象傳" states: "The image of water placed on top of wood stands for the image of well." There are three explanations for this composite image: (1) water comes from underground in the way the sap in a tree moves upward; (2) a wooden device is lowered to the bottom of a well to draw water upward; (3) a wooden frame deep in the well allows clear water to seep upward.[54] All three explanations stress an upward movement that indicates the direction of water in a well. Just as a weather vane (a typical Peircean index) points to the direction of wind, so the hexagram image of *jing* indicates the movement of water inside a well. More are symbolic representations: *qian* for horse, *kun* for cow, *zhen* for dragon, and so on. The doubling of trigrams involves juxtapositional representation, just as in the organization of words into discourse. The hexagram statements cover all four types of representations. In addition, the signs in the *Zhouyi*, whether they are hexagram images or hexagram statements, all possess the three characteristics Peirce attributes to a sign: material quality, pure demonstrative application, and appeal to a mind.[55]

I have stated earlier that the *Zhouyi* text is a grand semiotic system consisting of two subsystems: hexagram images, and hexagram and line statements. The text is quite extraordinary in the sense that it is made up of images and words—visual and verbal signs. The fact that the text has two different systems of signs makes the interpretive process in relation to the sages' intention much more complicated than a text of words only. In principle, I do not believe in pretextual intention as something useful or enlightening, but I accept what is called "in-text" intention—possible purposes that can be conveyed by and constructed through the reading of the text. In terms of this position, the in-text intention of the *Zhouyi* is what traditional *Zhouyi* scholars call "the sages' intention." The addition of this third term further complicates the interpretive process and turns the text into an unlimited hermeneutic space. According to the accepted theory, this is how hexagrams and hexagram statements came into being: "The *Zhouyi* as a book has its root in the hexagram images. . . . It originated from the sages' looking up and down. It is also said that the sages designed hexagrams and observed their images, and attached words to clarify auspicious and inauspicious situations. If the attached words came from observing hexagram images, then, the extant hexagram and line statements all resulted from the sages who, having intently observed the hexagram images, composed the attached words."[56] In terms of this possible source of *guaci*, I will schematize the relationship of *yi*, *xiang*, and *yan* into the following model:

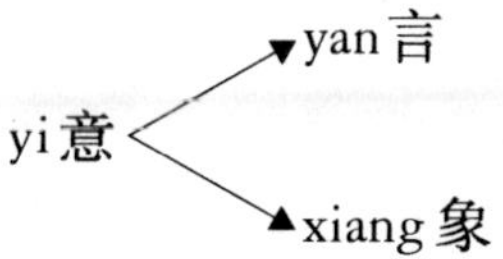

Yan covers hexagram and line statements; *xiang* is hexagram images; *yi* refers to the sages' intentions. If statements came from observing images, there is definitely a correlation between *yan* and *xiang*. To ignore *xiang* while solely concentrating on *yan*, one can only get part of the sages' intentions. In the hermeneutic tradition of the *Zhouyi*, the whole system of representation may be reduced to these key terms: (1) the sages' original intention; (2) hexagram images; (3) hexagram statements and line statements; (4) commentaries. The sages' thoughts are the starting point, which consists of *yi* (ideas) in the sages' mind. Sages wanted to convey their thoughts to posterity. They employed two systems to convey their ideas: (1) hexagram images; (2) hexagram and line statements. The two systems are the material means of transmission. The commentaries are more elaborate elucidations made by later generations to explicate the sages' two systems. They represent what scholars believe to be the interpretations of the sages' original thoughts. As such they are the meanings resulting from numerous readings. The relationship among these key terms proceeds along these lines: the sages observed the universe and wanted to impart the insight derived from their observation; they produced hexagrams and statements to convey their observations; commentators read the sages' hexagrams and statements and produce exegeses of what they think constitutes the sages' intentions. We can observe the same relationship among the elements of writing and reading: the author observes the world and produces a text; his observation is conveyed through the text; the reader reads the text to understand what is meant by the text; critics help the reader by offering informed readings. Indeed, *Zhouyi* hermeneutics is not different from the hermeneutics in reading. In each case, the universe may be viewed as both the stimulus for composing a hexagram/text and the context in which a hexagram/text was produced. From the perspective of reading and interpretation, the hexagram images may be viewed as the repressed original context, which has successfully resisted the lapse of time. Around hexagram images there has unfolded a great debate that started two millennia ago and still continues (more about this debate will be discussed in the next chapter). Scholars participating in the debate fall into two schools: *Xiangshu pai* (Image-Number school) and *Yili pai* (Meaning-Principle school). Despite their different paradigms of interpretation, each was able to generate multiple readings, thereby testifying further to the open nature of the *Zhouyi*.

Ideas of Openness in *Zhouyi* Intellectual Thought

The openness of the *Zhouyi* comes from its being a semiotic system whose principle of composition warrants unlimited semiosis, as well as from different strategies of reading that attempt reasoned correlations between a divination result and its given situation. Thus, the openness of the *Zhouyi* results from open representation and open interpretation, which form two sides of the same coin. In Chinese history, inquiries into the two sides of the same coin formed one of the two great hermeneutic traditions: *Zhouyi* hermeneutics. In their inquiry into the nature, genesis, and function of the *Zhouyi*, scholars have produced a staggering amount of insight and blindness. Curiously, their insight is often blended with blindness. And often, their blindness to the limitations of their approaches turns out to give rise to insight. To explore how the openness of the *Zhouyi* may help us construct an open poetics, we need to consider the blindness and insight in the *Zhouyi* hermeneutic tradition. I believe that even their blindness may often lead to some of the most fascinating insights into literary openness and the art of making art.

In Chinese history, there have been a few scholars who have intuitively appreciated the open nature of the book. Cheng Yi 程頤 (1033–1101) said: "[In interpretation,] one should not confine a hexagram to a single thing. If one sticks to one thing, then the three hundred eighty-four lines would only represent three hundred eighty-four things. That would be the end of it all."[57] Zhu Xi 朱熹 (1130–1200) promoted Cheng Yi's idea and developed it into what he called an "empty object": "The *Zhouyi* is an empty object. Before there is a certain event, it states in advance a certain principle. Therefore it can cover many principles in their entirety. When one uses it in observing people and conducting affairs, he will find it fitting for everything."[58] To advance his idea of "empty object," he contrasted the *Zhouyi* with other classics like the *Book of Songs, Book of Documents*, and the *Spring and Autumn Annals*. In his opinion, the persons, things, and events carried in the other classics were real persons, things, and events. Because they were real, they came to be recorded in those classics. The events recorded in the hexagram and line statements might have been real, but they were employed to represent certain ideas and principles. Since the events were not recorded for the sake of recording those events, they only serve as empty formulas that may represent similar events. He further claimed that the *Zhouyi* only expresses abstract ideas: "The *Zhouyi* only aims at expounding a rationale in an unsubstantiated manner; it only hypothesizes what it would look like with this rationale."[59] He also compared the *Zhouyi* to a mirror: "The *Zhouyi* is like a mirror which can reflect any object that appears." By comparing the *Zhouyi* to a mirror, Zhu Xi had not only understood its open nature but also sensed its similar nature and function to literature. "When the *Zhouyi* talks about an object, that object is not a real object. For example, when it speaks of a dragon, that is not a real dragon. In other books, what is mentioned is a real fact: filial piety is filial piety; benevolence is benevolence."[60] Here, Zhu Xi credited the book with a quality that borders on the fictionality of creative works. His insight coincides with Aristotle's distinction between history and poetry: "The true difference is that one relates what has happened, the other what may happen."[61] Certainly, his characterization of the *Yi* as an "empty object" finds reverberations in the modern conception of a literary text as an empty basket into which one can throw anything, a kind of empty stand upon which one can hang clothes of different colors and styles.

Zhu Xi, however, seemed to have realized that the perceived empty quality emanates from representations. And representations are not restricted to natural correspondences alone. He recognized that the principle of correspondences could explain some relationships between hexagram images and statements. For example, there is a corresponding relationship between horse and robustness, or cow and compliance: "It is common sense that a horse stands for robustness and a cow for compliance."[62] But it could not explain some other situations. For example: "When one investigates the hexagram images in accordance with the hexagram statements, if *tun* hexagram has a statement of horse but has no image of *qian*; *li* hexagram has a statement of cow but has no image of *kun* . . . these are cases that cannot be known [by the principle of correspondence]."[63] When they could not find explanations in "Shuogua," the Han scholars devised various techniques to make hexagram images and statements match. Zhu Xi disapproved of the far-fetchedness. For this reason, he approved of Wang Bi's 王弼 (226–49) and Cheng Yi's exegetical approach, which deviated from that of the Han scholars. Nevertheless, he disapproved of the opposite tendency in Wang Bi's and Cheng Yi's exegeses: "When I examine their ideas, however, they seem to insist that the images that the *Yi* has adopted cannot be retraced to their origins and they were like the *bi* and *xing* images in the *Book of Songs* and the parables in the *Mencius*. If so, then the composition of 'Shuogua' has nothing that is related to the *Zhouyi*. Moreover, it has made redundant the belief that the hexagram images were invented by imitating body parts near at hand and various objects in the distance. I therefore have doubts about their ideas, which seem unable to offer a full explanation." Metaphors and parables worked on the principle of correspondences, too. Thus, Wang Bi's and Cheng Yi's approach entails exegetical methods based on another sort of correspondences: the correlation of a hexagram statement to a similar idea perceived by the interpreter. Zhu Xi seemed to have realized that some hexagram images might have been designated in an arbitrary way in the remote past: "The images of the hexagrams must certainly have originated from some sources. The belief in those sources must have once existed in the records of the grand official-diviners. As their sources cannot be retraced, we are compelled to accept the loss."[64] For this reason, he expressed this idea on another occasion: "The *Yi* as a book is full of borrowed analogy and hypothetical sayings."[65]

A Semiotic Model of Reading and Representation

The awesome amount of exegeses turned out by the *Zhouyi* scholars does not just testify to the openness of the classic. If we subject their exegeses to a semiotic study, we may extrapolate some useful insights for constructing a semiotic model of signification and representation. In this section, I will focus on some aspects of *Zhouyi* scholarship with the aim to arrive at a semiotic model of openness. The ancient Chinese paid a great deal of attention to the rectification of names. In the *Confucian Analects*, when one of Confucius's disciples asked him what would be his priority if the Prince of Wei should request him to administer the government, the Master replied that "it would certainly be to rectify names/language."[66] When the disciple asked further for the reason, the Master replied, "If [name] language is incorrect, then what is said does not concord with what was meant; and if what is said does not concord with what was meant, what is to be done cannot be effected."[67] After Confucius, Xun Zi, Mo Zi, Gongsun Long, and other scholars of the *Mingjia* (the School of Names) engaged in elaborate discussions of the significance of name/language. Though their main interest lay in the social, logical, and regulative functions of naming and language, the intensity of their interest suggests that they were aware that naming is related to language but language is not nomenclatural in nature. In modern language theory, Saussure corrects a common error in viewing the nature of language; that is, people often "regard language, when reduced to its elements, as a naming process only—a list of words, each corresponding to the thing that it names."[68] The *Zhouyi* scholars over history have demonstrated this insight in their discussion of the naming of the book without expressing it in conceptual terms. And in their discussion, they were not only aware of the slippery nature of naming/language, but also practically worked out a way of reading that may be said to share the basic rationale of what Peirce calls "semiosis."

The title, *Zhouyi*, has been extensively discussed in most of the major studies of the book. It is a term open to different but equally valid interpretations. The different interpretations were largely predicated on the multivalent nature of the two characters *zhou* and *yi*. According to extant scholarship, the character *zhou* has two basic meanings. (1) It means "comprehensive, all-encompassing." Zheng Xuan of the Eastern Han explained in his discourse: "The title of the *Zhouyi* means that the Way of the Changes is comprehensive and encompasses everything."[69] Lu Deming 陸德明 (550–630) of the Tang also affirmed this explanation: "*Zhou* is a dynasty name. It means all-reaching, all-encompassing, and all-possessing. Now it is used to name the book because of its all-comprehensiveness."[70] (2) It stands for the dynastic title of the Zhou (1045–256 BC). Kong Yingda 孔穎達 (574–648) of the Tang disagreed with scholars who explained the character *Zhou* as "comprehensive" and criticized their explanation as "groundless." In his preface to the *Zhouyi zhengyi*, he said, "Though Zheng Xuan offers such an explanation, it has no textual evidence to support it."[71] Instead, he offered his own explanation: "The *Zhouyi* is entitled *Zhou* because it took the place name of Qiyang. . . . When King Wen composed the *Book of Changes*, he lived in Youli. At that time, the virtue of the Zhou had not arisen yet and it was still the era of the Yin. Therefore, he entitled the book *Zhouyi* so as to make a distinction from the Ying. Since it was amplified by King Wen it was named *Zhouyi* in the same way the *Book of Zhou* and the *Rites of Zhou* were entitled so as to distinguish it from books remaining from the previous dynasty." In his opinion, the *Zhouyi* is so called because it is a work composed by the founder of the Zhou dynasty and hence became a representative work of the Zhou. Kong Yingda's remark provided a new and convincing explanation to the title and has since had wide influence. But he did not endorse the other explanation; he insisted on the correctness of his own explanation and questioned the validity of a view held by other scholars who adopted both explanations: "By adopting Zheng Xuan's explanation, ancient scholars hold that the title refers to both the dynastic title of the Zhou and the meaning of all-comprehensiveness. Although they did not wish to abandon either explanation, their practice may not be plausible."[72] His comment represented a trend in *Zhouyi* hermeneutics that attempted to curb the multivalence of an open system. Kong Yingda's explanation was in its turn attacked by other scholars. Jia Gongyan 賈公彥 (fl. 650) in his annotation to the *Zhouli* (*Rites of the Zhou*) rejected Kong Yingda's explanation and reverted to Zheng Xuan's explanation: "Neither the *Lianshan* nor *Guizang* was said to be named after place names; both were named after their contents. If so, then the 'Zhou' in the *Zhouyi* is not a place name. The *Zhouyi* is headed by the hexagram *qian*, and *qian* is heaven which is capable of covering the four seasons. It is for this reason that the *Book of Changes* was entitled the *Zhouyi*."[73]

In my opinion, both explanations are valid as far as the character's signification in a particular historical contexts goes. To affirm one explanation at the expense of the other is to fail to see the title as an open epithet amenable to different interpretations on the local level. In the larger context, it is a failure to see the open nature of the whole work as an open system. The controversy over the character *Zhou* confirms the open nature of the *Zhouyi* and represents two tendencies in *Zhouyi* hermeneutics: one trend consciously or unconsciously recognizes the open nature of the *Zhouyi* as a system of representation; the other (un)consciously wants to recover the so-called sages' original meaning as transmitted by the *Zhouyi*.

The other character in the title, *yi*, is even more polysemous. The *Yiwei* 易緯 states: "Confucius said that the *Yi* is about simplicity, transformation, and no change."[74] Zheng Xuan reiterated this definition in his "Yizan 易贊": "As for the name of the *Yi*, the one character contains three meanings: the first meaning is 'simplicity'; the second 'change'; the third 'no change.'"[75] Here, the third explanation itself is also ambiguous because it may mean "no change" and "not easy" at the same time. Some other sources claim that it has four meanings. After some careful study, I have found that it actually refers to four strands of implications, three etymological definitions, and one phonetic definition, all of which are interrelated in a multidimensional web.

(1) It means "change, transformation, indeterminacy." Kong Yingda's *Zhouyi Zhengyi* opens with this statement: "The character *yi* is a general name for all transformations and a different epithet for changes."[76] The *Xicizhuan* states: "The divine has no perimeters and the *Yi* has no form." Han Kangbo 韓康伯 (332–380) supplied this annotation: "Perimeters and forms all depend on tangible objects. By contrast, the divine cannot be measured by the *yin* and *yang*. The *Yi* will adapt to changes only. It cannot be elucidated with perimeters and forms."[77]

(2) It means "constancy, no change." The *Xicizhuan* opens with this statement: "The heaven being high and earth being low, *qian* and *kun* were determined. The low and high being established, the honorable and humble are positioned. Movement and stasis being constant, the hard and soft are distinguished." Kong Yingda annotated thus: "Heaven is *yang* and characterized by movement; earth is *yin* and characterized by stasis. Each

having its constant parameters, the hard and soft are distinguished and determined."[78] The *Zhouyi* is about the operations of the universe. The laws governing the transformations of myriad things are constant and unchanging. For this reason, the *Zhengyi* states, "By 'constancy' it means that the positions of heaven and earth are determined and cannot be exchanged."[79]

(3) It means "simplicity and easy to understand." The *Xicizhuan* states: "*Qian* is known by its easiness; *kun* is enabled by its simplicity." Han Kangbo explained this to mean: "The Way of heaven and earth is good at starting something without doing anything and good at accomplishing something without laboring at it. This is why it is regarded as easy and simple."[80] The *Xicizhuan* further states: "By 'easiness' it means 'easy to know'; by 'simplicity' it means 'easy to follow.'" Kong Yingda paraphrased this saying: "'*Qian* is known by its easiness; *kun* is enabled by its simplicity.' This saying is talking about the form and nature of *qian* and *kun* . . . since *qian* and *kun* are endowed with those characteristics, it would be easy for people to deport themselves in following the principles."[81]

(4) It implies "complexity and profundity." The *Xicizhuan* states: "The *Yi* is equal to heaven and earth. Hence it is capable of encompassing the Way of heaven and earth. Looking up, one can use it to observe the heavenly patterns; looking down, one can use it to observe earthly markings. Therefore, it is capable of knowing the rationale behind tangible and intangible objects and understanding the law governing life and death."[82] The universe is a macrocosm; the *Yi* is a microcosm. The microcosm is a representation of the macrocosm and is in a position to facilitate our understanding the operations of the macrocosm.

The three etymological definitions provide three different but plausible sources for the denotations and connotations of the character:

(1) In Xu Shen's 許慎 (30–124) *Shuowen* 説文, the first possible source of definition reads: "'Yi' came from 'lizard,' a house lizard which stays at a house. The character is a pictogram."[83] This definition not only provides an etymological source for the character but also alludes to a different source of its philosophical implications. A lizard is known for its ability to change its colors. Thus, the idea of "change" and "transformation" might have come from observing the physical conditions of lizards.

(2) Xu Shen's *Shuowen*, quoting from an earlier source, provides a second definition: "The combination of *ri* and *yue* gives rise to the character *yi*. It symbolizes the *yin* and *yang* principles."[84] It defines the word as a combination of the sun and moon which in their turn represent *yang* and *yin*, the two underlying principles of the universe. Many scholars accept this as a definition of *yi*: "The word *yi* is composed of the two characters, *ri* and *yue*." The *Cantongqi* 參同契 states: "The combination of *ri* and *yue* becomes the word *yi*. The hard and soft are evenly matched."[85] Yu Fan

虞翻 agreed with the *Cantongqi* saying: "The word *yi* grows out of placing *yue* under *ri*."[86] He was saying that the combination of the sun graph on top and the moon graph at the bottom produces the character 易. Later scholars like Lu Deming 陸德明, Sun Xingyan 孫星衍 (1753–1818),[87] Zhang Xuecheng 章學誠 (1738–1801), Zhang Huiyan 張慧言 (1761–1802),[88] Chen Menglei 陳夢雷 (1650–1741),[89] Liu Shipei 劉師培 (1884–1919), Yao Peizhong 姚配中 (1792–1844),[90] and others all adopt this etymological definition. Liu Shipei viewed this definition as covering both the title and theme of the book: "*Ri* (sun) and *yue* (moon) combined gave rise to *yi*—this is the name and significance of the *Yijing*."[91] A modern scholar's annotation of the *Zhouyi* sums up their views and considers this definition very reasonable: "The definition of *yi* as the combination of *ri* and *yue* is a most reasonable one. The word *yi* represents the image of *ri* on top and *yue* at the bottom."[92] In some other scholarly sources, the etymological definition is mixed up with a philosophical definition. The *Xicizhuan* provides an example: "The principles of *yin* and *yang* are matched with the sun and the moon."[93] From all these views, we can see that the character *yi* is a word produced with the graphic principles of *xiangxing* 象形 and *huiyi* 會義.

(3) In a slightly different etymological definition, some scholars suggest that the character was not formed with *ri* and *yue* but with *ri* and *wu* 勿; *wu* means objects 物. Xu Shen's definition in the *Shuowen* states: "Another saying has it that the radical under *ri* came from *wu* 一日，從勿."[94] The combination means that *ri* and *yue* are immanent in things, therefore standing for the images of things. Some other scholars completely reject the above view as having no solid foundation.[95] A modern scholar, citing the character on oracle bones as support, suggests that "The rise of the sun is the definition of *yi*."[96]

In addition to the etymological definitions, I wish to supply a supplementary phonetic definition: "The word '*yi*' is its homophon '*yi*' 易者一也." Though I do not know whether any other scholar has made this definition, it has reasonable grounds in traditional scholarship. Philosophically, I can cite Yao Peizhong's saying for theoretical support: "The One is the first. The first is the origin of the *Yi*. Hence, if one does not know the One, it is not worthwhile to talk with him about the *Yi*."[97] Phonetically, punning definition is an age-old practice in traditional scholarship. Suffice it to quote one example: *De zhe de ye* (To be virtuous is to gain).[98]

Having classified the four meanings and four definitions of the word *yi*, I must mention two different classifications. One modern scholar has situated the word *yi* with its implications in the large context of the *Xicizhuan*, the *Laozi*, and the *Zhuangzi* and classifies the multiple meanings of *yi* into four categories: "easy and simple," "unity of opposites," "mutual exchange," and "constant transformation." He explains the working principle like this: the birth, proliferation, and development of myriad things in the universe began with the Oneness of "easy simplicity"; the one Great Ultimate gradually divided itself into two principles of *yin* and *yang* or from the One grew the opposition between the two images of heaven and earth; because of the impact of the "mutual exchange" of the *yin* and *yang* principles or the two images of heaven and earth, myriad things were able to proliferate and "transform" infinitely.[99] From a methodological perspective, Mao Qiling maintained that the *Zhouyi* as a book of changes has its essence in the internal transformations of hexagram and line images. He classified the transformations into five categories and designated them as "five changes": (1) *bianyi* 變易 (change through *yin-yang* mutations); (2) *jiaoyi* 交易 (change through trigram connexions); (3) *fanyi* 反易 (change through trigram inversion); (4) *duiyi* 對易 (change through trigram exchange); (5) *yiyi* 移易 (change through line exchange).[100]

The scholarship centering around the discussion of the word *yi* has formed a multidimensional semiotic operation that has far-reaching significance for the study of literary openness. The etymological definition of *yi*, since it is the basis of scholarship and comprises the two graphic principles of *xiangxing* (imitation) and *huiyi* (synthetic compounds), is in fact the nodal point on which the other meanings intersect. I think it is the mother of all existent meanings because it is the source of all implications. The *Yiwei* 易緯 made a very sagacious remark: "The name of the *yi* has four meanings all of which originated in the combination of *ri* (the sun) and *yue* (the moon)."[101] To a larger extent, the various meanings of the word result from the proliferation of the signifier in various directions. In this sense, the explication of the word *yi* not only forms an open system of signification but also contains an open way of reading. Firstly, the signifying process started with etymology. The *ri* radical 日 stands for the sun and the *yue* radical 月 stands for the moon. Both radicals are pictograms, imagistic representations of the sun and the moon. This leads to the signified images in the universe. The *Xicizhuan* states: "The book of *Yi* is about *xiang* or images. The images are the resemblances of things." This is equivalent to saying that the system of the *Zhouyi* grew out of images. Of all the images in the universe, the two most important ones are the sun and the moon: "Of all the clear and bright images suspended in the universe, nothing is more important than the sun and the moon."[102] Secondly, since the sun and moon are so important, through a synecdochic representation (part for the whole), the sun and the moon became symbols for the whole universe. Then, through another signifying process, this time a metonymic representation (concrete quality for abstract quality), the sun became the principle of *yang*, and the moon the principle of *yin*. The *Xicizhuan* states: "The meanings of the *yin* and *yang* are correlated with the sun and moon."[103] Then through a metaphoric representation (one quality stands for another similar quality), *yang* stands for heaven and *yin* stands for earth. Thus through a detour, the sun is associated with heaven while the moon is associated with the earth. Thirdly, the sun rises and sets every day; the moon waxes and wanes every month. The four seasons come and go in a cycle, as one scholar puts it: "The changes of the *Yi* means that spring, summer, autumn, and winter come and go in cycles."[104] The cyclical movement symbolizes the constant changes of the universe. This gives rise to philosophical implications. Fourthly, the sun rises at dawn and sets at dusk; the moon waxes and wanes in a set cycle. There is a constant and unchanging law. When the cyclical pattern is viewed as a law, it becomes a cultural phenomenon. Fifthly, the movement of the sun and moon are commonly seen phenomena of the universe. This gives a commonsense impression of "simplicity." Last but not least, the universe is a macrocosm; the *Yi* is a microcosm. The microcosm is a representation of the macrocosm and by studying it one is in a position to understand the operations of the macrocosm. The *Yi* as a system of representation is as complicated as the universe because it is a representation of the universe and operates on the same complex principles that underlie the operations of the latter. For this reason, we are often troubled by the ambiguity of the word *yi* when it appears in classical texts. It is often difficult to decide whether the word in a particular situation means the operating principles of the universe, or the philosophy of the *Zhouyi*, or the title of the book, or simply the book itself.

My above account reveals three fascinating points about the word *yi*. The first point is about the self-generating power of the character through juxtaposition. The combination of *ri* and *yue* (or *wu*) produces an entity capable of generating new meanings quite beyond the original combination. Since the self-generating operation largely relies on signification, it is a semiotic entity whose self-generating power comes from the interactions of signs. The second fascinating point is the unity of two directly opposite meanings existing in the word *yi*: "transformation and constancy," "simplicity and complexity." The fact that the same word *yi* can generate two entirely opposite meanings through signification prompts me to venture the opinion that the signifying process for the implications of the word *yi* displays a signifying tendency that is deconstructive in nature, if we are to accept the reductive definition of Deconstruction as a signifying act that reverses its surface meaning. The third fascinating point is that signification is open and may point in many different directions. This is where openness is at its most interesting juncture.

The multivalence of the character *yi* suggests that the elaboration of the title of the *Zhouyi* not only forms an open system by itself but also throws some light on the ways multivalence and polysemy in the Chinese tradition are produced. In a way, it anticipated many of the characteristic features of open signification in the Chinese tradition. Out of the explicit and implicit denotations and connotations of the word *yi*, we may construct an embryonic model of signification and representation that will be found to underlie the general system of signification and representation in the Chinese tradition. *I conceive of this model as a nodal point that links multiple signifying channels on different dimensions: imagistic, phonetic, etymological, epistemological, abstract, paradigmatic, syntagmatic, and diagonal. One can change from one channel to another channel, or switch from one level to another level, or shift from one dimension to another dimension. With every change, switch or shift, the meaning of a reading changes.* As a model of representation, the composition of *yi* embraces not only the three principles of representation found by C. S. Peirce to cover all ways of sign representation but also creates an additional principle, which is a unique principle of Chinese writing and art making:[105]

(1) Iconic representation. The pictograms *ri* (sun) and *yue* (moon) are respectively imagistic imitations of the sun and the moon. (2) Symbolic representation: the pictograms *ri* (sun) and *yue* (moon) have three levels of symbolic representation. At one level, the pictograms represent the abstract principles of *yang* and *yin*. At another level, they represent highly abstracted images of the *yin* and *yang* principles: − − stands for *yin*; — stands for *yang*. At still another level, they are language symbols. (3) Juxtaposition: the placing of *ri* on top of *yue* makes the principle of juxtaposition. This principle has a great significance for the signifying mechanism of Chinese representation. I cannot overemphasize its significance for signification. It underlies the two graphic principles of Chinese character formation: *xingsheng* (shape-sound combination) and *huiyi* (synthesis of component radicals). It plays a great role in the creation of artistic objects, visual and verbal, and anticipates and provides inspiration for such modern artistic techniques as montage, collage, and ideogrammic method. (4) Indexical representation. "Indexical representation," says Mitchell, "explains 'standing for' in terms of cause and effect or some 'existential' relation like physical proximity or connectedness."[106] The juxtaposition of *ri* 日 on top of *wu* 勿 is a mutated juxtaposition of *ri* 日 on top of *yue* 月. We may say that the mutation indicates a relation of cause and effect: the existential relation of physical proximity of *ri* and *yue* causes *yue* to change into *wu*, thereby indicating a downward movement of sunlight and its effect on the myriad things in the universe, which is another meaning of the word *yi*.

Because the character *yi* incorporates all the possible principles of representation, it embodies a model of representation destined to be open and unlimited. As an open paradigm of representation, it is capable of generating all the above-mentioned meanings and implications. Some have similar ramifications; some yield different associations; still others produce opposite and contradictory reverberations. This paradigm of multidimensional network summarizes many of the insights that I have teased out of Chinese hermeneutic theories and has significance not only for conceptual inquiries into openness but also for practical readings of literary texts.

The Source of the *Zhouyi*'s Seductive Power

The *Zhouyi* is a complex open work of representation. Its openness comes from a variety of factors. First, it is a network woven with both visual and verbal signs. Second, the symbolism of a sign is polysemously designated. Third, the signs relate to each other in indeterminate relationships on multiple levels. Fourth, the network is amenable to different but often equally valid interpretative strategies. Last but not least, the system has a tolerant quality that permits new views to be assimilated into it as new components. All these factors allow the book to become an open system of representation, which provides inexhaustible opportunities for new interpretations. As a system of representation, its makers might not have consciously willed it to be open at the beginning, but as time went on, its open nature became more and more evident. Many of its interpreters over history seem to have recognized its open nature, but few of them were willing to accept it as an open system. Even today, many scholars still believe that the book was originally intended as a reservoir of mysteries or secret messages. Quite a few studies proclaim that the book has some mysteries waiting to be resolved. And some scholars bemoan that the numerous approaches to the book only serve to further and further shroud its mystery. Evidently, these scholars have been blind to the open nature of the book. This blindness is attested by the fact that from time to time, we encounter a study which claims that it has decoded the secret messages.

As the *Zhouyi* is an open system, it would be an illusion for anyone to claim that he has cracked the mystery of the hexagrams or found a way to unlock the mystery of the book. By now, I am in a better position to claim that the mystery of the book lies in its openness, in its capacity to be interpreted in as many ways as scholars' ingenuity allows. In a way, the source of fascination of the *Zhouyi* shares the same ground as Shakyamuni's wordless communication with his disciple Kasyapa. The common ground is the establishment of an open context of communication and its accompanying open space for interpretation. But the *Zhouyi* is more meaningful than the *Chan* legend of the Buddha's wordless communication in a number of aspects. The wordless communication may at first arouse an intense interest in the viewer who may, nevertheless, completely lose his interest on the ground that the gesture may signify nothing. A meaningful gesture without some hints at its implications would run the risk of being dismissed as meaningless. The problematic nature of the wordless transmission has in fact been criticized by some scholars, including one *Chan* master, Wumen Huikai (1183–1260), who questioned: "If he [the Buddha] says there is a transmission of the true *dharma* eye, then that yellow-faced old geezer would be cheating country bumpkins. But if he says there is no transmission, then why did he approve of Mahakasyapa alone?"[107] With this critical spirit, Bernard Faure analyzes the Buddha's wordless communication, Bodhidharma's (fl. 470–528) dialogue with Emperor Wu of the Liang (r. 502–49), and Huike (487–593), the second *Chan* patriarch's silent response to Bodhidharma's inquiry about his understanding of the *dharma*. He points out the self-defeating effects of silent communication and its possible nullity: "[T]he nondiscursive strategy had on the whole obvious advantages for those masters who, having nothing to say, could always pretend that they were emulating Vimalakirti's silence."[108] By contrast, the *Zhouyi* possesses both meaningful gestures and accompanying hints. The hexagram images are the meaningful gestures while the hexagram and line statements are pregnant hints. Both gestures and hints form an elaborate open system of signification and representation. The more one studies it, the more one is seduced by it simply because he may become more and more convinced that the whole system really has some esoteric knowledge to impart. Because of its unlimited openness, the *Zhouyi* will continue to fascinate scholars of the world in spite of any attempt to view it as a closed system with some finite messages.

The *Zhouyi* is not a literary work. Precisely because of its nonliterary nature, *Zhouyi* hermeneutics possesses greater universal significance than schools of literary hermeneutics in Chinese culture. Even from the perspective of literary hermeneutics, *Zhouyi* hermeneutics deals with the same issues of representation in literary texts and may feed plenty of insights into literary composition and exegeses. One of the insights is that it has made us aware of a text's materiality in the production of meanings and its capacity for allowing scholars to approach it from multiple perspectives. Because of the interaction between visual and verbal signs, *Zhouyi* hermeneutics has blurred the boundaries between literary and nonliterary texts and provided us with the inspiration to adopt a semiotic approach to any texts, literary or otherwise.

Elucidation of Images: Ancient Insights into Modern Ideas of Reading and Writing

In chapter 1, I deferred the discussion of Wang Bi's 王弼 (226–49) conceptual inquiry into reading and writing. The major reason for the deferment is that I must situate it in the larger context of *Zhouyi* hermeneutics and examine it against the local background of a great debate in studies of the *Zhouyi*. The larger context is the conceptual inquiries into the problematics of reading and writing started by Mencius and Zhuangzi (see chapter 1). The local background involves two opposite contentions: *zhongxiang shuo* 重象説 (emphasizing images) and *wangxiang shuo* 忘象説 (forgetting images). The two contentions define two opposite exegetical trends in *Zhouyi* hermeneutics. The debate, when reduced to its core, essentially centers on ideas in Wang Bi's seminal discourse "明象 Elucidation of Images." Where a scholar stands in the debate largely depends on whether he supports or opposes Wang Bi's thesis in this discourse. Although the immediate aim of Wang Bi's discourse was to clarify the relationship between hexagram images and statements, the debate between his supporters and critics has linguistic, philosophical, and literary significance beyond the immediate context of *Zhouyi* hermeneutics and the larger context of Chinese tradition. First, it captures the two opposite trends in Chinese hermeneutics: Mencius' intentionalist theory and Zhuangzi's mistrust of language transmission. Second, it anticipates modern debates on signification, representation, and hermeneutics. By studying the central issues on the elucidation of images in relation to modern language philosophy, we will be able to see how a strand of hermeneutic impulses broke away from interpretive closure and yielded fascinating insights into modern ideas of reading and writing.

Situating the Hermeneutic Controversy

Up to the third century, the notion of "emphasizing images" occupied an undisputed position supported by the commentary of the *Zhouyi* itself. The *Xicizhuan* 繫辭傳 states, "The *Zhouyi* is a book about images; the images are symbolic resemblances of things."[1] The *Xicizhuan* also states, "The eight trigrams having been arranged in proper order, images of myriad things are immanent within."[2] These statements suggest that at its core, the *Zhouyi* is a book born out of attempts to represent myriad things and conditions under heaven through imagistic symbolism. Since *xiang* constitutes its core, without *mingxiang* (clarification of images), the *Zhouyi* cannot be adequately interpreted. The *Zhouyi*, however, is not just a book of *guaxiang* (hexagram images) and *yaoxiang* (line images); it has *guaci* (hexagram statements) and *yaoci* (line statements) which are written in words. Confucius is quoted as saying: "The sages established images to fully express their thought, designed hexagrams to fully express the true and false conditions of affairs, and attached verbalizations to fully express what they wanted to say."[3] This statement establishes the order in which the *guaxiang*, *yaoxiang*, *guaci*, and *yaoci* came to be composed. The *xiang* or image(s) formed the core of the *Zhouyi* and drove the hermeneutic tradition for several millennia. As *xiang* occupies an important position in the *Zhouyi* hermeneutic tradition, in the numerous attempts to clarify the relationship between *guaxiang* and *guaci*, the notion of emphasizing images naturally developed into a hermeneutic hegemony. It is a closed position because it assumes that the sages' intentions may be retrieved by pondering the relationship between hexagram images and statements.

With the appearance of Wang Bi's exegesis and especially his discourse on the elucidation of images, the hegemony of the closed hermeneutic position was seriously challenged and eventually overcome. Wang Bi's discourse is of seminal value not only because it ushered in an open hermeneutic trend in *Zhouyi* hermeneutics in particular, but also because it made an important contribution to the inquiry into language philosophy and hermeneutics in the Chinese tradition in general. It has been recognized as an important contribution to the study of the *Zhouyi*, but as a contribution to Chinese linguistic and literary thought, it has not yet received its due recognition. The reasons for the lack of a full recognition of Wang Bi's discourse are many, but one of them seems to be related to the controversy over the latter part of the discourse. Scholars generally do not disagree on the meaning of the first part, but around the second part, they have split into two major schools: the *Xiang-shu* 象數 (Image-Number) school and *Yi-li* 義理 (Meaning-Principle) school. Before Wang Bi, all scholars of the *Zhouyi* emphasized the importance of *xiang*. After him, "ignoring images" 忘象説 became so popular that the *Yi-li* school overwhelmed the *Xiang-shu* school. Nevertheless, the latter never disappeared and saw a few flourishing periods especially during the Song and Qing dynasties. Around the subject of *mingxiang*, there unfolded a great debate. Some scholars argued for the perspicacity of Wang Bi's insight while some others argued against its validity. Still others held a middle ground, trying to reconcile the opposing views and offering a compromise interpretation. In the heated debate over Wang Bi's view on how to clarify the *Zhouyi* hexagram images and statements emerged a cluster of remarks and discourses. In the following, I will conduct a close reading of Wang Bi's discourse in conjunction with discourses of other scholars and through detailed analysis in terms of modern semiotic, linguistic, and literary theories, assess the contributions made by those thinkers to Chinese language philosophy and hermeneutics. In addition, I will explore how two major paradigms of interpretation evolved from the elucidation of images in the *Zhouyi* and how the notion of forgetting images represents a shift in hermeneutic trend from interpretive closure to hermeneutic openness.

Traditionally, the differences between the Image-Number school and Meaning-Principle school can be summed up as the following. The Image-Number school, as the name indicates, is mainly concerned with exploring the internal relations between hexagram and line images and hexagram and line statements in particular and the interrelations between the *jing* or text proper and the *zhuan* or appended verbalizations. The central argument of this school contends that every word of the *Zhouyi* text was intentionally created and originated in the hexagram and line images. It therefore places great emphasis on the imagistic and numerical aspects in its interpretation of hexagram and line statements. By contrast, the Meaning-Principle school paid little attention to the relationship between the hexagram and line images and the hexagram and line statements. In fact, Wang Bi, its initiator, openly advocated "forgetting images" so as to get correct interpretations. Instead, it focuses on the natural, social, ontological, and epistemological rationale believed to inhere in the text of the *Zhouyi* and places great emphasis on exploring the significance revealed by the text in its interpretation of the book.

The Image-Number school was the older of the two. Before the appearance of the Meaning-Principle school, the Image-Number school had already established itself as the mainstream scholarship of the *Zhouyi* and enlisted the support of almost all the famous *Zhouyi* scholars. When

Wang Bi, the founder of the Meaning-Principle school came on the scene, he had two roads to take: he could either follow the beaten track traveled by the Image-Number scholars or blaze a new path of his own. As a young genius in his early twenties, Wang Bi chose the second road and started what may be called "a revolution in *Zhouyi* scholarship." Truly, his pioneering effort was a revolution in the sense that it challenged the established tradition and started a new tradition that professed to break away from the old tradition. In his revolution, the principal theme is: one should forget the hexagram images and concentrate on finding the meanings of the statements 忘象求意. Thus, the central difference between the two schools lies in whether one sets great store by or pays little attention to the images in the *Zhouyi* text.

In essence, however, I suggest that what lies at the heart of their differences is a shift of reading paradigms, a change that reminds us of a similar move adopted respectively by structuralist scholars and poststructuralist scholars. The Image-Number scholars are image bound; in their attempt to unlock the supposedly concealed meanings of the sages through correlative readings of the hexagram images and statements, they may be said to be intention bound and text bound. And since they emphasized the importance of hexagram images as containing the original intentions of the sages, they may also be said to be author centered. The Meaning-Principle scholars also paid lip service to the intentions of the sages, but they were more concerned with how to generate new interpretations of the *Zhouyi* in relation to changing circumstances. Hence, they are context bound. Here we must note that their context is not the original context but possible contexts and new context(s). As they were not bound by the images of the text, they related the text to the infinite context of the universe, society, and human conditions. By allowing the interpreter to have his initiative, they may be said to be reader centered. From the perspective of reading, I may suggest that the controversy between the Image-Number school and the Meaning-Principle school was endowed with a significance beyond their immediate context and even beyond the Chinese tradition. In many ways the contention between the two schools anticipated the contemporary debates over the central issues of reading. In terms of whether one should emphasize image-number or thought-principle, Wang Bi's annotation of the *Zhouyi* signified a shift of emphasis in the hermeneutic tradition from iconic representation to linguistic representation. The shift in turn led to an age-old contention between two paradigms of interpretation: a conservative author-oriented paradigm and a radical reader-oriented paradigm. This is the theoretical background against which the debate between the two schools ought to be viewed.

Despite their different notions of relevant factors in exegeses, both schools were able to come up with reading strategies that turned out an awesome amount of interpretations. The paradoxical situation in which the conservative Image-Number scholars looked as radical as the revolutionary Meaning-Principle scholars came about not simply because of the open nature of the *Zhouyi* text. It also came from two different approaches to the coding in the text. As far as coding is concerned, the Image-Number school's paradigm of exegesis may be called "overcoded reading." That is, it overemphasizes the efforts believed to have gone into the making of the *Zhouyi* text, which may not have been the case at all. On the other hand, the Meaning-Principle school's paradigm of exegesis may be termed "undercoded reading" because it seems to suggest that the intense efforts believed to have gone into the correlation between images and statements might not have been there in the first place; and even if there were such efforts, they should not hinder a reader's exegesis in terms of his own circumstances.

Mingxiang as a Hermeneutic Issue

Ostensibly, *mingxiang* (elucidation of images) arose as a result of the need to address the problematic relationship between hexagram images and statements, but in essence it is concerned with the broad issues of thinking, language, and writing. The *Xicizhuan* quoted Confucius as saying, "Writing cannot fully express speech; speech cannot fully express thought."[4] This supposedly Confucian saying perceptively identifies the gap between speech and writing, language and thought and started the inquiry into signification and representation in *Zhouyi* hermeneutics. Kong Yingda's 孔穎達 (574–648) annotation of the Confucian saying shows how the necessity of *mingxiang* first arose: "Writing is that which records speech. Speech is complex and diverse. The speech of the Chu differs from that of the Xia; and there are places where there is speech but there may be no words. Even though one wants to record speech in writing, writing is unable to fully express what is said. This is why it is said: 'writing cannot fully express speech.' Moreover, thought, profound and tortuous, may not be fully described in speech. This is why 'speech cannot fully express thought.'"[5] Kong Yingda recognized the inadequacy of written language for conveying spoken language and thought. He seemed to believe that the symbolism of the hexagram images can express profound thought that cannot be conveyed through language and reveal the inner conditions of the myriad things in the world.

Guo Yong 郭雍 (1103–87) of the Song also stressed the importance of images for conveying meaning: "The *Xicizhuan* says, 'The *Zhouyi* is a book about images.' It also says, 'The sages established images to fully express their thought.' This generally means that the meanings of the *Zhouyi* cannot be comprehended in their entirety; therefore, images are created to fully convey them. As thought cannot be fully expressed, if one engages only in pondering words, he will get empty talk."[6] Shang Binghe 尚秉和, a modern scholar, agrees with this opinion: "When thought cannot be fully expressed, hexagrams can fully convey it. Speech cannot be fully expressed, hexagram images can fully reveal it. Hence '[the sages] established images to fully express their thought and designed hexagrams to fully express the true and false conditions of situations.'"[7] All of these scholars seem to say: thought is nebulous; words are inadequate to express it; only *xiang* can fully express it; language, spoken or written, can only help express it. With this understanding, they seem to prefer the symbolism of iconic and indexical representation to verbal representation. Wang Bi's discourse signified a shift of emphasis in the hermeneutic tradition from iconic representation to linguistic representation. The shift in turn led to an age-old contention between two paradigms of interpretation: a conservative author-centered paradigm and a radical reader-oriented paradigm.

Why does the significance of the debate over how to clarify the relationship between hexagram images and hexagram statements go beyond the local issue of *Zhouyi* hermeneutics to cover the relationships between thought and symbol, symbol and language, language and literature, creation and interpretation? Stephen Owen rightly points out: "[T]he rhetoric of Chinese exegesis encourages running through serial relations in several directions to clarify the exact terms of those relations. What Wang Pi discovers in doing this has important implications for understanding the *Book of Changes*, for a general theory of languages, and particularly for poetry."[8] In my opinion, Wang Bi's discourse may be the first systematic discussion of signification and representation in the Chinese tradition. Only when we tackle Wang's discourse from the combined perspective of thought, language, representation, and interpretation can we come to an adequate understanding of his view and to an adequate assessment of his contribution to traditional Chinese language philosophy and literary thought. On top of all this, we can extend Wang Bi's theory and the discussions initiated by his discourse to a general theory of traditional Chinese language philosophy and representation.

The difficulty for relating *mingxiang* and *Zhouyi* hermeneutics to a modern theory of signification and representation may come from the fact that these discourses were first and foremost aimed at clarifying the local

issues pertaining to the hexagrams and their associated images, the hexagrams and attached statements, hexagram lines and line statements. What
enables us to overcome this difficulty is the semiotic notion that any
humanly constructed system, be it a language, or a sign system, or even a
food menu, can be analyzed in terms of semiology, the general science
of signs. In his *Course in General Linguistics*, Saussure proposed a general
science of signs which he called semiology. He envisioned it to embrace
the study of almost all human systems of signs: images, gestures, the sign
language of deaf-mutes, musical sounds, artifacts, rites and ritual, daily
routine, polite formulas, and traffic signs.[9] Roland Barthes, working in the
direction pioneered by Saussure, used semiotics to study mass media, film,
advertisements, toys, food, menu, clothing, photography, striptease, and
wrestling, as well as language and literature. Barthes's major contention
about the legitimacy of these diverse subjects as proper subjects of study
is that they all contain an inherent system of signification.[10] Wang Bi's
and other scholars' discourses are concerned with the *Zhouyi*, which is
doubtless a system of signs and signification. As an elucidation of the
images of the *Zhouyi*, which encompasses both signs and words, their discourses can certainly be viewed as studies on the mechanism of language
and reading in general.

Wang Bi as an Innovative Synthesizer

Wang Bi did not articulate his theory of hermeneutics without any
reference to previous theories. In fact, he situated his inquiry in the context
of *Zhouyi* hermeneutics as well as his predecessors' conceptual inquiries
into reading and writing. It is a scholarly consensus that Wang Bi was an
enthusiastic promoter of Lao Zi's and Zhuangzi's Daoist system of thought,
especially in his annotation of the *Zhouyi*. In terms of this consensus, his
theory of reading should be a Daoist one heavily influenced by Lao Zi's
and Zhuangzi's theory of hermeneutics, especially the latter's radical linguistic skepticism and preference for wordless communication. A casual
look at his discourse seems to confirm this view. In his discourse, we find
an overt use of Zhuangzi's metaphors for words ("fish-traps and rabbit-
snares") and an implicit amplification of Zhuangzi's view of language and
verbal communication. By contrast, we do not see any overt reference to
Mencius' ideas. I, however, venture to argue that Wang Bi's theory of
reading certainly came under the influence of Zhuangzi, but he did not
reject Mencius' theory of reading altogether. In this section, I will demonstrate that Wang Bi is not a partisan scholar but a synthesizer. Adopting
a syncretic approach to his predecessors' views, he drew inspirations from

both Mencius and Zhuangzi and synthesized their insights into a theory of hermeneutics that builds on the strength of his predecessors and explores the questions left by them.

Wang Bi's discourse begins with a discussion of the relationship among *xiang* (image), *yi* (thought), and *yan* (language): "The image is that which brings out the thought; language is that which elucidates the image. To fully express ideas, nothing is more effective than images; to fully convey an image nothing can excel language. Language is born of images; therefore, one can observe images by following language. Images are born of thought; therefore, one can observe thought by tracing images. Thought is fully conveyed through images; images are made explicit through language."[11] The opening passage is doubtless about thought and representation. When a human being has a thought in his mind, it is a cluster of nerve stimuli that are invisible, unnamable, and indescribable. If he wants to convey his thought to another person, he must resort to representation. There are various ways of representation: body language (gestures, facial expressions, actions, etc.), symbolic language (use of tokens, a rose for love, an ax to grind for belligerence, a chip on the shoulder for provocation, etc.), and language per se (spoken language and written language). Of the various languages that are semiotic systems, the linguistic system is the most convenient tool to convey one's ideas, desires, and feelings. This is precisely what Wang Bi meant in his opening statement.

Wang Bi posited a correlation of three terms: thought, image, and language. His idea came from the *Xicizhuan*: "The sages established images to fully express their thought, designed hexagrams to fully express the true and false conditions of affairs, and attached verbalizations to fully express what they wanted to say."[12] But to configurate the three terms in an organicist structure is entirely Wang Bi's invention. It is to his credit that he correlates the three terms in such a systematic manner that their relation corresponds pretty well to the correlation of the basic terms of signification in the Saussurean linguistics. In Saussure's theory of the sign, signification is done through the sign, which requires a relation between two terms, a concept and an image. The linguistic sign is a "two-sided psychological entity" that consists of a concept and a sound image. The concept is derived from thought; the image may be either a sound image or a visual image or a mental image. Their relationship is shown in the following diagrams:[13]

Concept   tree

--------   -------

Image   

This model is further abstracted into the opposition between the signified and signifier. There are two slightly different versions of this model: Saussure's model and Lacan's modified model.

Saussure's model	Lacan's model
Signified	Signifier
———————	———————
Signifier	Signified

There is no essential difference between Saussure's model and Lacan's model though the signifier and signified exchange their positions. I have adopted Lacan's model because it has some subtle implications that conform to the topography and inner workings of the mental apparatus. In Lacan's model, the bar (——) separating the signifier and signified represents repression and resistance to signification.[14]

Although Wang Bi did not schematize the relationship between thought and image, thought and words, in terms of Saussure's sign structure, his correlation of the terms implies the opposition between the signifier and signified. While Saussure proposes the opposition between concept and image, signifier and signified, Wang Bi deployed the opposition between *yi* 意 (thought) and *xiang* 象 (image), *yi* 意 and *yan* 言 (words). The following diagrams may serve to show how close Wang Bi's notion comes to Saussure's theory of the sign:

Image	Xiang 象	Signifier	Yan 言
———————	———————	———————	———————
Concept	Yi 意	Signified	Yi 意

Here, we may see that *yi* is equivalent to Saussure's concept and the signified in that it is invisible and inaccessible because it comes from the mind. *Xiang* and *yan* are equivalent to the signifier as they are material representation of *yi* (thought). By material representation I mean that they are visible and accessible signs whether they are hexagrams images or hexagram statements.

In Wang Bi's discourse, he conceived of the correlation of *yi* (thought) and *xiang* (image), *yi* (thought) and *yan* (words), in such an innovative way that his conception is remarkably comparable to the modern theory of signification. I consider this to be his greatest contribution to a Chinese theory of signification. Thought is the origin; image is a way to represent thought; and language is a way to express the meaning of an image, hence becoming another way to represent thought. Thought is the mother of ideas; images and language are means to convey ideas. The movement from thought, through image, to language constitutes a complete process of signification. This process of signification is a two-way movement. From the speaker's (writer's) point of view, one can trace the movement from thought through image to language. From the listener's (reader's) point of view, one can reverse the process by retracing the movement from language, through image, to thought. This process of signification is succinctly expressed by Wang Bi: "Language is born of images. Therefore one can observe the image by following the language. Images are born of thought. One therefore can observe the thought by following images. Thought is fully expressed through images; images are made obvious through language." In the local context of *Zhouyi* hermeneutics, Wang Bi's reconceptualization adequately captures the transmitted tradition of how the hexagram images and statements came about. In the general context of representation, Wang Bi's notion anticipates the modern theory of sign representation and verbal representation. The schema below shows how *yi* (thought), *xiang* (image), and *yan* (language) are related to one another:

Yi (Thought) → Xiang (Images) → Yang (Words)

images are born of thought	words are born of images
images are to bring forth thought	words are to elucidate images
thought is fully expressed in images	images become manifest through words
nothing is more effective than images in fully conveying thought	nothing is more effective than words in fully conveying images
one observes thought through images	one observes images through words

In tracing the movement from *yi* to *xiang* and from *xiang* to *yan*, Wang Bi made another remarkable achievement with regard to the origin of language. By noting "images are born of thought" and "words are born of images," Wang Bi is free from a common error in views of language. As Stephen Owen rightly points out: "On the level of a theory of language, Wang Pi's passage suggests that words do not name 'things'; words are a stage in the processes of mind, 'born from' the images of things."[15] Wang Bi's view of the relation between *yi* and *xiang*, *yi* and *yan* anticipates Saussure's theory of the linguistic sign. What is a linguistic sign? Saussure argues against a common error in viewing the nature of linguistic sign. People often "regard language, when reduced to its elements, as a naming process only—a list of words, each corresponding to the thing that it names."[16] The Biblical story of Adam naming beasts is a well-known version of the normenclatural nature of language. It is a remarkable achievement for Wang Bi to avoid the common error and suggest an alternative perspective to examine the nature of the linguistic sign. By viewing language as something born of the mind, Wang Bi pioneered a way of studying language distinctly different from that of Confucius, Xun Zi 荀子, Mo Zi 墨子, Gongsun Long 公孫龍, and other scholars of *Mingjia* (the School of Names), whose chief concern is with the social, logical, and regulative function of language.[17] I suggest, Wang Bi's view of the origin of language and language's relation to thought and image might have been influenced by the dominant expressionism in Chinese aesthetic thought, the notion that poetry is the natural, spontaneous outpouring of emotions from the mind.[18]

My analysis shows that Wang Bi is not a partisan scholar but a synthesizer. Adopting a syncretic approach to his predecessors' views, he drew inspirations from Confucius, Mencius, and Zhuangzi and synthesized their insights into a theory of signification and representation that blends the insights of his predecessors with those of his own. Situated in the whole context of his discourse, his model is not unlike the hermeneutic one based on Roman Jakobson's model of verbal communication, consisting of the addresser, the addressee, code, message, contact, and context.[19] Like Mencius, who viewed reading as an act of communication between the author and reader, Wang Bi considered representation and interpretation as a complete process of communication. What differentiates him from his predecessor is that he treated communication as consisting of two interconnected processes of representation, one belonging to the encoder (author) and the other to the decoder (reader). He dealt with representation on the part of the author first. His opening statement shows him to side more with Mencius than with Zhuangzi, for he presented an argument directly against Zhuangzi's radical linguistic skepticism. His idea is a creative reconsideration of the paradoxical nature of language and a rethinking of the relationship between language and thought, both of which have been identified in the *Xicizhuan*.

Like Mencius, Wang Bi believed that the reader can, with the aid of language and representation, get back to what was on the mind of the author: "Language is born of images; therefore, one can observe images by following language. Images are born of thought; therefore, one can observe thought by tracing images." This is another way of stating the core of Mencius' theory of reading: "to use one's understanding to trace it back to the author." He also practically accepted Mencius' belief in the adequacy of language (words and signs) for communication: "To fully express ideas, nothing is more effective than images; to fully convey an image nothing can excel language." His recognition of language's communicative power problematizes a scholarly consensus that, in the debate over whether language can exhaustively express ideas, Wang Bi was firmly on the side of those who believed in the negative thesis.

The Controversy over "Forgetting Images"

After an innovative synthesis in the opening, Wang Bi began to propose new ideas of his own. The originality of his ideas have given rise to a great controversy that continues to this day. The central point in the controversy is his statement that "one can forget images after he gets the thought 得意忘象" and its accompanying statement that "one can forget words after one gets the image 得象忘言." Both statements come from the second passage in Wang Bi's discourse: "Thus, language is what illuminates the images; once one gets the image, the words are forgotten. Images are what preserves the ideas; once one obtains the ideas, the images are forgotten. In a like manner, a snare is what serves to catch rabbits; once one catches the rabbit, the snare is forgotten; and a fish-trap is what serves to catch fish; once the fish is caught, the fish-trap is forgotten. If it is so, then, language is the snare for images; the images are the fish-traps for ideas." Here, many scholars, classical and modern, start to disagree with Wang Bi, accusing him of having made a dubious proposition. During the Song dynasty, Guo Yong 郭雍 (1103–87) questioned the correctness of Wang Bi's view: "As a book, the *Yijing*'s rationale and language all come out of images. There has been no one who forgets the images but gets to understand the book!"[20] Wang Yan 王炎 (1138–1218) of the Southern Song also challenged Wang Bi's move to ignore the images of all hexagrams except *jing* 井, *ding* 鼎, *yi* 頤, and *shike* 噬嗑: "The sixty-four hexagrams are similar in nature. Why is it appropriate to discuss the images of four hexagrams while ignoring and leaving undiscussed the images of all the rest?"[21] Zhu Xi 朱熹 (1130–1200), who had a good understanding of the Golden Mean, questioned Wang Bi's view, but refrained from a point-blank criticism for lack of evidence.[22]

There are more upholders of Wang Bi's view than questioners. The defenders and critics have been locked in a thousand-year-old controversy. Each side sticks to its position; neither side is able to convince the other. I believe, the reason the controversy has not been satisfactorily resolved is mainly because each side appeals to impressionistic common sense; neither side resorts to rigorous methods of logical analysis. Before we take a stand in the controversy, we need to review briefly the complex issue of *xiang* (image) again. As I have mentioned earlier, *xiang* has a congeries of denotations and connotations. On its local level—that is, the elucidation of the *Zhouyi*—both *xiang* and *yan* are believed to be the carriers of the original intentions of the sages. Thus, the sages' original thoughts in creating the hexagrams are immanent in *xiang* (hexagram and line images), the pure sign system, and accessible through *yan*, the semiotic system conveying the meanings of images couched in language and covering *wuxiang* (natural phenomena), *shixiang* (social phenomena), and *yixiang* (poetic images). Since the sages, the originators of the various kinds of images are long gone, their ideas (conceptual values of the book) have to be discovered by retracing the process of signification—that is, going back from words through images to thought. In this reverse way, *yan* or language and *xiang* or images become the indispensable tools for recovering the lost meanings intended by the sages.

Wang Bi's way of viewing images as the tool for conveying thought and of language as the tool for illuminating images is remarkable even by modern standards, for it conceives of a correct relationship between thought and language before the appearance of the modern linguistic theory that language is the tool without which thinking is impossible. As Saussure states: "Philosophers and linguists have always agreed in recognizing that without the help of signs we would be unable to make a clear-cut, consistent distinction between two ideas. Without language, thought is a vague, uncharted nebula. There are no pre-existing ideas, and nothing is distinct before the appearance of language."[23]

In Zhuangzi's original statement, he implied that "rabbit-snares" and "fish-traps" are metaphors for language. Wang Bi adopted Zhuangzi's metaphors and affirmed the idea that language is a tool for thinking and representation. Zhuangzi, in using metaphors, was aware of the metaphorical nature of language (the gap between language and thought), and mistrusted the function of language. He therefore advocated abandoning language as a communicative tool and implicitly called for a mode of communication that does not use language. Wang Bi agreed with Zhuangzi on the nature of language and accepted the gap between language and thought, but he did not share Zhuangzi's radical linguistic skepticism and total mistrust of verbal communication. He wanted to put to creative use the paradoxical nature of language as a means of communication. Hence, Wang Bi made a radical proposal:

Thus, he who stays fixed on the language will not be the person who gets the images; he who stays fixed on the images will not be the person who gets the idea. Images are born of thought; should images be preserved, what is preserved is not the images of the original thought. Words are born of images; should words be preserved, what is preserved is not the original words. If this reasoning is correct, then he who forgets the images is the one who obtains the idea; he who forgets words is the one who obtains the images. To get the original thought depends on forgetting images; to get images rests on forgetting words.

Wang Bi's critics do not understand why one has to forget *xiang* in order to preserve *yi* and why one has to forget *yan* in order to keep *xiang*. His defenders offered a number of explanations. A most common and coherent one reads: "Fish-traps and rabbit-snares are tools; fish and rabbits are the objects sought. Having gotten fish and rabbits, one can set aside his fish-trap and rabbit-snare. This is why Wang Bi says, 'To establish images to fully convey one's thoughts, one can forget the image after he gets the thought. To create a hexagram by doubling two trigrams to convey one's disposition, one can forget the trigrams.'"[24] This line of defense seems theoretically sound. After all, representational material is only a tool, be it image, sign, or language. But if we probe into the theoretic foundation of representation further, we will discover a problem articulated by Wang Bi's critics. True, representational material is the tool for thinking, but it is a special tool. It is special because the tool is inseparable from the work accomplished. The tool and the work accomplished are one and the same thing, like the two sides of a sheet of paper. One cannot cut the two sides apart without destroying the paper, as Saussure vividly puts it in his discussion of language representation.[25] The representational material in Saussure's discussion is language sound rather than image or sign, but the pertinence of his theory is the same.

Some of Wang Bi's critics voiced their criticism in a line of thought that is very modern. Shao Yong 邵雍 (1011–77), critical of Wang Bi's view concerning the relationship between *xiang* and *yi*, *yan* and *xiang*, said in an ironic tone: "As images and numbers are fish-trap and rabbit-snare, so words and thoughts are fish and rabbits. It is all right to forget the fish-trap and rabbit-snare after one has captured fish and rabbits. If one abandons the fish-trap and rabbit-snare to capture fish and rabbits, he will never see his catch."[26] Wang Yan directly criticized Wang Bi's use of fish-trap and rabbit-snare metaphors to justify the move to ignore images: "To discard the fish-trap and rabbit-snare, one cannot capture fish and rabbits. Wang Bi himself knew it was impossible to get ideas without images. He, therefore, digressed by saying, 'Should the intended meaning be *robustness*, why must one start with an image of the horse in the hexagram image? If the category aims at compliance, why must one start with an image of a cow?' This amounts to saying that one can discard the fish-trap and rabbit-snare before he captures fish and rabbits."[27]

I have suggested that Wang Bi's view of the relationship of thought, image, and language comes very close to the modern theory of linguistic sign. But on a very crucial aspect of the linguistic sign, his critics may claim that their notion of representation in terms of sign and language comes closer to modern language philosophy than his notion. Let us look at the structural model of sign again. Any signification postulates a relation between two terms, a signifier and a signified. In the process of signification, it is not simply a case of the signifier expressing the signified. There is a third term. It is the correlation that unifies the two terms. The third term is the sign which is the associative total of the signifier and signified. This is the signification pattern of any semiotic system:

Signifier	Xiang 象	Yan 言
--------- Sign	---------- 意象 (Image)	-------- 文/字 (Word)
Signified	Yi 意	Yi 意

A sign is a unified entity of a signifier and a signified; an image, a unified entity of an idea and an image; a word, a unified entity of a concept and a written symbol. Without exception, what is visible or tangible in a sign or a word is the material aspect, the sound image, or the written symbol. The Chinese literary concept *yixiang* 意象 (image) is a remarkable invention because it captures both the seen and unseen, image and thought. In the *Xicizhuan*, *xiang* and *yi* are still separate: "The sages establish images to fully express ideas." Liu Xie 劉勰 (466–538) joined the two together to make an important aesthetic concept in his *Wenxin diaolong*: "A master artist with unique insight would brandish his ax in accordance with his vision of an idea-image. This is the primary technique for the mastery of writing and the great end in the planning of a writing."[28] The evolution of the concept *yixiang* 意象 (idea-image)[29] shows vividly how the ancient Chinese mind grasps the inseparableness of idea and its material body, the word. In the evolution from the separate *yi* and *xiang* to the joint concept *yixiang*, we can certainly see Wang Bi's contribution. But by invoking the inseparableness of the signifier and signified, a critic of Wang Bi's view may claim that in his insistent proposition, "once one gets the idea, he can forget the image," he falls one step short of the joint concept of *yixiang*.

How is it so? On the local level of the *Zhouyi*, the *yi* or thought is doubly inaccessible because the sages are long gone and the intended meanings of the hexagrams can be accessible only by means of hexagram symbols and line statements. On the general level of signification, the same is true. In terms of the opposition between signifier and signified, it is clear that although the *yi* and *xiang*, (*yi* and *yan*, too) are separate terms, they form a unit with two inseparable sides. As I have shown through the model of the sign, the two sides, *yi* and *xiang* or *yi* and *yan*, are inseparable in the sense that the two sides of a sheet of paper are inseparable. From this point of view, *guaxiang* and *yaoci* are not mere tools like the rabbit-snare and fish-trap. In real situations, the snare and fish-trap can really be forgotten once rabbits and fish are caught. But in language and semiotic signification, the tool (*xiang*, *yan*) coexists with the work it accomplishes. If one forgets the tool, he loses the work done.

This is exactly the insight Zhuangzi tries to convey through his allegory. Wang Bi's use of the metaphors, the rabbit-snare for *xiang* and fish-trap for *yan*, comes from Zhuangzi, but he seemed to have ignored a most subtle aspect of Zhuangzi's implication. Wang Yinglin 王應麟 (1223–96) once made this remark: "Wang Bi's notion of forgetting images is but the remnant vestiges of Zhuangzi's idea."[30] Perhaps he somehow felt that Wang Bi did not get the essence of Zhuangzi's idea. The *locus classicus* of rabbit-snare and fish-trap is a statement in the *Zhuangzi*: "The fish-trap is a tool to catch fish. Once the fish is caught, the fish-trap is forgotten. A rabbit-snare is a tool to catch rabbits. Once the rabbit is caught, the snare is forgotten. Language is a tool to hold ideas. Once ideas are conveyed, language is forgotten. Where on earth could I find a person who has forgotten words to have a word with him?"[31]

Ostensibly, Wang Bi's idea is a rewording of Zhuangzi's original idea. In fact it deviates in an important aspect from the original meaning. The last sentence of Zhuangzi's statement is an exclamatory question. It implies that it is impossible to get hold of a person with whom one can communicate without the aid of language. Hence it is an illusion to think that one can get *yi* and forget *yan*. Zhuangzi was arguing against the common illusion. Although Zhuangzi did not categorically say language and thought are inseparable, his question suggests it: ordinarily, people conceive of language as a tool in the way one uses a fish-trap or a rabbit-snare. This conception is a specious illusion. One cannot retain *yi* without *xiang* or without *yan*. Once one gets hold of *yi*, *xiang* or *yan* will stick to the *yi* whether he likes it or not; or to put it in another more appropriate way, whether he is aware of it or not. Martin Heiddeger, in his metameditation on the nature of language, touches on a phenomenon in language communication that comes close to the situation in Wang Bi's proposition, "once one gets the idea, he can forget the image." He points out that human beings' "relation to language is vague, obscure, almost speechless." In our everyday life, we have a paradoxical relation with language. Though we are so close to language and speak it every day, we scarcely notice the existence of language. We become conscious of the existence of language only when we "cannot find the right word for something that concerns us, carries us away, oppresses or encourages us."[32] To a certain extent, it may be because of the vague and obscure relation to language that Wang Bi talked about the illusory perception that one can forget *xiang* and *yan* after he gets *yi*.

Wang Bi's critics may invoke another modern theory to argue against his view. They may say that Wang Bi, like most scholars before modern times, had fallen victim to the conventional view of language as a container that holds meaning. According to this container theory, the process of signification is like this: an addresser has an idea, which is a message. He encodes it and puts it in language, which is the carrier. An addressee comes along, gets the container (language), and decodes the message in the container. Once he gets the message, the container (language) is cast away. In terms of this fallacy, the critics' accusation seems to be legitimate. The two sentences from Wang Bi's discourse seem to be another way of expressing this container theory: "Therefore after establishing a *xiang* to fully express *yi*, one can forget the *xiang*; having doubled the trigrams into a hexagram to fully convey one's mood, one can forget the trigrams. Thus, anything that touches an object of the same category can serve as the image of the category; anything that matches an idea can serve as the symbol of the idea." The whole passage may be paraphrased this way: Since sages set up *guaxiang* to express their ideas, doubled trigram to express their sentiments, and employed things and situations of the same category to represent the category, hexagram images and hexagram statements are only means to the end. As they are external to thoughts, one should not stay fixed on them. Once the meaning of a hexagram image or a hexagram statement is understood, the image and statement can be forgotten. This line of thought again plays into the hands of his critics.

A Distinction between Meaning and Significance

My close examination of Wang Bi's and his critics' views in terms of rigorous language philosophy seems to favor the latter. But his defenders would wonder, How could Wang Bi, an acknowledged genius and a perceptive scholar, have missed Zhuangzi's subtle point? More pertinently, they may ask: If Wang Bi's notion of "forgetting images" is as faulty as the critics claim, then there would be a contradiction in his discourse. Indeed, if we recall Wang Bi's statement at the beginning of his discourse—"To fully express ideas, nothing is more effective than images; to fully convey an image nothing can excel language. Language is born of images; therefore, one can observe images by following language"—we will see that his advocacy for forgetting images does not come logically from his reasoning and would contradict his opening thesis. How could Wang Bi contradict himself in a short discourse? Few scholars seem to have paid enough attention to this seeming contradiction. Liu Dajun, as an exception, notices the discrepancy between Wang Bi's opening statement and his concluding statement. He, however, argues that it is only a seeming discrepancy.[33]

I here suggest that in the advocacy of "forgetting images once the meaning is comprehended," Wang Bi had another aim in mind, which can be logically deduced. I want to argue that precisely because he understood that representation is not a conveyance belt that can send information from the author to the reader without any loss, he employed Zhuangzi's parable to advance a radical theory of hermeneutics the revolutionary nature of which lies in its shift of emphasis from the author to the reader. In other words, he advocated a new, reader-oriented paradigm that seeks to break away from the conservative author-centered paradigm of reading.

His supporters defended his position by claiming that Wang Bi did not advocate forgetting images before getting ideas; he advised people to forget images only after ideas are first understood. This defense is feeble, for Wang Bi categorically declared: "To get the original thought depends on forgetting images; to get images rests on forgetting words." In my opinion, neither his critics nor his defenders have understood the profound insight in Wang Bi's idea for several reasons. First, Wang Bi is truly a genius (acknowledged in his own time), whose insight into representation and interpretation went far ahead of its time. Second, because they were too narrowly focused on Wang Bi's claim in relation to the *Zhouyi* and did not place his idea in the larger context of signification and representation. Third, Wang Bi came to an understanding shared by contemporary hermeneutics. The goal of hermeneutic understanding is not what a work meant to its original audience or author but what it may mean to us in the present—though this does not imply that one can do whatever one wants with the text. Fourth, on the basis of this understanding, Wang Bi made a subtle distinction between representation (creation) and interpretation (recreation).

Up to passage 3, Wang Bi was more concerned with the author's representation and emphasized the positive side of language, especially its suggestiveness. Like Mencius, he believed that language is an effective tool for representing the author's ideas. But starting with the third passage, Wang Bi began to shift from the author's representation to the reader's interpretation and emphasized the impossibility of matching the author's ideas with the reader's understanding due to the slippery nature of language. Passage 3 as a whole should be understood in this direction. Because

language is metaphorical, representation implies an alienating distanciation. What is represented by the author cannot be fully re-presented by
the reader. We need to pay attention to the pronoun *qi*, which refers to
the author. "Images are born of ideas" refers to the author's representation.
"He who preserves the images" is the reader. In a like manner; "words are
born of images" refers to the author's creation. "He who preserves the
words" is the reader. Therefore, we can paraphrase Wang Bi's statement
thus: "He who sticks to the literal meaning of words is not a reader who
can get the author's created image. He who sticks to the image is not a
reader who will be able to get the author's original meaning." Wang Bi
pointed out the inherent reason: "Since images were born out of [the
author's] ideas, if one sticks to the image, what he sticks to is not the
[author's] original images. Since words were born of the [author's] created
images, if the reader sticks to the words, what he sticks to are not the
[author's] original words." This understanding reveals Wang Bi's profound
insight into the mismatch between representation and interpretation. Representation consists of images and words. Images and words are the
material elements that an author employs to represent his ideas. They are
the carriers of his ideas but not the ideas themselves. To use an analogy,
water consists of hydrogen and oxygen particles in a special makeup, but
hydrogen and oxygen particles are not water. Images and words in a representation are like hydrogen and oxygen particles in water. If one sticks
to images and words, he cannot get the ideas represented by images and
words any more than a thirsty person who inhales hydrogen and oxygen
particles can quench his thirst.

Having confirmed that images and words are not equal to the
author's original ideas, Wang Bi continued to argue in a radically provocative manner: "If this is true, then, a reader who forgets the images will
(likely) get the author's original ideas. A reader who forgets words will
(likely) get the meaning of the author's created images." This provocative
statement reveals Wang Bi's profound insight into interpretation. He
seemed to have realized that interpretation is another form of representation or re-creation. The images and words are the materials provided by
the author for the reader to reconstruct the original ideas of the author.
Images and words have their conventional meanings, but the author's representation has specific meanings peculiar to the circumstantial conditions
that have made the representation possible. If a reader sticks to the conventional meanings of images and words, he is unlikely to obtain the
special meaning conveyed by the author through the use of images and
words. This means that in a paradoxical way, to get (close to) the author's
original meaning is conditional on forgetting the (literal meaning of)
images; and to get (close to) the meaning of images is conditional on for-

getting the (literal meaning of) words. Hence, Wang Bi made his most radical claim: "To get the original ideas depends on forgetting images; to get images rests on forgetting words." In the context of interpretation, "forgetting images" and "forgetting words" mean the rejection of conventional and standardized meanings of images and words, requiring the reader to take his own initiative to generate new meanings that may be close to the author's original meanings.

I have tried to bring out Wang Bi's genius, which reveals itself in the remarkable realization that reading is not a simple process of getting the message from a representation, and what one gets in reading is not equal to what is meant in representation. His realization can be illustrated with a concrete example in *Zhouyi* hermeneutics. Let's suppose that the sage wanted to express the idea of "robustness." He had three ways at his disposal: the iconic, indexical, and symbolic. In one way, he might point at a real horse to express his idea because a horse is conventionally associated with strength. This way of representation is both indexical and iconic. But since it is inconvenient and often impossible to use a real horse, he might draw a horse or compose a hexagram image to stand for "horse." The representation by means of a likeness or diagram, according to Peirce, is an iconic representation. In another way, he might simply use the word *zhuang* (robust) to convey the idea of strength. This is the symbolic way of representation. Wang Bi's argument seems to say, since the purpose of interpretation is to get the idea of robustness, why bother about the representational material? Interpretation is not simply a process of getting an object out of a container; it is a complicated process of re-creation. For re-creation to yield its result, one needs to forget the material signs that carry the idea. If one stays fixed on the materiality of horse either as an image or a real animal, what he gets is the idea of the animal, not the idea of robustness.

Previously, scholars have failed to make sense of Wang Bi's "forgetting images and words" because they did not notice Wang Bi's profound insight into the distinction between representation and interpretation. When the process of reading or re-creation is not distinguished from the process of composition or creation, problems arise. *The conflation of creative process and reading process has serious consequences for later generations' interpretation of Wang Bi's discourse. To a great extent, the unresolved controversy over Wang Bi's view stems from this conflation of creative process and interpretative process.*

Wang Bi's distinction is both implicitly and explicitly stated throughout his discourse. In his further argument, he implicitly stated his distinction: "Therefore after establishing a *xiang* to fully express *yi*, one can forget the *xiang*; having doubled the trigrams into a hexagram to fully convey one's mood, one can forget the trigrams." Each of these two sentences touches representation and interpretation. In each sentence, the first part refers to representation while the second part refers to interpretation. They may be paraphrased this way: since sages set up *guaxiang* (hexagram images) to express their ideas, doubled trigrams to express their sentiments, and employed things and situations of the same category to represent the category, hexagram images and hexagram statements are only the means to the end. As they are the means to convey thoughts, one should not stay fixed on them but instead conjecture beyond their surface meaning.

Wang Bi's advocacy for forgetting images in one's attempt to understand the author's ideas rests on the theoretical basis that representation and interpretation are two related but different processes of mental action. The statements "images are born of thought, words are born of images," "nothing is more effective than images in fully conveying thought," "nothing is more effective than words in fully conveying images," "words are that which illuminates the images; images are that which preserves the ideas," "[the sages] established images to fully express their thoughts and doubled the trigrams to fully express their emotions" all refer to the process of creation. They are concerned with sages' representation of their thoughts. As a statement about representation, Wang Bi touched on an important facet of representation. Any representation, whether it is sign representation or language representation, is always a substitution. What we get is not what is meant because representation, as the word suggests, is always accomplished through an act of designation.

In Wang Bi's discourse, the remarks "once one gets the image, the words are forgotten," "once one obtains the ideas, the images are forgotten," "he who forgets the images is the one who obtains the idea," "he who forgets words is the one who obtains the images," "the hexagram images may be forgotten," and "the line images may be forgotten" all deal with the interpretation of sages' hexagram images and hexagram statements. Hence, they refer to the process of reading or recreation. The judgmental remarks "Images are born of thought; should images be preserved, what is preserved is not the images of the original thought. Words are born of images; should words be preserved, what is preserved is not the original words," are well-reasoned insights born out of his observation of the differences between representation and interpretation. They are equivalent to declaring that what the reader gets in interpretation is not equal to what the author means in creation.

Wang Bi's subtle distinction between representation and interpretation finds an explicit expression in his differential use of *Yi* 意 and *yi* 義. His distinction becomes self-evident in the remainder of his discourse:

Thus, anything that touches an object of the same category can serve as the image of the category; anything that matches an idea can serve as the symbol of the idea. Should the meaning be "robustness," why must there be an image of the horse in the hexagram image? If the category suggests compliance, why must there be an image of a cow? Should the line image conform to compliance, why must there be the image of *kun* which stands for a cow? If the meaning corresponds with "robustness," why must there be the image of *qian* which stands for a horse? Nevertheless, there are some deluded people who designate *qian* as a horse and investigate the hexagram image in accordance with the hexagram and line statements. When the statement suggests a horse but the hexagram image does not yield a *qian* trigram, spurious opinions run rampant and are difficult to keep track of. When the method of "internal trigram" is insufficient for explication, the method of "hexagram changes" are introduced. When "hexagram changes" fall short, the method of five agents are put forward. Once these methods fail to capture the original ideas of the sages, more methods try to be cleverer and more intricate. Even if a theory incidentally makes the image and statement match, the meaning it comes up with has nothing to recommend itself. All this simply results from preserving the images but ignoring ideas. If one forgets the image so as to seek the ideas (conveyed through words), then, the meaning will come to light.[34]

The word *yi* 義 appears five times. All of them refer to the meaning or significance created by the interpreter. The ending sentence, which contains both *yi* 意 and *yi* 義, puts Wang Bi's distinction between representation and interpretation beyond any doubt. The first *yi* with a "heart" radical obviously refers to ideas in the mind of the author, which becomes meaning while the second *yi* with a "me" radical refers to the reader's construction of the author's possible ideas that becomes significance. The first *yi* results from creation while the second *yi* pertains to reading. This passage confirms not only Wang Bi's distinction between representation and interpretation but also his conception of the difference between author's *yi* 意 and reader's *yi* 義. His distinction is incredibly modern and its value may be duly appreciated when we compare it with E. D. Hirsch's distinction between "meaning" and "significance." "Meaning," according to Hirsch, "refers to the whole verbal meaning of a text, and 'significance' to textual meaning in relation to a larger context, i.e., another mind, another era, a wider subject matter, an alien system of values, and so on. In other words, 'significance' is textual meaning as related to some context, indeed any context, beyond itself."[35]

In "anything that touches an object of the same category can serve as the image of the category; anything that matches an idea can serve as the symbol of the idea," Wang Bi practically intuited the two fundamental principles that underlie semiotic representation (metonymy and metaphor) and the two basic mental functions (displacement and condensation). In the statement "anything that touches an object of the same category can serve as the image of the category," there is obviously a sign-to-sign relationship that is the basis of metonymy; in the statement "anything that matches an idea can serve as the symbol of the idea," there is a sign for sign relationship that is the basis of metaphor. Let us compare Wang Bi's idea with Jacques Lacan's psycholinguistic definition of metaphor and metonymy: "[I]t is in the word-to-word connection that metonymy is based"[36] and "One word for another: that is the formula for the metaphor."[37] Lacan is famous for reinterpreting Freud's ideas of "condensation" and "displacement"—two fundamental principles of the psyche—in terms of linguistic theory of signification. He links metaphor to the replacement of one word for another, relating this substituting process to the Freudian concept of condensation. He links metonymy to the connection of word to word, and relates this connecting process to the Freudian concept of displacement.[38] Wang Bi did not employ such technical terms as displacement and condensation, but his proposition shows the way the mind tries to cope with signification and representation to be essentially similar to the theories proposed by Freud and Lacan. "Anything that touches an object of the same category can serve as the image of the category" indicates that the mind, faced with the difficulty of representation, veers off from a nebulous idea to a concrete image, thus making that image stand for the indescribable idea. This veering off from a nebulous thought to an image is the displacing of mental energy from one object to another, hence essentially the same as the psychological function of displacement. The resultant representation is a metonymy or synecdoche. The remark "anything that matches an idea can serve as the symbol of the idea," shows that the mind, in its attempt to find the right representational carrier for that which is to be represented, superimposes its nebulous thought onto an object that suits its purpose. The superimposition of an idea onto a signifier similar in nature displays an act of substituting or condensing, hence essentially similar to the psychological function of "condensation."[39] The resultant representation is the birth of metaphor. Compared with the general remark in the *Xicizhuan*: "The sages established images to fully express their thought, "Wang Bi's proposition marked a significant step forward in the attempt to fine-tune the process of representation. This is truly an admirable achievement.

The use of *yi* 義 rather than *yi* 意 in "anything that touches an object of the same category can serve as the image of the category; anything that matches an idea can serve as the symbol of the idea" reveals another facet of Wang Bi's genius. With regard to how to conduct abstract representation, Confucius was quoted as saying: "The sages established images to fully express their idea." But as to why "establishing images can fully express one's ideas," he did not elaborate. Wang Bi offered a theoretic insight into the rationale of imagistic representation: "Anything that touches the category of something can be used to be its image." In an attempt to represent an idea one can use an object that belongs to the category of objects. Thus, representation is essentially an act of correlation through analogy. The Chinese concept *lei* 類, in Wang Bi's discourse, is perhaps the closest term to the act of correlation through analogy. In probing the question of which concept in Chinese is equivalent to analogy, Owen points out, "The most apposite term in Chinese is *lei* 類, 'natural category': these correlations of pattern were not made by a willful act of analogy but rather occurred because their elements were, in essential ways, 'of the same kind.'"[40] What is most intriguing in the Chinese concept is that it may have denotations for either metaphorical or metonymic substitution, depending on how one looks at the correlative connections. (I will deal with this in detail shortly.) In Wang Bi's conception of how an image becomes a symbol for an idea, a specific part stands for a general category. In the Chinese tradition, this theory of representation is the theoretical basis of *xing* (inspired interest). Wang Bi's statement reveals the essence of representation and therefore obviously refers to imaginative creation.

In "anything that matches an idea can serve as the symbol of the idea," the word *yi* 義, as I have suggested, is indicative of interpretation or re-creation. Interpretation is essentially a re-presentation of ideas in a work of creation. How to re-present those ideas? Re-presentation is basically the same as representation; the difference lies in that it is a representation by the reader. And in the local context of the *Zhouyi*, it was mostly done in words, as Confucius's saying states, "to attach verbalizations to fully express what one wants to say." But why can words re-present sages' ideas? Again Confucius did not provide answers about its rationale. And again Wang Bi did. His answer is: "Anything that matches an idea can be used to re-present the idea." Thus, re-presentation of ideas is basically a metaphorical act: the replacement of an idea with a similar idea. Lacan has argued that just as there is nothing, except a condition imposed upon the signifying material, to distinguish condensation and displacement, metaphor and metonymy are essentially the same as far as the psychological function is concerned.[41] Wang Bi's discourse reveals the same insight. Both metaphor and metonymy are the same psychological act to locate similar relationship between two disparate categories. Metaphor tends to gather different categories into a whole, while metonymy tends to relate different categories to each other. Metaphor downplays the difference and emphasizes similarity in relationship, while metonymy recognizes similarity but declines to cover difference in relationship. To employ an analogy, metaphor is like a person who says, "we are all members of the same family"; metonymy is like another person who says, "we are individuals in the same family." Wang Bi seemed to have suggested that the difference really lies in the different stages of the whole verbal communicative process, which consists of representation and interpretation. Representation is a metonymic act to view ideas (literary work) as a natural growth of the world; interpretation is a metaphorical act to view one's reading as an approximation of the ideas or literary work. Representation is also a metaphorical act in the sense that one views a literary work as an approximation of the observed world. Interpretation is also a metonymic act in the sense that one views one's interpretation as a natural outgrowth of the text. Wang Bi's statement suggests that condensation and displacement are two chief principles of representation for both creation and interpretation. In modern Chinese, the concept *xiangzheng* 象徵 (symbol or symbolism), which grew out the combination of *xiang* and *zheng* in Wang Bi's statement, is but a further extension of Wang Bi's insight. In literary criticism, we often deem interpretation as re-creation. The theoretical foundation of this view rests on the fact that literary creation and interpretation employ the same principles of representation in the psyche and are both approximations.

Wang Bi's realization that both representation and interpretation are interconnected approximations leads logically to another realization that what the reader gets in reading cannot possibly match what the author has meant in writing. On this theoretical basis, he considered it a legitimate move to forget images and to engage in re-creation. The freedom sanctioned by the mismatch between representation and re-presentation allowed him to make an imaginative leap and call for a radical theory of reading: "If one forgets the image so as to seek the ideas (conveyed through words), then, the meaning will come to light." In the passage before this concluding sentence, Wang Bi rejected the Han scholars' theory of reading that sticks to the transmitted tradition and interpretive strategies. Here, *xiang* literally refers to the hexagram images, and the approaches to *xiang* refer to transmitted conventional reading strategies like "internal trigram 互體," "trigram change 卦變," and "five agents theory 五行" employed by the Han scholars in their reading of the *Zhouyi*. By declaring "Even if a theory incidentally makes the image and statement match, the meaning it comes up with has nothing to recommend itself. All this simply results from preserving the images but ignoring ideas," Wang Bi revealed the root cause of the Han scholars' problematic approach: faced with the description of a horse in hexagram statement, instead of trying to find out the ideas behind the image, they riveted their attention on the image and forgot about what ideas that image might possibly represent. Thus, Wang Bi's dual thesis of "forgetting images" and "forgetting words" is, in the final analysis, *an imaginative extension of Zhuangzi's rejection of books and language as the carrier of the Dao*: "Although people of the world cherish words, still I don't think words are worth cherishing because what people treasure is not that which deserves cherishing."[42] What he advised people to forget is the supposedly authorial intentions. Original intentions of the author are impossible to ascertain. The so-called transmitted interpretations claim to be based on the original intentions, but they are as misleading and often as irrelevant as supposed authorial intentions. Paradoxically, by forgetting these supposedly authoritative interpretive strategies, one may be able to produce readings that approximate the original intentions. In so advocating, Wang Bi emphasized the initiative of the reader and viewed the reader's re-creation as a legitimate step in reading.

Premodern Husserlians and Heideggerians

Wang Bi and his Meaning-Principle school were not unaware of the significance of hexagram images for the interpretation of the *Zhouyi*. In the opening of his discourse, he emphasized the importance of images for conveying meaning.[43] In his practical reading of the *Zhouyi* text, he also demonstrated the usefulness of hexagram images in the interpretation of the *Zhouyi* text. There is little doubt that his reading of four hexagrams— *jing* 井, *ding* 鼎, *yi* 頤, and *shike* 噬嗑—was conducted in the reading paradigm of the Image-Number school.[44] But his imagistic reading was only restricted to these four hexagrams. Later scholars felt puzzled about why he only discussed the images of four hexagrams while ignoring and leaving undiscussed the images of the rest. The answer is found in Wang Bi's awareness of the death of the author and its implications. He seemed to say that the hexagram image may or may not necessarily be related to the hexagram statements. Even if it is related to a statement, who can tell which is the original relation since scholars have already constructed so many possible relations? Now that the sages, the original composers of the *Zhouyi* text, are gone, the original relation can never be recovered. It is therefore lopsided to overemphasize the importance of hexagram images. The Image-Number scholars, with their eyes fixed on the hexagram images as imparting the sages' ideas, were putting themselves in shackles when they exerted themselves to make the image match the idea supposedly expressed in the hexagram statements. Moreover, we as readers of the

Zhouyi are not primarily concerned with hexagram images but with what a hexagram may mean. For these reasons, Wang Bi advocated forgetting images and seeking ideas in words: "If one forgets the image so as to seek the thought (conveyed through words), then, the meaning will come to light."[45]

In terms of Hirsch's distinction between "meaning" and "significance," Wang Bi's distinction has reverberations and ramifications beyond the immediate context of his discourse. If we bring the philosophical debate behind Hirsch's distinction to bear on the two radically different approaches to the clarification of the image, we may say that the debate between the "Image-Number School" and "Meaning-Principle School" anticipated the modern debate in hermeneutics between the Husserlians and Heideggerians. While Husserl posits a mental function of intentionality, the mind's capacity to "bracket" a realm of experience to be contemplated over time, Heideggerians take Dilthey's hermeneutic circle as the model and argue for the impossibility of bracketing off a part of experience from the whole experience of life. In the literary realm, followers of Husserl and Heidegger have adopted two distinctly different approaches to intention and meaning. The Husserlians conceive of meaning as a wordless act, willed by the author, that is fixed in a series of signs for all time and may be understood through the same system of signs. The Heideggerians contend that meaning, including authorial meaning, is not as stable and determinate as the Husserlians claim. The reason it is not is precisely because it is the product of signs that have something slippery about them. It is difficult, if not impossible, to know what an intention or meaning is. Moreover, an author's intention is itself a complex text, which may be variously interpreted like any other text.[46] In a way, scholars of the Image-Number school may be viewed as premodern Husserlians, while scholars of the Meaning-Principle school may be regarded as premodern Heideggerians.

Having made such a bold claim, I feel that the two epithets are not exactly appropriate. Perhaps we should call them respectively author-centered exegetes and reader-centered exegetes. Scholars of the *Xiang-shu* school upheld a traditional model of reading that views communication as a process of conveyance. What is represented can be conveyed to the intended destination without any loss of original information. In this connection, their error is similar to that of the traditional literary theorists who believe that the author has an intention, encodes it, then puts it in the container of a text; the reader reads the text, decodes it, and gets the message from the container. In this model of reading, interpretation, or correct interpretation is equal to representation. Wang Bi and his Meaning-Principle school followers differ from them not just in whether one should ignore hexagram images. In claiming, "If one forgets the image so as to seek the thought (conveyed through words), then, the meaning will come to light," Wang Bi seemed to have believed that one should be concerned not with what is intended but with what is produced in reading. In Wang Bi's theory of hermeneutics, *yi* or thought 意 is *not* equivalent to *yi* or meaning 義. For this reason, we can put him in the ranks of reader-oriented theorists like Roland Barthes, Wolfgang Iser, Umberto Eco, Jacques Derrida, Norman Holland, Stanley Fish, and Jonathan Culler. Wang Bi also seemed to have understood that just as the signified is not equal to concept, so thought is not equal to meaning. Thought is something within the mind of the author, while meaning is something else in the mind of the reader who interprets the "something." Moreover, representation and interpretation involve four factors: the author, the reader, the text, and context. Of the four factors, two of them are indeterminate: the author's intention is unknown; so is the original context. The unknown original intention, the loss of original context, and above all, the process of signification have made it inevitable that *thought is not equal to meaning; meaning is not equal to significance; yi* 意 *is not equal to yi* 義.

Because of the different attitudes toward intention and context, the Image-Number school and the Meaning-Principle school represent respectively two paradigms of exegesis. To illustrate this point, I will draw two different schemata:

Schema A:

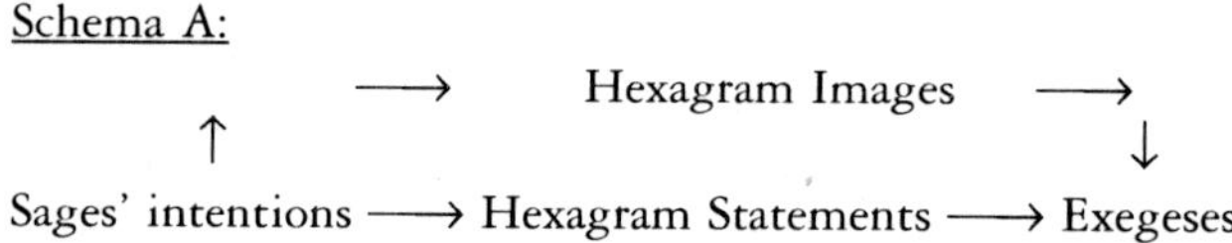

Schema B:

Sages' intentions → Hexagram Images → Hexagram Statements → Exegeses

The sages' thoughts are expressed through two channels, the hexagram images and hexagram statements. There are three possibilities. (1) the images and statements of a hexagram are used to express the same thought; hence there is a correlation between the two. (2) The images and statements of a hexagram are used to express different aspects of a thought; hence there is no correlation between the two. (3) The thought is first expressed through the image, and then the image is verbalized in the statement; hence there is a movement from thought through image to statement. The three possible ways of composition gave the *Zhouyi* text an indeterminacy that turns it into an open space of hermeneutics even before any interpretation takes place. Most scholars, however, seem to uphold the last possibility. Shang Binghe's statement represents this dominant view: "All the statements of the *Zhouyi* were born out of hexagram images. When Han Xuanzi went to the State of Lu, he did not say that he saw the *Zhouyi*, but instead said that he saw the *Hexagram Images* and the *Spring and Autumn Annals of Lu*. Truly, 'the *Zhouyi* is a book on images, and the images are symbolic representations.' This saying means that innumerable as the things under heaven are, the hexagram images can symbolically represent them all."[47]

In terms of this dominant view, the Image-Number school's paradigm obviously fits more comfortably into Schema B because it takes into consideration both aspects of the text. The correlation between hexagram images and statements implies that an interpretation must be based on a negotiation among the sage's intention, the textual evidence, the reader's reading, and the original context. The resultant interpretation is a circumscribed exegesis, and hence less open. The dominant view, however, is only a possible one. Some scholars have denied the absolute validity of this view. Zhu Bokun 朱伯昆, a renowned scholar on the *Zhouyi*, challenges the dominant view: "Is there a logical, intrinsic, and absolutely certain coordination between hexagram and line images and hexagram and line statements? The *Zhouyi* scholars of ancient times all agree that there is such an absolutely certain relationship. They, therefore, respected the *Zhouyi* as a book by sages. I, however, agree with another view: so far as the content of the whole book is concerned, there is no logical, absolutely necessary relationship between hexagram and line images and hexagram and line statements."[48] He analyzed some key hexagrams to prove the validity of his claim. Obviously, the advocacy of "forgetting images" came from a similar assumption. This assumption was in fact the theoretical basis of the Meaning-Principle school's paradigm of reading, which can be illustrated with a different diagram:

Sages' intentions $\longrightarrow$ Hexagram Statements $\longrightarrow$ Exegeses
(Hexagram Images)

In this diagram, hexagram images are bracketed. Exegeses do not have to pass through the channel of images but directly come from the sages' intentions. This diagram may tell us why Wang Bi's advocacy of "forgetting images" was popular. By getting rid of one possible channel of signification, the Meaning-Principle scholars were able to emancipate themselves from a straightjacket and to have a freer hand in their interpretations. In this sense, Wang Bi's advocacy is truly a "revolution in *Zhouyi* scholarship." However, because of the riddance of images, exegeses are mainly born out of the reader's confrontation with the text; they are largely colored by the reader's intention and making. While the text's intention is fully considered, the author's intention is largely bracketed if the accepted theory about the origin and nature of the images is true. Because of the bracketing, an exegesis of a hexagram statement seems to ignore the original intention of the sages on the ground that the sages' intention is impossible to know.

From my analysis, it can be seen that Wang Bi's paradigm is reader oriented and function driven. Some later scholars have noticed this utilitarian purpose. Zhu Xi commented: "The creation of hexagram images has its sources; their function has use value. They do not simply serve as parables. On the one hand, the scholars of the Western and Eastern Han were not content until they could locate their sources. As a result, their exegeses are stagnant as well as irrational. On the other hand, scholars since Wang Bi were not satisfied until they could clarify their functions. Because of this, their interpretations are careless and groundless. Both ways of exegesis are faulty for their lopsidedness and both result from their inability to reserve their skepticism for further investigation."[49] Zhu Xi's evaluation seems to have touched on the crux in the controversy: the Han scholars, determined to search for the sources of the images, were concerned with representation while Wang Bi's followers, setting their mind on how to read hexagram images and statements, were preoccupied with interpretation. They were entangled in a tug-of-war because each side pulled at one end of the representation-interpretation stick. The tug-of-war gave rise to two models of reading: one traditional (in the sense of a pursuit of original intention), the other modern (in the sense of present-day theories of reading).

The Death of the Author and Rise of the Reader

Scholars of the Image-Number school and the Meaning-Principle school base their models of reading on two different understandings of the author's intention. The former adhere to sages as textual authority and insist on seeking the original intentions as they believe that the sages' intention was fixed in image, number, and words. In this sense they are like Husserl who believes that meaning is an "intentional object." Although it is not objective like any tangible object, it is not subjective either. It is a sort of "ideal object" that could be represented in a number of ways, but still retain the same meaning. To them hexagram images are just this kind of "intentional object." Terry Eagleton's comment on Husserl's notion of meaning may throw some light on the Image-Number scholars' notion of sages' intentions and their representation in hexagram images and statements: "[T]he meaning of a literary work is fixed once and for all: it is identical with whatever 'mental object' the author had in mind, or 'intended,' at the time of writing."[50] By contrast, the Meaning-Principle scholars seem to have held a different notion of the author's intention and its relevance for exegeses. In advocating ignoring hexagram images and concentrating on the verbal statements of the *Zhouyi* only, they seem to have acknowledged the death of the sages. In this sense, they share the same stance as those modern reader response critics who have argued that with the appearance of writing, the presence in voice loses its origin and the author ceases to exist, entering into a figurative death. As Barthes puts it in his famous essay "The Death of the Author," "Writing is the destruction of every voice, of every point of origin."[51] Writing or literature covers a field that "has no other origin than language itself, language which ceaselessly calls into question all origins."[52] Under this condition, the text can no longer be viewed as a container or a place where the reader can find the original meanings of the author: "a text is not a line of words releasing a single 'theological' meaning (the 'message' of the Author-God) but a multi-dimensional space in which a variety of writings, none of them original, blend and clash."[53] With the "death" of the author, the text becomes public property for readers who have been liberated from the confines of author(rity) and enjoy the freedom to interpret it in accordance with the interpretive strategies of a given community.

Of course, nowhere in his works can we find that Wang Bi or any Meaning-Principle scholars declared the death of the author. The contemporary reading theory about the author's death may serve to provide us with a new perspective to examine the paradigm of reading he advanced nearly two thousand years ago. In his short span of life, Wang Bi was recognized as an avid reader of the works of Lao Zi and Zhuangzi. His annotation of the *Laozi* is a concrete proof of his intense interest. Whether one approves or disapproves of his annotation of the *Zhouyi*, all scholars agree that his comments were set forth in the light of Lao Zi's and Zhuangzi's theories. *Siku tiyao (Abstracts of Writings in the Siku Quanshu)* states: "Wang Bi completely expelled images and numbers, and expounded the *Zhouyi* in accordance with Lao Zi's and Zhuangzi's theories. . . . His annotation originated from an admiration for nonbeing. As a result, the *Zhouyi* became merged with the *Laozi* and *Zhuangzi*."[54] One modern scholar agrees with this assessment: "Wang Bi's annotation of the *Zhouyi* disregarded images and numbers and took the *Laozi* and the *Zhuangzi* as its guiding principle. As a result, the intentions of the Han version of the classic got gradually lost."[55] If Wang Bi was well versed in the *Laozi* and *Zhuangzi* and annotated the *Zhouyi* in the spirit of Lao Zi's and Zhuangzi's philosophical views, I can make an educated guess that he must have read the well-known dialogue between Lun Bian (Wheelwright Bian) and Duke Huan,[56] and Zhuangzi's understanding of the problematic relationship between the author and his writing must have had a great impact on his "Revolution in *Zhouyi* Scholarship." The essential spirit Zhuangzi expressed in this parable is exactly what Barthes means by "the death of the author." If we put in perspective Wang Bi's good knowledge of the *Zhuangzi* and his subscription to Zhuangzi's philosophy, it is perhaps not far wrong to claim that like the wheelwright, Wang Bi must have been aware of the implication of the literal and figurative death of the sages. Even if we discount any direct link between his advocacy of "forgetting images" and the parable of the wheelwright, we must admit that his "Revolution in *Zhouyi* Scholarship" was conducted precisely in the spirit of the wheelwright parable and signifies the maturity of the metaphysico-aesthetic trend in Chinese hermeneutics.

Wang Bi's advocacy of a revolution in *Zhouyi* scholarship arose from another major concern. Despite the fact that the Image-Number scholars were able to devise numerous ways to interpret the relations between the hexagram and line images and hexagram and line statements, their actual interpretations were characterized by one serious drawback: there was not much that was new. This drawback came about simply because their ways of interpretation were restricted by a handicap: the need to identify the sages' original intentions by correlating the images with the text. By contrast, the Meaning-Principle school, in their move to ignore the images, had a much freer hand to produce new and interesting readings. In his preface to Wang Bi's commentary, Kong Yingda succinctly sums up the major reason why Wang Bi's commentary has been popular.[57] He seemed to have believed that Wang Bi's strategies of interpretation were warmly welcomed because they were capable of producing new interpretations.

Wang Bi's advocacy for forgetting images and language is fairly sound from the perspective of interpretation. The defense of Wang Bi's "forgetting images after getting the meaning" in terms of a reaction against Han scholarship is, however, only half right. The sages' thoughts are expressed through two channels, the hexagram images and hexagram statements. I have pointed out above that there are three possibilities concerning the relationship among sages's thought, hexagram images, and statements. Though most scholars uphold the last possibility, the dominant view is only one of the possibilities. Wang Bi would agree with them on only an aspect of it: "The *Zhouyi* is a book of images. The sources of images are located in the mind. When there is an idea in the mind, it is illuminated with an object which serves as its symbol."[58] Now that the sages are gone, it is impossible to determine which of the three possibilities is applied to a given hexagram. In cases in which images and state-ments were not originally intended to match, Wang Bi's advocacy for for-getting images is certainly valid. In cases in which there is a correlation between images and statements, his advocacy is wrong. But it is impossi-ble to ascertain which is the original relationship. In a way, Wang Bi's "forgetting images after getting the meaning" may have resulted from his awareness of the indeterminate nature of the correlation.

When I said earlier that the defenders of Wang Bi's "forgetting images after getting the meaning" are only half right, I mean that they saw only half the picture and underestimated Wang Bi's revolutionary potential. Having given a detailed analysis of Wang Bi's discourse in rela-tion to other scholars' views and in terms of modern semiotics, I will examine the quarrel between Wang Bi's Meaning-Principle school and the Han scholars' Image-Number school a little further. Scholars of the Image-Number school adhere to sages as textual authority and insist on seeking the original intentions. Hence they fall under the "intentional fallacy" and their merits and demerits constitute an interesting paradox. W. K. Wimsatt and Monroe C. Beardsley argue in their well-known essay: "The poem is not the critics' own and not the author's (it is detached from the author at birth and goes about the world beyond his power to intend about it or control it). The poem belongs to the public. It is embodied in lan-guage, the peculiar possession of the public, and it is about the human being, an object of public knowledge."[59] Although their concern is with poetry, their argument is applicable to the text of the *Zhouyi* because both are a form of writing, a type of semiotic system. Barthes's declaration of "The Death of the Author" is but another way of saying that with the "death" of the author, the text becomes public property for readers who have been liberated from the confines of author(rity) and enjoy the freedom to interpret it in accordance with interpretive strategies approved by an interpretive community.

The *Zhouyi* hexagrams and statements have been passed on to us in the form of writing. As forms of writing or written symbols, its authors or the sages are literally dead. There is no author(rity) to stipulate the orig-inal, pristine meanings of hexagrams. To a great extent, Wang Bi adopted a self-conscious approach to the death of the sages and accepted their death both literally and figuratively. The sages must have intended the hexagram images to mean something, but now the sages are gone, those intended meanings are also gone, never to be recovered. Talking about the source of images, Zhu Xi expressed an opinion implicitly voiced in Wang Bi's view: "As their sources cannot be retraced, we are compelled to accept the absence." Huang Ze 黃澤 of the Yuan seemed to have understood Wang Bi's implication: "In the study of the *Zhouyi*, one must clarify the images.

This is certainly a correct notion that cannot change. But the images are impossible to clarify. Hence the idea of forgetting images arose. To advocate forgetting images is a remark Wang Bi cannot help but make."[60] Chen Feng 陳澧 (1810–82) made a similar comment: "Among scholars who study the *Zhouyi* and take elucidation of images as their own task, no one can match Huang Chuwang. He made long and arduous efforts, but was still unable to understand the images of female cattle, baby and mother cows. He therefore viewed one cow as small and one following another. Is he any different from Wang Bi who could not clarify images and had to forget them? That the images cannot be clarified is an honest saying."[61] These comments suggest that Wang Bi did not willfully discard images but advocated a theory of interpretation based on his understanding of the slippery nature of images and words.

After a careful study of the Image-Number school's origin-oriented approach and the Meaning-Principle school's function-oriented approach, Zhu Xi offered a third approach: "The images of the hexagrams must have originated from some sources. The belief in those sources must have once existed in the records of the grand official-diviners. As their sources cannot be retraced, we are compelled to accept the loss. Instead, we may directly seek the meanings of the images in the light of images expressed by hexagram statements so that they serve as sufficient evidence for determining whether a divination is auspicious or inauspicious, just as Wang Bi, Master Cheng, and my *Zhouyi benyi* have stated. This approach is also permissible."[62] Previously, some scholars have accused Zhu Xi of sitting on the fence. I, however, think that Zhu Xi's position is a sensible one and is compatible with a transactive approach to reading that emphasizes interpretation as a negotiating process. Just as the original sources of the hexagram images cannot be retraced, so the authorial intention of a text cannot be recovered. But this does not mean that we can completely ignore the sources of hexagram images, nor can we completely ignore whatever might have been the author's intention at the time of composition. Zhu Xi's advice is equally valid for reading a text. To seek meanings of a text in the light of the meanings expressed by the text would not deviate entirely from the "in-text" intention of the author while at the same time leaving a text open to other possible readings.

Conceptual Significance of the Paradigm Shift

Wang Bi's differentiation between *yi* (ideas) and *yi* (meaning) facilitated the shift of emphasis from the author to the reader and provided the theoretical justification for multiple exegeses. In contemporary theory, the reason thought and meaning are not equivalent is because of the slippery nature of language in representation. In the binary opposition between the signifier and signified, signified is not a concept, it is only another signifier whose signified is still another signifier and so on to infinity. Just as signified is not equal to concept, so thought is not equal to meaning. Whereas thought is something in the mind of the addressor, meaning is something else produced by the addressee in response to a message. The thought of the addresser cannot be conveyed to the addressee without some loss because the means of communication is a semiotic system, be it a sign system or a linguistic system. Thought must be expressed through signification; meaning must also be generated through signification. In the process of signification, because of the constant sliding of the signifier on the chain of signification, every reading is always a rereading (or misreading); even a correct reading is inevitably a near miss. Hence every understanding is theoretically a form of misunderstanding. Wang Bi did not express the slippery nature of representation overtly, but in saying "anything that touches an object of the same category can serve as the image of the category; anything that matches an idea can serve as the symbol of the idea," he was aware that representation is made through metaphor or metonymy or other symbolic means, and in each case, an image (or word) that stands for an idea is that idea only for the originator who intends it and may become an different idea for another person. His distinction between *Yi* 意 (meaning) and *yi* 義 (significance) implies that what is represented cannot be fully recaptured. For this reason, he advocated a spontaneous reading: what one reads is what one gets. "Should the meaning be 'robustness,' why must there be an image of the horse in the hexagram image? If the category suggests compliance, why must there be an image of a cow?" This is what he meant when he advocated "forgetting *yan* after getting *yi*." In the final analysis, the *yi* 意 (meaning) *is not really the author's* yi *(ideas) but a conjectured* yi 義 *(meaning or significance) generated by the reader with the hints of* yan *(language).*

Wang Bi has been proclaimed by many as a revolutionary who swept away the far-fetched interpretations of the Image-Number school. The reason he advocated ignoring the images and seeking the original meaning of the sages in statements only is partly because he disliked their specious interpretations and partly because he accepted the sages' death and emphasized a new model of reading. In this respect, his advocacy is revolutionary and comes close to the modern call to view a text as an infinite potential space for reading and interpretation. From the viewpoint of reading and interpretation, Wang Bi's call for ignoring images and words emancipated scholars who had been confined within the circumscribed space of images and numbers. Wang Bi did not proclaim, as the modern theorists do, that the author is dead, but an equivalent is implied, for by following his advocacy, scholars of the Meaning-Principle school practically turned their back on the textual authority of the sages and produced interpretations that are largely recreations, and in some cases pure creations. Under the influence of Wang Bi's theory, there arose a scholarly situation characterized by Zhu Xi: "In their interpretation of classics, Han scholars made their deductions and interpretations in strict accordance with the classics. Scholars of the Jin did not follow suit. Instead, they departed from the classics and created classics by themselves."[63] Wang Yan came to a similar understanding of why Wang Bi's commentary has been popular: "Wang Bi discarded images and refused to discuss them. Scholars of later generations liked his theory for its simplicity and convenience."[64]

After the Jin, Wang Bi's theory became the conceptual justification of reader-initiated interpretations. His advocacy for forgetting images liberates later generations from the confines of images and give them a freer hand to interpret the hexagram statements. In their interpretation of the *Zhouyi*, the scholars of the Image-Number school are circumscribed within the perimeters defined by the relation between hexagrams and statements. The scholars of the Meaning-Principle school followed Wang Bi's advocacy of forgetting *xiang* and rid themselves of one restraint. As a result, they were having a freer hand than the scholars of the Image-Number school. For this reason, Liu Dajun rightly points out that Wang Bi's reading of hexagram images laid the theoretical foundation for free and far-fetched interpretations.[65]

In the *Zhouyi* hermeneutic tradition, some scholars understood that the strengths and weaknesses of both the Image-Number school and Meaning-Principle school were the inevitable drawbacks of two opposite paradigms of interpretation: the conservative author-centered model and the radical reader-oriented model. Theoretically, neither paradigm is capable of recovering the original meanings of the sages because the sages' intentions are simply irrecoverable in the process of reading. Zhu Xi, for one, was aware that every reading is a rereading colored by the reader's background: "Confucius's reading of the *Book of Changes* is not that of King Wen; nor is King Wen's reading that of Fu Xi. Yichuan's commentary on the *Zhouyi* is evidently his own understanding of the book."[66] Huang Ze 黃澤 (1260–1346) of the Yuan disputed any attempt to restore and recover the pristine meanings of the images: "The meanings the scholars sought for the images are by no means the original meanings of King Wen and the Duke of Zhou."[67]

Among later scholars of the *Zhouyi*, Wang Yan provided a fairly balanced view of composition and interpretation that takes into account both the author's intention and the reader's intention, the author's creation and the reader's re-creation, and the suggestiveness of language: "The classics by the sages are concise in words but broad in implications; or profuse in words and profound in meanings. The reader may not comprehend them in full. It is not that King Wen and the Duke of Zhou made deliberate attempts to hide their intentions which therefore lie latent, but that they made their opening by the use of words, deposited their intentions beyond the domain of words. If those who are determined to study think intently and comprehend by themselves, then the implications that lie hidden and undeveloped may be constantly contemplated with no danger of boredom."[68] Here, Wang Yan viewed the compositions by the sages as a potential space made possible by the infinite possibilities of *xiang* or images (iconic signs), in which the reader can exercise his imagination and come up with inexhaustible understandings. The width and depth of understanding largely depend on the initiative of the reader. Moreover, he seemed to have implied that it is impossible to completely understand the original intentions of the sages. Wang Yan's remark is of central importance for Chinese theories of reading because it intersects with aesthetic suggestiveness in the mainstream of literary thought—especially Zhong Rong's famous saying "The text may come to an end but the implications are more than plenty"[69] and Yan Yu's 嚴羽 similar notion "the words may come to an end but their implications are limitless"[70]—thus effecting a connection between *Zhouyi* hermeneutics and literary hermeneutics. Moreover, he seemed to emphasize both the author's conscious efforts at making potentially open space for reading and the reader's initiative in exercising his imagination to come up with inexhaustible understandings. The scope of hermeneutic space depends both on the breadth and profundity of the author and on the initiative and ingenuity of the reader. Wang Yan's remark shows that, by the Song, Wang Bi's revolutionary ideas were no longer heresy.

Concluding Remarks

The inquiry into the problematic relationship between the images and words of the *Zhouyi* made significant contributions to the development of traditional Chinese language philosophy and hermeneutics. Of all the participants in the debate, Wang Bi is certainly the one who made the greatest contribution. The debate over "forgetting images" and "restoring images" represents two major trends in Chinese language philosophy and hermeneutics. By declaring "If one forgets the image to seek the ideas (conveyed through words), then, the meaning will come to light," Wang Bi seemed to prefer symbolic, abstract representation and reader-centered paradigm of reading. On the other hand, when Guo Yong declared: "The Classic says, 'To appear [or too be seen] is to be called *xiang* (image).' If it is so, then, nothing except the image is capable of making the *Dao* appear [or be seen],"[71] he was emphasizing an underlying trend in Chinese thought: iconic, visual representation, and author-centered interpretation. The wide acceptance of Wang Bi's theory marked the shift of trend in reading and interpretation, which professes to be text centered and reader oriented, and values aesthetic suggestiveness and hermeneutic openness in literary creation and interpretation. Moreover, it marked a triumph of the "other" tradition, the metaphysical-aesthetic tradition, over the dominant intentionalist tradition. Wang Bi's discourse is a proclamation as well as a conceptual justification of this triumph and should be treated as a milestone in the development of open aesthetics in Chinese tradition.

Part III

Shijing Hermeneutics

The *Shijing* and Open Poetics

The second major hermeneutic tradition in China is *Shijing* hermeneutics, which centers on the enormous amount of exegeses of the poems in the *Shijing* or the *Book of Songs* in Arthur Waley's popular translation. No other literary work in the Chinese tradition has exerted as profound an influence and maintained as lasting an appeal as the *Shijing*. For more than two millennia before modern times, this anthology was central to practically all aspects of Chinese life and culture. After China entered modern times, it did not cease to hold its fascination but continued to exert an influence on men and women of letters. The reasons for its lasting value and charm are many. I wish to suggest a new one: the *Shijing* has been able to retain its unshakable position in the Chinese tradition largely because it is an anthology full of poems endowed with hermeneutic openness that allows readers of different times to use different aspects of it for different purposes.

My view finds support first of all in the multiple function of the *Shijing*. Although Confucius was not the first to comment on the importance of the *Shijing*, he may be the first to recognize its many functions.[1] He even claimed that without learning the *Shijing*, one would find oneself at a loss in conversation.[2] Following Confucius's cue, some attributed to it a moral and ethical value. Confucian scholars considered it an indispensable instrument for moral education. The *Liji* 禮記 speaks of the *Shijing* as being capable of cultivating civilized virtue.[3] Some attributed a political significance to it. The Great Preface claimed that the *Shijing* was a mirror that reflected the social mores and conditions of the time and was capable of offering insights for harmonizing human relations and regulating government.[4] Some discovered a philosophical value in it. Huang Xun 黃標 (c. 1177) of the Southern Song said: "The principle of the *Shijing* has been present since the existence of heaven, earth, and the myriads of things. The cracking of thunder, the cessation of wind, and the stimulation of the myriads of things—all are endowed with the principle of the *Shijing* before they are manifest. The smiles of infants and the songs of children—all contain the sentiments of the *Shijing* in their latent form."[5] Modern scholars assign to it historical, sociological, anthropological, and ethnographical values. Of course, its greatest value lies in its literary quality. Yao Jiheng 姚際恒 (1647–1715) suggested that the *Shijing* is the fountainhead of all literary genres in China and served as the model and inspiration for later Chinese literature.[6] In literary thought, it stimulated a critical awareness which grew out of the study of the poems. *Shijing* hermeneutics formed the basis of the dominant expressive theory of literature and laid the foundation stone for a classical and formal approach to literary criticism. The heterogeneous functions that the *Shijing* has been identified to perform over history suggest that this classic is an open classic like the *Zhouyi*.

Literary Openness in the *Shijing*

The *Shijing* is a collection of poems that possess varying degrees of openness. An overview of all the poems informs us that some poems are more open than others. All the poems in the *Song* 頌 section are obviously less open because the contents are often verifiable in terms of historical data. In a way, in spite of their short length, their narration takes on a quality not unlike that of Western epics. Some poems in the *Daya* 大雅 section are less open than poems in the *Feng* 風 and *Xiaoya* 小雅 sections, for their context of composition and purpose of composition can often be verified in historical documents like the *Zuozhuan*, *Guoyu*, and *Shangshu*. In some poems, the Zhou kings' names, their wives' names, their ancestors' names, and their ministers' and generals' names are mentioned. In some others, even poets' names are stated. Poems in the *Feng* section are most open for these reasons: (1) their authors are unknown, at least unverifiable although some conjectures may be made; (2) the original purpose for composing these poems are unknown; (3) the contexts in which these poems were composed are vague and indeterminate; and (4) the signifying elements of individual poems are multivalent, the structuring principles are open-ended, and the possible themes and effects are open.

It is impossible to analyze all the *Feng* poems to demonstrate the openness of the *Feng* section. In fact, it is also unnecessary. The openness of the *Feng* poems is derived from a complex way of poetic making, which can be illustrated by a detailed analysis of a few poems in relation to the hermeneutic tradition. "Guanju," the first poem in the *Shijing* anthology will serve my purpose. It is perhaps the most well known of all the poems in the collection, as well as the most studied poem. Its eminent position does not simply come from the fact that it is the first poem. I consider its greatness as coming from its capacity to generate open interpretations. Its exegetical tradition allows me to claim that it is the first open poem in Chinese history.

In the chapter on insights of openness in Chinese thought, I analyzed a reputedly Confucian passage in the *Hanshi waizhuan* 韓詩外傳. In response to Zi Xia's 子夏 question of why "Guanju" came to be the first of the anthology, Confucius is believed to have lavished high-sounding praises on the poem. And Zi Xia exclaimed with a sigh: "Great Indeed! 'Guanju' is the basis of heaven and earth."[7] After reading this account, I am somehow reminded of the critical evaluation passed on James Joyce's *Ulysses*. According to the accepted opinion, Joyce's novel was like a jigsaw puzzle meant to represent practically everything under the sun, from the various stages of human development and the organs of the human body to the colors of the spectrum. Any reader who has read the "Guanju" poem briefly will feel puzzled: How can a short poem be so great as to embody so many great things, some of which are of transcendental qualities? After studying the poem for some time, he/she may quickly come to the conclusion that this is an exaggeration entirely out of proportion. However, if one has the patience to survey all the exegetical materials concerning the poem, he/she will admit that there may be an element of truth in the above account. The reputed Confucian exaggeration may be read as another way of saying that the poem has a self-generative quality and is quite open to interpretations. In the following sections, I will demonstrate to what extent Confucius's praise of the poem's multiplicity was no exaggeration and how that multiplicity came about.

What has endowed "Guanju" with self-generativeness? To give the reader a hint at this point, I only wish to say that since it contains no words to indicate its historical context, it can be subjected to many ways of historicization and contextualization. It has no definite reference to historical persons, therefore it can refer to any persons from that historical period. It is formally so constructed that later comers can always find ways to relate it to given aspects of life in which they happen to have an interest or to add a new twist to existent readings. The openness of the poem does not simply inhere in itself but resides in the endless interpretations. A brief survey of the major interpretations over history will help us to better understand the open nature of the poem. Of the major interpretations, the poem has been construed to cover, among other things, individuals and society, government and politics, mores and morality, family relations and human relations, customs and habits, physical passion and spiritual sublimation, eulogy and satire. The interpretations are not always compatible with each other. In fact some directly conflict and contradict each other. This again is another way of saying the poem is quite open. In the following section, I will briefly review the major interpretations and how they came about:

(1) It is a eulogy of exemplary virtue. The Great Preface, the cornerstone of the Mao school of *Shijing* exegesis, set the basic theme of the poem that has been doggedly adhered to by most later exegeses. Within this general frame, it was, first and foremost, read as a eulogy of the virtue of the queen consort, or the king, or both.[8] Zheng Xuan, and Kong Yingda,[9] Cheng Yi 程頤,[10] Lü Zuqian 呂祖謙,[11] Chen Huan 陳奐[12] and many others followed the line laid out by the Mao commentary and only added some minor details to further the theme. Xu Qian 許謙 (1270–1337) of the Yuan expressed a slightly different opinion, viewing the poem as praising the virtues of both the queen consort and King Wen with an emphasis on the latter.[13] Yan Can of the Song did not depart far from the Mao Commentary either, but he read the poem into a theme on the harmony not between husband and wife but among ladies in the king's harem.[14]

(2) It is a satire. Specifically, it attacks King Kang, or King You, or King Zhou of the Shang. The Lu school of commentary stated: "The Dao of the Zhou being on the decline, the poet composed 'Guanju' [as a satire] on the king's late rising habit."[15] The Han school claimed that "'Guanju' is a poem which satirizes current affairs."[16] Sima Qian 司馬遷 (145 BC–86 BC) also regarded the poem as a satire meant to use the past to criticize the present.[17] Ouyang Xiu of the Northern Song kept the sting of the satire.[18] But he said the satire was conveyed through a contrast between past virtue and present depravity.[19] Wei Yuan 魏源 (1794–1857) of the Qing agreed with the three schools and Sima Qian and believed that the poem is a satire the spearhead of which was directed against the depraved social conditions at the end of the Shang.[20]

(3) It is a poem about activities in a prenuptial school for brides-to-be. Hao Yixing 郝懿行 (1757–1825) worked out an interesting theme which did not entirely depart from the moral frame, but it added a dramatic twist to the normative interpretation. In his opinion, the poem is a poetic narrative of how female virtue was taught at a public school for girls to be married.[21]

(4) It is a musical tune of the inner chamber originally sung by ladies to praise or persuade their lords. Chen Huan said: "'Guanju' is a song of

the inner chamber."[22] In a slightly different form, it is viewed as a wedding song or epithalamium. Yao Jiheng argued that it may not necessarily refer to King Wen's marriage because no specific reference was made. He viewed it as an epithalamium sung to celebrate the marriage of the Zhou king's eldest son. The harmonious marriage set a fine example for the governing of the state and regulating social mores.[23] Fang Yurun accepted Yao's view of the poem as an epithalamium, but he also added a new twist. He viewed the poem as a song of the inner chamber that was later to be put to political and moral application.[24] Yao and Fang departed considerably from the normative Confucian exegesis, but they were not free from the influence of the so-called *shijiao* theory of moral education.

(5) It is a song meant to seek the talented and worthy. Cui Shu 崔述 of the Qing did not completely reject the poem as a song about proper conjugal relation between husband and wife, but he added a metaphorical twist by saying that it is a poem about the search for worthy talent.[25] Zhai Xiangjun 翟相君, a modern scholar, who rejects the traditional theme of a queen consort's search for virtuous ladies for the harem, suggests a theme similar to that of Cui Shu. He thinks that it is a poem about searching for talents, recommending talents, and welcoming talents.[26]

(6) It is a love song of the folk style. Modern scholars of the May Fourth period started a new exegetical tradition that completely rejected the Confucian paradigm of reading. The scholars of the so-called Gushibian school generally view the poem as a love song of the folk style, in which a male is tormented by lovesickness. As to the exact subject matter, they differ to some extent. Hu Shi rejects Yao Jiheng's and Fang Yurun's view of the poem as an epithalamium and regards it as "a love song pure and simple."[27] Wen Yiduo 聞一多, however, believes that the poem is a love song created on the spot by a man with the aim to amuse a girl.[28]

The rejection of the dominant Confucian paradigm of reading opened the floodgates of the new *Shijing* hermeneutic stream. Following the inquisitive spirit of the Gushibian school, modern scholars have turned out interpretations that would have staggered Confucian scholars from Mao Heng to Fang Yurun. Yu Guanying 余冠英 describes the poem as one of unrequited love.[29] Chen Zizhan 陳子展 accepts the poem as a love song and considers it a narrative of a successful courtship of the upper class.[30] Some modern scholars accept the traditional view of the poem as an epithalamium, but add some modern sensibilities. Li Changzhi 李長之 states: "This is a song sung at weddings."[31] Wei Ziyun 魏子雲 further fine-tunes this view: "The poetic theme of the poem is one of a marching song about the love, courtship and marriage of a man."[32] Another modern scholar, however, argues against the view of the poem as an epithalamium and suggests that it was a poem on the moral education concerning marriages during the historical period when there was the custom of snatching a bride for wife by force.[33]

(7) With regard to the identity of the personas in the poem and the social ideology of the poem, there are two opposite views. Most scholars, ancient and modern, believe that the personas in the poem are from the upper social classes, possibly persons of nobility or even royal origin. Cheng Junying 程俊英 suggests that it may be a love song by the upper classes.[34] Huang Diancheng 黃典誠 agrees with this interpretation.[35] Lan Jusun 藍菊蓀 accepts the poem as a marriage song but views it as an epithalamium which sings praises of two countryside youngsters who fall in love of their own will.[36] Two other scholars argue against this opinion and suggest that the poem is the precursor of literary works about talented scholars and beautiful ladies.[37]

(8) It was a song describing the performance of spring plough. Recently, a scholar provides a seemingly incredible reading of the poem. After relating the details of the poem to the spring sacrificial ceremonies in the Zhou dynasty, he states: "This poem should be a song for the dances performed at the grand spring sacrificial ceremony, which dramatizes the whole process of agricultural production with the purpose of praying for bumper harvests."[38]

The Open Texuality of "Guanju"

My survey of the major views is far from exhaustive. It, however, has paved the way for an in-depth look into the internal mechanism of the *Shijing* poems, and for an advocacy of an open paradigm in reading the *Shijing* poems. The theoretical basis of an open paradigm of reading cannot rest on the different and differing interpretations alone. To declare simply that the "Guanju" is an open poem only resolves half of the problem. The other half, a more important half, involves the effort to see how these different and divergent readings came about. This more demanding effort requires us to examine the textuality of the "Guanju" poem. The openness of the poem was made possible by a variety of factors. One of them is its special textuality, which consists of many aporias. An aporia is a Greek word meaning "puzzle," "question for discussion," or "state of perplexity."[39] It is a term used by philosophers to identify an insoluble philosophical problem that continues to attract attention not only because it poses a challenge but also because it has already become part and parcel of philosophical thinking. In Aristotle's discourse, an aporia comes close to an impasse consisting in the equal validity of contrary arguments. The methodological function of positing conflicting arguments is to sharpen the statement of the problem and to prepare a solution.[40] In contemporary literary criticism, aporia becomes almost an equivalent of the undecidable. Deconstructive criticism maintains that a literary text, whether the author knows it or not, always contains one or several aporias that deconstruct the apparent message through close readings. Paul de Man, for example, pursues a rigorously close reading of a given text to ferret out its underlying aporia to illustrate how each text undercuts its own affirmation.[41] Many of the *Shijing* poems are texts full of aporias; "Guanju" is especially so. In a way, the reason it received the greatest attention in all exegeses and won the highest praise of all the *Shijing* poems may be because it is a text full of aporias:

"Guan, guan," cries the osprey,	關關雎鳩，
On the islet of the Yellow River.	在河之州。
A graceful and virtuous lady,	窈窕淑女，
Is a fit mate for a noble man.	君子好逑。
Long and short is water weed;	參差荇菜；
To left and right I search for it.	左右流之。
A graceful and virtuous lady,	窈窕淑女，
Day and night I search for her.	寤寐求之。
Seeking her with no success,	求之不得，
I pine for her awake or asleep.	寤寐思服。
Endless, endless is my longing;	悠哉悠哉，
I toss and turn in my bed.	輾轉反側。
Long and short is water weed,	參差荇菜，
To left and right I gather it.	左右採之。
A graceful and virtuous lady,	窈窕淑女，
I play my zither to befriend her.	琴瑟友之。
Long and short is water weed;	參差荇菜，
To left and right I choose it.	左右芼之。
A graceful and virtuous lady,	窈窕淑女，
I amuse her with bells and drums.	鐘鼓樂之。[42]

   I will conduct an examination of the aporias in the "Guanju" with the aim not primarily to come up with new interpretations, but to see how the signifying mechanism of the poem is capable of generating multiple meanings and how we can benefit from its making for the construction of an open poetics. "Guanguan" is the first aporia in the poem. It is a scholarly consensus that "guanguan" is an instance of onomatopoeia, representing the cry of an osprey(s). But as to what it signifies, opinions differ and sometimes conflict. The Mao Commentary considered the cry as the answering calls of a pair of ospreys: "Guanguan is a call of harmony."[43]

Zhu Xi extended the Mao annotation: "'Guanguan' is a call of harmony between a male bird and female bird."[44] In their opinion, the bird call signifies conjugal harmony. The reading of the cry as a sign of conjugal harmony would naturally lead to the interpretation that the poem is about the harmonious marital relations between the king and the queen, who set a fine example for all in the kingdom. Differing from Mao and Zhu, I would view the onomatopoeia as the mating call of two birds—a male calling for a female, or vice versa. To read the word as a representation of mating calls would lead one to regard the poem as a love song and interpret the song as an expression of unrequited love or lovesickness ending up in a happy marriage. There are two other existent explanations. Mou Yingzhen 牟應振 of the Qing annotated the onomatopoeia as: "Guaguan is like the expression 'jiaojiao.' It indicates that the male and female birds care for each other."[45] Yao Jiheng voiced a similar opinion, but he considered the onomatopoeia as a pun: "'Guanguan' is a call of harmony. Someone may say that 'guanguan' means two caring for each other. It is a way of expressing sense through sound. A new interpretation."[46] Wen Yiduo provides still another interpretation: "'Juju' is a metaphor for the girl. The cry of 'guanguan' represents her giggling voice."[47]

I wish to add more possible implications to the onomatopoeia. The cry may be a mating call, a warning, an invitation, or a cry for help. As a warning call, a female osprey warns a male osprey to keep off. This reading would still fit into the general drift of the poem. If one reads the cry as a female fish-hawk warning the male bird to keep away from her, then, the cry symbolizes a woman trying to fight off a man's advances, hence the man's lovesickness in the following stanzas. However, if one reads the cry as an invitation, he may interpret the poem in an entirely different way: a male bird finds a lot of food and wants to invite a female bird to share it with him; in the context of the whole poem, a man wants to seduce a woman with an offering of water mallow, but the woman refuses. So the man falls lovesick. Some cheap kind of material offer does not seem to satisfy the woman. She wants to marry a man with class. So he thinks of some other kinds of enticement that might give him class: the playing of a zither and bells and drums. Thus, the poem may well imply a disparity in social class between the man and the woman. I may even say that the man was a lowly laborer, a water plant gatherer, who tries wishfully to satisfy his unrequited love by imagining himself to be a lord who knows how to play the zither and can afford the entertainment of bells and drums. Still, if one reads the cry as a distress call, he may interpet the poem with a new twist: the man has been lovesick right at the start of the poem. Like a lonely water bird that calls for a mate, he expresses his lovesickness to an adorable lady, but the latter ignores his expression of love. The frustration further aggravates his lovesickness. With some ingenuity, we may read the bird call in some other ways.

The word *jujiu* 雎鳩 is another aporia. The consensus is that it is a bird, but as to what sort of bird, opinions differ. The Mao Commentary states: "'Jujiu' is a kingfisher."[48] Kong Yingda, quoting several sources, glossed the word as "vulture," "hawk," "eagle," and so on.[49] Among modern scholars, some think it is a mandarin duck; some think it is a wild goose; some others simply gloss it as "water bird." Altogether we have a good array of birds: osprey, kingfisher, fish-hawk, eagle, hawk, vulture, mandarin duck, and wild goose. Since different birds have different characters and habits, they evoke different associations in the reader's mind. Zheng Xuan said: "The kingfishers are a kind of birds. The male and female cherish profound affection for each other and yet they keep proper segregation."[50] Kong Yingda extended Mao and Zheng's annotation saying something to this effect that just as the water birds have steadfast love for and yet keep segregated from each other, so the queen and king loved each other dearly but did not indulge themselves with each other. How can we relate this Confucian explanation to the supposed moral habits of the water bird? Qu Wanli spells out the Confucian allegory in plain words: "About this kind of birds, the male and female have profound affection for each other. They do not mate at places where there are people. It seems as though they understand rites and propriety."[51] As we do not know for sure whether ospreys have these qualities, modern scholars tend to view Mao-Zheng-Kong's gloss as twisted explanations to suit their aim of moral education. Their twisted annotations are obviously far-fetched. Whether it is a hawk, or an eagle, or a fish-hawk, or an osprey, since these are birds of prey, they are unlikely to arouse a sense of demure beauty associated with a beautiful lady. For this reason, Confucian scholars had to twist the image to fit their scheme of interpretation. Liu Xie must defend the distortion by appealing to a rhetoric of oblique reference: "In the 'Guanju' poem, the fish-hawks observe the segregation of the sexes, therefore they become an oblique reference to the virtue of the queen consort."[52]

The undecidable identity of the bird may give rise to different and entirely opposite associations and interpretations. Mandarin ducks and wild geese may give one the association of elegance, grace, and faithfulness. But the image of a hawk, vulture, and fish-hawk may give one the impression of coarseness, uncouthness, and even cruelty—qualities far removed from the female virtue of the queen consort. As birds of prey, they fit well into my previous reading of the cry as a warning to keep off. For this reason, some scholars prefer to view the water birds as mandarin ducks or wild geese and have gone to some length to prove that these birds do have these qualities. One modern scholar argues that the bird could not be a hawk, or a vulture, or any bird of prey because the *guanguan* sound could be uttered only by birds with a flat beak like a duck. After a meticulous investigation, philological, anthropological, archaeological, and anecdotal, he draws the conclusion that *jujiu* is the ancient name for a wild goose. He also provides a lengthy account of his own observations to prove that wild geese possess the instinct for faithfulness cherished by devoted lovers.[53]

The two personas in the poem, *junzi* and *shunü* constitute another key aporia. Who is the noble lord or gentleman? Who is the good, fair lady? Are they general epithets or do they refer to specific individuals in history? Most traditional commentators believed that the lord refers to King Wen; the good lady refers to his wife Taisi. But if one accepts the view that the poem was composed at the transitional period from the end of the Shang and the beginning of the Zhou, the lord could be Taiwang 太王, Wang Ji 王季, or King Wu 武王. Accordingly, the good lady could be any of their consorts. Some other commentators offered different but possible options. Wei Yuan, for example, was of the opinion that the lord was not King Wen but the Duke of Zhou.[54] The different candidates for the lord and lady point to another facet of openness in the poem. Modern scholars generally believe that *junzi* and *shunü* are general epithets. Here they also disagree with one another. Some suggest that they were members of the aristocracy. Some others believe that they are young country people. Still others argue that they may refer to young people in general. As a result, their identity is not just vague; it is open to the reader's imagination.

The word *yaotiao* 窈窕 is an aporia by its textuality. The Mao Commentary glosses it: "'Yaotiao' means 'serene and demure.'"[55] Zheng Xuan followed the Mao Commentary but added a slight twist: "reside serenely and demurely in a secluded palace."[56] Kong Yingda further elaborated on this line of thought: "'Yaotiao' describes the conditions of the virtuous lady's palace, which is secluded and peaceful."[57] Following this way of glossing, the lady was believed to live in the imperial harem. Yao Jiheng glossed it somewhat differently. By tracing the philological origins of the "house" radical and citing the use of the word in various poems, he claimed: "'Yaotiao' is derived from 'xue' (cave). . . . It means the same as saying 'secluded boudoir' in later generations."[58]

There is a real shift of meaning. Instead of living in the deep imperial palace, the lady now is a girl living at home in her boudoir. The different readings caused quite a bit of controversy among the traditional annotators. If one accepts the "deep palace," then, it entails the reading that the lady is a consort, at least a wife of a feudal lord, already married. If, however, one glosses the word as "boudoir," then, the girl is not married and may not be Taisi, or a consort of a feudal lord. Fang Yurun expressed still another idea. In his opinion, the word is related to the boudoir, but it does not necessarily refer to it. The expression only describes the demure and graceful qualities of the girl.[59] A modern scholar accepts Yao Jiheng's and Fang Yurun's annotation but gives it a new twist. In his opinion, the traditional annotation of *yaotiao* as "beautiful," "graceful," "peaceful," "demure," is incorrect. The most appropriate annotation should be "living in seclusion and feeling lonely." In line with this annotation, *yaotiao shunü* means a beautiful lady who is confined in a boudoir and feels very lonely.[60]

This annotation, however, may also advance a different reading. The girl is from an upper-class family in which the Confucian requirement for moral behavior was strictly observed and marriages were arranged by parents. She is confined to the boudoir segregated from males outside of the family. A young man from the lower class accidentally got a glimpse of her and fell in love with her. But the class difference posed a barrier between them and the strictly observed male and female segregation prevented them from meeting each other. The young man was tormented by lovesickness and had to find solace in daydreaming. In his daydream, he imagined himself becoming a gentleman well versed in the arts of an educated gentleman and succeeded in marrying the girl in a pompous wedding with bells and drums. From this point of view, the poem may be viewed as a precursor for the legends of Zhuo Wenjun and Sima Xianru (179–117 BC) and anticipated the love story in "The Story of Yingying 鶯鶯傳." In this kind of reading, the poem's theme is one of lack of freedom in one's choice of love.

The water plant is still another aporia; at least its function in the poem works like an aporia. It raises several questions. First of all, what is it? Secondly, how is the water plant related to the personas in the poem? Thirdly, is it something the poet saw or recalled while composing the poem? And last but not least, who was gathering the plant: the fair lady or the gentleman or the poet or someone else? The different answers to these questions leave the situation completely open. Lu Ji 陸璣 explained it as a water plant whose leaves float on the water while its root reaches to the river-bed. To soak it in wine makes a delicious dish.[61] The Mao commentary viewed the water plant as an edible water grass used as sacrificial food at the ancestors' temple. Accordingly, it held that the gatherer is the fair lady. Kong Yingda extended Mao's commentary: "The queen consort said that the disorderly water plant required concubines to assist her in the effort to get it. For this reason, she made up her mind to seek more virtuous ladies."[62] Thus, the gatherer becomes plural. It involves both the queen consort and the king's concubines. Some other scholars annotated it as a kind of medicinal herb. For this view there are two slightly different versions. One view holds that the water plant can be made into an aphrodisiac that gives male potency. The other view holds that the aphrodisiac was for females. It gave the female sexual attraction. To follow this line of annotation, a reader would naturally view the plant as a sexual symbol in the poem.

I do not wish to deny this possible reading. Nevertheless, I suggest that the plant may have another possible implication. If we treat the plant as simply an edible grass poor people gather to supplement their scanty food, it may open up a new perspective. The plant may give a hint at the status of the speaker of the song. Given the edible quality of the plant, we may say that the gatherer may not be the queen consort or the king's concubines. For even if the plant is gathered for sacrifice, it is unlikely that the queen consort and the concubines would personally attend to its gathering. From this point of view, the gatherer(s) might be a girl or some other country folk who picked the plant to supplement their diet. In this connection, the gatherers, whoever they might be, are not people of the upper classes. It might be a country lass from a peasant family. It might be a country lad who picked the water plants for food. Or it might be a group of country youth picking water plants together. If we take the gatherer to be a single country lad, we may have this reading: on a certain day, a lad went to pick water plants on the river. He saw a beautiful girl by the bank who might or might not be picking water plants, and fell in love with her. If we take the gathering activity to be done by a group of young folks, we will have a different interpretation: on a certain spring day, a group of country youth were picking water plants on the bank of the river. While engaged in the picking, they were having a good time, chatting, laughing, and flirting with each other. A lad fell in love with a lass, and became lovesick. This kind of reading would lend support to the view that this poem is not about the love and marriage of the upper classes, but about the love and courtship of country folk.

If we treat the activity of plant picking as a *xing*, how is it related to the whole poem? We may suggest an interesting correlation: the water plant is soft and supple, thus symbolizing the delicate and obedient qualities of the consort. For a similar reason, Hao Yixing and Cui Shu also considered the water plant as a *xing* and related it to the female virtue of the lady. Hao Yixing made an implicit remark: "The water plant is soft and clean. Female virtue resembles it."[63] Cui Shu made an explicit statement: "To create a *xing* out of the water plant is because the plant is in the water, clean but difficult to pick. Being clean symbolizes the woman's chastity; being difficult to pick symbolizes the difficulty to seek her."[64] Both Cheng Yi and Cui Shu attributed a moral implication to the image of the water plant. We may disregard their moral implication and simply take their suggestion at its face value. The water plant with its supple, soft, and pure qualities symbolizes the lady's physical beauty. From a different angle, I may say that since the water plant was picked for food, its edibleness symbolizes her desirableness, thus relating edibleness to sexual connotations. In the male picker's mind, water plant picking has the same implications as picking a flower. Thus, the repeated action of water plant picking is endowed with a sexual connotation, associations not far removed from the English idea of "deflowering." Here, a highly moral theme may turn into a sexual escapade. Other aporias are the terms *qinse* (zither) and *zhonggu* (bells and drums). The Mao Commentary states: "It is appropriate to befriend her with *qin* zither and *se* zither." Zheng Xuan gave the Mao explanation a twist and viewed zither as a symbol of friendship between the queen consort and the other palace ladies. Yao Jiheng rejected Zheng Xuan's explanation as total nonsense because he thought it was impossible to compare the friendship between the queen and the palace ladies to the harmony associated with a zither. In his opinion, "To befriend with the *qin* zither and *se* zither means exactly husband and wife."[65]

In addition to the above aporias, I need to mention in passing the word *he* (river). To most scholars, the word *he* is decidable because scholarship has argued that in all the *Shijing* poems it refers to the Yellow River. But a modern reader who does not know this historical information may read *he* as a general reference to an indeterminate river. He may defend his reading with the argument that if one reads the poem as a folk love song with no particular reference to dating, authorship, and historical context, it makes sense to regard *he* as a river in its general sense. There is no lack of precedence for such a reading. Even an erudite like Zhu Xi glossed the term as a general reference: " 'He' is a general word for flowing waters in the north."[66]

To sum up, we are faced with a series of questions that often lead to opposite and conflicting answers. Is it a poem about sexual love or about moral virtue? If it is about love, then is it mutual affection or one-sided love? If the love is mutual, did the love culminate in a wedding or was the wedding only imaginary? If it is about marriage, is it a royal wedding or country folk's marriage? As far as the animus is concerned, is it a eulogy or a satire? As for its tone, is it one of jubilation, or one of wishful thinking, or one of frustration? The different and divergent interpretations suggest that this is not an "either . . . or" case, or a "both . . . and" case, but an open situation. Since some interpretations are opposite, I would say that it keeps the options suspended and leaves the decision to the reader, to chance, or to imagination. The aporias not only make possible different interpretations but also make it possible for the poem to deconstruct itself. About the outcome of the love affair in the poem, it is generally believed that the poem represents a successful love story that ends in happy marriage. Chen Zizhan, for example, views the outcome of the love story as a positive one: "The poem consists of three parts which describe the process of the courtship and its progress from initial falling in love through courtship to success."[67] I, however, may use the aporias in the poem and read the poem as a lyric narration of unrequited love. At most it narrates a love story with imaginary fulfillment.

As for whether the events described in the poem are real or imaginary, we have two opposite accounts. The general view holds it that it might have been a lyric narration of a real event. Dai Jun'en 戴君恩 (c. 1613), a scholar from the Ming, however, suggested that the content of the poem is an imaginary situation, not a real event.[68] His reasoning makes some sense. The narrative supports his argument. The narrative strategy of the poem bears some resemblance to the cinematographical technique of *montage*. The shifting of scenes from stanza to stanza and from line to line, and especially the shifting of images between "osprey," "plant picking," "waking and sleeping," "tossing and turning in bed," "zither playing," and "beating of bells and drums" in the poem seems to point to the impossibility of its being a historical experience as suggested by some scholars. The poem might have been inspired by the cry of the osprey when the poet was standing on the river bank, but it seems impossible for the details of "osprey," "bed," "zither," and "bells and drums" to appear in the same historical situation. In my opinion, most of the action in the poem took place in the mind of the poet. So it is a kind of psychological realism rather than historical realism that went into the making of the poem.

In what follows I will offer a reading of the poem with the aim to demonstrate how the poem's undecidable elements may allow us to present a reading opposite to the accepted views. I want to argue that the poem is a poetical dramatization of the cause, effect, and imaginary resolution of the poet's love sickness. Lines 1 and 2 describe the setting, scene, and dominant imagery of the poem, which pave the way for the unfolding of the human drama in the later stanzas. The image of the osprey may not stand for the harmony between husband and wife, as Confucian annotations suggested, for two reasons. First, the fidelity attributed to the osprey may be a moral quality projected by Confucian scholars. The mandarin duck, a symbol of marital fidelity in Chinese culture, has been found to be as unfaithful as other animals in their mating habits. The osprey could not be an exception. Second, the poem does not state clearly whether the ospreys are paired. I suggest that the birds are not yet paired just as the speaker of the poem has not yet found a mate. Indeed, he is gripped by the longing for a good mate. Thus, the osprey's cry is a metonymy and represents the desire for mating in the natural world. It is a *xing* which gives rise to the cause of love sickness.

Lines 3 and 4 shift the scene from the natural world to the human world. If the image of the osprey is viewed as a *xing*, now a *bi* is implied though no such words as "like" or "as" are used. The mating call in the animal world, an objective correlative for the human desire for a mate, gives rise to the poet's love. Lines 5 and 6 describe the scene on the river bank. They involve a shift in point of view. Line 5 may allude to the woman who picked water vegetables. So it is a *xing* in which a metonymy is implied: the picked fringe stands for the woman picker. But in line 6, the fringe picker is the persona. In an oblique way, vegetable picking is endowed with the sexual connotation of picking flowers (deflowering). So a *bi* is introduced at the same time. In the *Shijing* poems, vegetable picking was mostly done by women just as mulberry leaves were picked by women. But there are poems in the *Shijing* that refer to male pickers (e.g., poems 108, 167, 188, 222). When a man appeared among women pickers in a poem or a story, usually a sexual motif is introduced. As an alternative reading, I may suggest that the fringe picker in this poem is not a woman but the poet himself. The action of catching the water vegetable of irregular length is compared to the search for the girl in lines 7 and 8. Perhaps, it is not easy to pick the irregular water grass, which flows left and right in the river, just as it is not easy to win the heart of the beautiful girl. The vegetable picking may also allude to the social status of the poet. In my opinion, he was a lowly person, and might even be a plant picker. Precisely because he was a lowly laborer, he did not hold the social position to propose to the beautiful and virtuous lady, a proper mate for a noble lord. Hence his love sickness. From another point of view, the water fringe is edible as the beauty of the girl is desirable. In this stanza, the phallic desire regresses to oral desire, a feature that characterizes the perception of bodily pleasure in Chinese literature and culture. We can find numerous examples in Chinese literature in which phallic pleasure is experienced and imparted in an oral way.[69] This poem might be the earliest example.

Stanza 3 vividly dramatizes the love sickness of the poet and alludes to its cause. "To seek her but not get her" may imply that the poet was not a man of noble status. In lines 11 and 12, as he was separated from the girl by social barriers, he suffered from acute love sickness. He could not keep his mind off the girl day or night. In fact, his love sickness during the quiet, lonely night was even more acute, for he could not fall asleep and could not help longing for her. In stanza 4, the poet, like many lovesick persons in the world, had to find a substitute to gratify his desire. He fell into a daydream. Freud who considered daydreaming a fundamental cause for the genesis of literature would be pleased to find support in this poem. The poet wanted to take some imaginary action. He imagined himself a noble lord or an educated literatus able to play the zither. Zither playing figures prominently in love stories of Chinese literature. We can easily recall the love story of Sima Xianru and Zhuo Wenjun in which the zither playing served as a go-between. By imagining himself playing the zither to attract the girl's attention, the poet found the means to be close to her, to befriend her, and finally to win her. His imagined social mobility, pathetic as it seems, adds a subtle flavor of irony and an element of comedy to the poem.

The last stanza marks the imagined resolution of love sickness. His daydreaming has reached its climax. His zither playing attracted the beautiful girl who was imagined to have fallen in love with him and have agreed to marry him. A grand wedding such as would befit a noble lord was arranged. Bells and drums were struck. Amidst an atmosphere of euphoria, the lowly commoner and the beautiful girl were joined in matrimony and lived together happily thereafter. My experimental reading directly contradicts the accepted view that the love was requited and the poem ended in happy marriage. In this sense, the poem may be said to evince a deconstructive turn. As a poem about an imagined solution to unrequited love, it may be said to be archetypal.

Textual and Extratextual Indeterminacy

In my above analysis, the openness of a *Shijing* poem is often derived from indeterminate or unknown factors within and without the text. I wish to classify the extratextual unknowns into one category and designate it as "outer context." To further illustrate the significance of outer context for a text's openness, I will draw a little comparison between two poems with the same title, "Huangniao or Yellow Bird": poems 131 and 187. In poem 131, the names of Duke Mu, and three sons of the Ziju clan are mentioned. This detail ties the poem to verifiable historical data. According to the *Zuo Commentary*, "Renhao, the Duke of Qin died. With him were buried alive the three sons of the Ziju clan: Yanxi, Zonghang, and Qianhu. All of them were the finest pick of the Qin. People of the state lamented over their fate and composed the poem 'Yellow Bird.'"[70] Scholars confidently dated the poem as one composed around 622 BC. With these details, the poem can have only one historical context. As a result, its space for interpretation is significantly reduced. The Mao Commentary regards the poem as a criticism of Duke Mu's inhumanity. No later scholars ever disputed this interpretation. Poem 187 also employs the image of a yellow bird to start the poem. Because its context is not clear, its hermeneutic space is larger. There are different interpretations. Mao Heng, Zheng Xuan, and Kong Yingda all argued that the poem ostensibly narrates the complaint of a deserted wife, who wanted to return to her home, family, and clan, but it hides an implied criticism of King Xuan who failed to enforce the marriage covenant between husband and wife.[71] Wang Su and Su Zhe read the poem as one in which a worthy talent decides to leave his prince for his home because of frustrated ambition. Some other scholars read the poem as one in which a self-imposed exile wanted to return to his homeland because of unfriendly treatment in a foreign land.[72] Zhu Xi, Yao Jiheng, Yan Can, and some modern scholars suggested this opinion. Some other scholars argue that the persona was not an exile but one compatriot who found it difficult to live peacefully with his neighbors in a time of moral decline. Fang Yurun held this view.[73] It is clear that poem 187 has a larger hermeneutic space than poem 131 because of the fact that while the latter contains specific details to indicate a clearly implied subject position, the former does not. Poem 131 may be a poem that supplies a clearer context than any other poem in the *Feng* section. Nevertheless, the clear context does not prevent it from being open. For example, the question regarding its attitude toward the practice of burying live persons with the dead remains open. Some scholars suggest that it objects to the practice as a whole. Some other scholars argue that it only objects to the burying alive of those three fine men of the state, citing the detail as support: "Could we but ransom him / There are a hundred would give their lives."

My little comparative study allows me to suggest that the magnitude of the open field of a poem is inversely proportional to its contextual clarity: the less specific the contextual details, the larger the open field. My comparison also shows that a literary text would normally supply some necessary elements to reconstruct a context, to imply a subject position, and to provide some constraints to delimit the readers' reading. But in the case of "Guanju" (and many other *Shijing* poems as well), the text is so full of aporias that both the extratextual elements and the introtextual elements are frequently undecidable. I wish to group the introtextual elements into the large category of "inner context." Within the text, I have already shown that it is full of unknowns: unverifiable time, unidentifiable place, and unknown personae. In this sense, "Guanju" differs from most poems in the *Daya* and the *Song* sections. Commenting on the "Guanju," Mou Yingzhen of the Qing made a remark that reveals the difference: "One may ask: why didn't you talk about King Wen and his consort in this poem? I answer: because there is no evidence for that. Poems in the *Daya* section depict King Wen's virtue and accomplishments as well as his marriage. There is also a fairly detailed account of the queen consort Taisi's family lineage. 'Guanju,' however, makes no mention of all this."[74]

In his comment on the same issue, Yao Jiheng made an insightful remark, which not only clarifies the issue in question but also provides a sound opinion concerning the openness of the poem as well as poetry reading in general: "Generally speaking, one who is good at reading the poem would understand it by correlating his own intuition with it rather than imparting his intuition in words. If he uses his own intuition to read the poem, he may view it as a poem concerning King Wen and his consort Taisi. He would not impart his intuition in words, because there is no evidence in the poem to confirm the possible reference to King Wen and his consort. Who can be certain that the personae are not King Tai and his consort Tairen, King Wu and his consort Yijiang? Only when one reads the poem in this way can he be said to be skillful at reading the poem."[75] We may also add: Who could be sure that the personae in the poem are not some country lad and lass, a poor scholar and a lady from a rich family, or the like?

A Notion of Open Field

Most of the undecidables I have dealt with should have posed no problem in ordinary discourse. They are simply words, but within the poem they become aporias. Therefore, the undecidability does not inhere in the words themselves, but resides in the structural system of the poem, which I wish to call an "open field." An open text is not just an open space of signification. It is an open field, like a magnetic field. Words become energized with openness in the same way iron chippings become magnetized under the force of a magnet. Iron chippings do not possess magnetic power by themselves. But once they are thrown into a magnetic field, they become tiny magnets endowed with magnetic power. The greatness of "Guanju" lies in its hermeneutic potential quite like the magnetic field of a giant magnet. Many *Shijing* poems are so ingeniously composed that their signifying structure forms such an open field. Now it is necessary to explore how this sort of open field is organized.

As a rough definition, I conceive of the open field as a complex system of signifying relations that are unstable, ever changing, and defy attempts to nail them down. In this open field, individual words are both free and under control. They are free in the sense that they have the capacity to form relations with other words; they are controlled in the sense that the act of forming relations is under the sway of certain signifying laws, some of which are designed by the author; some are derived from semiosis; still some may be devised by the reader. In a closed text, words are like dictionary entries, whose significance is fairly identifiable. In an open text, words become aporias, turned into indeterminate elements and forming undecidable junctures in the text. An open text signifies in the way a kaleidoscope works. After a kaleidoscope is made, every shake will produce a new array of colorful patterns. Or in semiotic terms, it is what Derrida calls "the seminal adventure of the trace," or "the play of the world" in which the general text always provides further connections, correlations, and contexts: "That is the joyous affirmation of the play of the world and of the innocence of becoming, the affirmation of a world of signs without fault, without truth, and without origin which is offered to an active interpretation."[76]

The construction of an open field of signification involves various composing strategies to put words into fluid, changeable, indeterminate relations. Many of the *Shijing* poems, partly due to history, partly due to the characteristics of poetic language, show a fascinating array of signifying strategies that find concentrated expression in "Guanju." Generally speaking, these open strategies fall into two large categories: extratextual strategies and introtextual strategies. I can point to three kinds of extratextual strategies: unknown author, unknown context, and unknown intention. Firstly, the authorship of the poem is open. Over history, there have been several views as to who composed this poem. One view has it that the poem was composed by King Wen's consort Taisi who sang this song to express her pleasure at King Wen's virtue, her wish to seek more virtuous ladies for the king, and her joy at finding them. Although Mao Heng, Zheng Xuan, and Kong Yingda did not explicitly uphold this view, they implied this in their commentaries and annotations.[77] Feng Fang 豐坊 (fl. 1523) of the Ming made an explicit statement.[78] Yao Jiheng pointed out that if one followed the exegeses in the Great Preface and the Minor Preface, the poem would be regarded as "the queen consort's own song."[79] Another view has it that the poem was composed by palace ladies in King Wen's court who sang praises of the virtues of King Wen and his consort Taisi. Zhu Xi held this view.[80] Wei Yuan disagreed: "The two 'Nan Sections' were folk songs of the Zhou state. They must have been composed by people of the state, and the Duke of Zhou collected them and set them to music. It was in no way a poem composed by the palace ladies."[81] One scholar attributed the poem to a historical person, a minister of King Kang, Duke Bao.[82] Another scholar agreed that it was composed by a minister of King Kang, but argued that the composer was not Duke Bao but Duke Bi.[83] Still another view holds that the poem may be a folk song composed by an anonymous person and then collected by the folksong collectors sent by the king. Yao Jiheng, Fang Yurun, and modern scholars like Hu Shi, Gu Jiegang, and Zheng Zhengduo uphold this view.[84] The different views with regard to its author gave rise to different interpretations.

Secondly, the time in which the poem was originally composed is open. Most traditional commentators believed that the poem was composed toward the end of the Shang and at the beginning of the Zhou. Some believed that it was composed at a time when the Zhou dynasty was on the decline. Altogether, there are four views: the poem may have been composed at King Wen's time, or at Wang Ji's time, or at King Kang's time, or King You's time. Thirdly, the original authorial intention is unknown. Modern literary theory has convincingly demonstrated that authorial intention is unreliable and often misleading in the interpretation of a literary text. In the case of "Guanju" and most *Shijing* poems, the authorial intention is doubly unreliable and misleading because it is simply anybody's guess. As my survey shows, there are many speculations about the original intentions of the poem, but none of them is reliable for the simple reason that they are impossible to verify. Indeed, the existent speculations are conflicting and contradictory, revealing by themselves their unreliability. In this sense, I may say that the authorial intention is completely open. From an entirely different cultural perspective, the different versions with regard to the pretextual intention of the poet serve to argue for the validity of the "intentional fallacy."

In reading "Guanju," we are faced with a poem with unknown author, unknown date, and unknown intention. Moreover, we do not even know its implied reader, implied author, and implied context. These unknowns make interpretations open. If it was composed at King Wen's time, it might have been a song singing the virtue of King Wen or his consort Taisi. Hence it would be a eulogy. But if it was a song composed at King Kang's time, it would be a satire. If one accepts the view that the dating of the original version is unknown, then, the poem would be a love song composed at a particular time but meant for all historical ages. It is largely because of these extratextual unknowns that readers throughout history have been able to approach it from different angles and appropriate it for their own political agendas, moral programs, and personal consumption. From this point of view, the poem comes close to an archetypal text with universal significance, classless, value free, bias free, transcending culture, time, and space, with an unadulterated reverence for love, life, and human experience. The poem is not just multivalent; it is open. Only when it is open is it capable of generating meanings compatible with, complementary to, conflicting, and contradicting each other, and of lending itself to different kinds of appropriations.

I have stated earlier that the words become aporias only after they enter an open field the construction of which involves strategies to put words in indeterminate but meaningful relations of signification. The structure of "Guanju" exemplifies its construction. The poem is constructed on an open structure with a series of signifiers that interact with each other in ways not specified, but are left to the reader or chance. The relations among those signifiers will be established only after the reader makes a decision to read the poem from certain subject positions. The signifiers are reciprocally active upon each other. If the significance of one signifier is construed in a different way during the process of reading, the significance of other signifiers is likely to alter accordingly. And a new relationship needs to be found in order to make sense of the whole stanza and whole poem. Next, I will analyze the first stanza structurally to show how the open field is constructed. I will first cut the stanza into separate signifying units and then schematize their relationship into an open structure. To facilitate my discussion, I designate individual signifiers as A, B, C, D, E, F, G, H; blocks of signifiers as 1, 2, 3, and 4, and still larger blocks as I and II.

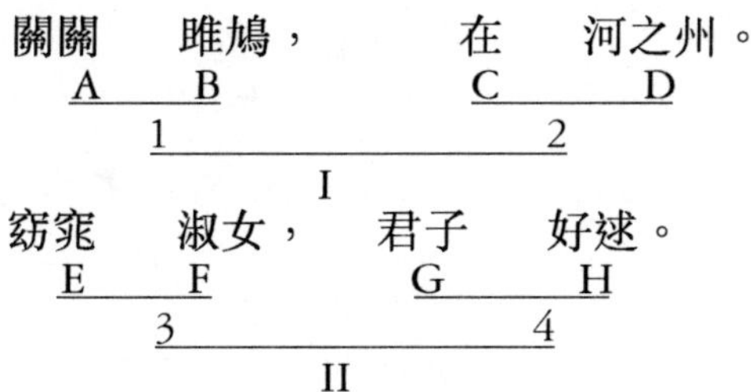

All the signifiers are related to each other in a complex system of signification and representation, either horizontally (syntagmatically) or vertically (paradigmatically), but the exact nature of their relationships are indeterminate. This indeterminacy, however, can be illustrated with another diagram:

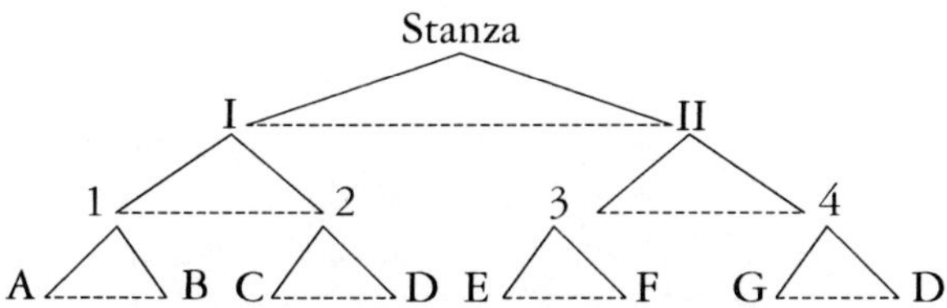

In the above diagram, the dotted lines indicate relations of uncertain signification and representation. In plain, discursive language, we may describe the uncertain relations as a series of questions: In what way does *guanguan* modify the osprey? Why is the osprey on the islet of the river? How does *yaotiao* modify the fair lady? How is the gentleman related to the fair lady? And finally, is there a meaningful relationship between a crying osprey on the islet of the river and the gentleman and his fair lady? My survey and my own speculative reading of the poem have demonstrated that all these questions can find no definite answers in morphology, syntax, signification, and representation. Morphologically, should we read *guanguan jujiu* as "*guanguan* cries the osprey" or "*guanguan* cry the ospreys"? In other words, is it only one osprey calling or two or more ospreys calling and answering each other? Syntactically, is *yaotiao shunü* connected with *junzi haoqiu* by an implied "is"? In the case of *haoqiu*, is *hao* a modifier for *qiu* or, as Wen Yiduo argues, should it be glossed as *fei* 妃, and therefore *hao* and *qiu* are parallel elements?[85] Conscious of the indeterminacy of the word in the context of the poem, Wen Yiduo expresses a different opinion on another occasion: "The original meanings of 'hao': as a verb, it should be glossed as 'man and woman love each other'; as a noun, it should be read as 'mate or spouse'; as an adjective, it means 'graceful and fair,' which is an extension of the original meaning."[86] Thus, he does not rule out the possibility of *hao* being an adjective. Yu Guanying also annotates *hao* as a verb: "'Hao': male and female amuse each other."[87] This annotation would significantly alter the meaning of the stanza. We may recall Wen Yiduo's annotation of *guanguan* as the laughing sound of girls. If we combine both annotations, we may come up with a new reading of the stanza: just as the ospreys on the islet of the river were having a good time crying happily together, so the men and women were enjoying themselves by amusing each other. Along the same line of thinking, I may add that *hao* may also be glossed as a verb, meaning "love or seeking love." In the context of the poem, this reading also makes sense: just as male and female ospreys seek each other out for mates, so the gentleman and the fair lady love each other as mates. In other stanzas of the poem, there are also a number of grammatical indeterminacies. For example, in *qinse you zhi*, there are three readings: (1) with *qin* zither and *se* zither [I] befriend her; (2) like *qin* zither and *se* zither [we] befriend each other; (3) [I] as *qin* zither and you as *se* zither befriend each other. The indeterminacy is also caused by the pronoun *zhi* 之 because we cannot determine its antecedent referent.

I am not going to discuss signifying and representational uncertainties any more, having already devoted enough space to them. Next I will undertake an analysis of the uncertain relationship between signifier block I and signifier block II. The indeterminate relation constitutes the most fascinating feature not only of this poem but also of many *Shijing* poems. In traditional literary thought, it is called *xing* 興, variously defined as "to start," "stimulus," and "arousal." I do not wish to go into a historical survey of the extant scholarship on the meaning of this word. I only want to investigate its signifying mechanism. In my article on *xing*, I suggest that for signifiers in a situation that may be called *xing*, there is an implied relation of analogy between elements involved. It is structured like a verbal analogy in a Graduate Record Examination: A : B // C : D, which, in discursive language, reads as: "A is to B as C is to D."[88] Here I must extend this idea further in consideration of openness and making. A *xing* is certainly structured like a GRE analogy, but there is a fundamental difference between the two. While in a GRE analogy, there is only one correct answer to the relationship between analogized terms, in a *xing*, the relationship is uncertain, indeterminate, and open to interpretations. There may be as many answers as the reader cares to find by putting his ingenuity to work. We may render the first stanza of "Guanju" into the following analogical pattern:

As the osprey(s) cry *guanguan* on the islet of the river,
So a secluded fair lady is a suitable mate for a gentleman.

The literal rendering leaves the analogy opaque. In other words, the analogy pattern is open. Because the pattern is open, readers can project possible and plausible significance into each of the signifiers. If one takes *guanguan* to be the answering calls of ospreys, then he would argue that it is about conjugal harmony. If one sees the ospreys as birds that are faithful companions, he may argue that the stanza is about marital fidelity. If one thinks that the ospreys are birds that keep proper segregation between the male and female, he would accept the Mao Commentary that the stanza is about the virtue of proper moral behavior. If one considers the osprey as an image of beauty, he would suggest that just as the osprey on the islet is beautiful, so the lady is gracefully desirable as a mate. Lü Zuqian was of this opinion: "'Guanguan' cries the osprey / On the islet of the River'— is employed to describe the shape and appearance. 'A fair and virtuous lady / A fit mate for the lord'—sings of the lady as truly a perfect spouse for a king."[89] If one views *guanguan* as mating calls, he is likely to suggest that just as the osprey has the animal instinct for mating, so humans have the instinct for love. If one sees the osprey on the islet in the middle of the river as a sign of seclusion, he would argue that the fair lady may be secluded in a boudoir. If one perceives the ospreys' cry as a sign of happiness, he may argue that just as the ospreys cry happily on the river, so a gentleman and a fair lady are having an enjoyable tryst. If one thinks that the osprey is a water bird the poet wanted to catch, he may suggest that just as the osprey on the islet of the river is impossible to catch, so the fair lady in seclusion is inaccessible as a possible mate. Zheng Qiao's 鄭樵 (1104–62) reading suggests this idea.[90]

That *xing* involves a correlative relation between elements in a text has been rigorously resisted by some scholars: Su Zhe,[91] Zheng Qiao,[92] Yao Jiheng,[93] and Gu Jiegang,[94] to name just a few famous ones. They vehemently denied that there is a necessary correspondence implied between the *xing* image and the discourse it arouses. Some other scholars adopt a position which holds that some *xing* images have a corresponding implication while others do not. Here I do not wish to go into an extended discussion of the pros and cons. I only wish to point out that to deny the correlative function of *xing* ignores an important feature of it. While *xing* is an open structure that allows for multiple interpretations, at the same time it imposes some textual constraint on far-fetched and unbridled interpretations. To deny the correlative function of *xing* would be equivalent to licensing the reader to read in whatever way he pleases. We have discussed the analogical implications of the osprey. If we accept the denial of implied analogy, viewing the cry of the osprey as a mere stimulus to start the poem, then, rampant interpretations would arise because *guanguan* is a bird call that may be construed to represent many implications. In addition to being symbols of physical beauty, conjugal harmony, moral virtue, and love instinct, the bird call may be an appeal for help, a signal for having found food, a warning of danger, a call to locate a mate, parent, offspring, sibling, friend, the group, and so on. All these implications are possible but not equal in plausibility. The criterion against which to measure the plausibility is the correlative function. Readings of the osprey as symbols of physical beauty, conjugal harmony, or love instinct are convincing because they find corresponding connotations in the context of the poem. Other readings are less convincing simply because they can only find weak echoes or no echoes in the poem. In this sense, I may put forward a paradoxical claim that a *xing* structure is both open and closed; its interpretations are both free and constrained. The same conditions apply equally well to an open field.

Paronomastic Reading and Writing

Now I will deal with one question: Is the openness in the *Shijing* poems naturally made or consciously intended? My answer is: I don't know, but I may make an educated guess. My guess is both. Considering the fact that the *Shijing* poems were believed to be folk songs collected, edited, and reedited by literary men including Confucius, it is very likely that some conscious efforts were made to leave some poems deliberately open. Poem 129 may be a case in point. Ji Ben of the Ming made this comment: "This poem speaks of this theme: a man should not regard staying away from humanity as the Way. From this we may say that it is a poem composed by a scholar."[95] Ji Ben's guess is fairly reasonable. I suspect that whoever the poet was, he might have played a word game to explore the possibility of openness. One tell-tale sign is the rhetorical expression, "that so-called someone." There is no way to ascertain the identity of this person: male or female, old or young, handsome or plain, tall or short, thin or plump, rich or poor. In normal circumstances, when we read a poem about a person, we should be able to visualize in our mind's eye an image of that person. We can compare this poem with poem 57, "Shuoren 碩人." After reading poem 57, we would be able to construct a picture of the lady, however different that picture may be, depending on each reader's construction. But after reading "The Reeds," we have no way of knowing what this person looks like. Nevertheless, that person is not airy nothing. Her/his desirability is unmistakable through the intensity of the ardent search. It is as though the poet left the image open, allowing the reader to concretize it as he/she pleases. This strategy for creating desirable images corresponds with the principle in Lao Zi's saying "A great image is rarefied in shape" and was frequently employed in poetry making by later generations.

Another sign of intentional openness is to be found in the attention paid to the material aspect of signifiers. The choice of words in some poems seems to suggest a conscious awareness of the interrelatedness of shape, sound, and sense of words through the mediation of the materiality of signifiers. This awareness is to be found in the prevalent use of characters and words with the same, similar, or equivalent shape, sound and sense. In poem 131, the *xing* image "yellow bird" settles on three different trees in each of the three stanzas, *ji* 棘 (thorn bush), *sang* 桑 (mulberry tree), and *chu* 楚 (brambles). I have mentioned earlier that the poem is a lamentation. As many commentators have pointed out, it is also a *cishi* 刺詩 (poem of criticism). In Chinese, *ci* literally means "to stab" or "to prick." The words *ji* 棘 and *ci* 刺 visually look similar, having the same radical. Both "thorn bushes" and "brambles" have thorns capable of pricking, thus alluding to the metaphorical meaning of criticism. "*Sang* or mulberry" is a homophone for *sang* 喪 (death, loss), *shang* 殤 (die young), and *shang* 傷 (wound, injury). Wen Yiduo has shown that in high antiquity, *sang* 桑 was sometimes used as a loan word for *sang* 喪. "*Jiaojiao* sing the yellow birds / As they light on the mulberry tree"—the two lines may be read as: the yellow birds gather at the burial ground, singing a dirge and mourning the loss of the three fine men who died young and whose death broke the heart of the people of the Qin state. The use of polysemous words endows poem 44 with an enigma amenable to a number of interpretations:

Two gentlemen went off in a boat,	二子乘舟，
Floating, floating is the scene/shadow.	汎汎其景。
Longingly I think of you;	願言思子；
My heart within is sore.	中心養養。
Two gentlemen went off in a boat,	二子乘舟，
Floating, floating is their passing.	汎汎其逝。
Longingly I think of you;	願言思子；
Oh may you come to no harm.	不瑕有害。[96]

In the first stanza, *jing* is the same as the radical of *ying* 影 and is often used interchangeably with the latter. Thus, the poem may refer to the scene of going away or the shadows of the goers. In the second stanza, *shi* 逝 may have a three-fold meaning: going away, passing away, and disappearing like immortals. The ambiguity of the *jing* and *shi* makes the poem multivalent. According to the traditional interpretation, the poem refers to a historical event. Duke Xuan of Wei wanted to kill his eldest son. His younger son came to know the plot. He warned his eldest brother who, nevertheless, refused to flee. In the end, both brothers met with tragic deaths. The people of the state lamented over their death and composed the poem.[97] With this historical context, the poem may be a eulogy of the two brothers' noble courage: They confronted death as though it were a journey by boat. But there is no textual evidence in the poem to support the historical context. The poem is so vaguely worded that we may say that the theme is quite open. It may depict the departing scene of two persons; it may express sorrow for their death; it may describe their apotheosis; or it could refer to all these denotations and connotations.

In "Guanju," the onomatopoeia *guanguan* could be replaced by *guagua*, the sound of a flat-beaked bird, but *guanguan* is a semantically pregnant word; for while *guagua* is only an onomatopoeia, *guanguan*, in addition to being an imitation of a bird's call, associates the sound with a series of meanings. Previously scholars have already suggested that *guanguan* is associated with *xiangguan* 相關 and *guanxin* 關心. I here suggest that it may also be related to *guanbi* 關閉 (enclosed and secluded within), suggesting "segregation" or "seclusion." Both meanings make sense in the context of the poem. In the same poem, *qiu* 逑 seems to be another meaningfully chosen word. All annotators agree that it is the same as *chou* 仇. If *chou* were used, it would not affect the rhyme scheme. That *qiu* was chosen may be because it is a double pun. It puns audio-visually with 求

(seek), a word that appears twice in the poem and forms the major action of the poem. In the context of the poem, one could say: "A fair and virtuous lady involves a good deal of seeking by the lord." In a way, this reading fits the tenor of the poem even better, because the image, action, and theme are all about seeking.

Since I have argued that the original intentions are impossible to recover, it may be objected that the different readings of the same character, word, or phrase might not have been consciously intended as I have described. At least, there is no proof. This objection is certainly fair. Nevertheless, even if we accept this objection, from the viewpoint of the reader, my analysis above has enough validity to suggest that it constitutes a way of interpretation I would call "paronamastic reading." Wen Yiduo has extensively explored the transformations of sound, shape, and sense in the texuality of many *Shijing* poems. In some cases, the word meant and the word used display discernible efforts at conscious making. Take poem 8, "*Fuyi* 芣苢," for example. It has quite a few different interpretations. The differences emanate from the word *fuyi*. It is believed to be a kind of plant, but Wen Yiduo proves that it is a word intended for "fetus" by way of intricate connections in terms of sound and shape: "Both *fu* 芣 and *pei* 胚 were characters evolved from *pi* 不; both *yi* 苢 and *tai* 胎 evolved from *yi* 以. The sound of *fuyi* came close to *peitai* [in high antiquity]. So the ancient folk believed that eating *fuyi* would be conducive to pregnancy and birth through a form of magic thinking in terms of analogical law (similar sound)."[98] His evidential research suggests that paronamastic writing might have been consciously intended. Even if we cannot ascertain whether paronomastic writing was used intentionally by the *Shijing* poets, it is safe to say that paronomastic reading is a valid strategy to open up hermeneutic space.

Chapter 6

Shijing Hermeneutics: Blindness and Insight

Like *Zhouyi* hermeneutics, *Shijing* hermeneutics has a number of interesting features. First, almost all great scholars in Chinese history have at least dabbled in *Shijing* hermeneutics. Second, just as the *Zhouyi* scholars split into two camps—the Image-Number school and the Meaning-Principle school—the *Shijing* scholars divided into two schools based on their support for or opposition to the Great Preface to the anthology: the *Zunxu pai* 尊序派 (Pro-Preface school) and the *Feixu pai* 廢序派 (Anti-Preface school). Third, each school has had its assumptions, agendas, predilection, and exegetical techniques. Fourth, each school has had its insights and blindness with regard to the poems in particular and to theories of interpretation in general. By investigating their assumptions, orientations, and methodologies underlying the different strands of *Shijing* hermeneutics, we may see from a vantage point why the anthology is full of open poems, how openness is achieved, and to what extent our efforts to locate a theoretical basis for the construction of an open poetics may benefit from the insights and blindness of *Shijing* hermeneutics.

In Search of Original Intentions

In the preface to *Shijing tonglun*, Yao Jiheng ranked the *Shijing* higher than other classics, but he also said: "Compared with the other classics it is the single most difficult text for exegesis."[1] Why is that so? Yao explained that the original purposes and themes of the poems in the anthology had got lost in transmission. As a result, scholars of later generations became blind men groping in the dark who produced many mistakes and follies. Yao Jiheng was one of the few premodern scholars who recognized that the *Shijing* poems are literary texts without origin and context. He argued that the *Shijing* exegeses were severely hampered by this lack. I, however, suggest that this lack is a double-edged sword. True, it hampered *Shijing* hermeneutics in some way, but at the same time it helped promote *Shijing* hermeneutics. Without this lack, the *Shijing* hermeneutic tradition would not have been as colorful as it is today.

Like any hermeneutic tradition, *Shijing* hermeneutics centers on readings of a text and involves a process of reading. The result of any reading is determined by many factors. Three essential ones are the reader, the text, and context. Any reading is an interactive process between the reader and the text within a context. The reader controls the reading process through his/her ideological affiliation, moral values, and personal predilections, but he/she is in turn controlled by the text. A reading without taking into account the text would yield a totally subjective exegesis that is most likely to be dismissed by other readers. The same is true of *Shijing* hermeneutics. No matter how a *Shijing* exegete may distort and twist his reading of a poem, he cannot totally dissociate himself from the text. Even some of the most ridiculous commentaries in the history of *Shijing* hermeneutics were based on the reading of texts. They may have some tenuous claims to legitimacy as readings, due to the loss of origin and context. In the history of *Shijing* hermeneutics, the staggering amount of commentaries, annotations, and criticism was made possible not entirely by the fact that the *Shijing* had been consistently respected as a Confucian classic. The *Shijing* is not the only Confucian classic. That only the *Shijing* rivals or may even surpass the *Zhouyi* in the huge amount of exegeses produced has something to do with the special conditions of the *Shijing*. Of the three essential factors in reading, the reader is the free agent; text and context are restraints. But in *Shijing* hermeneutics, the contextual restraint was lost and the textual restraint is considerably less restraining than in the case of other texts. So, the reader enjoys more freedom in the process of reading.

Like the *Zhouyi* scholarship, the *Shijing* exegeses have undergone an ever greater expansion that may well be called a snowball effect. The history of *Shijing* hermeneutics is one of contention, conflicts, and controversy. It is chaotic, disorderly, and discouraging. The *Shijing* exegetes over history attack each other and each of them claims that his reading of a particular poem is the most correct one. Some even claim that it is the only correct one. Few of them seem to have realized that most *Shijing* poems are literary texts without clear "subject positions."

In reading, a text will offer the reader some perspectives from which to read it. The perspectives are called "subject positions," which may include pretextual intention, compositional context, textual orientations, and textual effects. In *Shijing* hermeneutics, the subject positions for many poems are either too few or too many. To be more exact, the "too many" subject positions are the result of "too few" subject positions. Because many poems do not imply clear subject positions, exegetes scrambled for positions. Initially, there were the so-called Qi 齊, Lu 魯, Han 韓, and Mao 毛 schools of commentary circulating in the Western Han. Then in the Eastern Han, Zheng Xuan 鄭玄 (127–200), taking the Mao school of commentary as his basis and assimilating miscellaneous elements from the other three schools, produced an annotated text, *Maoshi Zhengjian* 毛詩鄭箋, with a subject position that dominated *Shijing* hermeneutics until modern times. By the time of the Tang, Kong Yingda 孔穎達 (574–648), at the decree of the emperor, organized a group of scholars who further edited and annotated Zheng Xuan's text into the standard text, *Maoshi zhengyi* 毛詩正義. The meaning of the title, "Correct Meanings of the Mao Version of the *Shijing*," unequivocally declared the subject position provided by the Mao Preface and Commentary to be the only correct guideline in *Shijing* hermeneutics. Nevertheless, it could not shut out dissenting voices. The dissent was voiced by scholars who challenged the correctness of the Preface. Over history, the Pro-Preface school and the Anti-Preface school were engaged in a long and protracted debate that parallels the debate between the Image-Number school and the Meaning-Principle school in *Zhouyi* hermeneutics.

Although the two schools have different agendas, considerations, and intellectual predilections, their approaches to the study of the *Shijing* were determined by the same paradigm of reading. It is a political and moral paradigm, which views the *Shijing* as a reflection and expression of a bygone political and moral order. Although there were attempts to depart from this paradigm, up to modern times, deviations were never significant enough to transgress the limits of the paradigm. This is so even with the heated debate between the two schools. Ostensibly, the debate was characterized by an intensity which smacks of deconstructive criticism in modern theories of reading. In fact, it was a furor stimulated by the scramble for position in the race of *Shijing* hermeneutics to find some illusory origins. At its inception in the Western Han, *Shijing* hermeneutics had four subject positions. The Qi, Lu, Han, and Mao schools each represented a subject position. By the Eastern Han, the Mao school had nudged the other three schools off the race course and become the dominant subject position. Since then, *Shijing* hermeneutics has traversed a route more or less charted by the *Maozhuan* (the Mao Commentary) and *Zhengjian* (Zheng

Xuan's annotations). But within this tradition, there appeared more frantic acts of jockeying for position in the search for origins. Even scholars of independent mind like Yao Jiheng, Cui Shu 崔述 (1740–1816), and Fang Yurun 方玉潤 (1811–83), who transcended the controversy over the debate between the "Maoxu" upholders and detractors, were unable to deviate from the search for origins.[2]

My critical survey of *Shijing* scholarship before modern times seems to support one Song dynasty scholar's opinion of the situation: "The six classics all suffered under commentaries and annotations. The *Shijing* suffers the most."[3] Modern scholars have adopted an even more negative attitude toward the exegetical tradition of the *Shijing*. Gu Jiegang 顧頡剛 compares the *Shijing* to a valuable ancient monument that had been deeply buried in wild grass and profuse shrubs.[4] Zheng Zhenduo 鄭振鐸 compares the *Shijing* commentaries and annotations to layers upon layers of rubble, which, if it is not swept away, will hinder the original nature of the *Shijing* from being unearthed.[5] Hu Shi simply dismisses the exegetical tradition as a heap of rotten account books that "have never been subjected to a general settling."[6]

My purpose in conducting this critical survey is meant not only to historicize the chaotic and disorderly conditions of *Shijing* exegesis but also to show that this complex situation was brought about by the search for origins in a lost context. It has been an accepted critical opinion that if one wants to pick his way out of such chaotic conditions, one may view the different and divergent exegeses as centering around the struggle between those scholars who uphold the Mao Preface as the key to the poems and those scholars who reject the preface as misleading. This is certainly true, but my critical review reveals that the controversy over the Mao Preface was really one over a search for origins. I contend that this is the ultimate source of all the controversies.

For most *Shijing* exegetes, be they Preface-upholders or Preface-detractors, their real interest in the *Shijing* is motivated by the desire to know the original meanings and conditions of the poetic anthology. All the exegetes, ancient and modern, share the idea that every poem in the collection has a pristine origin or meanings that can somehow be recaptured through proper exegesis. Mencius was perhaps the first to express this idea.[7] The Mao school of commentary was a concentrated expression of the attempt to get at the intentions behind the poems. As Van Zoeren puts it, one of the central claims of the Preface is "the insistence that the Odes fully inscribe the authentic aims or *zhi* of their authors,"[8] and the fundamental approach to the study of the Odes, as adopted by the Mao school of exegetes is characterized by "the concern with the motivations that lay behind texts and utterances."[9] Even Ouyang Xiu 歐陽修

(1007–72) who was the first to raise doubts about the authenticity of the Mao Preface was motivated by the desire to search for the original and unitary meaning of the *Shijing*, which, in his opinion, had become lost and confused due to the decline and dispersal in the long process of transmission. The title of his study, *Shi benyi* 詩本義 (the Original Meaning of the *Shijing*), testifies to his view of the intention of the poet as the foundation and origin of the poems. In his distinction between *ben* (root) and *mo* (branches), he clearly privileged the intention of the poet over the reconstructed significance by the reader.[10] Fang Yurun, despite his remarkably independent mind and original interpretations, was not free from this search for the original intentions: "I have determined not to stop seeking until I have obtained the original intentions of the ancients, irrespective of the Preface, the Commentary, and previous exegeses. I will follow what is correct and rectify what is wrong. My book is entitled 'To Trace the Origin,' because I wish to trace the *original intentions of the ancient poets*."[11]

Modern scholars have also embarked on the same search for origins. Zheng Zhengduo has a high opinion of Yao Jiheng's, Cui Shu's, and Fang Yurun's *Shijing* exegeses, but he still thinks that their studies fall short of revealing the original features of the *Shijing*, because "the original features of the *Shijing* cannot be found in their books."[12] Western scholars also joined this search for original intentions. Marcel Granet, who may be credited with starting the modern trend of *Shijing* hermeneutics in the West, is a case in point. Like many modern scholars, Granet was puzzled by the canonical interpretation: "How was it that the scholars—and excellent scholars at that—were unable to interpret their native language?"[13] His inquiry into how the mistake arose leads to an allegorical methodology of reading derived from ideological commitment: "They were not merely scholars; there is more of the official than the lover of literature about them; they put the poems at the service of political ethics and thereafter were unable to admit their popular origin." Because canonical interpretation "leads to misconception of the text," Granet proposed to set it aside and to treat the poems as folk songs. He believed that if one remembers the folk origin of the odes, "it is possible to go beyond the simple literary explanation, and beyond the symbolic interpretation, *to discover the original meaning of the odes*."[14] Granet did not seem to realize that his methodology of reading, like that of the canonical interpretation, offers but another subject position to read the poems. For all its strength and fascination, his reading method is no more capable of uncovering the original meanings of the odes than the traditional scholarship because the original intentions are beyond anyone's efforts to recover.

The motivation to get at the original meanings of the poems has given rise to the widely divergent commentaries, annotations, and interpretations. A modern scholar rightly points out: "Some proclaimed themselves as having obtained the original heart of the poets; their every word is to the point. Some have entitled their books as *zhengyi* (correct meaning), *benyi* (original intention), *tonglun* (comprehensive discussions), *bianwang* (recongnizing absurdities). They all believe: 'Everyone else is wrong; only I am correct.' . . . As a result, the *Shijing* has been the subject of a long debate lasting several thousand years. There has been so far no definitive interpretation of it."[15]

Gu Jiegang, after criticizing the ancient *Shijing* exegetes for making a mess of the book, raises one thought-provoking question: "While only a few engaged themselves in making the mess, why did most scholars fail to rise to oppose them? Instead, why did the majority destroy their own rational faculty and blindly follow those few?" He provides an answer: all scholars lacked the necessary historical knowledge for studying the *Shijing* and therefore all ended up following Mao-Zheng's far-fetched interpretations.[16] Like Granet, Gu Jiegang believed that if one had adequate historical knowledge, he could get at the original meanings of the poems. His position is based on another ideological assumption: if one knows what happened in history, he would know the truth. It never dawned on him, great scholar that he was, that the poetry as language could provoke readers to infinite interpretations. His position is unsatisfactory because it largely ignores the fact that most of the *Shijing* poems are literary texts, not historical documents. Thus, even with adequate historical background knowledge, scholars have so far failed to answer another question: Why were those few classicists able to distort the *Shijing*? Indeed, what is there in the *Shijing* that enables them to interpret these poems according to their wishes? This question forces us to examine the internal mechanism of representation which enabled scholars over history to read the poems in accordance with their beliefs and purposes.

Two Paradigms: One Orientation

An overview of *Shjing* hermeneutics through history tells us that in spite of the dazzling variety of interpretations, they can be grouped under two large categories which represent two basic paradigms of reading. The first paradigm holds the belief that the *Shijing* poems were reflections of a bygone age and hence it tends to read the poems as moral and political expressions. The second paradigm holds the belief that the *Shijing* poems were poetic expressions of individuals in a bygone age and hence it tends to read the poems as personal vehicles of self-expression. Traditional exegetes before modern times generally worked within the confines of the first paradigm. Ouyang Xiu, Zhu Xi, Yan Can 嚴粲 (fl. 1248), Yao Jiheng, Cui Shu, and Fang Yurun did make some excursions into the second paradigm, but no sooner had they ventured out of the first paradigm than they hastily withdrew back into it. The real paradigm shift in reading only came after the May Fourth movement. When modern scholars subjected all historical documents of high antiquity to a relentless scrutiny and cast an enormous doubt on various aspects of ancient history, it was natural that they would reject the first paradigm and engage in readings in the light of the second paradigm. Although traditional and modern scholars worked with different paradigms, they have shared a common ground: the poems were originally created with a purpose which, though deeply buried under layers and layers of historical debris, can somehow be recovered. Modern exegetes have evinced varying degrees of openness in their readings, but on the whole, they do not seem to subscribe to the notion that a literary text is endowed by its textuality with an openness that makes different and divergent readings possible; nor do they seem to realize that the *Shijing* poems, due to their special historical, linguistic, and aesthetic conditions, are endowed with an openness greater than poetry produced in "normal" circumstances. By "normal," I mean that the author, pretextual intention, and historical context are known. Because of the belief in the possiblity of recovering original intentions, the two paradigms were built on the same epistemological base and oriented toward the same goal—the recovering of the lost authorial intentions.

Here I will analyze a modern scholars' criticism of "Guanju 關雎" to show that modern readings are trapped by the same blindness (a belief in the recoverability of original intentions) as those of traditional scholars. Lan Jusun 藍菊蓀, in his reading of "Guanju," argues against Chen Zizhan's 陳子展 view that it is a poem which sings of a love story between a man and a woman of the upper class. In his contention, he demonstrates admirable literary sensibility in the annotation of the key words *junzi* 君子 and *shunü* 淑女: "The implications of a word in the *Shijing* must be determined by examining the circumstances under which it is used. They cannot remain permanently stable." He goes on to say: "The word 'junzi' is generally a common address for the aristocracy and for negative characters, but it can also be used as a respectful address for the laboring people and for positive characters." After some thoughtful reasoning, he draws his conclusion on the theme of the poem, which is "not one singing praises of a successful love affair between a man and a woman from the upper social class. On the contrary, it is a poem eulogizing the successful love of the lower class. Subjectively, I feel that to understand the poem in this direction is relatively more fitting for the facts of that time."[17]

What is problematic is his claim that his reading is more valid because it corresponds with the pristine conditions under which the poem was first composed. To his claim, I would raise the question. How do you know your reading fits the facts of a bygone era? How can you ascertain that the theme is derived from facts at the time of the poem's composition? Chen Zizhan, whose reading was criticized by Lan Jusun, voices an opinion that manifests some measure of awareness of the blindness of most *Shijing* scholars: "In my opinion, at present, even among *Shijing* 'experts,' no one would have the audacity to say for sure that he is unlikely to be subjected to the ridicule leveled at the blind man in the legend, who attempts to pass judgment on an inscribed horizontal board [before it is even hung]."[18]

I venture to argue that the *Shijing* commentators and critics, from Mao Heng and Zheng Xuan through Zhu Xi, Yao Jiheng, and Fang Yurun, to Gu Jiegang, Wen Yiduo 聞一多, and Qu Wanli 屈萬里, all have their insight and blindness. Each of them has shown some fascinating insight through their commentaries, annotations, and interpretations. However, all of them have shared one common blindness—that is, they all think that each of the *Shijing* poems has a pristine meaning emanating from the original intentions of the poet. All of them are blind to the textual conditions of the poems, which are composed in indeterminate poetic language and with open structuring principles. In this chapter, I want to demonstrate that any attempt to seek the original intention or meaning of the poets is an illusory act because the *Shijing* is a collection of poems most of which have unknown and unknowable origins.

Indeterminate Subject Position

In my analysis of "Guanju" in the previous chapter, I have located a variety of factors contributing to the poem's openness. Representative as the poem may be, it does not exhaust all the possible open strategies. In some other *Guofeng* poems, we may find open strategies of a different kind. Poem 129, "Jianjia 蒹葭," may be considered the first *menglong shi* 朦朧詩 (opaque poem) in Chinese history. Niu Yunzhen 牛運震 (1706–58) of the Qing characterized it as "the first mysterious poem in the *Guofeng* section."[19] Generally speaking, the consensus is that this is a poem about a search. In this sense, it shares the same theme or topos as "Guanju." But its difference from "Guanju" is significant. In reading "Guanju," one will gradually develop a subject position with which to view it as the poem unfolds. One reads of falling in love first, then the tormented mental state in love, then courtship, and finally wedding (real or imaginary). In "Jianjia," however, there is no clear subject position even after one finishes reading the whole poem. What one gets at the end of the poem is a search. As for the object of search, it is anybody's guess. There are three extant views. (1) The object of search is a moral principle. Most Confucian commentators implicitly held this view. Lü Zuqian explicitly stated: "The so-called 'someone' is the same as saying 'this so-called principle.' It refers to the Rites of the Zhou."[20] (2) The object of search is a virtuous person, or a recluse. Feng Fang, Yao Jiheng, Hao Yixing, Fang Yurun, and other scholars hold this view. (3) The object of the search is a love(r). Modern scholars tend to adopt this view. I wish to add a fourth category. The object of search may be a metaphysical object, desire, self, being, the Way, or whatever one names his personal quest. The existent interpretations are only a few readings out of an unknown number of possible readings. The poem is so worded that the object of the search is completely veiled in a cloud of mystery. We are faced with a long series of unanswered and unanswerable questions. Is it a person or an object, or a moral principle, or a hallucinatory feeling? If it is a moral principle, is it loyalty or integrity or propriety? If it is an idea, is it a search for the meaning of life or death, or the original being, or simply the unattainability of desire? If it is a hallucination, is it the effect brought about by alcohol, or drugs, or religious fervor? If it is a person, is it a person of virtue or an object of love? If it is a love object, is it an object of affection or an object of sexual desire? If it is an object of affection, is it a parent or a child, or a sibling, or a friend, or a master? If it is an object of sexual love, is it a male or a female? If it is a male, is it a husband or a lover? If it is a husband/lover, is it someone who is dead or a lover who jilts the poet? If it is a female, is it a girl secluded in a boudoir, or a lost wife who is dead, symbolically separated by the barriers between humans and ghosts, or a mistress under the strict control of her husband, or a fairy/goddess separated from the poet by the barriers between mortals and immortals, or simply someone who does not even know she is being loved by another? If it is love in the common sense, is it an impossible love separated by personal incompatibility, social barriers, family feuds, or whatever? In fact, the poem is so mysteriously contrived that we do not know for certain whether the object of search is a male or female, not to mention his/her identity. From this point of view, the poem is entirely open. The series of questions I have raised could be used as clues or guidelines for interesting readings. With some ingenuity, one can follow each of the suggested clues and come up with an interesting reading. As another experimental reading, I wish to read the poem as a search for the meaning of life.

Thick grow the reed leaves; 蒹葭蒼蒼，
Their white dew turns to frost. 白露為霜。
That so-called someone 所謂伊人，
Must be somewhere along this stream. 在水一方。
I went up the river to look for him/her, 溯洄從之，
But the way was difficult and long. 道阻且長。
I went down the stream to look for him/her, 溯游從之，
He/she seems to be in the mid-water. 宛在水中央。

Luxuriant grow the reed leaves; 蒹葭淒淒，
Their white dew is not yet dry. 白露未晞。
That so-called someone 所謂伊人，
Is at the water's side. 在水之湄。
Upstream I sought him/her, 溯洄從之，
But the way is hard and steep. 道阻且躋。
Downstream I sought him/her, 溯游從之，
He/she seems to be at the islet in the water. 宛在水中坻。

Splendid grow the reed leaves, 蒹葭採採，
Their white dew ceaselessly falls. 白露未已。
That so-called someone 所謂伊人，
Is at the water's edge. 在水之涘。
Upstream I sought him/her, 溯洄從之，
But the way is hard and tortuous. 道阻且右。
Downstream I sought him/her, 溯游從之，
He/she seems to be on the shoals of the water. 宛在水中沚。[21]

The first two lines give us a rough idea of the season. Zhu Xi dated the poem as one composed in autumn.[22] There is certainly textual evidence to support his dating. When the reeds are in shape and have not yet begun to wither, it must be autumn. The little detail that the dew has turned to frost implies that it is late autumn. In ancient China, autumn was a time of harvest as well as a time of sentimental emotions: sorrow, moodiness, and contemplation. In this poem, the image of autumn may cut both ways. It may be associated with the poet's review of his life and his mood of contemplation. Here the autumn may also have a metaphorical meaning. It may refer to the poet's late mid-life. The dew, an image of life-giving force, turns into frost, the image of white hair, chilliness, feelings of bleak desolation. The seasonal change made the poet sentimental and contemplative: What have I done in my life? or What is the true meaning of life? These questions start him on a search: "That so-called someone / Must be somewhere along this stream of water." What does the stream stand for? It is undecidable, but within my scheme of reading, it stands for time, the river of time.

To use flowing water as a metaphor for elapsing time is a practice that occurs across cultures. In the *Analects of Confucius*, the sage was thus quoted: "Standing on the bank of a stream, the Master said: 'That which passes is like the flowing water which never stops, night or day.'"[23] Like Confucius, the poet might stand beside a stream, struck by the resemblance of flowing water to elapsing time. The meaning of life, it might seem to him, must lie somewhere in the passing of one's life in particular and the elapse of time in general. "I went up the river to look for it, / But the way was difficult and long." Time passes from the past through the present to the future. He went against the current of the river—that is, going back into the past. The past has no beginning, stretching beyond the dawn of life into human unconsciousness. "I went down the stream to look for it, / It seems to be in the mid-water." He went along the current of flowing time into the future. The meaning of life seems to lie in the future, but not quite. The word *wan* (seems) indicates that it is not the real meaning of life.

The poet continued his search. The second and the third stanzas are almost a repetition of the first stanza with some variations. The repetition may point to the intensity of the search. Three stanzas represent three attempts at a search into the passing of time. Three really means numerous. The three stanzas may be construed as representing three searches in three different periods of the poet's life: youth, mid-life, late mid-life and early old age. The three periods were put in reverse order— old age first, mid-life second, and youth last. The subtle changes in the conditions of the "reeds" and "dew" may be cited to support this sequential order. The three reiterative words, *cangcang* 蒼蒼, *qiqi* 淒淒, and *caicai* 採採, all describe the reed's condition of growth. The Mao Commentary glossed *cangcang* as "luxuriant"[24] and used this meaning to gloss the other two. Kong Yingda and other traditional commentators all agreed with Mao. Modern scholars also accept this glossing. They only concretize the meaning. Wen Yiduo annotates: "All three words describe fresh and bright color."[25] Other modern scholars annotate the three words as "green or dark green." I have some doubt about the indiscriminate glossing, because it does not make much sense. I, therefore, offer a slightly different glossing.

Though the three words may denote more or less the same condition of growth, there may be degrees of difference. Xu Shen's *Shuowen* defines *cangcang* as "the color of all vegetation."[26] He did not specify what color. *Cangcang* generally refers to the color green, but it also denotes the color of "white gray" as one describes the color of an old man's hair. *Qiqi*, according to the *Ciyuan*, means "the look of rising clouds."[27] *Cai* 採 is often an equivalent of *cai* 彩, which means "bright." Although Zhu Xi agreed with

Mao, Zheng, Kong, and other scholars, he did touch on an aspect that often escapes our notice. In his dating of the poem he said, "The reed had not yet withered; the dew had just started to turn to frost."[28] The reed had not yet withered but it was about to wither, in the same way the poet was not quite old but was about to step into his old age. While we cannot distinguish the nuances of the three words by examining them alone, we can locate their nuance in the context of the poem, and especially through their adjacent and related words, "the white dew turns to frost," "the white dew is not yet dry," "the white dew still falls." The "dew" is usually a word associated with freshness and freshening agents, energy and energizing agents, and life-giving qualities. In the context of the poem, it may be an image related to the poet's life energy. Its changing conditions may obliquely refer to the poet's different stages in life. That the dew falls profusely may indicate that the poet's life energy was at its best, thus referring to his youth; that the dew is not yet dry may refer to his middle life; that the dew turns to frost may refer to his being at the threshold of old age.

Thus, the changing conditions of the "reeds" and "dew" may suggest that the three stanzas represent three searches in the reverse order of the poet's life span. The variations "in mid-water," "at the water's side," and "at the water's edge" all suggest that the object of search—that is, the meaning of life—is uncertain and ever changing. The third group of variations, "it seems as though in the mid-water," "it was as though on an islet in mid-water," and "it was as though on the shoal," may point to the poet's changing perception of his goal during his life span. In his youth, he perhaps thought that the meaning of life was easy to obtain, just like a trip to the beach. In his middle life, he became less optimistic. The goal of his search retreated onto the islet in the middle of the water, and hence was less accessible. In his late mid-life and early old age, it dawned on him that the meaning of life was located nowhere but in the process of living one's life: just as the goal of the search was located right in the middle of the water, the flowing river of time. My reading shows a synchronic search within a diachronic search: a contemplation of one's own life against the backdrop of life in general, in the endless stream of time that has no beginning and no ending. A conclusion from my reading would be that the meaning of life is inaccessible; the older and more experienced one becomes, the more strongly one feels its inaccessibility. If I wish, I can read the poem as a search for one's being, second self, lost self, or even the Way. Ji Ben 季本 (1485–1563) offered an interesting reading of the poem in this vein.[29]

From Allegory to Open Readings

My study of *Shijing* hermeneutics not only problematizes the accepted paradigms of reading but also highlights the blindness of the exegetes, which proves paradoxically to be their valuable insight into reading. In their groping for the pristine meanings of the *Shijing* poems, the exegetes were completely free from the formalist conception of the literary text as a free-standing, self-contained, autotelic enclosure. In a closed conception of the text, one does not need to go outside it to decode the meanings. He/she can bracket all that is outside the text—biography, history, politics, culture, author, reader, and so on—and concentrate on the text alone. But my study of the chosen poems and their exegeses show that if one does not go outside the text, the poems would just be mysterious puzzles. The "Reeds" is an epitome of this condition. When one connects the poem with associations warranted by the poem, it begins to open itself up, yielding different interpretations. The "Reeds" is like a cake of Chinese bean curd. It is bland, having almost no taste, but it will take on different flavors when different ingredients are added. It is a supreme example of a text of literary openness.

In their studies of the critical methodology of Confucian exegetes, modern scholars, Western scholars in particular, believed that they were using an allegorical or symbolic mode of reading. James Legge and Herbert Giles, who were the first Western scholars to introduce the *Shijing* to the West, pointed out this mode of reading without actually using the word "allegorical."[30] Granet may have been the first to use the word to describe the canonical interpretation.[31] Since then, allegorical reading has become the term to describe the traditional mode of reading and the word "allegory" has been employed by quite a few scholars including Arthur Waley and C. H. Wang.[32] Recently the word "allegory" has given rise to interesting discussions in the field of Chinese poetics. It became the center of contention in the works of Andrew Plaks,[33] Pauline Yu,[34] Stephen Owen,[35] Zhang Longxi,[36] and Haun Saussy. What exactly does "allegorical interpretation" mean in the context of *Shijing* hermeneutics? "One meaning of the use of 'allegorical' to describe the old school of exegesis," Saussy summarizes for us, "is simply to announce this fact: more than do 'symbolic' or 'moral,' the word stresses the mismatch of text and commentary."[37] Pauline Yu strongly argues against viewing the Confucian mode of reading as allegorical on the ground that "the traditional commentators read the poems in the *Classic of Poetry* not as fictional works composed ad hoc to create or correspond to some historical reality or philosophical truth, but as literal vignettes drawn from that reality. They are not making the poems refer to something fundamentally other—belonging to another plane of existence—than what they say, but are revealing them to be specifically referential." For this reason, she proposes to call the traditional mode of reading "contextualization" rather than "allegorization."[38]

"Contextualization" is another way to describe the hermeneutic scramble to jockey for subject positions in search of origins, but as Saussy points out it is "potentially misleading."[39] To be fair to Pauline Yu, her notion of context is an asserted context by the critic/commentator even though she does not dwell on this point. What is potentially misleading is that contextualization seems to suggest that whatever the commentators say it is true, it must be the case. I would add some prefixes to give the term a fine-tuning. My discussion above has shown that most of the *Shijing* poems do not have a context, for the original context of the poems was long lost, never to be recovered. The indeterminate extratextual and introtextual conditions of the *Shijing* that I have elaborated constitute an open context within which exegetes have enough room to construct as many new contexts as they have the ingenuity to accommodate their political views, moral values, and personal predilections. In a way, all exegetes throughout history, ancient and modern, have adopted the same reading mode in their approaches to the poems. All were engaged in earnest efforts to contextualize the poems. But because of the irrecoverably lost context, their effort at contextualization amounts to nothing less than supplying new contexts for the poems. Thus, their efforts are "recontextualization," which involves a good deal of artificial ingenuity and creative invention. In this sense, all *Shijing* critics are inventors of the contexts within which the poems were supposed to have been composed. As inventors of contexts, the exegeses of the commentators and critics differ from each other only in degree but not in kind. Because of the open context of the *Shijing* poems, all interpretations are also efforts at "pseudocontextualization," and all results of these efforts are only approximations and near misses.

How can we have a fair assessment of traditional *Shijing* hermeneutics as a whole? Modern scholars of the Gushibian school have almost completely rejected the traditional exegeses. The negative images these scholars have used to describe them—"a heap of rotten account books," "wild grass that has buried the monument," and "layers upon layers of rubble"—suggest that they are considered as something having no intrinsic value. Their evaluation has much legitimate ground but is not entirely fair, especially when one looks at the traditional commentaries from the viewpoint of literary studies. One of the accusations modern scholars have leveled at the traditional exegeses is that traditional exegetes, with few exceptions, treated the poems in the *Shijing* as expressions of political and moral allegories and almost completely ignored the original features of them as literature. This accusation is certainly legitimate. However, if we accept the poems in the *Shijing* as literary texts, we are compelled to give traditional *Shijing* hermeneutics, including the most distorted and far-fetched commentaries and annotations, a place in the history of *Shijing* studies. My argument is based on this: from the viewpoint of reading literature, the original intentions or meanings of the poems have vanished into oblivion with the passing of their authors. The death of the poets makes it impossible to recover the original intentions of the poems. It is an illusion to think one can somehow reconstruct the context within which the poems were written and thereby recover the pristine meanings of the poems. Every reading is a unique reading because every reader will inevitably bring his/her own background to bear on the poem, thus adding elements alien to the poem. In this sense, all readings, traditional or modern, are equal. For example, Hu Shi adopts a radical stance toward the traditional commentaries. But his reading of some *Shijing* poems manifests the same kind of distortion and misreading. His interpretation of "Getan 葛覃" reads: "It describes a scene in which female workers, having been granted a leave, were eager to return home." His interpretation of the poem "Xiaoxing 小星" borders on a joke: "The poem is the most ancient record of the life of a prostitute."[40] In terms of reader response criticism, we cannot say that Hu Shi's reading is wrong, but we must admit that his reading is by no means superior to Mao Heng's commentary on or Zheng Xuan's annotation of the same poems. In terms of contemporary theories of reading, modern readings differ from traditional exegeses only in degree, not in kind. For they are near misses too. The hermeneutic tradition initiated and guided by the Great Preface and the Mao Commentary is not entirely wrong, for it only represents the time-honored effort to supply contexts; what is wrong is its insistence that it provides the only correct subject position.

Given the special conditions of the *Shijing*, it is impossible to come up with a single "correct" reading of a *Shijing* poem. By "correct," I mean that a reader's interpretation completely matches the original intentions of the author. There may be many "correct" readings. For this reason, we need to make a paradigm shift in *Shijing* hermeneutics and adopt a new mode of exegesis, which I wish to call "an open paradigm of reading." My use of "open" may give the impression that there is no point in making distinctions between interpretations. Just as there are possible and impossible contexts for the poems, so there are possible and impossible interpretations. Impossible interpretations result from readings which, purely reader centered, disregard textual constraints and Aristotle's "law of probability."[41] Possible interpretations are the results of readings that work within the hermeneutic space circumscribed by the text. Possible interpretations are certainly superior to impossible interpretations. The status of possible and impossible readings is not permanent. As scholarship advances, a possible reading may become impossible while an impossible reading may become possible. For a hypothetical example, in my discussion of poem 131, if later scholars prove that the reconstructed sound of "mulberry" in high antiquity does not have any trace of similairity to *sang*, then, my reading of the stanza as alluding to "death," "die young," and "broken-hearted" should be ruled out. For an opposite case, the traditional interpretation of poem 8 as one alluding to pregnancy and childbirth seems an unlikely reading. Zheng Qiao dismissed it as a pedantic quirk: "'Fuyi' is believed to be a poem about a woman's fond desire for children. Not a shred of evidence in the poem supports this idea."[42] Zhou Fu 周孚 (1135–77) who wrote a rebuttal of Zheng Qiao's *Shi bianwang* defended the traditional interpretation by quoting the *Erya*'s 爾雅 description of the plant as a herb conducive to birth.[43] Gu Jiegang in his postface to Zhou Fu's book considers Zheng Qiao's dismissal as forceful and convincing.[44] That the traditional reading is an impossible one seemed established, but Wen Yiduo's evidential research turns the impossible into a possible reading.

All possible readings, be they ancient or modern, are equal because they fall within the hermeneutic space of the text. But to vary George Orwell's famous saying, I may say that some readings are "more equal" than others. There are strong readings and weak readings, interesting readings and dull readings. The extent to which a reading is strong and interesting is determined not by subjective response, but by a number of factors. A strong interpretation comes from a fresh, interesting, and innovative reading that not only takes advantage of the open context and open textuality of a given poem but also takes into account its signifying elements and textual evidence. "The validity of interpretation," as Zhang Longxi rightly points out, "is therefore not absolute but temporary and contingent, and the best interpretation is the one that accounts for the most elements in the process of reading, offers the most coherent explanation of the text, and simply makes the best sense of the literary work as a whole."[45]

A Writing Model of Intertextual Dissemination

In my study of the controversy between the Pro-Preface school and Anti-Preface school in *Shijing* hermeneutic tradition, I only made a cursory mention of the "Great Preface" to the *Shijing* (Shi daxu 詩大序) and did not examine its concerns in relation to *Shijing* hermeneutics. I deliberately deferred a discussion of it because, as a foundational text in Chinese literary thought, the Great Preface has a significance not only for the

Shijing poems in particular but also for Chinese poetry and poetics in general. Although it consists of only a few hundred words, it is the cornerstone for Chinese literary criticism and raises a number of seminal concerns in Chinese literary theory. As Stephen Owen aptly puts it, it "was the most authoritative statement on the nature and function of poetry in traditional China."[46] Because of its significance, I have reserved it for the construction of a paradigm of reading and writing. As the first treatise exclusively devoted to poetics in China, the Preface has had adequate appraisal of its significance over history. In the past two millennia, however, scholarly appraisal has been confined to two related aspects. One aspect deals with its function as a piece of literary criticism. In this respect, it has been viewed as a synthesis of the transmitted interpretations about the *Book of Songs* up to the Han times.[47] The other aspect centers on its significance as a piece of literary theory. On this theoretical level, it has been regarded as the first sustained inquiry into the nature and function of poetry in early China. Both aspects are concerned with the content of the discourse. So far, practically no one has paid any attention to the implied significance of its formal presentation.

In fact, its formal presentation has been lowly valued. Due to the undervaluation, the Preface has been misunderstood and even charged with a number of faults. One common fault attributed to the Preface is its alleged loose structure. Because of this fault, scholars feel that they are entitled to rearrange the sections of the Preface according to their understanding and reassign the divisions to different places of the *Book of Songs*. In history, the most drastic rearrangement was carried out by Zhu Xi (1130–1200), the Confucian synthesizer of the Song dynasty. He dismantled the whole piece and reassigned the opening and ending sections as a "minor preface" to "Guanju or the Osprey," the first poem of the *Book of Songs*.[48] In a recent study, Steven Van Zoeren holds an even less favorable view of the structuring principle of the Preface: "Characterized by a choppy and allusive argument that moves abruptly from one subject to another and punctuated by connectives at precisely those points where connections seem weakest, this is a text that may frustrate even a sympathetic reader."[49] Like other scholars, he recognizes the Preface as a "composite, layered text structured according to a rhetoric of exegesis," but fails to appreciate its internal unity and coherence and even considers it to be characterized by a "confusion" due to "textual corruption."

I venture to suggest that the Great Preface is a well-conceived and coherently argued treatise on poetry. Moreover, its way of presentation in relation to its content contains an implicit statement on a paradigm of reading and writing, which may perhaps be appropriately called "intertextual dissemination." This paradigm of reading not only set the pattern for reading the *Book of Songs* but also influenced the hermeneutic development of the Chinese tradition. In this section, I do not attempt to tackle the complex issue of how the paradigm of reading influenced exegesis of other canonical works. I will limit my discussion to an exploration of how the Preface is constructed on an overarching structure and how it implicitly advances a paradigm of openness, which anticipated facets of contemporary theories of reading and writing.

On its surface level, the Great Preface doubtless gives the impression of haphazard looseness. The writer, whoever that might be, seemed to have embarked on a joy ride and followed whatever direction that he happened to have chosen. One explanation for this phenomenon is that it has been stipulated by the fact that he had to synthesize the existent materials related to his subject and as the materials are so diverse, he was compelled to string them loosely together. I, however, suggest that the writer had a controlling idea and a deliberate design in mind, and after thoroughly digesting the existent materials, he constructed his discourse in accordance with that controlling idea and design. The controlling idea is political and moral criticism and the design of formal presentation is the time-honored approach of *xungu* 訓詁, a complex philological approach to ancient Chinese texts. While *xungu* was originally a way of exegesis, the writer of the Great Preface turned it into a way of composition as well as interpretation.

Nowadays, both in China and in the West, the philological approach to literature has somehow become an old-fashioned scholarship. I, however, argue that the philological approach is not as far removed from postmodern approaches as some people think. As a time-honored branch of learning, the Chinese philological approaches to texts share with modern approaches to literature some fundamental similarities. The complexity of this scholarship is far beyond my ability to give it an adequate characterization.[50] Here I only want to make a modest attempt to locate some common ground between Chinese philological approaches and contemporary critical paradigms. The most noticeable point of contact between Chinese philology and modern approaches to literary study is the attention paid to the written conditions of a literary text: the material aspects that have gone into the making of discourse. In Chinese philology, attention is directed to the sound, shape, sense, and constitutional principles of a discourse. In Chinese philology, there are some fundamental principles of exegesis. Two of them are: "to seek meaning through the shape of a word" and "to seek meanings through the sound of a word."[51] As I have demonstrated in the study of the *Zhouyi* and *Shijing* hermeneutics, the two fundamental principles of philological scholarship are responsible for the generation of different and conflicting readings. In the composition of the

Great Preface, the author turned the two fundamental principles into the warp and woof that are used to weave a theoretical text, thereby creating a unique writing principle that shares some affinity with modernist and postmodern notions on the materiality of the sign. In terms of postmodern textual studies, the materiality of discourse is called textuality, a term suggesting that a text is a material entity made of words rather than abstract concepts. I venture to suggest that the widely used techniques in Chinese philology are, in some ways, compatible with the postmodern idea of textual study. What distinguishes textuality from philology is that the former openly acknowledges the tendency of language to produce not a simple reference to the world outside language but a multiplicity of potentially different, conflicting, and even opposite signifying flux in the process of writing and reading. So conceived, postmodern textual study argues against representational and interpretive closure and rejects the conception of the text as an autonomous and autotelic entity with a definite original intention.

In another significant way, Chinese philology is comparable to intertextual study. Julia Kristeva conceives of the text as a network of sign systems implicated in other systems of signifying practices. She describes intertexuality as a "permutation of texts" within the semiotic practice of textual stratification and as a typology of arranging different textual layers within historical and social texts.[52] In a way, the Great Preface is precisely composed with such a notion. In the philological approach to literature, a traditional scholar would concentrate on finding earlier occurrences and original sources (*loci classici*) of textual elements and would then come up with an interpretation of the text on the basis of this source study. This shares a common ground with a restricted strand of intertextuality, which focuses on the relations between several texts. However, the philological style of textual study often involves little more than influence tracing, a tendency intertextuality seeks to displace. Kristeva, therefore, prefers the term "transposition" to "intertextuality" because "the passage from one signifying system to another demands a new articulation of the thetic— of enunciative and denotative positionality."[53] Moreover, an obsessive concern with original sources and allusions seldom asks how a source is used or modified. Hence, the philological approach often misses textual effects of irony, parody, and distortion in its interpretation. What is most alien to philological-style textual study is the notion of unlimited semiosis or dissemination, the concept of the text as tissue, "hyphology" or a spider's weaving,[54] and deconstruction or the notion of the necessary intertextuality of all discourse because each text is an interweaving or "textile of signifiers" whose signifieds are by definition intertextually determined by other discourses.[55]

Having stated some similarities and differences between Chinese philology and postmodern textual study, I have found in the philological approach to literature a most fascinating phenomenon: while in theory it would not accept intertextuality and deconstruction, much less conceive of these concepts, it, in actual practice, transcends its own limitations and arrives at some insight that is postmodern in nature. The major exegetical traditions of Chinese literature—such as *Zhouyi* hermeneutics, *Shijing* hermeneutics, *Jin Ping Mei* scholarship, and *Hongloumeng* scholarship— abound in this kind of blind or unacknowledged insight. In many cases, such insights are self-consciously acknowledged. In the remaining space of this section, I will conduct a rereading to show how the Chinese insight has its seminal form in the Preface and how it exemplifies a strand of critical thought that can be turned into a paradigm of reading and writing. To tease out this paradigm, I need to analyze the entire Preface in detail. Let me start with the first paragraph:

> "Guanju" is about the virtue of the queen consort; it is the beginning of the *Feng* (airs/suasion). It is the means by which all under heaven are influenced (swayed) and the relations between husband and wife are properly regulated. It is, therefore, sung at the gatherings of common folks as well as feudal lords. *Feng* means wind (airs/suasion) and teaching. Wind (suasion) is the means to sway [people]. Teaching is the means to transform [people].[56]

"The Preface of Mao" is built on a structuring principle that may be called intertextual dissemination. It starts with a summary of an alleged theme in "Guanju," the first poem of the *Shijing*. Since "Guanju" is also the first poem of the "Feng 風" section, the Preface refers to it as "the beginning of Feng." The word *Feng* becomes a multivalent word in immediate discursive development: "it is that which influences (feng) all under heaven so as to make correct husband-wife relations." Now *feng* is no longer a noun but becomes a verb which means "to sway" or "to influence." With this connotation, the word intersects with Confucius's words: "The virtue of a gentleman is that of wind; the virtue of a small man is that of grass. When a wind passes over grass, it would bend the grass without fail."[57] The metaphor of grass swaying under the force of a wind vividly imparts the educational power of moral virtue. From this intertextual source, the Preface defines *feng* as "influence 風也" and "teaching 教也." The definition is a repetition of the same word, *feng*, which represents two facets of meanings: one literal, one metaphorical. The literal meaning involves the natural power of natural wind; the metaphorical meaning refers to the moral power of virtue: "the wind is to sway grass; teaching is to transform people." The second paragraph shifts from the analysis of a poem to a consideration of its generic source:

> Poetry is where the intent of the mind goes. Lodged in the heart it is intent; expressed in words, it is poetry. When an emotion moves within one's heart, it will take its form in words. If words are inadequate to express it, one will sigh over it. If sighing is not adequate, he will express it in a song. If a song is still not adequate, he will dance it by moving his hands and tap it out by stamping his feet.

"Guanju," which stands for the "Feng" section, in turn stands for the *Shijing* via a synecdochic extension. Structurally, it is natural to enter upon a discussion of *shi* 詩 in the second paragraph. Here, *shi* is also a double word. It refers to both the *Shijing* in particular and to *shi* (poetry) in general. The definition of *shi* is a tautology: "Poetry is where the heart/mind goes 詩言志." Some scholars have argued through philological study that *shi* 詩 and *zhi* 志 are cognate with each other.[58] The Preface confirms their symbiotic relation by pointing out that "lodged in the heart it is intention; uttered in words it becomes poetry." This statement links intertextually with a previous source about the origin of poetry, "Shundian 舜典" in the *Shangshu* 尚書: "Poetry expresses one's inspiration/ambition; songs chant the words; tunes depend on chanting; rhythm harmonizes tunes."[59] The Preface probes further into the source of poetry and finds it to be *qing* (or emotions): "Emotions move in the heart and take form in utterances." This probing enlarges the scope of *zhi* and anticipates a new view of poetry by Lu Ji 陸機 (261–303): "Poetry follows from emotions and is sensuously intricate."[60] The rest of the second paragraph deals with emotions, their transformations through different media, words, voices, and gestures. Here, we have a case that is not just an intertextual echoing of a previous statement; in fact, it is a reworking of two passages from the *Liji* 禮記.[61] The analysis of the source of poetry, "emotion," effects a natural transition to the third paragraph:

> Emotions are expressed in sounds. When the sounds form a pattern, they are called a tune. The tunes of a well-ordered society are peaceful and joyful; its government is harmonious. The tunes of a chaotic society are resentful and angry; its government is perverse. The tunes of a conquered state are sorrowful and nostalgic; its people are miserable. Thus, nothing comes close to poetry in correctly assessing gains and losses, moving heaven and earth, and touching ghosts and spirits. Kings of ancient times used it to regulate relations between husband and wife, complete filial piety and respect, perfect human relations, beautify moral education, and change mores and customs.

The third paragraph continues with the discussion of *qing* and the transformations, their power and consequences. It cites different functions to prove that *shi* is the supreme form of persuasive power. Again, the statement reworks previous sources and finds echoes in the *Liji* 禮記[62] and in Xun Zi's 荀子 (*c.* 300–230 BC) "Discourse on Music."[63] But the originality of the paragraph is not to be underestimated. First, it makes an effortless transition from previous sources on music to a statement of the function of poetry. Second, it employs a powerful rhetoric to make a moral and utilitarian view of poetry sound natural. Then the focus returns to the examination of poetry:

> Poetry has six forms: the first is called *Feng*; the second is called *Fu*; the third is called *Bi*; the fourth is called *Xing*; the fifth is called *Ya*; and the sixth is called *Song*. Those above (in power) use poetry to transform those below; those below use it to indirectly criticize those above. Criticism is governed by *wen* (patterns) and remonstrance is made obliquely. He who criticizes [in this way] incurs no culpability, but his [oblique] criticism is enough to warn the listener. For this reason, a form of poetry is called *Feng* (airs/remonstrance).

The examination of *Shi*'s definition and function leads to an examination of its manifested forms and modes of representation in the fourth paragraph: *Shi* has six categories of *yi* (meanings): *feng, fu, bi, xing, ya,* and *song*. The notion of six *yi* again touches upon an intertextual relation as it comes from the *Zhouli*: "The Grand Master . . . teaches six forms of *shi: feng, fu, bi, xing, ya,* and *song*."[64] While the *Zhouli* lists six kinds of poetry, the Great Preface proposes six categories of meanings. The change from *liushi* to *liuyi* signifies the author's awareness that the six terms not only refer to six kinds of poetry but also represent different forms of classification. Though the Preface does not classify the six terms into two distinctive groups in terms of their function, it does imply a classification to be more clearly made by Kong Yingda in his *Maoshi zhengyi*.[65] Of the six terms, *feng, ya,* and *song* deal with the three sections of the *Shijing; fu, bi,* and *xing* are three modes of representation. When we examine the passage closely, we are bound to find that the demarcation is not as neatly drawn as Kong Yingda described. Feng certainly matches the section of "Guofeng" or "Airs of the States," but in the Preface, it does not exclusively refer to the airs of the states. In fact, the writer was still preoccupied with the word play of *feng* to make it cut both ways. The fourth paragraph continues to play upon the word *feng* 風. "The people high up use the wind to transform people down below; the people down below use the wind to satirize people high up." There appears a new meaning of *feng*, based on punning or homophone, which is "諷 criticize indirectly."

By the time the kingly way decayed, rites and propriety were abandoned, moral education of the government lost, the government of the state altered, and the customs of the family changed, mutated *Feng* and *Ya* arose. [Through them,] the scribe of a state saw clearly the traces of success and failure. He lamented the decay of human relations, bemoaned the cruelty of punishments and government, sang of what he had felt in his heart so as to persuade those above. He was able to understand the cause of changes and longed for the old customs. Mutated airs, therefore, started from emotions but did not go beyond the bounds of rites and propriety. It is people's natural propensity to start composing mutated airs; it is because of the beneficent influence of former kings that the airs stayed within bounds of rites and propriety.

The decline of government and morality causes the *Feng* to change its original function. Hence there appear "mutated airs 變風." "Those above (in power) use poetry to transform those below; those below use it to indirectly criticize those above. Criticism is governed by *wen* (patterns) and remonstrance is made obliquely. He who criticizes [in this way] incurs no culpability, but his [oblique] criticism is enough to warn the listener. For this reason, a form of poetry is called *Feng* (airs/remonstrance)." In the preceding statement, what is emphasized is how to embellish one's remonstrance so as to make criticism oblique, palatable, easy to accept. On this account, *feng* is still a mode of expression. The "mutated *Feng*" (mutated airs) and "mutated *Ya*" are more concerned with content. They are, therefore, directly related to the *Feng* and *Ya* sections of the *Book of Songs*.

Because the three modes of expression, *fu*, *bi*, and *xing* were only mentioned in a cursory way in the Preface, some scholars question their appropriateness in the Preface. In my opinion, since the Preface focuses on a political and moral inquiry into the genesis, nature, and function of *Shi*, the three modes of representation are not content oriented, hence they are mentioned only in passing, never to be discussed again in the rest of the discourse. As *feng* is a multivalent word, which is both content oriented and formally implicit, it fulfills the political, ethical, and utilitarian function of poetry while at the same time satisfying the formal needs of direct expressions and oblique criticism. It, therefore, still occupies the center stage of the discourse:

Thus, the poems that sing of the affairs of a state tied to a single person are called *Feng*. The poems that speak of the affairs under heaven and take forms in the airs of four directions are called *Ya*. *Ya* poems are proper songs that speak about the causes for the rise and fall of a kingly government. As there are greater and lesser governments, so the *Ya* songs have major and minor forms. The *Song* poems are songs that sing praises of the good conditions of flourishing virtue and inform the ancestral spirits of the achievements and meritorious deeds. These four forms of poetry are called the four beginnings; they are the ultimate perfection of poetry.

In contradistinction to "changed wind/mutated airs" is the proper wind/moral virtue: "The *Ya* poetry is about propriety 雅者，正也." Now, through an intertextual allusion and a word play, the Preface links songs in the *Ya* section with government. First, it alludes to a saying in the *Analects of Confucius*: "Ji Kangzi asked Confucius about the art of government. Confucius replied, 'Government is about propriety' (政者正也)."[66] Then, the Preface plays on the word *zheng*. Through a homophonic relation, *zheng* (propriety) evolves into *zheng* 政 (government), and *wang-zheng* 王政 (king's government). Just as there are major and minor forms of government, so there are Major *Ya* and Minor *Ya* sections. Moral virtues and proper government must be eulogized and reported to the divine spirit. Hence there is the *Song* 頌 section. Some scholars have found that *song* is cognate with *rong* 容.[67] Their close relation is identifiable in the same vowel sound "ong." In fact, they were frequently borrowed for each other in early texts. Thus, to sing the praises of someone is to describe his flourishing virtue in poetic language. Once again, the word play is employed both as a way of exegesis and as a way of writing.

The paragraph ends by calling *Feng, Daya, Xiaoya, and Song* the "four beginnings." The discussion of the four sections centers on the *zhi* or content of the *Shijing*. The content-oriented discussion not only justifies the meager mention of *fu, bi,* and *xing* but also implies that the three terms are three modes of expression and therefore do not fall within the author's utilitarian consideration of the *Book of Songs*. Finally, the discourse returns to the subject of the opening paragraph, which is practical criticism of some poems:

> Thus, the transformation in "Guanju" and "Linzhi" belongs to the kingly airs. They are thus associated with the Duke of Zhou. The Nan form of poetry speaks of how the transformation moved from north to south. The virtue in "Quechao" and "Zouyu" belongs to the airs of feudal lords. They are that by which former kings conducted moral teachings. Therefore they are associated with the Duke of Shao. "Zhou Nan" and "Shao Nan" represent the way of proper beginning; they are the basis of kingly transformations. Thus, the joy in "Guanju" is one of finding a virtuous lady as consort for the lord; the anxiety is concerned with recommending the worthy; there is no indulgence in her beauty. The poem sings of the sorrow over her seclusion, longs for worthy talent, and nurses no harmful thoughts for the virtuous. This is the theme of "Guanju."

The mention of other representative poems like "Linzhi," "Quechao," "Zouyu," and two "Nan" sections of the *Shijing* not only problematizes Zhu Xi's redivision but also shows without doubt that the author was concerned with literary criticism in general. Thus, the last paragraph marks a return to the subject matter at the opening of the Preface. It is still directly related to the text proper through the word *feng*. The *Feng* section consists of two Nan subsections and the airs of fifteen states. As though the author anticipated the question from future generations: why were the two Nan subsections not titled "state airs"? The author answered: the two Nan subsections are also *feng* or airs. One is "kingly wind/king's airs"; the other "lordly wind/lord's airs." The Preface ends with an elaborate thematic analysis of the "Guanju," an act of wrapping up, which correlates with the opening to provide a sandwich frame for the whole discourse.

Previous scholars seem to have failed to see the deliberate and elaborate efforts that have gone into the overarching structure of the Preface. Their redivision of the text not only does a disservice to our understanding of it but also blind us to the implicit paradigm of writing that can be brought out by a careful reading. Basing myself on the above rereading, I wish to conclude that the Preface was well thought out, carefully planned, and skillfully written. As is fitting for an introductory preface, it took the whole anthology of the *Shijing* as its object of study, but at the same time it did not lose sight of a larger aim: a treatise on the moral and utilitarian function of poetry. The writer(s), whoever it or they may have been, assumed the triple role of a theorist, a critic, and a scholar. The resultant discourse is a mixture of literary theory, literary criticism, and scholarship. In a way, since it results from a rethinking of much existent material, it may be viewed as a mixed discourse of metatheory, metacriticism, and metascholarship.

My rereading also shows that the composition of this discourse followed a mode of writing that builds on textuality, borders on intertextuality, and emphasizes the interweaving of signifiers in a way akin to dissemination. It even displays a deconstructive tendency. The dissemination of *feng* in the discourse produces a gamut of meanings: wind, moral influence, customs/mores, airs/songs, satire, proper wind, mutated wind, wind of four directions, kingly wind, and lordly wind. Among these different strands of meaning, some are compatible with each other, some are different, and some are antithetical. For example, the proper wind is quite opposite to mutated wind as their implied meanings connote. Proper wind pertains to proper government, moral virtues, and positive values; the mutated wind results from social disorder, moral decay, and negative topics. Proper wind means eulogy; mutated wind implies criticism. In terms of social relations, *feng* can either refer to the suasive influence of the ruling class or to the popular sentiments of the ruled. If the influence is moral, then *feng* can serve as a bridge between two opposite classes. If the influence is depraved, then *feng* can serve to reveal the gap between two conflicting classes.

In the space of a few hundred words, the Preface explores the genesis, nature, function, and form of poetry in general and the *Shijing* in particular. For the latter, it opens up the oeuvre and relates it to its possible social, political, and moral context. Some modern scholars may accuse it of distorting the content of "Guanju," but it provides a paradigm of reading that rejects the closure of a literary text. Chinese literary thought has always been viewed as an unsystematic, impressionistic jumble of disparate intuitions. The Preface has not escaped this assessment. My analysis shows that this judgment is far from accurate. Not only is it carefully and coherently structured, but it also rests on a systematic synthesis and creative innovation. In many ways, the whole text is truly a fabric interwoven with words, phrases, and passages, some of which came from the author's own mind, and some from other sources. Scholars have generally accepted Cao Pi's 曹丕 (187–226) "Discourse on Literature 論文"[68] as the first systematically and self-consciously written discourse on literature in the Chinese tradition. My analysis has offered enough reason to suggest that the accepted view should be modified. The Preface is not just a random treatise in Chinese literary thought; it is the first milestone in the development of Chinese literary theory. Since it attaches great importance to the signifying mechanisms of discourse, it may also be considered an embryonic form of open poetics, the underlying principles of which are multidimensional semiosis and intertextual dissemination.

Part IV

Literary Hermeneutics

Chapter 7

Open Poetics in Chinese Poetry

This part deals with another major hermeneutic practice in the Chinese tradition, which may be loosely called literary hermeneutics. As I have already dealt with the conceptual and critical insights in Chinese poetics in chapter 2, it will not examine critical data on poetics in the main but will focus on the reading of some chosen poems. The main objective, however, is not to produce new and interesting readings but to reveal mechanisms of hermeneutic openness in the making of poetry. By getting into the formal structures of the chosen poems, the linguistic system of classical Chinese language, and the signifying mechanism of poetic discourse, I attempt to tap the sources of hermeneutic openness in classical Chinese poetry, tease out insights of open representation, and formulate a poetics of openness in the reading and writing of poetry.

Spatial Form and Linguistic Economy

Poetry is a verbal art. Its artistry is perceived in terms of time and sequence. But when we talk about the openness of poetry, we are unavoidably perceiving it as a spatial form that has various dimensions. A poem consists of words on the page. The words in the poem are not simply symbols of meanings; they are placeholders of relations and occupy space on the page. The construction of a poem involves arranging words in a certain order, a move not different from the construction of a building. Mies Van Der Rohe, one of the founding masters of modern architecture once remarked: "Architecture is a language having the discipline of a grammar. Language can be used for normal day-to-day purposes as prose. And if you are very good you can be a poet."[1] The aesthetic equivalence between architecture and poetry suggests that poetic structure has to do with the coordination of different parts into a unified entity, which in poetry means complex syntactic relations of words. Hence, poetic openness is a linguistic issue. Since poetry, especially Chinese lyric poetry, is short and seldom displays a narrative thrust, the spatial arrangement stands out more conspicuously than in narrative poetry or prose.

In the formulation of his modern architectural theory, Mies Van Der Rohe proposes a principle central to his architectural theory: "Less Is More." In terms of architectural designs, this saying means that in contrast to the heavily decorated premodern style architecture, the modern-style architectural buildings with minimal internal and external decorations are compensated by more space, better light, fresher air, and increased practical value. In a way, a classical Chinese poem composed with minimal morphological and syntactical restraints resembles the modern-style architecture in its sparseness of ornamental decorations. In constructing words into an aesthetic edifice, ancient Chinese poets adopted a principle of linguistic economy that has been summarized by James Liu as "the principle of saying more by saying less, or, in its extreme form, saying all by saying nothing."[2]

Saying nothing is silence. Silence in a text is not absence of words in spatial terms. It is the unspoken. "The unspoken is not merely what is deprived of sound," Heidegger remarks, "rather, it is the unsaid, what is not yet shown, what has not yet appeared on the scene. Whatever has to remain unspoken will be held in reserve in the unsaid. It will linger in what is concealed as something unshowable."[3] Here, Heidegger's concept of "reserve" dovetails with *hanxu* (subtle reserve or suggestiveness) in traditional Chinese poetics. Heidegger also suggests that the silence that enables people to listen is more significant than all the noise of signification. His idea imparts the notion of the so-called thunderous silence. When a silence is as loud as thunder, its impact is not sonic but psychological. Thus, the linguistic economy that contributes to the openness of hermeneutic space relies on ordering principles that are psychological as well as spatial. The exploration of openness and open poetics is, therefore, a psychological as well as a linguistic undertaking. To be more exact, it is a semiotic undertaking.

By "semiotic," I am referring to Julia Kristeva's idea of poetic language as the workings of a "semiotic system" predicated on an integration of ideology, psychology, and linguistics. In her inquiry into poetic language, Kristeva agrees with Jacobson that poetic language cannot be viewed as a "deviation from the norm" of language. Instead of considering it to be a subcode of the linguistic code, she views it as standing for the infinite possibilities of language. From this position she argues, "literary practice is seen as exploration and discovery of the possibilities of language; as an activity that liberates the subject from a number of linguistic, psychic, and social networks; as a dynamism that breaks up the inertia of language habits and grants linguists the unique possibility of studying the *becoming* of the significations of signs."[4] In existent scholarship of Chinese poetry, great emphasis has been laid upon the role of poetic language as a means of representation. We need to make a shift from this to an emphasis on the workings of poetic language as a signifying practice, as a semiotic system generated by a speaking subject with conscious and unconscious motivations and within a social, cultural, and historical context.

In this chapter, I will explore how poetic openness is achieved in actual practice and to what extent openness is contingent upon multifarious ways of orchestrating textual elements in a poem. I suggest that openness in traditional Chinese poetry largely stems from the complex and multiple ways in which poetic language signifies and represents in given contexts—historical, social, cultural, and so on. Through different forms of coordination, poetic Chinese is capable of maximizing the three imaginations of the sign[5]—symbolic (involving symbolic consciousness), formal (involving paradigmatic consciousness), and functional (involving syntagmatic consciousness)—and producing signifying units that are open in the sense that they self-generate meanings beyond the original intentions of their makers. For my purpose, I am going to select some well-known poems and poetic lines (mostly short lyric poems), analyze their signifying mechanisms, and study their role in producing literary openness. My analysis will follow a gradually deepening procedure. First, I will identify some obvious elements that contribute to the openness of a poem. Then, I will examine less obvious elements hidden in the cracks and gaps between words. Finally, I will delve into the depth of the poetic mind to reveal how the poetic unconscious compresses copious thoughts into a potentially open space.

The "Eye" of Openness

In traditional Chinese poetic criticism, there is the literary term *shiyan* 詩眼 (the eye of the poem). This term came from the critical study of five-character line poetry in the Tang. It was believed that the artistry of five-character line poetry resided in a key word of a poem. This key word is called the "eye of the poem." As the term evolved, its connotations broadened. Now it may refer to the most brilliant key element in a poem.[6] As Kao Yu-kung and Mei Tsu-lin aptly put it, "Just as the eye is the focus of the face, so the poem's eye is the spark, the life, in a poem."[7] I may extend the metaphor in another direction and say that just as the eye of a person is the window to the soul of that person, so the eye of a poem may lead to a profound insight into the inner workings of that poem.

In traditional *shihua* 詩話 (Poetic Talks), the eye of the poem is generally a verb. In Wang Anshi's poetic line, "Spring wind again *greens* the southern bank of the Yangzi River 春風又綠江南岸" and Jia Dao's poetic line, "A monk *knocks* on the door under the moonlight 僧敲月下門," "green" (here a causative verb) and "knock" are recognized as the "eye" of the poems. In the epilogue to this study, I will demonstrate that each of the two words gives the two poems a profundity as well as a multiplicity of implications. In this respect, the eye of the poem becomes the eye of a poem's openness. For this reason, I venture to invent a critical term, "the eye of openness." This term, however, differs significantly from the eye of the poem in traditional literary criticism. First, not all eyes of the poem can be an eye of openness, because in many cases the eye of the poem is the exact word to capture the essence of a person, a scene, or a sentiment. In this respect, the eye of the poem limits the play of signification rather than promoting it. Second, while the eye of the poem is mainly a linguistic term, the eye of openness is a psycholinguistic term. As the metaphor "window to the soul" suggests, it enables the reader to peep into not only the meaning of the poem but also the inner workings of the poetic mind at the time of composition. In this sense, it comes close to a term in Freud's theory of dream interpretation, "nodal point." A nodal point is a juncture in a dream "upon which a great number of the dream-thoughts converge," and which reveals several meanings in connection with the formation of a dream.[8] Another difference is that while the eye of the poem is often a verb, the eye of openness may be any textual element: a verb, a noun, a phrase, a poetic line, or even a certain formal structure. It is an element in a poem that links the content of the poem with other elements within the text and with elements in the context. In a word, it is a window upon the soul of the poem as well as the poet.

Aporia as Eye of Openness. In Xin Qiji's 辛棄疾 (1140–1207) *ci*-poem "Qingyu an-Yuanxi 清玉案-元夕," the eye of openness is an indeterminate pronoun. For my purpose, I need to quote only the second half:

Moth and willow hair ornaments,   蛾兒雪柳黃金縷
    gold-threaded robes

Dispersed into a giggling throng with a trail   笑語盈盈暗香去。
    of fragrance.

In the crowd I searched for him/her   眾里尋他幾百度，
    countless times,

All of a sudden, as I turned my head,   驀然回首，
I caught sight of that person   那人卻在
In a place where lantern lights were dim.   燈火闌珊處。[9]

In classical Chinese, *ta* 他 may refer to a third person, either male or
female. The referent *naren* 那人 is as ambiguous as its antecedent. The use
of an ambiguous persona reminds us of similar practice in "The Reed,"
poem 129 in the *Shijing*. Since the gender identity of the persona is unclear,
the word in the poem is an aporia. So far there have been two accepted
interpretations. One is literal: this is a love poem describing a search for
a loved one. The other is allegorical: the poet entrusts his own lofty and
noble integrity to an unconventional person who distances himself from
the limelight of power.[10] If we relate the poem to the poet's frustrated
political career, we may read it differently and view the object of search as
his alter ego. In still another different light, we may read the poem as a
metaphorical description of the poet's inner struggle: the elaborate description of the splendid atmosphere suggests that the poet is not free from the
temptation to join the crowd. Only after considerable inner struggle does
he find his rightful place of being. In this sense, the object of search
becomes the lost self. When we take the gender ambiguity of *ta* literally,
there may be some other interpretations. If we take *ta* as referring to a
female third person, the object of search may be a secret love object. Since
ta in modern Chinese usually refers to a third person, male, a modern
reader who has no knowledge of the gender ambiguity of the word in
history may regard the person being sought as a male persona. From this
point of view, when we relate this persona to Xin Qiji's political career,
a different reading is possible. Throughout his political career, he
vehemently advocated the political position to cross the Yangtze River and
recover the land occupied by the invading barbarians. But his advocacy
found little support among the ruling bureaucrats. Those in power sup-
porting his advocacy were either persecuted or demoted. Thus the poem
may be read as: the poet wishes to find a person in power sympathetic
to his political position, but to his consternation, he finds that person
banished from the center of power.

    The title of a poem as eye of openness. The title of any text plays a sig-
nificant role in conveying the theme and subject position of that text. In

classic Chinese poetry, the title often functions in the same way as a caption relates to a picture. In viewing a picture, the images on the canvas may certainly convey represented meanings, but due to the multiple meanings of an image in relation to other images, the general theme of a picture is open to different and even conflicting interpretations. However, a caption by the painter gives the painting a fairly clear theme. In a poem, a title not only implies a subject, a theme, an attitude, a context, or a style, but also gives the reader a subject position to read the poem. Without a title, the meanings of a poem would often be totally indeterminate. This is especially so with poems of allegorical intentions. Zhu Qingyu's 朱慶餘 (b. 791) popular poem is a typical example:

The bridal chamber was lit up with red candles last night.	洞房昨夜停紅燭，
The bride waits for dawn to meet parents-in-laws in the hall.	待曉堂前拜舅姑。
After doing her makeup, she asks the groom in a low voice:	妝罷低聲問夫婿：
Have I drawn my eyebrows in a hue catching popular taste?	畫眉深淺入時無？[11]

Without a title, a reader would think that the poem vividly describes the nervous mental state of a newly wed bride who is going to pay her respects to her parents-in-law. The title of the poem, "Respectfully Presented to Secretary Zhang Hong of the Ministry of Water Works as the Examination Approaches 近試上張弘水部," however, enables us to realize that it is a poem depicting the anxiety of a civil service examination candidate and functions as a test balloon to the examiner.

A title would normally impose a subject position on the poem and its reader. There are cases, however, in which a title or caption, instead of imposing a definite position, leaves the subject positions open. In certain situations, a special title may perform a disorienting function and turn a poem into a poem that invites the reader to go beyond the surface meanings. For example, poems with "untitled" as title are composed with a simultaneous presence of conflicting intentions and emotions. The poet wants to express his pent-up emotions, but for certain reasons has to conceal his intentions. Nevertheless, he is afraid that readers may not get what is imparted in the poem. He, therefore, self-consciously entitles his poem "untitled." The untitled title speaks more pregnantly than a specific title. In Chinese poetry, premodern and modern, there are quite a few poets who use the "untitled" title to convey intended meanings and messages that are difficult to express because of political, social, personal, and moral constraints. Li Shangyin 李商隱 (813?–58) and Lu Xun (1881–1936) are two poets who are fond of this practice. Lu Xun wrote altogether fifty-nine ancient-style poems, of which eleven are entitled "untitled." Li Shangyin composed a group of poems called *wuti* 無題 (untitled). The following is one of them:

<table>
<tr><td>Meeting is difficult, so is parting.</td><td>相見時難別亦難，</td></tr>
<tr><td>East wind feeble, myriad flowers fall.</td><td>東風無力百花殘。</td></tr>
<tr><td>A silkworm spits silk until it dies.</td><td>春蠶到死絲方盡，</td></tr>
<tr><td>A candle drips tears till it turns to ashes.</td><td>蠟炬成灰淚且乾。</td></tr>
<tr><td>Facing the mirror at dawn,
　one fears the hair color may change.</td><td>曉鏡但愁雲鬢改，</td></tr>
<tr><td>Singing songs at night,
　one should feel cold in the moonlight.</td><td>夜吟應覺月光寒。</td></tr>
<tr><td>'Tis not far from here to Mount Peng.</td><td>蓬山此去無多路，</td></tr>
<tr><td>The blue bird diligently passes greetings.</td><td>青鳥殷勤為探看。[12]</td></tr>
</table>

There have been quite a few interpretations of this poem: veiled appeal to an official in power, secret love affairs with court ladies, or passionate relations with Daoist nuns.[13] All these interpretations are possible, but I venture to argue that the title, "untitled," may be a self-conscious effort on the part of the poet to come to terms with his uncontrollable passion and chaotic thoughts and to disorient the reader from guessing at the true intention in composing this poem. Understandably, the poet's pretextual intention might be one that seeks to hide his intention. Here is a case different from the similar situation that I have extensively analyzed from the *Shijing*. In the older tradition, some poems start to have multiple themes due to the loss of context and subject position. In the case of Li Shangyin's untitled poems, he succeeded in creating the loss of context and subject position by deliberately calling the reader's attention to his move to leave the poem untitled. From the reader's point of view, the untitled title liberates the reader from the constraint of relating the details of the poem with their supposed referents and of pinning down the poem on a single theme. The poem is practically open. What is "east wind"? What does "myriad flowers" refer to? Who is the subject worrying over the changing hair color in the mirror in line 5? Who is the subject feeling cold in the moonlight in line 6? Are they two personas or the same persona? Is the poem a lamentation over unrequited love or a eulogy for uncommon devotion? Last but not least, is it an appeal to a man in power or an allusion to a secret love affair? In a paradoxical way, "untitled" is really a multivalent title. It invites the reader to give the poem a title. Insofar as the untitled title leaves the poem open, I may say that it is the "eye of openness."

Absence of coda as eye of openness. All poems will come to a formal closure. As in ordinary verbal situations or musical performances, the poet will provide some signals to serve as coda to his poem. Without the coda, the reader will feel dissatisfied with the poem in the absence of a sense of appropriate cessation. Babara Smith, who conducts an excellent study of poetic closure, states: "As in music, so also in poetry, the coda is most often found as a special closural device when the structure of the work does not itself determine a conclusion."[14] The coda announces the cessation of further development and imparts a sense of completion and finality that people generally value in a piece of verbal art. Before the appearance of postmodern art, coda is almost indispensable for giving unity and coherence to the reader's reading of a poem by supplying a vantage point from which to have a comprehensive view of all the discursive elements and to perceive the overall design of the poem as a well-conceived work of art. In traditional Chinese poetry, however, there are poems in which there is no coda, and moreover, its absence is largely deliberately intended for special artistic effects. One of the poems in Han Musical Bureau poetry, "Mulberry Tree by the Path 陌上桑," is a case in point. The poem is quite long, and since it is well known, it is unnecessary to quote it in full. Instead, I will just summarize its theme and concentrate on its elements of openness, especially the ending. The poem narrates the story of Luofu, a beautiful woman from a common folk's family, who ingeniously and successfully resists the seduction by a powerful bureaucrat. The whole poem consists of three sections. The first section is a depiction of Luofu's beauty. The descriptive strategy used may be said to be one of suggestiveness. The poet did not directly describe the beauty of the heroine Luofu but indirectly portrayed it through the responses of the onlookers, thus leaving it open to readers' imagination:

The travelers who see Luofu	行者見羅敷，
Lay down their loads to stroke their beards.	下擔捋髭須。
The young people who see Luofu	少年見羅敷，
Take off their caps to flaunt their headband.	脱帽著帩頭。
Those who till forget their ploughing,	耕者忘其犁，
Those who hoe forget their hoeing.	鋤者忘其鋤。
Coming home they are angry with each other	來歸相怨怒，
For nothing but because they've seen Luofu.	但坐觀羅敷。[15]

In the first section and in the whole poem, not a single word is said about Luofu's actual physical beauty, but the responses of the personae leave an open space for the reader to imagine how beautiful she is. In this sense, this poem exemplifies Sikong Tu's dictum of *hanxu* (reserve): "Not a single word is written, / [it] Fully captures wind and flow."

The second and third sections narrate the prefect's attempted abduction and Luofu's resistance. By pretending to have a husband who holds high office and by enumerating his extraordinary personal qualities and talents, she puts the official in a humbled position and successfully wards off a possible kidnapping. The entire third section is her enumeration of her husband's virtue. Just as the reader wonders how the official would respond and how the poem would end, her pronouncement comes to an abrupt stop, bringing the poem to an end without a coda. Because there is no coda, the poem becomes open both in form and theme. It is formally open as it does not have a structure that appears to be complete, integral, and coherent. Thematically, it is open because the absence of coda leaves an open space for the reader to imagine an ending. The commonly accepted reading is that Luofu successfully resists the seduction. Along this line, one can imagine how elated Luofu is and how dejected the official is. But I can argue for the opposite. The official could not be an imbecile who is easily fooled. Since he has lackeys in the poem, he could find out the truth. Then, he could frame a crime against Luofu for deceiving the superior, a crime punishable by arrest, and do whatever he wanted to do with her. Perhaps, the poet might have been aware of this possible outcome. So he deliberately left no coda. Thus, the absence of coda is the eye of openness. This poem is full of open elements. Apart from those that I have already discussed, another one is that the poet did not tell whether Luofu is really married or whether her husband is really a high-ranking official. These unspecified elements may be said to constitute deliberate making of openness.

Metaphysical suggestiveness as eye of openness. Poem number 5 of Tao Qian's 陶潛 (365–427) "Wine Poems 飲酒" has widely been regarded as one of the great poems in Chinese lyricism:

I build my hut in the human world,	結廬在人境，
But hear no noise of passing traffic.	而無車馬喧。
You would ask me how it is so?	問君何能爾？
With the mind afar, my hut is remote.	心遠地自偏。
Picking chrysanthemums by the eastern hedge,	採菊東籬下，
I in leisure caught sight of the southern hills.	悠然見南山。
The mountain air is pleasant at sunset,	山氣日夕佳，
When flying birds return together.	飛鳥相與還。
In this there exists a real meaning,	此中有真義，
I wish to identify but find no words.	慾辨已忘言。[16]

Its eye of openness may be said to consist in metaphysical suggestiveness. This poem is greatly appreciated largely because of the scholarly consensus that it expresses an exhilarating emotion of lofty detachment, natural insouciance, and effortless communion with nature. Scholars particularly like the middle couplet, "Picking chrysanthemums by the eastern hedge, / I caught sight of the southern hills in leisure." To me, however, the last couplet is the most meaningful and pregnant. As James Hightower puts it, "A fundamental truth seems to have been communicated, even as the poet suggests, without having been formulated in words."[17] Kao Yu-kung and Mei Tsu-lin express an accepted opinion: "When T'ao Ch'ien wrote his famous line . . . he was [not only] restating Chuang-tzu's idea, but also expressing a view prevalent at his time."[18] They were referring to Zhuang Zi's advice to "forget words once one gets the meaning." Zhu Ziqing expresses an opinion that touches on a different aspect of Zhuangzi's thinking: "The 'real meaning' refers to 'real thought'; and 'real thought' is certainly 'original heart'; so it also refers to 'nature.'"[19] James Liu's reading of these last two lines adds a twist: "The point of the last line is not so much that the poet wishes to speak but cannot find the words as that he has reached the stage of understanding that no longer requires words."[20]

All the quoted opinions are certainly correct. In my opinion, however, the last couplet is not a mere recognition of the inadequacy of language or one's inability to use language for adequate representation. It is, among other things, a strategy to make the poem suggest more than its words on the page signify. The referent of *cizhong* 此中 is ambiguous and we don't know whether it refers to the meaning of one poetic line or to the total meaning of the poem. As a move to caution the reader that what he has expressed in the poem contains more than meets the eye, he may be said to have opened a metaphorical window unto his heart, through which the reader may get a meaningful glimpse of his life, career, and temperament. This poem enables me to more fully appreciate Said's idea: "[T]he text is a multidimensional structure extending from the beginning to the end of the writer's career. A text is the source and the aim of a man's desire to be an author . . . and in a whole range of complex and differing ways it incarnates the pressures upon the writer of his psychology, his time, his society."[21]

I am sure that few readers would finish the poem without struggling to guess at what the fundamental truth might be. To get the answer, the reader would need to not only examine the text itself but also go out of the text to examine Tao Qian's life, personality, and works. In a perceptive study of the relationship between one's poetry and one's self, Stephen Owen views Tao's autobiographical poetry as a "perfect mirror" that reflects his doubleness, his secret motives, and his inner self beneath a surface role.[22] Tao's poem under my discussion is such a mirror. In a way, it may be viewed as a window that allows us to have a glimpse into his life, self, and true nature. We may say that the poem expresses a sense of freedom after the poet rejects the world of Red Dust and returns to live among the mountains. As his poem number 1 of "Return to Lead a Farmer's Life" tells: "After long being locked in a cage / I was able to return to nature."[23] We may also say that the poem celebrates the poet's love of simplicity and insouciance. On the metaphysical level, we may say that the poem eulogizes the ability to achieve transcendence amidst immanence. On the psychological dimension, we may say that the poem speaks of a state of mind in which the poet forgets himself amidst natural scenery; a mental state highly treasured and constantly sought by the recluse: the "realm without self and other," a higher order of life in which one forgets wealth and poverty, glory and shame, nobility and humility, superiority and inferiority. In addition to all the above, we may say that it touches on what Romain Rolland calls the "true source of religious sentiments," "a sensation of eternity, a feeling as of something limitless, unbound—as it were, 'oceanic.'"[24] Freud explains the "oceanic" feeling as the crisis of self-object differentiation, a sense of "limitlessness and of a bond with the universe," which had once been the mother.[25] This feeling of an indissoluble bond, of being one with the external world as a whole must have been the source of Tao Qian's love of nature. Or we may say that the poem celebrates a return to the natural existence of an infant before what Lacan calls the Mirror Stage when it does not differentiate self and other. The added interpretations find support in the poem: the engrossed self-absorption, the returning birds, the communion with mother nature, and self-forgetfulness, and above all, in his inborn love of nature as expressed in his other writings: "I have since childhood had no desire for the secular world. By nature I have a love for mountains and hills."[26] In a way, we may even say that this poem anticipates an idea in his "Ziji wen 自祭文," the view of the human world as a traveler's inn and of death as the original home: "Mr. Tao will bid farewell to the inn on his journey and forever return to his original home."[27] Nevertheless, the poet does not clearly state these ideas. The celebration of freedom, the love of simple life, the sense of homecoming, and the effortless union with mother nature—all may be said to be the "true meaning." But the poet would not specify for the reader. By concluding the poem with the last couplet, he leaves the poem open and challenges the reader to speculate on what the true meaning is. Thus, the greatness of the poem lies not only in what has been expressed, but moreover in what has not been said.

Indeterminate subject as eye of openness. In the chapter on *Shijing* hermeneutics, I spent much time discussing the construction of poems in such a way that the subject matter or theme or persona in a poem is left completely open to the reader's response. In the *Shijing* tradition, however, the making of openness was largely done in an unconscious manner. By contrast, the making of openness was often deliberately carried out in Chinese lyric poetry after the *Shijing*. Some of this kind of poems were composed with difficult-to-determine motives on the part of the poets. One such example is a *ci* poem by Bai Juyi 白居易 (772–846):

<table>
<tr><td>A flower and yet not a flower.</td><td>花非花，</td></tr>
<tr><td>A mist and yet not a mist.</td><td>霧非霧。</td></tr>
<tr><td>It comes at midnight</td><td>夜半來，</td></tr>
<tr><td>   and leaves at daybreak.</td><td>天明去。</td></tr>
<tr><td>Coming like spring dreams,</td><td>來如春夢不多時，</td></tr>
<tr><td>   it does not stay long.</td><td></td></tr>
<tr><td>Going away like morning clouds,</td><td>去似朝雲無覓處。[28]</td></tr>
<tr><td>   it leaves no traces.</td><td></td></tr>
</table>

In this poem, the poet gives us a sketchy description of something or someone. It is neither a flower nor a fog. Is it the moon or a secret love(r) in tryst? Or is it a description of a dream or hallucination? The poet does not specify but forces the reader to exercise his/her imagination. The mysterious nature of the poem leaves the reader in a mental state of suspense filled with wonder and aesthetic pleasure. We cannot determine what motivated the writing of this poem. The poet might have been engaged in a word game or might have expressed an emotional attachment to a secret object. The first four lines are structured on the pattern of a paradox. The last two lines are structured on the pattern of a simile. Since the eye of openness is not overtly named, it is an indeterminate structure.

Symbiosis of Opposite Aesthetic Feelings

Another kind of literary openness to be found in some Chinese poems is the existence of conflicting emotions and aesthetic feelings. Chen Zi'ang's 陳子昂 (659–700) "Song on Climbing Youzhou Terrace 登幽州台歌" is a case in point:

<table>
<tr><td>Before me, I do not see the ancients;</td><td>前不見古人；</td></tr>
<tr><td>After me, I do not see newcomers.</td><td>後不見來者。</td></tr>
<tr><td>Brooding on the infinity of heaven and earth,</td><td>念天地之悠悠，</td></tr>
<tr><td>With tears streaking down, I stand alone.</td><td>獨愴然而涕下。[29]</td></tr>
</table>

Since I first read the poem in my teenage years, I have always had a mixed response to it. On the one hand, I find in the poem a strong note of sadness, melancholia, and even despair. But on the other hand, I intuitively feel a powerful aura of grandeur radiating out of the poem, which borders on heroism and the sublime amidst pathos. I know that my intuitive feeling conflicts with the accepted interpretation of the poem, a version of which is adequately rendered by Stephen Owen in his excellent study of the early Tang poetry: "The poem is a straightforward and moving description of the isolation of the individual in space and time, cut off from past and future, dwarfed by the immensity of the universe."[30] According to the accepted interpretation, the poem has a theme that is pessimistic, self-abased, and even pathetic in tone. But I have never found this interpretation satisfactory. If we recontextualize the poem, we will be able to detect, beneath the facade of pessimism, self-debasement, and pathos, another dimension of heroism, heroic forbearance, and the tragic sublime. According to the biographical account, on the day the poem was composed, he climbed onto the Jibei Tower and recalled the heroes of the past. Inspired by their heroic deeds, he composed a few poems with tears streaking down his face.[31] The recalling of heroic personages in history infused him with the sadness of a frustrated hero, but at the same time inspired him to write a heroic poem, which presents the poet as a pioneer who stands tall and proud against the background of the eternal universe. Thus, the tone of the poem could not be entirely one of pessimistic sorrow but one mixed with heroic forbearance. The poem signifies with conflicting connotations. We may have two different readings with two conflicting themes. One of the readings is exemplified by the accepted interpretation, which suggests that the poet is on a journey, but he stops and broods on his loneliness. I want to follow the conventional reading but wish to see the poem as describing a metaphorical journey through time and space, life and history. On the one hand, we may imagine the poet embarking on his journey in a conventional way—conventional in the sense that it is a journey that everybody takes in his short life span. The ancients who had come into this world earlier than the poet had started on the journey earlier; and the newcomers who are born later than the poet embark on the journey after the poet. In this conventional reading, the poet finds himself in a setting where he sees neither the earlier travelers nor later comers. He is in a no-man's land, surrounded only by the limitlessness of the universe. In addition to the feeling of loneliness and directionlessness, he feels the universe as an absolute power in contrast to his insignificance. He cries; his tears are the tears of despair and frustration, the tears of someone who feels lost.

On the other hand, we may read the poem in an unconventional way. The poet is still on his life journey through time and space, life and history, but he is not on the beaten track trodden by everyone. He is a pioneer, a pathfinder, and a trailblazer. Because he is on a road that no one has traveled before, he sees no predecessors before him. Because of the difficulty involved in embarking on this new trail, he finds no latecomers who would

follow his footsteps. He is undertaking an endeavor that has neither precedent nor will have recurrence (*kongqian juehou*), as depicted by the Chinese
saying "*qian wu guren, hou wu laizhe* (There are no ancients ahead nor followers behind)." He stands metaphorically alone in time and space, towering over life and history. The universe is infinitely great, but he does not
have the feeling of being dwarfed by it. On the contrary, by blazing a new
path through the wilderness, he shows himself to be a winner. In observing the disparity between the infinite greatness of the universe and the
insignificance of human beings, he is infused with a strong sense of the
sublime. This is not merely a quality the poet attributes to the absolute
greatness of the universe, but is more significantly related to the poet
himself. In contemplating the "endlessness of Heaven and Earth," the poet
is discovering the sublime in his own valiant path blazing. This sublime
experience is precisely what is described by Kant: "[W]e willingly call
these objects sublime, because they raise the energies of the soul above
their accustomed height and discover in us a faculty of resistance of a quite
different kind, which gives us courage to measure ourselves against the
apparent almightiness of nature."[32] When tears streak down his cheeks,
they are not the tears of despair but tears of painful pleasure. If there is
an element of sadness, it arises from the realization that no one else
can share his sublime sensation. This sadness is what Kant calls "negative
pleasure."[33]

Chen Zi'ang's poem is indebted to a passage of a poem attributed to
Qu Yuan 屈原, "Yuanyou 遠游":

Pondering the endlessness of Heaven and Earth,	惟天地之無窮兮，
I lament the long toiling of human life.	哀人生之長勤。
Those gone before I will never reach,	往者余弗及兮，
Of those to come I will never hear.	來者吾不聞。[34]

In his subtle comparison of Chen's poem with its source, Owen makes this
remark: "The poet of the *Yüan-yu*, whom Ch'en believed to have been Ch'u
Yüan, resolved his grief over human mortality by a flight through the
heavens to a state of transcendence; Ch'en Tzu-ang resigns himself to solitude and tears, but the pathos of the situation is heightened by the background of the *Yüan-yu*."[35] This remark touches upon a significant aspect
of the total theme in Chen Zi'ang's poem. Another aspect is subtly
imparted through the conflicting message of which I have just given a
detailed analysis. Owen rightly points out that though three of the four
lines in Chen's poem can be traced to their source in Qu Yuan's poem, the
greatness of Chen's poem is not diminished. What makes a poem of substantially borrowed source great? I think, Chen recast the borrowed mate-

rials in an entirely different light. As a result, the two poems differ from one another not just in degree but in kind. Although the source poem is characterized by a sense of transcendence, its tone is basically one of helplessness and lamentation. The contrast between the eternity of the universe and the long toiling of human life and especially the lamentation over such a contrast suggest that the poet is unable to transcend, either imaginatively or emotionally, the limitations of mortals. It certainly has no sense of the sublime subtly expressed in Chen's poem, the boldness of vision, the heroic spirit of daring to measure one's limited power against the absolutely limitless universe. In a word, it lacks the heroic abandon 豪放 and the sublime beauty of *yanggang* 陽剛之美 . In my opinion, it is the presence of the sublime that has transformed Chen's poem into something that is different from its borrowed source. Of course, I do not mean to say that Chen's poem is completely dominated by the sublime beauty of *yanggang*. On the contrary, I fully acknowledge the presence of pathos, delicate restraint 婉約, and the beauty of *yinrou* 陰柔之美. The feeling of being dwarfed by the endlessness of heaven and earth is certainly one pertaining to the beautiful, because it arises from a disinterested contemplation, which is what the beautiful leads to. The most fascinating point of Chen's poem, I contend, is the simultaneous presence of and interrelation between the sublime beauty of *yanggang* and the delicate beauty of *yinrou*. What can be identified as the sublime can also be identified as the beautiful. Chen's poem is aesthetically more satisfying than its source because it retains the source poem's state of transcendence and enlarges the aesthetic spectrum by incorporating two opposite kinds of beauty. As it suggestively covers the two aesthetic poles of the sublime and the beautiful, it is capable of arousing in the reader a full range of responses from the most heroic to the most pathetic, depending upon an individual's mental setup under particular circumstances and at a particular time. Thus, in the final analysis, what has made it possible for Chen's poem to be loved by generation after generation is its full aesthetic suggestiveness.

Metaphysical Emptiness

In Chinese poetic tradition, Wang Wei's 王維 (701–61) poetry has been highly regarded through the ages. There are many reasons for his lasting fame. One of the major reasons, I suggest, is the aesthetic suggestiveness and the accompanying poetics responsible for its seemingly unlimited hermeneutic space. Wang was a poet, a painter, a calligrapher, musician, and to a lesser extent, a philosopher. He was at home in all these artistic and intellectual domains. His poetry naturally grew out of his combined interest in all these branches of learning and benefited from the insights reaped from the different media for poetic representation. In this subsection, I am not going to show the impact of these branches of learning on his poetry; rather I wish to concentrate on a single short poem to illustrate the aesthetic openness of Wang Wei's poetry and to probe its poetics of making. The chosen poem is "Deer Enclosure 鹿柴." With only four five-character lines and a total of twenty characters, the poem has fascinated readers over history and across cultural boundaries. The lasting charm, I suggest, is its open hermeneutic space, which invites different interpretations. To facilitate discussion, I will give a literal rendition:

empty mountain / not see people	空山不見人，
but hear / people speak / sound	但聞人語響；
returning light / enter deep wood	返景入深林，
again shine / green moss / top	復照青苔上。[36]

The poem does not tell the reader much. Indeed, one can hardly read the poem into a theme or central idea. It is practically blank, or as the first character indicates, empty of clearly stated ideas. In this sense, the poem has attained the aesthetic status of the two conditions that I have elaborated in an earlier chapter: the *se* zither of the Purity Temple and the great broth of the sacrificial feast. Just as the *se* zither of the Purity Temple has a lingering sound and the great broth has a lasting taste, so Wang Wei's poem, because of its emptiness, is filled with a gamut of indeterminate meanings. Let us engage in a little exegetic exercise to see what possible meanings we can find in the poem.

An accepted and easy interpretation of the poem is that it is a vivid depiction of the natural scenery of a place near Wang Wei's villa, a place called "Deer Enclosure." In the empty mountain, there is not a single person to be seen, but there are faint human voices. The sunlight at dusk peeps through the trees and shines on the green moss. The faint noise only accentuates the profundity of quietude. We can find this interpretation in any standard anthology.[37] This interpretation represents the surface meaning of the poem. Since we know that Wang Wei was a devout Buddhist devoted to Chan Buddhism, a person with a philosophical mind, this interpretation can only scratch the surface of the poem.

Because Wang Wei was known to have converted a big part of his estate to a Buddhist monastery, the poem's title may have a Buddhist connotation. Literary history informs us that Wang Wei did own a place near his residence called "Deer Enclosure." Though I do not know for sure how the place got its name, it is reasonable to believe that the title of the poem has an oblique reference to the Deer Park in Sarnath, India, where the

Buddha preached his first sermon to the public. In terms of this reference, though we may not say that Wang Wei meant to view the Deer Enclosure near his villa as a replica of the Deer Park in India, it is reasonable to speculate that he perhaps considered this place as having the peaceful tranquillity of a Buddhist sacred place. Along this line of thought, we may even say that Wang Wei might have nursed the idea that he had attained Buddhahood, which many Buddhist believers had striven to achieve: the empty mountain is symbolic of the emptiness of life and being, and the tranquil serenity is the state of mind of someone who has attained enlightenment.

A reader may object to this interpretation by pointing out that as a devout Buddhist, Wang Wei could not have been so arrogant as to consider himself as having attained Buddhahood. At most, he might have regarded himself as having reached the desirable state of enlightenment. In this light, the poem represents a profound spiritual experience. François Cheng, for one, views the poem as a description of a walk on the mountain and at the same time, "a spiritual experience, an experience of the Void and of communion with Nature."[38] Octavio Paz who holds this view argues that this is a Buddhist nature poem. The light of the setting sun is an allusion to the Amida Buddha. Or to be more exact, it refers to the "light from the Western Paradise." The theme of the poem, then, is that "at the end of the afternoon the adept meditates and, like the moss in the forest, receives illumination."[39]

I might differ from the above interpretation by arguing that this poem is inspired by an exercise of *zazen* 坐禪 and depicts the process of such an exercise. The words in the poem are the words of a *gong'an* 公案 (*ko-an* in Japanese). My interpretation finds support both in and out of the poetic text. Extratexually, Wang Wei was said to have made good friends with some eminent Buddhist priests. According to history, he studied Chan Buddhism for ten years with the Chan master Daoguang (689–739) and wrote stele-inscriptions for both Daoguang and the Sixth Chan patriarch Huineng 慧能 (638–713). Textually, the poem resembles a Chan *jiyu* 偈語 (Buddhist hymn) in more ways than one. First, its content matches the usual theme of a Buddhist hymn. A *jiyu* is a "verse, used to sing the praises of the Buddha or to re-state succinctly major points of Buddhist doctrine."[40] Second, its stylistic form fits exactly that of a Chan hymn. A Chan hymn always consists of four phrases or lines to a verse, no matter how many characters are in each phrase or line. A recall of Huineng's legendary Chan verse on the Bodhi tree would establish the stylistic affinity beyond doubt: both were written in a four-line, five-character verse form. Third, just like other Chan poems, Wang Wei's poem is structured on contrasting opposites, antitheses, and negation of the negations (empty/full, no one/someone, light/shadow, to/fro, depart/return, etc.). Fourth, the general tone is one of universality, impersonality, and timelessness—all qualities leading to an enlightened mental state of transcendence.

I may continue the religious line of thought and give it yet another twist. Since this poem was written in Wang Wei's late life, it might have represented his contemplation of old age. As sunset is often taken as a symbol for one's old age, the returning light may refer to an old man's wisdom. Accordingly, the "deep wood" may symbolize the unconscious of the human mind contemplating the meaning of life, society, and the universe. The "mountain" may symbolize one's achievement in life. The "green moss," a lowly form of life, may stand for the insignificant status of human beings. As the light of wisdom enters the deep recess of the mind, the poet suddenly realizes how insignificant a human being is. His worldly achievement is empty, devoid of meaning, even though it may look magnificent in one's lifetime.

All the above interpretations have resulted from our efforts at situating the poem within the context supplied by Wang Wei's biographical information. If readers know nothing of Wang Wei's biographical information and must rely on close readings of the words on the page, the poem may be read in an entirely different light, giving rise to a series of different interpretations. A modern reader accustomed to city life may find this poem pleasing because it offers an entirely new landscape. He/she may view the poem as describing the scene of an outing and its impact upon the mind of the participants. In contrast to the hustle and bustle of the city streets full of people and traffic, the mountain is empty of human beings. But it is not entirely empty, for the presence of human voices suggests that the visitors to this place are shrouded out of sight by the green foliage and trees. The natural scene is more enchanting at dusk. As the last glow of the sunset penetrates the dense foliage and throws its remaining light on the inside of the forest, even the green moss seems to take on a life of its own.

In a different light from the Buddhist view of life as a void, a reader may come up with an opposite interpretation. The mountain looks empty, but it is full of hustle and bustle. Under the cover of dense foliage and trees, different kinds of life forms exist ranging from the highest order on the food chain, the human beings, to the lowest form, the green moss. Their existence is hidden from the casual eye and will reveal itself from time to time. The voices one can hear may be the voices of woodcutters, huntsmen, or farmers. If one sets his mind on finding their presence, he will be able to locate them. Even the green moss, the lowest form of life, which grows in dark and damp places, will manifest its liveliness and meaningfulness when the sunlight penetrates through the dense foliage and reaches those places seldom visited by human beings. Thus, the implied theme of the poem is that the world is not empty; life is full of meaning. The significance of existence will only reveal itself at the right time, in the right place, and to the right person.

I have provided enough interpretations of this poem. Now I need to do a little summing up with regard to the poetics of making pertaining to the poem. I suggest that in composing this poem, Wang Wei might have had as his theoretical basis the Daoist or Chan Buddhist conception of life, being, and art. The technique involved in making the poem is one of constructing the words and lines in such a rarefied manner that the poem does not have a totalizing structure or unified vision. But precisely because of this, the poem is amenable to different and conflicting interpretations. To borrow some of the sayings in contemporary literary thought, Wang Wei's poem may be said to be an empty basket, an empty shelf, and an empty schema. The first character of the poem, *kong* (or empty), does not simply modify the mountain, but may serve as an emblem of the poem: it conveys an empty message and is therefore open. Su Shi's Chan-style contemplation of the art of poetry adequately captures the metaphysical emptiness of Wang Wei's poem: "If you want your poetry to be superb, / You should not detest emptiness and quietude. / In quiet you can feel the movement of myriad things. / With emptiness your poetry can embrace a million scenes."[41]

Serial Form and Oriented Openness

Darwin once said: "A dream is an involuntary poem." This means that the openness of a dream is unconsciously intended. My study of Chinese poetry warrants an inversion of Darwin's saying: "A poem is a voluntary dream." This implies that frequently, the openness of a poem may be consciously produced. In the Chinese poetic tradition, there are many instances in which poets were engaged in a consciously oriented composition of poems with open possibilities. Su Hui 蘇蕙 (fl. 334–94), a woman poet of the fourth century, in order to repair the estranged marital relationship with her husband, composed a palindromic verse and had it woven in silk. According to a description by Wu Zetian (624–705), the only female emperor in Chinese history, "On a piece of silk a mere eight inches square, she wove more than two hundred poems of more than eight hundred characters."[42] Her embroidered verse is called "Xuanji Diagram of Palindromic Verse." What has fascinated generations of poets is that the diagram has a life of its own, capable of generating new poems out of the existent characters. Su Hui was quoted as saying, "As it lingers aimlessly, twisting and turning, it takes on a pattern of its own. No one but my beloved can be sure of comprehending it."[43] Zhu Shuzhen, a thirteenth-century woman poet who studied the verse with great care, describes its self-generating procedure:

> When each character is repeated once, a four-character poem emerges. One then goes on to the Second Square, which can be equated with the Purple Palace. Four-character palindromic poems are located here. The four rectangles growing out of the four sides of the Second Square form five-character palindromic poems, while in the four squares [off?] of the corners of the Second Square one finds four-character palindromic poems. In the four rectangles growing out of the four sides of the Third Square are four-character poems, if only the last character of one line is repeated as the first character of the next line. (These lines, however, cannot be read in reverse.) In the four squares adjacent to the corner of the Third Square are three-character palindromic poems. The perimeter of the Third Square and the perimeter of the entire diagram are all seven-character palindromic poems which can be read in different directions following the boundaries.[44]

On the surface of the diagram, there are about two hundred poems, but as one can read horizontally, vertically, and in whatever directions, and as characters on the embroidery can form different coordinations, the number of poems one can get is many times the original number. According to one account, a Daoist priest, after meticulous study, obtains 3,752 poems of varying length (three-character, four-character, five-character, six-character, and seven-character poems).[45] Her verse not only succeeded in repairing and strengthening her marital relationship but also left behind a marvelous form of poetry that reminds one of the postmodern serial form in literary composition. In contemporary Western poetry, the postmodern serial form is one of the major forms that strives for an oriented and conscious production of openness. The serial form is based on serial thought, of which Eco gives a succinct description: "[A] series, qua constellation, is a field of possibilities that generates multiple choices. It is possible to conceive of large syntagmatic chains (such as Stockhausen's musical 'group'; the 'material' ensemble of action painting; the linguistic unit extracted from a different context and inserted, as a new unit of articulation, within a discourse where what matters are the meanings that emerge out of the conjunction and not the primary meanings of the syntagmatic unit in its natural context; and so on)—chains that offer themselves as ulterior instances of articulation in relation to their initial articulation."[46]

Joseph Conte, who has made an excellent study of postmodern serial form, states: "[T]he postmodern theorist proposes an open structure that welcomes possibility, choice, and chance. Serial thought is the expression of a world concept that lies, luxurious in its possibilities between the systematic and the anarchic."[47] Some scholars have suggested that the serial form is indebted to Ezra Pound's *Cantos*. As Robert Von Hallberg argues: "William's lead [in the locale of Paterson] is an Ariadne thread through the wayward serial structure Olson took from the *Cantos*."[48] Since Pound's creative principle for the *Cantos* was heavily indebted to classical Chinese poetry, it is not far-fetched to say that postmodern serial form is related to ancient Chinese poetry in some way. Indeed, many of the characteristic open features of serial form are to be found in classical Chinese poetry as well. If Su Hui's Xuanji Diagram is an exceptional form of palindromic poem and cannot be cited as evidence for the fluidity of Chinese poetic form in general, in the following section, I will conduct a discussion of a few Chinese poems to show how Chinese poets made use of poetic Chinese to create a form that is inherently more open than the Western serial form. One of the chosen poems is Meng Haoran's 孟浩然 (689–740) "Mooring at the Jiande River 宿建德江":

Moving the boat and mooring it at a hazy islet,	移舟泊煙渚，
The traveler feels a renewed sorrow at dusk.	日暮客愁新。
The wilderness is wide and the sky low over trees;	野曠天低樹；
The river is clear to reflect the moon close to him.	江清月近人。[49]

Sequentiality is necessary for all poetry to make sense, but certain classical Chinese poetic forms and postmodern serial form exceed sequential signification. In a Chinese poetic game, one can rearrange different words of a poem in any order and is still able to obtain a meaningful poem. Meng Haoran's poem is a good illustration. To save space, I will only read the poem backward from the last word:

The man moves close to the moon on the clear river.	人近月清江。
The trees are low and the sky is wide over the wilderness.	樹低天曠野。
Fresh sorrow lodges like a stranger in the setting sun.	新愁客暮日。
The smoke on the islet makes the moored boat move.	渚煙泊舟移。

Conte points out: "In classical thought, the form is systematic, hierarchical, and preconstituted. But serial thought, as Boulez argues, 'creates the objects it needs and the form necessary for their organization each time it has occasion to express itself.' The serial form constitutes itself on the instant from a set of mobile and discontinuous objects; and it may reconstitute itself at the next instant from a varied set of objects. Each new combination produces a new meaning, reorients itself as a new aesthetic object."[50] The poetic form in Meng's poem is precisely such a pliant form. I as a reader can enter the poem almost at any point, from the first word, the second word, the third word, or whatever, or read the poem from the last word back to the first word. Each different entry produces a new meaningful poem. Although the general tenor of each reading has some affinity, the details are quite different. Those details are significant enough to generate different interpretations. This free-rolling feature endows the poem with a circular or cyclical structural pattern with a potential of self-generativeness. My suggested experimental reading is of course a word game. Its purpose, however, is to show to what extent poetic Chinese is fluid and in what way the Chinese poetic form is similar to postmodern serial form.

I have argued in the above that the fluidity of poetic Chinese enables the poet to compose poems in largely paratactic rather than hypotactic structures. Through the parataxis of poetic structure, a Chinese poem achieves openness both through sequence and serial form. In this respect, the composing principle of ancient Chinese poetry is not different from postmodern serial form, which is also predicated largely on paratactic relations. Conte is of the opinion that hypotaxis and parataxis distinguish a sequence from a series:

> A sequence is a hypotactic structure (meaning, "arranged one under another") whose elements are subordinate to or dependent on other elements for their meaning. . . . The series, however, is a paratactic structure (meaning, "arranged side by side") whose elements, although related by the fact of their contiguity, are nevertheless autonomous. For example: a line of parked cars assembles itself on the street each evening shortly after six p.m. The cars are related by their bumper-to-bumper contiguity and by their general participation in this phenomenon. Yet the make and model of the cars differ and their order along the curb frequently changes; occasionally, one arrives or departs at an odd hour. Their relationship is serial, or paratactic, subject to a multiplicity of combinations.[51]

Conte's analogy of parked cars is an intriguing way to explain the rationale of serial form, but in my opinion, the recombinatory pliablity that I have demonstrated with Meng Haoran's poem would be a better alternative. In a sense, the Chinese mode of representation sanctioned by poetic Chinese has the versatility of a crossword puzzle. Like an English letter, the monosyllabic Chinese character occupies a set space on the page and enjoys more freedom in combination with other characters than English words. In a crossword puzzle, one can find letters forming words horizontally, vertically, diagonally, and interconnecting with other letters to form new words. A near equivalent in English writing is James Joyce's neologisms in *Finnegans Wake*. Eco describes the novel thus: "*Finnegans Wake* is an open work. For this reason it is a *scherzarade* (game, charade, tale of Sheherazade), *vicocyclometer, collideoscope, proteiform graph, polyhedron of scripture, meanderthale* and, finally, *a work of doublecrossing twofold truths and devising tail-words.*"[52] Joyce makes full use of the combinatory power of English syllables to coin words which signify in a way some Chinese poems (especially *huiwenshi* or palindrome poems) signify, horizontally, vertically, diagonally, reversely, creating a new poem with each word as the start. In Chinese history, there have been numerous poems conceived in this manner. They have frequently been dismissed as word games, but very often serious messages are conveyed through this mode of writing.

I wish to point out that this mode of writing made possible by poetic Chinese is responsible for a large measure of deliberate openness in Chinese poetry and may lend great support to the openness of serial thought. Conte points out: "Serial thought recognizes that each conjunction of objects has a meaning; that the objects are capable of rearrangement; and that subsequent arrangement also has a meaning which is in no way 'secondary' to its initial articulation. Nor does the initial articulation determine the pattern or arrangement of those that follow. This recombinatory quality does not negate form; it acknowledges its pliability in an expanding, relative universe."[53] Classical Chinese poems were often written down on paper without punctuation and with an order contrary to the modern way of reading (i.e., from right to left and from top to bottom). Coupled with this formal presentation, some ancient Chinese poems may be said to have accomplished a postmodern serial form long before serial form was invented. Here, I wish to mention a literary anecdote in Chinese history. Ji Yun 紀昀 (1724–1805), one of the most famous literati of the Qing dynasty, was once copying a poem for Emperor Qianlong. The poem was Wang Zhihuan's 王之渙 (688–742) famous "Liangzhou ci 涼洲詞":

The Yellow River ascends far into the white clouds.	黃河遠上白雲間。
A lonely city is circled by mountains thousand yard high.	一片孤城萬仞山。
Why should a Qiang flute sadly play the "Willows" tune?	羌笛何須怨楊柳？
You know that spring wind can't pass the Yumen Pass.	春風不度玉門關。[54]

By accident, he omitted the last word of the first line. The emperor found this out and accused him of committing the crime of deceiving his majesty.

With a little ingenuity, Ji Yun successfully glossed over his slip of the pen by saying that he was not copying Wang Zhihuan's poem but writing a *ci*-style poem, which should be punctuated as follows:[55]

The Yellow River ascends far.	黃河遠上，
A stretch of white clouds,	白雲一片，
A lonely city and mountains thousand yard high.	孤城萬仞山。
Why should the Qiang flute complain?	羌笛何須怨？
Willows and spring wind	楊柳春風
Can't reach the Yumen Pass.	不度玉門關。[56]

This anecdote has been passed on from generation to generation. It, nevertheless, has a significance beyond its anecdotal value. Ji Yun's clever punctuation accomplished more than saving his neck; it represents a premodern form of productive rather than consumptive reading, a reoriented production of new meanings, and a maximal use of poetic language's possibilities of recombination. In a practical way, it touches upon a form of serial thought that Boulez talks about in musical composition: "Here (within serial thought) there are no preconstituted scales—that is, no general structures within which a particular thought could inscribe itself. A composer's thought, operating in accordance with a particular methodology, creates the objects it needs and the form necessary for their organization each time it has occasion to express itself."[57] Boulez's idea of serial thought was pertaining to musical composition. Eco extends it to any artistic composition and considers it to be the theoretical basis of any open work: "This hypothesis of an oriented production of open possibilities, of an incitement to experience choice, of a constant questioning of any established grammar, is the basis of any theory of the 'open work,' in music as well as in every other artistic genre. The theory of the open work is none other than a poetics of serial thought."[58]

As if by coincidence, traditional Chinese poems were composed with a principle much like the postmodern serial form that both Barthes and Eco have identified as being capable of open creation. Ancient Chinese poets may not have consciously conceived of anything like serial thought, but I believe that some of them must have intuitively felt something in that direction. Discussions of Su Hui's Xuanji Diagram supports my view. Wu Zetian's comment, "Whether one read vertically or horizontally, in whatever direction, verses would emerge with nothing missing at all,"[59] shows an insight into reading that projects creative impulse from the axis of combination to the axis of selection. Zhu Shuzhen's insight into the principle of the diagram also testifies to the awareness of the coordination between paradigmatic and syntagmatic relations: "Finally, I awakened to the principle of the diagram. Following vertical longtitudes and horizontal latitudes, I sought the verses, and as I had expected, it read fluently."[60] Su Hui's own words, "As it lingers aimlessly, twisting and turning, it takes on a pattern of its own,"[61] seem to suggest that she was consciously experimenting with a poetic form in which there is no preconstituted sequence within which a particular thought could inscribe itself but only an arrangement of mobile signs, whose combination is free rolling and produces a new constellation of meanings each time the given signs are coordinated in a certain way.

Of course, what had enabled Chinese poets to accomplish something like serial form in their poetic practice is a special characteristic of poetic Chinese. Poetic Chinese can be described in semiotic terms as a poetic form in which the syntagmatic relation of the sign is flexible and fluid. This quality comes close to syntagmatic imagination of the sign. Barthes describes a "syntagmatic imagination," which no longer sees the sign in terms of its "depth" (or symbolic) relation, but in terms of "its antecedent or consequent links, the bridges it extends to other signs."[62] Barthes argues for the aesthetic complexity with which signs combine. Such literary forms as the series are the product of "a 'stemmatous' imagination of the chain or network." They function as "an arrangement of mobile, substitutive parts, whose combination produces meaning, or more generally a new object."[63] In exactly the same way poetic Chinese functions to produce multivalence and polysemy.

My analysis of the chosen poems suggests that poetic Chinese is weak in formal logic. Indeed, it is not ruled by a formal logic but by a logic of combinations. This logic is based on an undeclared "rule": every word can be combined with any other word in a discourse so long as the combinations make sense in a certain context. This combinatory logic resembles serial form in Conte's analogy of parked cars along a pavement: there is no restriction on the model, make, and arrival time of a car for it to be part of the formation of an array of cars: "The series demands neither summation nor exclusion. It is instead a combinative form whose arrangements admit a variegated set of materials."[64] Whereas, as Conte suggests that "the series is an open form in large part because it does not require the 'mechanic' imposition of an external organization," in Chinese poetry each character is a module that acquires its position in the process of signification through combination with other characters. The openness of traditional Chinese poetry is largely based on the complex and multifarious ways in which one word finds its different coordinates with other words. The coordination is not entirely decided by a conscious intention but often by unconscious linguistic processes. This will be the topic of the next chapter.

Chapter 8

Linguistic Openness and the Poetic Unconscious

Literature is a language art. Poetry is even more so. Zhu Ziqing 朱自清 (1898–1948), Chinese scholar and poet, makes this apt remark in his study of poetic language: "Essentially, poetry is nothing more than language, a pure language."[1] In this sense, to understand poetry is to understand pure language. In contemporary hermeneutic theory, the linguisticality of understanding has been commonly accepted. Understanding has generally been viewed as an interpretation, and that interpretation is the explicit form of understanding. The language used in interpretation represents a structural moment of interpretation.[2] From this point of view, understanding a text is a moment in which a reader makes attempts to structure language into meaningful ideas. Language thus occupies a central position in reading and interpretation.

In his metaphysical reflection on the essence of language, Heidegger pronounces this famous saying: "Language is the house of Being."[3] Following his line of thought, Gadamer conceives of the motive of Being as "being brought to language" and proclaims that "Being comes to language by opening itself up."[4] In their existential hermeneutics, language is no longer viewed as the tool that people generally hold it to be; it constitutes in itself the subject-matter of a "world"[5] and moreover implicitly brings that subject-matter to disclosure: "What language properly pursues, right from the start, is the essential unfolding of speech, of saying. Language speaks by saying; that is, by showing."[6] The showing and saying that language performs constitute the very essence of language. In literature, the "world" created by language is a text. Language not only creates the world of the text, but also already endows it with the potential of disclosing itself. Moreover, it maps the hermeneutic space enclosing and uniting the reader in the process of reading. Because of the latent tendency of language to reveal, hermeneutic experience precludes closure and encourages openness to new experience. As Gadamer puts it, hermeneutic experience "has its own fulfillment not in definite knowledge, but in that openness to experience that is encouraged by experience itself."[7] In this chapter, I will explore how language (un)consciously structures our creation and perception of a text and how it turns a text into an open hermeneutic space.

Openness and Poetic Language

In my discussion of the various possible interpretations of Wang Wei's poem, I did not analyze in detail the impact of linguistic ambiguity or indeterminacy upon the magnitude of hermeneutic space. If we concentrate on this aspect, we may come up with some new readings. For example, the poem displays the characteristic omission of personal pronouns in Chinese lyricism. François Cheng considers the omission as a "matter of conscious choice" and suggests a philosophical dimension to the process of composition: "It gives birth to a language that places the personal subject in a particular relationship with beings and things. In erasing itself, or rather in choosing only to imply its presence, the subject interiorizes the exterior elements."[8] I fully agree with Cheng, but wish to look at the matter from a purely linguistic point of view and see to what extent the ambiguity of poetic Chinese contributes to the enlargement of hermeneutic space. To facilitate my discussion, I would render the poem in the following version:

> The empty mountain sees no man,
> But hears men's voices resound.
> Returning shadow enters deep wood.
> Reciprocal light ascends green moss.

In the conventional interpretation of the poem, it is generally agreed that the first-person pronoun "I" which stands for the poet, is omitted. So the poem should be interpreted and translated by restoring the "I" in English. François Cheng offers a different interpretation. In his opinion, the suppression of the pronoun indicates that the poet identifies with the mountain. He also suggests that in the third line, the poet "is the ray of the setting sun that penetrates the forest." But in the actual reading of the poem, Cheng retracts the bold steps taken and falls back on the accepted view concerning the omission of the pronoun: "From the point of view of content, the first two lines present the poet as still 'not seeing'; in his ears the echoes of human voices still resound. The last two lines are centered in the theme of 'vision': to see the golden effect of the setting sun on the green moss."[9]

I wish to go beyond the existential identification of the poet with the natural scene and suggest a new reading. The poetic language warrants the reader to approach the poem from an anthropomorphic perspective. Simply put, I mean that it is not that the poet identifies with the natural scene but that he treats the elements in the natural scene as humanized and personified subjects. The mountain does not have eyes. Therefore it does not see human beings inhabiting it. It has no ears, but it can feel the resounding of their voices. The first two lines may be construed as showing an intimate relationship between the mountain and its inhabitants. In this connection, the mountain is really a metonymic representation of nature, mother nature, or the empty Dao. It is empty, yet it gives rise to myriad things, including human beings. The last two lines describe a mutually dependent process. The returning shadow is reciprocated by the returning light. Without the shadow there would be no light. Thus, the shadow and light form a complimentary pair of opposites. Syntactically, the parallel of the two is made possible by a reading of the word *shang*. Peter Boodberg argues that the last word of the poem, *shang*, is a verb that means "to rise," though scholars generally accept it as meaning "above, on top, or top."[10] Thus, we could read the last line as 復照上青苔. Here, *fuzhao* is not a verbal phrase but a noun phrase. From a prosodic point of view, this reading is very likely, for in order to make *shang* rhyme with *xiang*, the poet has to invert the word order. The restoration of the natural word order would produce a perfect parallel structure for the last two lines. Moreover, the new reading would give the last line a cinematic effect: the returning light accompanied by the approaching shadow moves gradually up the moss-covered trees or mountain slope.

My new reading further opens up the hermeneutic space of the poem. It is not at all unnatural. At least, it seems as natural as, if not more natural than, the accepted readings. What makes this reading acceptable is not cultural or contextual ambiguity but linguistic ambiguity. Starting from this section, I will shift my focus and explore open hermeneutic space from the perspective of poetic language in relation to the three imaginations of the sign, to which I referred in the opening section of this chapter. I suggest that the openness of classical Chinese poetry, especially regulated poetry, is in great measure attributable to the indeterminacy of poetic language. To deal adequately with openness and open poetics in Chinese poetry, we cannot avoid discussing the salient features of poetic Chinese.

In the *Art of Chinese Poetry*, James Liu makes a statement: "[I]t (Chinese) makes possible the expression of thought and emotion with the greatest economy of words. The poet can compress several meanings into one word, and the reader has to choose the meaning that seems most likely to be uppermost in the poet's mind, as well as probable subsidiary meanings, while excluding irrelevant meanings of which the word is capable in other contexts. This of course also happens in English, but not, I believe, to the same extent as in Chinese. In this respect, Chinese is a better language for writing poetry."[11]

This position has in fact been expressed before him by Ernest Fenollosa and Ezra Pound; both of them are of the opinion that Chinese is a better vehicle for writing poetry than the inflected European languages.[12] This view has been seriously disputed by scholars, Chinese and Western. Burton Watson, for example, engages James Liu in a minor dispute with regard to the advantages of Chinese in the composition of poetry. Specifically, Watson singles out two features of poetic Chinese: no indication of number and no indication of tense, and discusses the advantages and disadvantages. Watson makes this choice in order to match a claim by James Liu. In the *Art of Chinese Poetry*, Liu states: "As Chinese does not require any indication of 'number,' the poet need not bother about such irrelevant details and can concentrate on his main task of presenting the spirit of a tranquil spring among mountains. Moreover, the absence of 'tense' in Chinese enables the poet to present the scene not from the point of view of any specific time but almost *sub specie aeternitatis*: we are not invited to watch a particular spring night scene viewed by a particular person at a certain point in time, but to feel the quintessence of 'spring-night-ness.'"[13] Watson, while granting a partial validity to Liu's assertion, questions the validity of its privileging the general over the particular in the minds of the twentieth-century reader influenced by Imagism and W. C. William's motto "no idea but in things." "He would object," Watson says, "that unless one can 'get the picture' he will not know what mood or idea the poet is trying to convey; that it is of great consequence indeed whether 'bird,' for example, is singular or plural, since one bird is suggestive of loneliness, but a flock of them are more likely to seem either menacing or jolly, depending upon how one feels about the birds to begin with."[14]

Watson's objection to Liu's claim is grounded in the concern that "what are in fact mere accidents of language should not be mistakenly singled out as the source either of literary shortcomings or of some unusual felicity of expression."[15] Watson's objection has two problems. First, if the use of certain words in a certain poem is not mere accident but a deliberate attempt to convey a special effect, the situation would be entirely different. Second, as far as reader response is concerned, ambiguity of number, tense, gender, case, and so on, would certainly enlarge the hermeneutic space of a particular poem. It may be right to dispute the claim that Chinese nouns are intrinsically more poetic than those of Western languages, which are specific in those linguistic areas, but it would be equally correct to say that a poem composed with no specificity in those areas would have a larger hermeneutic space than another poem composed with those linguistic areas clearly spelled out. It is, of course, problematic to equate large hermeneutic space with artistic excellence, but we must admit that the magnitude of hermeneutic space is a distinct feature of artistry, and hence an indication of aesthetic quality. For this reason, I must say that Watson's following statement is a lame attempt to dispute Liu's claim: "And if we are to claim that Chinese nouns are intrinsically more poetic than those of English because they lack number, and are hence more universal, we must by the same reasoning claim that English nouns are more poetic than those of, say, French or Italian because they lack gender, a claim that few Frenchmen or Italians are likely to allow."[16] The ambiguity of gender is of course significant in the composition of a poem. As I have shown in reading Xin Qiji's poem, a view of *ta* as referring to a male persona produces a drastically different reading of the same poem than if we assume it to refer to a female. By using gender as a point of argument, Watson is in fact admitting that a poem with gender ambiguity offers a larger hermeneutic space than a gender-specific poem.

When we examine the claim that the Chinese language (classical Chinese or poetic Chinese) is a better medium for writing poetry, we must not lose sight of the other aspect of the claim. Liu admits that classic Chinese has "a serious drawback in expository prose."[17] One may also claim that classical Chinese as a legal language is much less accurate and precise than English or French. Thus, while an inflected language loses on the swings of hermeneutic openness, it gains on the roundabout of precision and accuracy. Of course, Liu's argument has a weakness in privileging the universal over the particular. A less problematic way of viewing the question under discussion might be that the lack of linguistic precision—clearly defined number, case, tense, gender, voice—may turn the words in a Chinese poem into a series of cues to what that poem is about. A reader may take different positions to view those cues and interpret the poem from different subject positions. The cues may be viewed as singular or plural, male or female, past, present, or future, passive or active, subjunctive or literal, depending on each individual's mindset at the time of reading the poem. Thus, the poem becomes one with a fairly open hermeneutic space which covers the universal and the particular, literal and figurative, transcendental and specific, precise and ambiguous. In this respect, Watson's view of a Chinese poem in terms of painting analogy is an appropriate one: a poem composed in poetic Chinese is "a blank canvas . . . inscribed 'tree,' 'birds,' 'mountain,' 'water' in the appropriate areas, upon which we are asked to execute our own realization of the scene."[18]

If one is still not convinced by my suggestion that poems composed in poetic Chinese are endowed with a larger hermeneutic space than poems written in English or French, I may turn to a literary game in poetic Chinese for further support. In such a game, we randomly select several classical Chinese poems, cut each poem into separate words (characters), and then put all the scraps of paper into a bag. If one randomly picks from that bag a certain number of words in accordance with the number requirements of a particular poetic style, say, that of a quatrain, he can punctuate the picked words and get a poem in that style. Of course, the burden of explanation or of supplying the diacritic elements, lies with the reader. In other words, the characters only have a paradigmatic relation and the syntagmatic relation between each and all the characters has to be supplied by the reader. In this game, that bag may be viewed as a miniature of Saussure's "inner storehouse of language,"[19] and in that limited space, words are floating in a spatial relation to each other, and may have various ways of combination just like bits and pieces of broken glass in a kaleidoscope. Every shake will produce a new and wondrous pattern. In actual poetic composition, the so-called palindrome poems 回文詩 constitute the most radical case in the maximal use of the characteristic features of poetic Chinese. A palindrome in English can only run to a line or two. But Chinese palindrome poems may run to a sizable number of lines. Furthermore, in reading a Chinese palindrome poem, the reader can enter the poem from any place in the discourse and read either forward or backward. Starting from any point of entry, he/she will embark on a different journey, one likely to yield totally new meanings and surprising discoveries. Different entries may produce different versions out of the same poem.

In a way, this kind of reading is akin to the method of reading developed by Barthes. It is perhaps the most drastic and radical form of what Barthes calls "segmentational reading." In his *S/Z*, Barthes invents a method for reading classical narrative works, which he calls segmentation. He cuts up the text into a series of fragments called *lexias*, which form the basic units of reading. Then he allows the fragments or *lexias* to freely combine so as to signify and represent in ways different from the uncut old text. He breaks open the old text to reveal the repressed codes, voices, and meanings, emphasizes the relative autonomy of each of the textual fragments, and permits all the cultural utterances in the text to speak.[20] Segmentation opens up a whole new field of signification, with new meanings which may have been there all along, but the existence of which had been hidden behind the linear organization of the text. From the reader's point of view, segmentation opposes the closure of the text and frees the reader from the predetermined subject position. What Barthes has done with the narrative work, the Chinese have done with palindrome poems and to a lesser extent with other lyric forms. As my exercise in the exegetical reading of Wang Wei's poem has demonstrated, and as additional readings in the next section will further demonstrate, the Chinese segmentational reading, if I may use that concept, has been made possible by the relative autonomy or free-standing quality of Chinese characters, and moreover by such features as those discussed by James Liu[21] and François Cheng[22] and other Chinese linguists: freedom from morphological restraints with regard to article, number, gender, case, voice, mood, verbal conjugation, and so on, and minimal syntactic requirement through omissions of personal pronoun, prepositions, comparatives and verbs; frequent use of word-order inversion, complements of time, empty words in place of verbs and so on. Needless to say, some of these features are permissible only in poetic Chinese.

Openness and Syntactic Ambiguity

Among the three imaginations of the sign, I have so far paid more attention to the symbolic imagination. Starting from this section, I will work more on the paradigmatic and syntagmatic imaginations. In their three excellent essays on Tang Recent Style poetry, Mei Tsu-lin and Kao Yu-kung have made extensive studies of the relationship among syntax, diction, imagery, meaning, metaphor, and allusion in Tang poetry. The major concern for one of the essays, "Syntax, Diction, and Imagery in T'ang Poetry" is a question: What is the function of syntax in poetry? In their conclusion to this essay, they examine four views taken from the Western tradition: T. E. Hulme's view of syntax as unpoetic, Ernest Fenollosa's view of syntax as action, Susanne Langer's view of syntax as music, and Donald Davie's view of syntax as an instrument of discursive articulation.[23] After their examination in relation to Tang poetry, they conclude that the Western scholars' views are confirmed by their study. To my surprise, none of them mention another obvious function of syntax in poetry: poetic syntax can be used consciously or unconsciously to create ambiguities and to enlarge hermeneutic space. This overlooking of an obvious function is the more surprising because Kao and Mei have observed, as many other scholars have noticed, that Tang poets frequently violate normal word order in their poetic compositions by means of the so-called measure of license: "the language of Recent Style poetry enjoys a considerable measure of license in the domains of form and grammatical construction." From the viewpoint of my inquiry, the measure of license is one of the factors that have contributed to the construction of open hermeneutic space in Chinese poetry. Linguistically, the measure of license is not primarily a poetic license but a measure allowed by syntactic rules in poetic Chinese, because many cases of the so-called violation of grammatical construction for the sake of prosody are in fact permitted not so much by poetic license as by syntactic fluidity and condensation of grammatical structures. In the following space, I will reexamine a few poetic examples analyzed by Mei and Kao and in the process of reexamination demonstrate how syntactic ambiguity not only contributes to the openness of classical Chinese poetry but also sheds light on the mental functions of the poetic (un)consciousness.

In their syntactic analysis of Du Fu's poem "Jiang Han 江漢," Kao and Mei provide a number of syntactic readings of the first four lines, which are literally rendered into English:

Jiang Han / think / returning guest	江漢思歸客，
Heaven earth / one rotten scholar	乾坤一腐儒。
a streak of cloud / heaven / share distance	片雲天共遠，
lasting night / moon / share solitude	永夜月同孤。

In their reading of lines 1 and 2, they resist two "natural" interpretations: (1) "by Yangtze and Han, a homesick stranger," in which case "Yangtze and Han" becomes the place-condition; and (2) "a homesick stranger (who is) by Yangtze and Han," in which case "Yangtze and Han" becomes, in Chinese, the premodifier of "a homesick stranger." Instead, they view the first lines as two images in juxtaposition, in which the reader could get two simple images and a sharp contrast between the vastness of the two rivers and the smallness of the human figure.[24] I do not know for sure why they resist the two "natural" readings. In my opinion, both are possible readings. In addition, I want to offer another possible reading. I suggest that lines 1 and 2 constitute a juxtaposition which amounts to a complete sentence structured on the common nominal predicate pattern: A者, B也 (A is B). Thus, the two lines can be read as: The guest homesick by the Yangtze and Han is a rotten scholar between the heaven and earth. This reading makes sense because "homesick guest" and "rotten scholar" are one and the same person—that is, the poet. In my reading, the first two lines are not primarily concerned with presenting images but with making a statement, the poet's perception and assessment of himself.

Lines 3 and 4, they maintain, have syntactic linkage but the syntax is scrambled. In their opinion, the two lines should be read as "片雲共天遠，永夜同月孤". As an illustration of their opinion, Mei

and Kao offer two readings: (1) "the streak of cloud is as far as the sky";
(2) "under the sky, I am as far (away from home) as the streak of cloud."
Linguistically, I may provide an additional reading by restoring an omitted
"I." Since the first and second lines present the poet as a homesick person
by the Yangtze and Han and a withered pedant between heaven and earth,
we can imagine how lonely he is. This sense of solitude is echoed and
strengthened by lines 3 and 4. For this reason, I offer a different reading
of the lines: 片雲之天/共(余)遠，永夜之月/同(余)孤, which can be
translated as: "The sky with a streak of cloud shares my distance from
home; the moon of endless night shares my solitude." From this point of
view, the ambiguity is the result of omission, not that of scrambled syntax.
By the same token, their second reading of line 3 as consisting of "dis-
continuity, ambiguity, and dislocation" is somewhat too restrictive,
because it underestimates the leverage allowed by poetic syntax.

In the reading of another poetic line: "lonely boat / one moored /
homeward heart 孤舟一系故園心," Mei and Kao regard the line as two
independent clauses in juxtaposition or as a continuous sentence: "In one
case, the grammatical structure emphasizes the contrast between the boat
tied up and the thoughts racing homeward, and in the other, the casual
connection between two kinds of immobility, the boat being moored and
the poet being tied to the boat."[25] They maintain that "it is perfectly
natural to interpret 'homeward thoughts' as the direct object of 'tied up.'
" To complement their two readings, I may suggest another that is not
only linguistically sound but also aesthetically profound. I read it as: "the
homeward heart is tied onto a lonely boat 孤舟一(葉)系(著)故園心."
In other words, the lonely boat may not be tied; it may be floating in the
distance. The poet projects his homesickness onto the moving boat so that
he imagined the boat could carry his homeward heart home. While Mei's
and Kao's reading emphasizes stasis, hinting at the poet's inability to
change his predicament, my reading stresses movement, showing the
poet's resolve to act even though he could act only in his imagination.
Syntactic ambiguity permits both interpretations.

My analysis of the above examples shows that ambiguity in classical
Chinese poetry is often caused by the omission of particles or pronouns.
In short and densely structured lyric poems, every word counts. Particles
and pronouns are often dropped to give space to more information-carrying
words. The omission may give rise to syntactic ambiguity, but make the
poetic structure terse and pregnant with implications. In many cases, the
poet may have deliberately made use of syntactic ambiguity to enlarge
the poetic space. The line "white cloud / bright moon / mourn / Lady Xiang
E 白雲明月吊湘娥" is a case in point. It is not clear whether the white
cloud and bright moon are mourning Lady Xiang E, or whether someone

or the poet is mourning her under the white cloud and bright moon. I think, the poet may have deliberately created the ambiguity so as to give the line a richer meaning. The first reading turns the line into a case of personification or even pathetic fallacy. When the white cloud and bright moon are mobilized by the poet to mourn Lady Xiang E, the situation is truly overflowing with pathos. If we move from linguistic analysis to literary analysis, this line may yield some other meanings. The "white cloud," because it is part of the sky, may stand for heaven. "White" in Chinese culture is a color of mourning. The "bright moon" appears in an evening sky. Thus, it may serve as a metonym for the evening sky. When the daytime sky and evening sky mourn Lady Xiang E, this poetic line may be said to have an added temporal dimension: the lady is being mourned by the universe day and night.

The poetic openness that I have discussed is largely achieved through minimal syntax. Minimal syntax as a theory for poetic composition was promoted by T. E. Hulme, father of Imagism.[26] It is characteristic of much of the Imagist poetry produced in England and America from 1910 to 1930 and of the Symbolist and Post-Symbolist poetry in France. It is worthwhile to note the similarities in the manipulation of syntax for special effects between classical Chinese poetry and French Symbolist poetry, as pointed out by Pauline Yu: "Symbolist and post-symbolist poets . . . in addition to employing a difficult syntax which impedes forward movement, also prefer the copula and juxtaposition, both of which leave temporal or causal relationships undefined, and frequently leave ambiguities and oppositions unresolved, relying on a principle of equivalence rather than logical sequence. Moreover, their poems are often noun-heavy, to create an overall effect of simultaneity."[27]

The idea of minimal syntax has support in Bergson's philosophical inquiry into time and in psychological studies of dreams. Many scholars have noticed the similarities between poetry and dreams in their imaginative resourcefulness and, moreover, in their lack of rigorous syntactic structures. To a certain extent, Imagist and Symbolist poetry represents a conscious striving toward the condition of dreams. If I were to invert a saying by Darwin, "A dream is an involuntary poem," we could say, a poem is a voluntary dream. The affinity is more apparent in Modernist poetry which, composed with scrambled syntax, often earns the notoriety of being a dreamer's ravings 夢囈. The syntax of classical Chinese poetry is quite similar to the unconventional syntax of Modernist poetry, which reminds one of the signifying mechanism of dreams discovered by Freud in his *Interpretation of Dreams*: a dream uses a language that does not have the syntactical rules of the daytime language. The single rule of composition in dreams is juxtaposition, which stands for all the syntactic rules of daytime language such as logic, sequence, coordination, and subordination.[28] Juxtaposition causes ambiguity but gives the dream a large possibility for interpretation. In a similar way, juxtaposition in poetry also endows a poem with a larger potential space for the reader to exercise his imagination.

Dream Language and the Poetic Unconscious

Having discussed syntactic ambiguity of poetic Chinese for openness, I venture to suggest that Chinese poems that have open hermeneutic space tend to signify and represent in a way akin to dream scripts. This proposition may surprise some scholars, but a comparison of the signifying mechanisms of dreams with representational mechanisms of poems with open space will allow this proposition to stand on solid ground and enable us to probe into the source of openness. Dreams gain their representability through juxtaposition of dream images. Most Chinese poems with an open hermeneutic space employ juxtaposition in a similar way: nouns, noun phrases, and verbal phrases placed side by side with minimal syntax. They have a spatial quality, a vague syntactic relation, and a sense of indeterminacy—all these are precisely the impressions we get in dreams. It is a truism that a poem is a compressed discourse. Poetic Chinese certainly contributes to the process of compression, but that which compresses diverse elements into a poetic discourse is an agency in the poet's mind, which I wish to call the poetic unconscious, or the "soul of openness" in keeping with the term that I invented at the beginning of this chapter, the "eye of openness." Nowadays, scholars generally reject the static view of the unconscious as the seat of the id, a seething cauldron full of drives, and accept the dynamic conception of the unconscious as "an abstraction, an invisible 'place' in the mind, or an unseeable system of energy flowing beyond consciousness."[29] This dynamic system has its own forces and energies that push toward consciousness or unconsciousness, expression or repression. In his advocacy for a return to Freud, Lacan argues that "What the psychoanalytic experience discovers in the unconscious is the whole structure of language."[30] He develops his notion into an elaborate theory of the unconscious, which may be summarized by his famous aphorism "the unconscious is structured like a language."[31] This aphorism means that the operations of the unconscious follow the axes of combination and selection as a language does. In Lacan's notion, we not only see his indebtedness to linguistics but more importantly the close relationship between language and the unconscious. He demonstrates that if the unconscious, as Freud describes it, exists, it functions linguistically, rather than symbolically or instinctually, as scholars used to believe. Levi-Strauss, who was a major influence on Lacan, thinks that the unconscious is responsible for imposing structural laws upon basic inarticulate elements, such as emotions, memories, and impulses—the raw materials of poetry.[32] In terms of Freud's, Levi-Strauss's, and Lacan's theories of the mind, I feel tempted to equate the poetic unconscious with the unconscious. Of course, this is not the place to explore the relationship between the unconscious and the poetic unconscious. What I have in mind is that by exploring the relationship between language and the unconscious, we may come to a better understanding of the poetic mind that is responsible for the act of compressing poetic discourse into a densely packed hermeneutic space. Moreover, with a combined approach that unites psychoanalysis, linguistics, and semiotics, we may be in a position to answer a few thoughtful questions Kao and Mei raised in their application of Jacobson's theory of poetic equivalence to the study of Chinese poetry.

The unconscious is just the opposite of the conscious. Its logic is fundamentally different from that of the Cartesian reason and self-identity. It is characterized by what is unknown, unknowable, and that which cannot be totalized. Nevertheless, the unconscious can be indirectly approached through unconscious psychic acts: slips of the tongue, slips of the pen, jokes, puns, the poetic dimension of language, forms of nonsense, and last but not least, dreams. Freud once made this famous remark: "The interpretation of dreams is the royal road to a knowledge of the unconscious activities of the mind."[33] In his comment on Freud's discovery of the unconscious language, Lacan reaffirms Freud's view: "Thus in *The Interpretation of Dreams* every page deals with what I call the letter of the discourse, in its texture, its usage, its immanence in the matter in question. For it is with this work that the work of Freud begins to open the royal road to the unconscious."[34] Creative writers like William Shakespeare, William Blake, Oscar Wilde, Paul Valéry, Stéphane Mallarmé, and Richard Wagner; thinkers like Charles Darwin, Friedrich Nietzsche, Sigmund Freud, Carl G. Jung, Ernst Cassirer, Roman Jacobson, and Jacques Lacan; critics like Northrop Frye, Erving Babbit, John C. Ransom, Lionel Trilling, and Norman Holland—all concur on the intrinsic relationship between dreams and creativity. Lacan emphasizes even more the kinship of poetry, dream, and the unconscious. For him, reading poetry is the closest one can come to accessing the unconscious. For him, too, poetry is a kind of dream through which the poet accesses his unconscious desires. Poetry gives to the poet not its meaning, but rather a plethora of signifiers with which the poet attempts to construct a rebus of his own meaning, to paint a disguised and scrambled portrait of his unconscious desires.[35]

Lacan's view of poetry is in keeping with creative writers' views of poetry. Wordsworth defines poetry as the "spontaneous overflow of powerful feelings."[36] The spontaneous emotions pouring out of streams of consciousness defy reason, logic, sequence, causality, and other necessary elements required for the clear expression of everyday communication. They cannot be pinned down with exact and precise words. In a way, Chinese poetic language duplicates the thought process in dreaming because it is less mediated than highly inflected languages. By the same token, Chinese poetic language is a fitting vehicle for the expression of poetic thought which, because it consists of streams of consciousness, is hazy, ambiguous, illogical, and multidetermined. With minimal morphology and syntax, poetic Chinese works in a way similar to the signifying process of dream language.

Dream language differs from ordinary language in its lack of recognized grammatical rules and logical order. Poetic Chinese resembles dream language in its lack of hard and fast syntax, looseness in logical order, and openness to different interpretations. In *The Interpretation of Dreams*, Freud asks this question: What representation do dreams provide for "if," "because," "just as," "although," "either—or," and all the other conjunctions without which we cannot understand sentences or speeches? His answer is as follows: "[D]reams have no means at their disposal for representing these logical relations between the dream-thoughts. For the most part dreams disregard all these conjunctions, and it is only the substantive content of the dream-thoughts that they take over and manipulate. The restoration of the connections which the dream-work has destroyed is a task which has to be performed by the interpretative process."[37]

Scholars of Chinese literature have arrived at a similar conclusion albeit this conclusion pertains to Chinese lyric poetry. Kang-i Sun Chang's excellent study of Chinese *ci* poetry is full of examples of how paratactic rather than hypotactic syntax dominates the composition of a *ci* poem.[38] Here I just want to quote Watson's view: "The [Chinese] poem is constructed almost wholly of these one-line units or building blocks; only rarely, most often in the last couplet, does the poet use a run-on line. Moreover, to continue the metaphor, these blocks are fitted together with little or no grammatical mortar; parataxis rather then hypotaxis is the rule. Occasionally an 'although' or a 'moreover' may be inserted, but for the most part the logical connectives must be supplied by the reader. Poems that comprise a single sentence, such as are not uncommon in English, or those in which the entire syntax is kept in suspension until the final syllables, as in Japanese, are unknown."[39]

If this comparison still fails to convince the reader of the similarity of poetic Chinese to dream language, I may provide a direct relation between dream language and poetic Chinese, confirmed by psychoanalytic research. In his study of dreams, Freud discovers an inherent relationship between dream language and ancient languages such as Chinese and Egyptian hieroglyphics. One common feature of dream language and ancient languages, he notes, is their lack of syntactic connectives that explain relations between words or between images.[40] Although Freud's understanding of Chinese is very limited and reductive, his observation touches upon an interesting aspect of classical Chinese in poetry. Poetic Chinese bears a strong resemblance to dream language in that highly abstract and logical relations such as whether/or, if/then, because, although, just as, and concepts associated with time, are not clearly marked, and the intended logical implications must often be recognized in the process of interpretation.

Poetic Chinese may be compared to dream language in a number of aspects. The most decisive one is that the building blocks of poetic Chinese are endowed with the characteristic qualities of dream symbols. Dream symbols are acoustic and imagistic signs. The multiple significance of a dream symbol is produced by acoustic and imagistic associations. Acoustically, a dream symbol is often a condensation of several meanings into one sound through the so-called *klang* association (sound association). Chinese is a highly homophonic language. Classical Chinese is even more so. One of the so-called *liushu* (six graph-making methods) is based on sound association: "The sixth is called *jiajie* (loan-borrowing). These are for words which originally had no graph of their own, and depend on the sounds to stand for something else."[41] In poetic creation, some poets consciously made use of sound association to create puns and word play to express double or multiple meanings. One well-known example is a poetic line in Liu Yuxi's 劉禹錫 (772–842) poem "Zhuzhi ci 竹枝詞": "道是無情還有晴 (情)."[42] This line may be literally rendered as "He says that there is no love, but there is sunshine." But the homophone of "love" and "sunshine" implies: "He says that there is no love, but his love is there." In Li Shangying's "Untitled" poem, which I have discussed for a different purpose, play on words forms a significant part of its art. The obvious word play is *si* (silk), which puns with *si* (thought). François Cheng even views the whole poem as being constructed on sound association.[43]

Visually, poetic Chinese signifies like dream language in its imagistic representation. By "imagistic" I do not mean that each Chinese character is a pictogram or has the pictorial quality as claimed by Fenollosa and Pound. I mean to say that a Chinese character is imagistic in the sense that it stands in and by itself, like an icon, and does not have to conform to the stringent morphological restraints such as number, article, case, gender, tense, voice, and conjugation required by an inflective language. A poetic discourse composed with these free-standing characters, functions, to a certain extent, like a picture composed with images. Watson's painting analogy of a Chinese poem, which I have quoted earlier, rightly captures this idiosyncratic feature of Chinese poetry. The relations among the characters in a Chinese poem are loosely determined, and are often subject to a determining effort on the part of the reader. Freud makes a special mention of this characteristic feature of Chinese in comparison with dream language: "They [dream symbols] frequently have more than one or even several meanings, and, as with Chinese script, the correct interpretation can only be arrived at on each occasion from the context. This ambiguity of the symbols links up with the characteristic of dreams for admitting of 'over-interpretation'—for representing in a single piece of content thoughts and wishes which are often widely divergent in their nature."[44] In this passage, Freud is employing the Chinese language as an illustrating example to show how a dream is composed of a series of repressed thoughts and can therefore be interpreted in various ways. I have reversed the analogy to demonstrate how the poetic unconscious compresses different strands of desires into a poem and endows it with a large hermeneutic space.

Juxtaposition and Multidetermination

When I claim that poetic Chinese comes close to dream language, and a Chinese poem with open space signifies in a way like a dream, I do not mean to say that a Chinese poem is as esoteric as a dream; nor is it my purpose to wrap Chinese lyric poetry in a mysterious veil. My aim is just the opposite: I want to tear through the enigmatic veil, to open up the poem to reveal its multidimensional signifying mechanism, and in the process of producing multivalence and polysemy, to advance a method of reading. Nothing facilitates my endeavor better than the illustration of a concrete example. In the space below, I will use Ma Zhiyuan's 馬致遠 (1250?–1324?) famous poem "Tian jingsha—qiusi 天淨沙—秋思" as an illustrative example:

Autumn Thoughts	秋思
Withered vines, old tree, dull crows.	枯籐老樹昏鴉。
Small bridge, flowing water, someone's house.	小橋流水人家。
Ancient road, westerly wind, a lean horse.	古道西風瘦馬。
The setting sun falls in the west.	夕陽西下。
A heartbroken man is at the heaven's edge.	斷腸人在天涯。[45]

Ma Zhiyuan's extant poems number over a hundred, but it is this short poem that has earned him lasting popularity. Wang Guowei, in his *Renjian cihua* 人間詞話, makes this comment: "With just a few words, the poem captures well the wonderful effects of the quatrain style poetry by the Tang poets. None of the *ci*-poets of the Yuan were capable of achieving this success."[46] In his *Song-Yuan xiqu shi* 宋元戲曲史, he agrees with the assessment of previous scholars and praises the poem as the supreme model for short poems in the style of dramatic lyrics.[47] I have read quite a few comments on this poem in Chinese literary studies, but to my disappointment, few scholars have explained adequately why this poem has such lasting popular appeal. Indeed, few are bothered with why it is a good poem. Wang Guowei's comment is equivalent to saying that the poem is good simply because it is good.

I suggest that the poem has a lasting popular appeal because it is constructed with a principle similar to Wang Wei's "Deer Enclosure." It is a poem with an open space for imagination. What makes it different from Wang Wei's poem is that its composing principle comes closer to the signifying mechanism of dreams. Almost entirely composed with imagistic words, it comes close to a dream scene. One scholar's analysis stresses the noun-heavy feature of this poem: "In the first three lines, nine images are used to construct the scene; all of them are notional words. In the last two lines, except for 'downwards' and 'at', all the rest are notional words too. The syntax is similar to the poetic lines: 'Cock's crow, thatched inn, and the moon; / human footprints, wood-board bridge, and the frost.'"[48] Although this scholar does not specify how the syntax contributes to the poetic qualities of the poem, the comparison with two lines from another famous poem, Wen Tingyun's 溫庭筠 (812–70) "Shangshan zaoxin (Leaving Mount Shang at Dawn)," touches upon a distinct feature of poetic syntax in classical Chinese poetry. The juxtaposition of a series of nouns without specifying their syntactical relations duplicates the signifying process of a dream scene, in which a series of dream symbols thrown together without logical connections makes the dream scene overdetermined with multiple meanings.

In his study of dreams, Freud makes a distinction between dream contents and dream thoughts. Dream contents are simply dreams that feature shifting scenes of pictographic images one sees in sleep. Dream thoughts refer to the process of thinking that lies behind dream content: "Their dominant element is the repressed impulse, which has obtained some kind of expression, toned down and disguised though it may be, by associating itself with stimuli which happen to be there by tucking itself in the residue of the day before."[49] Dream content is manifest while dream thought is latent. Their relationship is that between a translation and its original: "The dream-thoughts and the dream-content are presented to us like two versions of the same subject-matter in two different languages. Or, more properly, the dream-content seems like a transcript of the dream-thoughts into another mode of expression, whose characters and syntactic laws it is our business to discover by comparing the original and the translation."[50] The dream content and dream thoughts are intimately related, but they differ enormously not only in form but also in the magnitude of space: "Dreams are brief, meager and laconic in comparison with the range and wealth of the dream-thoughts. If a dream is written out it may perhaps fill half a page. The analysis setting out the dream-thoughts underlying it may occupy six, eight or a dozen times as much space."[51] Thus a dream scene is only the compressed form of copious dream thoughts.

All great literature is essentially a compressed form of writing. Classical Chinese poetry is even more so. Freud likes to compare an actual dream to the tip of an iceberg and the copious dream thoughts to the large bulk of the iceberg submerged in water. In a similar manner, we may say that the words of a Chinese poem on the page are but the tip of an iceberg. It is the reader's business to uncover the large bulk of meanings between, behind, and among the lines. Wen Tingyun's two poetic lines are open to several interpretations. What is the relationship between the "cockcrow" and the "thatched inn"? One may say the cock belongs to the inn; its function is to wake up the guests at dawn. In this context, the poetic line may mean that the guest arises and starts his journey early in the morning, earlier than the cock crows. Another possibility arises since the agent of the crowing is not specified. It could be the cry of a cock, but it could be that of a hen or hens. In this case, one may say that the hens cry because they are disturbed by the hustle and bustle of the early traveler. Thus, the crow may serve as an uninvited sendoff, further strengthening the desolate feeling of an early morning departure. Or the cockcrow is only a phenomenon the poet observes on departing early in the morning; he does not wish to specify the relationship. We need to attend to two other unspecified relationships: one between the moon and the inn and the other between the moon and the cock. Is the moon related to the inn because it shines upon the inn, or because the poet catches sight of it on coming out of the inn? As for the cock and the moon, are they related because the poet wants to indicate that when the cock crows, the moon has not yet set, or because both serve as indications of an early departure? With regard to the relationship among the footprints, wooden bridge, and the frost in the second line, there are a number of possibilities. Different possibilities may yield different implications.

The disparate elements in Wen Tinyun's two poetic lines are glued together by no syntax but juxtaposition. In short lyric poems, juxtaposition is not just a common technique to capture the copiousness of amorphous thoughts in writing; it also facilitates the activation of the three imaginations of the sign in reading. An examination of a couplet from Li Bai's poem "Seeing Off a Friend 送友人" will reveal how juxtaposition may hide symbolic, formal, and functional relations of the sign in the gaps between words: "floating clouds / wanderer's thoughts 浮雲游子意, setting sun / old friends' sentiments 落日故人情."[52] Scholars concur that each of these two lines involves a juxtaposition of two images with implied comparison omitted. Along this line, François Cheng gives a brilliant reading to reveal the hidden comparative relations.[53] Cheng's interpretation only covers an aspect of the possible relations of the juxtaposed four images. I wish to suggest another way of looking at the supposedly comparative relationship. I argue that the omission of a clearly marked syntactic relation creates a real gap between the juxtaposed images, which in turn constitutes a potential space for other readings. The juxtaposed images certainly imply a comparison (a metaphorical relation), but they may also conceal other relations that may subvert the accepted reading. For example, we may fill the gap with verbs other than "resemble" and render the two lines as: "the floating clouds incite/inspire/intensify the wanderer's thought" / "the setting sun weakens/soothes/dispels an old friend's feeling." The reading makes sense, for we may take the two lines to mean: while the floating clouds with its untrammeled freedom heighten the wanderer's resolve to rove, the setting sun with its soft rays soothes the friend's sadness at parting. Here, the images of "floating clouds" and "setting sun" not only function as *xing* or stimulus but also imply a symbolic relation. The poet chooses them to objectify his emotions. It is human feelings that correlate the disparate categories. The poetic unconscious causes the *xing* images to oscillate between metaphor and symbol, thus making it possible to have metaphorical and symbolic readings. "Floating clouds" and "wanderer" do not have any natural connection; the poet's "thoughts" about the similarity between the free-floating nature of the clouds and the roaming propensity link them together. The "setting sun" and "old friend's thought" do not have any logical or natural connection, either. They are connected because the poet sees in them an equivalence: the lingering of the setting sun on the western horizon is like the reluctance of his friend to part from him.

In a symbolic relationship, "floating clouds" and "setting sun" presuppose at least a weak functional connection. If we read them as common symbols, "floating clouds" should refer to "human life" in conventional symbolism (as the saying goes, "the human life is like floating clouds") or to "wealth and prosperity" (as the saying goes, "wealth and prosperity are like clouds"); "setting sun" to "fading glory" (as in "the lingering splendor of the setting sun") or "last stage in human life" (as in the poetic lines, "Boundlessly good is the setting sun; / Only to be Regretted that it is close to dusk"). In a symbolic reading, the first poetic line may be read as: because life is like floating clouds, the persona is gripped by the desire to wander. The second line may mean: because the setting sun symbolizes the short span of life, the old friendship may be shortened, too. But this symbolic reading fits uneasily into the context of the poem. We, therefore, must read the two lines in the other imaginations (or relations) of the sign: paradigmatic and syntagmatic.

In paradigmatic and syntagmatic relations, the two images signify vertically as well as horizontally. Within their vertical signification, "floating clouds" may be substituted with words of "anchorlessness" and "aimlessness"; "setting sun" with words of "ephemerality" and "remnant quality." Horizontally, they combine with other signifiers to produce a metonymic chain of deflections that signifies a progressive creation of metaphors. In addition to the metaphorical connections I have already mentioned, there are other possible metaphorical relations. Clouds float aimlessly. They may be seen as having an affinity to the wanderer's aimless roving. "Floating clouds" then may be perceived to hint that the wanderer's destinations are uncertain, or the wanderer is uncertain of where he plans to go. "Setting sun," which is at this moment about to disappear from sight, may be construed to mean that the friend's reluctance at parting will gradually vanish as time passes. This reading is possible in the context of the poem, especially if we consider the two ending lines: "Waving my hand, I depart from here, / Neigh, neigh cries my motley horse 揮手自茲去，嘯嘯斑馬鳴." These two lines suggest that having bidden farewell to his friend, the persona embarked on his journey alone with only his horse accompanying him. This reading directly contradicts the accepted reading and may be said to have accomplished a deconstructive turn. Finally, through a syntagmatic relation, the metaphorical meaning of the first line, the "insatiable wanderlust," may be brought into a paradigmatic relation with the metaphorical meaning of the second line, "friend's reluctance at parting," to form a poetic equivalence. As a result, there appears another metaphorical relation: "my friend's insatiable wanderlust is as strong as my reluctance to part from him." Some more relations may be discovered (created). Of all the discovered relations, some, located on the axis of selection, come from paradigmatic consciousness; some, located on the axis of combination, are the results of syntagmatic consciousness.

Metaphor, Metonymy, and Signifying Practice

My discussion of Li Bai's two lines may suggest a new way of looking at images in Chinese poetry. Poetic images in paratactically juxtaposed poetic lines, I argue, have the potential of being viewed from both the paradigmatic and syntagmatic angles. Because of the paratactical rather than hypotactical syntax, the word relations are ambiguous. As a result, poetic images may enter different orders of relations with each other and with the reader's subject positions and be understood either as symbol or metaphor or metonymy. This way of looking may explain the thoughtful questions Kao and Mei raised concerning Jacobson's theory of poetic function: "The poetic function projects the principle of equivalence from the axis of selection into the axis of combination."[54] In their application of Jacobson's theory, Kao and Mei are of the opinion that the principle of equivalence projected by the poetic function runs along the axis of combination, which means that equivalence is confined within said or written discourse or text. But in their study of Chinese poetry, they have found two types of phenomena central to recent-style poetry, which cannot be explained by examining the text alone:

> The first is the relation between an individual word and its semantic category. The word occurs in a poem, but the category occurs only by proxy. . . . The second is the frequent occurrence of covert metaphor and allusion. Both metaphor and allusion, it will be recalled, consist of two terms related by equivalence. In the covert variety, only one term occurs in the poem. The other term is merely hinted at, but an audience who shares the same tradition as the author clearly grasps the comparison. However, if we let the scope of equivalence relation extend beyond the poem, we have moved from text to context, and as a result, deserted the central dogma of new criticism and structural linguistics as it is commonly understood.[55]

This statement in Kao and Mei's study, conducted at a time when the New Critical and the Structuralist conception of literary text and criticism was just beginning to be challenged by poststructuralist theorists, shows that the two scholars were then aware of the limitations of structuralist linguistics and the structuralist concept of a text as an enclosed, self-contained, and autotelic space of unity and harmony. Had they not imposed on themselves an allegiance to the "spirit of structural[ist] linguistics," they could have gone beyond the structuralist study of poetry and embarked on the poststructuralist route to treat a text as an open space of different views, voices, values, and perspectives. Their introduction of tradition as a remedy for the limitations in Jacobson's theory is in fact part of what the poststructuralist theorists have advocated. But suppose that we confine our examination to the words on the page, can we still locate equivalences among disparate elements of a poem? My answer is yes. The affirmative answer, however, requires us to approach a text from the combined perspectives of psychoanalysis, linguistics, and semiotics, and especially from the vantage point of Lacan's redefinition of metaphor and metonymy.

After revising Freud's theory of dream condensation and displacement in terms of Saussurean linguistics, Lacan redraws a definition for metonymy and metaphor: "[I]t is in the word-to-word connection that metonymy is based"[56] and "One word for another: that is the formula for the metaphor."[57] Lacan's redefining of metaphor and metonymy has not only completely revolutionized our traditional understanding of metaphor and metonymy, but may also alter our understanding of imagery in Chinese poetry. It has liberated us from the confines of defining metaphor and metonymy in terms of certain relationships between tenor and vehicle in a discourse. In the case of metaphor, for example, it is no longer restricted to the Aristotelian way of seeing similarity in dissimilarity. In the case of metonymy, it is no longer restricted to the way of finding the part for the whole or vice versa. So long as it is a case of one word substituting for another, we have a metaphor; and so long as we encounter a word placed side by side with another, we have a metonymy. In this way, Lacan's redefinition provides theoretical support for my new way of looking at juxtaposed images in Chinese poetry.

The significance of Lacan's esoteric theory for our understanding of poetic imagery in Chinese poetry may be better understood with an analysis of Ma Zhiyuan's poem, a project that has been deferred so far. What is most fascinating about this poem is that even a literal translation is still able to convey the ethos of the original poem. The poem, composed with a minimal presence of grammatical restraints, presents a telegraphic style and offers a most convenient way to explain my view. I have divided the lines into units equivalent to Saussure's idea of terms rather than words. In the first line, "withered vines/old tree/dull crows," each of the slash symbols represents a metaphoric relationship because the terms on both sides of the slash imply an equivalence: withered vine and old tree can replace each other because both denote a sense of decrepitude. Old tree and dull crow have a similar equivalence: a sense of desolation. In the second line, the two slash symbols also represent an equivalence, but this time it is a positive one because each of the terms is related to one's home. The third, fourth, and fifth lines can be analyzed in a similar manner. In the third line, the equivalent quality is a sense of bleakness; in the fourth line, it is a downward movement; in the fifth line, it is a sense of pain. Up to this point, my analysis is still restricted to Jacobson's idea of equivalence. In the following, however, I will conduct my analysis in terms of Lacan's redefinition of metaphor and metonymy. The theme of the poem may be one of melancholy or homesickness. In terms of Lacan's definition of metaphor as "one word for another," we may say, in the poem, each unit or term can be viewed as a metaphor for the poet's homesickness. "Home-sickness" is the plain word that can convey the poet's mental state, but the word does not have any poetic evocativeness. It is replaced by a series of word units which, in the Chinese cultural context, evoke in the poet's/reader's mind the mental conditions of melancholy and homesickness. In a word-for-word substitution, we may render each term as: "the withered vines (old tree, dull crows . . . heaven's edge) stand for my homesickness." On the other hand, all the units share a word-to-word relation though the relation is not spelled out. By contiguity and contexture, the units may imply an unstated syntagmatic relation. If we are to bring out that relation, the units can be read as: "withered vines are on the old tree; the old tree is perched on by dull crows; Beneath the small bridge flows a stream of water; beside the stream stands a man's house"; etc.

Thus, the images in this poem can be viewed as both metaphor and metonymy, symptom and desire, and serve the different poetic impulses: lyricism and narrative. On the metaphorical axis, all the images are metaphors or symptoms of the poet's melancholy or homesickness. On the metonymic axis, the series of images shows the displacement of desire from one image to the next and implies a narrative impulse. This poem is also a good example to help us understand Lacan's examination of the differences between metaphor and metonymy in terms of their affects: "For the symptom is a metaphor whether one likes it or not, as desire is a metonymy, however funny people may find the idea."[58] In terms of this view, I may suggest that a metaphor implies that the poet has objectified his desire by finding what T. S. Eliot calls an "objective correlative," "a set of objects, a situation, a chain of events which shall be the formula of that particular emotion,"[59] while a metonymy implies that an object or situation is only an "other" of the poet's desire, not the fulfillment of his desire, and he therefore has to displace it from one signifier to another signifier, from one scene to another scene, and from one episode to another episode. Thus, the poem may seem to present a static picture, but just as dream content hides the logical connectives between dream scenes, so it also conceals a dynamic movement of a series of scenes with an implicit narrative impulse.

The narrative impulse was, of course, repressed by the poetic (un)conscious, which also suppressed syntactic relations among words, phrases, and logical connectives between poetic lines when the poem was composed. More than any other poem in the Chinese tradition, this poem approximates the conditions of a transcribed dream on the page. Dreams are shifting scenes with pictographic images. As a verbal construct, a poem cannot directly present pictographic images visually on the page, but Ma Zhiyuan's poem aspires to approximate visual presentation. For this purpose, he pushed the iconicity of Chinese characters to the limit. One of his methods is the already mentioned move to suppress any syntactic and logical connectives. Another move is to avoid using words that denote linear progression of time, especially verbs. Verbs generally convey a sense of process and the progression of time. But in this poem, there are only two verbs *xia* 下 and *zai* 在. Strictly speaking, there is only one verb, *xia*, for *zai* can be read as a coverb or preposition. Thus, the poem could be viewed as wholly consisting of nouns and noun phrases, which, through epistemological visualization, present visual images. The accepted reading presents a visual scene: An old tree hangs with withered vines. A crow perches on a branch of the old tree. Nearby flows a quiet stream upon which there is a small bridge. By the bridge stands someone's house. The poet is riding a lean horse on an ancient road. The westerly wind blows hard and the sun is setting. Now that he has traveled to such a distant land, he is filled with profound sorrow.

This reading is doubtless adequate and aesthetically pleasing. However, this is a static reading which suppresses the narrative impulse, shifting subject positions, and discrepant details. For a different reading, I suggest that we read the poem in the same way one views a dream, because the poem presents a series of visual images juxtaposed in indeterminate relations. Paradoxically, the suppression of ostensible linear progression of time does not impart the impression of a static picture. The montagelike technique of juxtaposition conveys a sense of dynamism that makes one feel as though he were watching a series of cinematic shots. The dynamic mode of presentation requires us to get into the cracks between words on the page and consider what has been ignored by the accepted reading.

In a dynamic reading, the poem may not be meant to present a static picture but a series of moving pictures. This means that the images in the poem do not belong to a single frame of reference and we should not be content with viewing the poem as a two-dimensional painting. Instead, we ought to conceive of its hermeneutic space as a multidimensional one. It is not only constructed with a sense of three dimensions but also with the dimension of time or narrative and a constant shift in focus. From this perspective, we should approach the poem not as we approach a Chinese landscape painting but as we watch a series of scenery shots in a film. The dynamic reading finds support in textual evidence. My analysis of equivalence in the lines suggests that the images constituting the five poetic lines may not be grouped together into a single category to symbolize sorrow and homesickness. Indeed, the disparate and discrepant nature of them suggests that we may typologize them into two or three or more categories by their denotations (conventional meanings) and connotations (inspired associations). Images of "withered vines, old tree, and dull crows" may form one group because they are all images with similar denotations and connotations. Images of "small bridge, flowing water, and man's house" may form another group because of their pleasant associations. Images of "westerly wind, ancient road, and lean horse" may form still another group because of their close relations with each other. "The sun sets in the west" is another different scene. It may be related to any of the above three groups; it may be a category standing on its own. Similarly, the image of a "heartbroken man at heaven's edge" may be related to the four poetic lines or may describe an independent scene.

My typology makes it possible for us to see the fragmentation of the poetic consciousness and the shifting in subject position. It is as though the poet acted like a film camera man or a film editor who orients the viewer from one angle to another. Line 1 leads the reader to see a scene with "withered vines, old tree, and a crow." Line 2 shifts to another scene with "small bridge, flowing water, and man's house." Line 3 may revert to the scene of line 1 or it may show another scene with "westerly wind, ancient road, and lean horse." Line 4 may revert the point of view to the scene of line 2 or may point to another scene. The last line may shift the point of view to lines 1 and 3, or it may introduce an entirely different scene. Within the lines themselves, there are shifts of focus. In line 1, "withered vine" indicates a near shot, "old tree" a distant shot, and "a crow" a snapshot. Since the number of "crow" in Chinese is not specified, it could be single or plural. It is not made clear either whether the crows are in flight or perching on the tree. If the crows are in flight, it may suggest a more distant shot. The other lines may be analyzed in the same way. The images in a line are bound together like a string of shots seen from the same angle and indicate that the poetic function is at work to locate equivalence.

For over six hundred years, scholars have generally believed that all the images belong to the same scene. But my reviewing of the poem in terms of the function of the poetic unconscious suggests an equally valid and perhaps more interesting reading of those images. The poetic unconscious dissolves consciousness into fragmented images and then juxtaposes them to generate new and original composite images and scenes in the same way the dreamwork fragments and recombines memories to create a dream scene. S. T. Coleridge calls this poetic function "secondary imagination," which "dissolves, diffuses, dissipates, in order to recreate."[60] In the case of Ma Zhiyuan's poem, all the images represent fragmented thoughts, and their connections need to be restored by the reader. There are a number of possible ways to coordinate the images into a meaningful syntactical relation. An obvious way is to read the poem as a radical example of minimal syntax in classical Chinese poetry through the avoidance of verbs. Linguistically, we could add "there are . . ." to the beginning of the poem and then the poem becomes a long-winded sentence and has a perfect grammatical structure.

But this is the basis of the conventional reading. One may approach the poem by restoring suppressed connections among the noun phrases and derive some unconventional readings. If we view the poet as the persona, we may get this reading: "When I saw the withered vines on an old tree with a crow perched on it, I thought of my house by a small bridge across a stream of flowing water. Braving the westerly wind, I am riding my lean horse on an ancient road. At the time of sunset, I am gripped by an acute spasm of homesickness." Or one may treat the poem as consisting of a series of shifting scenes. This time, the heartbroken man is not the poet but a family member, a loved one, or a friend. This reading is sanctioned by the subtitle, "autumn thought." If it is about thought, then the persona in the poem could be someone else. Even without the subtitle, the new reading is plausible, for it is not made clear the "heartbroken man" is the poet or someone else.

The poem presents a series of contrasting images: withered vine, old tree, and a crow on the one hand, small bridge, flowing water, and a home on the other hand. The contrast of paired images triggers his imagining of someone riding a lean horse on an ancient road. The setting sun with its associations of home return forms another contrast with the traveler far away from home. At sunset, even cattle and sheep return to their pens, but the traveler is at heaven's edge. I have, so far, directed my attention to the fluid form of the poem. Because it has no preconstituted form (or it does not show a particular form on the page), it may be called a formless form. As it is capable of creating forms necessary for a particular perspective and producing open possibilities, it works like a postmodern serial form. Once again, this quasi-serial form could not have resulted from a conscious serial thought, but might have arisen from the poetic unconscious structured by poetic language. I have only touched upon the potential linguistic mortar that fills the cracks between disparate elements of the discourse. If one were to interpret the images in the poem in terms of particular historical contexts and cultural associations, the poem would have many interpretations.

The "Soul" of Openness

Ma Zhiyuan's poem is not simply structured on juxtaposition. The potential relations between its words as revealed in my analysis exemplify a poetic technique I would call "linguistic suture." The iconic nature of Chinese characters, sparse morphological restraints of Chinese words, and syntactic freedom of poetic lines enabled classical Chinese poets to create linguistic suture, which comes close to the cinematic model of suture. "Suture" in ordinary language means "the process of joining two surfaces or edges together by or as if by sewing."[61] In film studies, "suture" is the term for the procedures by means of which cinematic shots are joined together to form a cinematic text, which in its turn confers subjectivity upon the viewers. Theorists of cinematic suture inform us that films are made by means of interlocking shots, and the juxtaposition of disparate images produces montage effects which result in a large potential space for the viewer to exercise his/her imagination. In filmmaking shot relations are viewed as the equivalent of syntactic ones in language discourse, as the agency whereby meaning emerges and a subject position is constructed for the viewer through the manipulation of shot relations.

In the making of Chinese poetry, word relations are achieved through the juxtaposition of language codes standing in for images, and subject positions are implied for the reader through linguistic suture, the consciously or unconsciously constructed relations among phrases, sense groups, lines, and stanzas. Linguistic suture in classical Chinese poetry, because of its radicalized move in the joining together of disparate and divergent arrays of words, images, and discourse elements, differs from cinematic suture considerably. The cinematic suture, as has been defined by some film theorists, refers to the moment when the subject inserts itself into the symbolic register in the guise of a signifier, and in so doing gains meaning at the expense of being.[62] This implies that suture imposes a subject position on the viewer. In my analysis of Ma Zhiyuan's poem, I have demonstrated that the linguistic suture at work does not necessarily impose a subject position for the reader though a reader may think so, as is attested by the accepted reading. Linguistic suture in my conception may imply many subject positions, thereby making the hermeneutic space in a poem indeterminate, free rolling, and, in a way, self-generative. This is perhaps a major source of literary openness of Chinese poetry and an issue at the core of the mechanism of open poetics.

The verbal structure of a poem constitutes only one level of poetic openness. The other level is the thematic structuring that involves the psychological activities of both the poet and the reader. From the poet's point of view, a poem with open implications results from a way of composition that may be called simultaneous presence of revelation and concealment, a compromise formation of fantasy and defense mechanism in the poet's mind: an uneasy balance between a strong desire to express pent-up emotions and an equally strong desire to repress those powerful emotions. Shen Deqian 沈德潛 (1673–1769) offers an insightful remark about this conflicting desire and the means to satisfy it: "There were hidden meanings in ancient people's minds that cannot but be expressed. They made use of poetry to convey them."[63]

Poetry is one of the best vehicles for conveying a compromise of conflicting feelings, desires, and intentions. Through compromise formation, a poem is endowed with openness and is comparable to the tip of an iceberg with the bulk of its latent meanings submerged between, behind, and, beneath the lines on the page. From the reader's point of view, the words in a poem are but signs which have their being through their connections to both their referents (the object to which a sign refers) and interpretants (the idea a sign produces in the mind). In Peirce's conception, an interpretant is the mental effect or thought generated by the relations between sign and object. It itself is a sign. It may produce a further sign, and a further interpretant through the process of interpretation.[64] Eco calls this successive production of new interpretants that defines the meanings of interpretation "unlimited semiosis." My reading of the chosen poems shows this unlimited semiosis to be the source of openness from the reader's perspective. Words on the page join the author and the reader in a dialogue and effects what Gadamer terms the "fusion of horizons." The workings of poetic language that integrate the author's representation and reader's interpretation are the sources of unlimited meanings and may thus constitute the "soul" of openness.

Toward A Self-Conscious Open Poetics in Reading and Writing

"All roads lead to Rome." My study has confirmed the assumption proposed in the introduction: Chinese hermeneutic theories have traversed a road of development from exegetic closure to interpretive openness similar to that of Western hermeneutic theories. It, however, reveals that the Chinese hermeneutic tradition arrives at that destination through a somewhat different route. While Western hermeneutic openness arises from conceptual inquires into the nature and function of reading and interpretation, stimulated by the advancement of modern theories in linguistics, semiotics, psychoanalysis, representation, and communication, the Chinese counterpart comes into being as a result of aesthetic concerns with suggestiveness in literature and art, metaphysical meditations on the inadequacy of language for representation and communication, the mismatch between critical precept and critical practice, and a self-conscious use of Chinese language's properties for multiple implications.

Despite the differences, my study has reaffirmed Gadamer's insight that hermeneutic experience is invariably open. The reaffirmation entails the necessity to answer two important questions: To what extent is an open reading acceptable? and Is hermeneutic openness a positive or negative aesthetic category? In this epilogue, by examining some cases of literary inquisitions in Chinese history and some legendary cases of poetry making in Chinese literary thought in relation to contemporary theories of reading and writing, I will attempt to clarify some hitherto vague and controversial issues in the postmodern inquiry into the nature, function, and value of hermeneutic openness and explore what benefits we may derive from a self-conscious awareness of hermeneutic openness.

How Open Is a Literary Text?

My study has demonstrated that a text is not an enclosed space of unity, harmony, or even a balance of opposites, but rather an open space of different views, voices, values, attitudes, and ideologies that invites different and conflicting interpretations. While this helps us open up a literary text to produce new readings out of old texts, it cannot but compel us to ask, How open is a literary text? In the past half century, the notion of textual openness has emancipated the reader from the confines of reading defined by traditional reading theories including the New Critical close reading. The New Criticism got rid of all extratextual factors in the study of a literary text: author, reader, society, and history, all must go; what is allowed to stay is the text, and the text only. Most of the theorists in favor of openness have upheld the New Critical riddance of the author as the sole producer of meaning but criticized the riddance of reader, society, and history. They resituated the text within a particular social and historical context, and reinstated the reader as a proper subject of literary study.

Some reader-oriented theorists went so far as to enthrone the reader in an unprecedented position as the sole producer of all meanings. As Terry Eagleton wittily puts it: "The true writer is the reader. . . . The readers have now overthrown the bosses and installed themselves in power."[1] What had been anticipated in William Empson's seven types of ambiguity has proliferated into different strands of literary openness. Now, a literary text is no longer a well-wrought object, but a space of indeterminacies, replete with elements that depend for their effect upon the reader's interpretation, and which can be interpreted in a variety of different and sometimes mutually conflicting ways. So perceived, a text is only a series of "cues" to the reader, inviting him/her to construct a piece of language into meaning. In a most radical way, some theorists maintain that a text is only a picnic for which the author brings nothing but words while the readers bring all that makes sense.[2] In this radical direction, Stanley Fish rejects the idea of meaning being "immanent" in the text's language as an objectivist illusion and insists that there is nothing whatsoever "in" the text itself.[3] His reasoning seems to suggest that a text is infinitely open and that the reader can make it mean whatever he/she likes.

This revolution in reading and interpretation has brought on a reaction from the least expected quarters. Eco, the first theorist to advocate a "poetics of openness," expresses in his more recent writings an unease at the way some leading strands of present-day literary theories, especially the school of Deconstructive Criticism, appear to him to license the reader to produce a limitless, uncheckable flow of readings. He characterizes the most radical reader-oriented reading theories as a "Hermetic approach"[4] and categorically declares that "the notion of unlimited semiosis does not lead to the conclusion that interpretation has no criteria."[5]

In my opinion, as far as open poetics is concerned, Eco's theory is the most interesting and instructive for the inquiry into hermeneutic openness. Interesting and instructive not just because he is the first to advocate a "poetics of openness" but also because he is a creative writer whose novels serve as the concretization of his theory of openness. What makes Eco's "poetics of openness" more fascinating is a series of ambivalent strands in his theoretical stance. First, he conceives of a work of art as both open and closed at the same time: "A work of art, therefore, is a complete and *closed* form in its uniqueness as a balanced organic whole, while at the same time constituting an *open* product on account of its susceptibility to countless different interpretations which do not impinge on its unadulterable specificity."[6] Secondly, having been one of the first theorists to call our attention to the role of the reader in reading, he has not completely expelled the author and insists on viewing reading as an interactive process between reader and text and giving the author a due role to play: "We have to respect the text, not the author as person so-and-so. Nevertheless, it can look rather crude to eliminate the poor author as something irrelevant for the story of an interpretation."[7] While some theorists declare confidently that the author is dead, Eco, like E. D. Hirsch (1967, 1976) and Norman Holland (1992), resurrects the spirit of the author (1992).

In his "Interpretation and Overinterpretation," Eco addresses in detail the question of whether the author has any privileged position as interpreter of "his" text. He accepts the New Critical doctrine that the author's pretextual intention, the purposes that may have led to the attempt to write a particular work, cannot serve as the criteria for interpretation, and may even be irrelevant or misleading as guides to a text's meanings. However, he argues that the Empirical Author must be allowed to rule out certain interpretations. In the context of present-day literary theory, Eco's position seems rather conservative and even more so than that of the New Critics, for as early as the mid-1940s the latter had already declared that once a literary text is published, it becomes a public property and ceases to be controlled by the author.[8] But Eco's conservative stance has a valid point as far as curbing the unbridled flow of far-fetched readings goes. In academia, the unbridled flow of interpretation may be a harmless game in which one may indulge oneself, but in the world of reality, unchecked open readings will cause problems. Let us imagine a country where there is no guarantee of the "first amendment." In such a country, if someone interprets a poem by a poet in as open a way as he wishes, the reading will surely spell trouble for the poet.

In Chinese history, there are numerous cases of *wenziyu* 文字獄 (literary inquisition). And the last Chinese dynasty, the Qing, is especially notorious for this phenomenon.[9] As an ethnic minority who conquered the previous Ming dynasty, the Qing rulers were so sensitive to their alien position that they became practically paranoid about the denotations and connotations of the two Chinese characters 明 *Ming* (bright) and 清 *Qing* (clear). In a curious way, the major techniques that the Qing censors who created cases of literary inquisition employed are exactly those used in radical reader-response readings. For example, one scholar was severely punished for writing these two poetic lines: "清風不識字，何必亂翻書" (Since the clear wind does not recognize words, / Why should it mess with the pages of my book?) This poetic couplet was misread as a satirical criticism of the Qing rulers, who were implicitly depicted as illiterate barbarians masquerading as arbiters of literary tastes. A distorted reading of the same words implicated another scholar-official's family in a literary inquisition long after his death. One of the charges against him is that he wrote these two poetic lines: "對明月而為良友，吸清風而為醉侯" (Facing the bright moon, one becomes a good friend. / Inhaling the clear wind, one falls a drunken lord.) In the same way, the "bright moon" was misread to refer to the salutary moral power of the Ming dynasty while the "clear wind" was misread to represent the unhealthy influence of the Qing dynasty. What made the case even more unfavorable for the dead scholar's family is that his great-great-grandson, on hearing that someone had reported the suspect lines to the authority, deleted the poetic lines from the published collection. His preemptive action seemed to have confirmed his great-great-grandfather's crime. But for a dramatic turn, the implicated family and some officials would have received a most severe punishment. Emperor Qianlong (r. 1735–95), who had personally engaged in creating many cases of literary inquisition, changed his mind this time. To consolidate the rule of the Qing and to win over scholars in his late years, he slackened censorship. In his imperial edict to the magistrate in charge of the case, he wrote: " 'Clear wind' and 'bright moon' are commonly used words in poetry and essays. How can one avoid using them?" Because of his change of mind, a great disaster faced by the scholar's family was averted.[10]

The powerful weapon wielded by literary inquisitors is the technique of distorted open reading. This weapon, however, is a double-edged sword. It can hurt others as well as the person who wields it. In a popular TV series recently shown in China, *Zaixiang Liu Luoguo* 宰相劉羅鍋 (The

Hump-Backed Prime Minister), there is an episode in which Emperor Qianlong is actively pursuing cases of literary inquisition. The hump-backed prime minister turns the table on him by pointing to the four Chinese characters on a horizontal inscribed board hanging over the Audience Hall of the Imperial Court: *zheng da guang ming* 正大光明. The inscription means "Be upright and above-board." But the prime minister tells the emperor that the last two characters can also be read literally as "Restoring the Ming dynasty." By so doing he successfully makes the emperor see the absurdity of literary inquisition.[11] My analysis of a few cases of literary inquisition in Chinese history is not solely meant to show the similarities between the techniques of open reading and those of literary inquisition. My concern is with these questions: Wherein lies the authority of writing? How can one formulate valid principles that authorize reading? and To what extent is an open reading acceptable, even in academia? In literary circles, extremist open readings may be used to advance sophistry and dubious theory. Although it is entirely groundless for some scholars to denounce Deconstruction as a terrorist weapon, in some conditions it may indeed be employed to persecute people or to exonerate wrongdoing. There is no doubt that the censors of literary inquisition privileged their own readings and ignored the intentions of their victims. In a similar way, radical reader-oriented theory of reading has stressed the rights of the reader and totally ignored the intentions of the author. My analysis of the literary inquisition and radical reading makes it clear that we ought to pay due respect to the rights of the author, too. After observing the contemporary theories of reading in the last decades, Eco expresses his uneasiness that the rights of the reader have been overstressed.[12]

If I may characterize the difference between Eco's poetics of openness and that of other theorists, I may say that Eco's open poetics emphasizes the author's intentional efforts to leave arrangements of some component parts of a work open to the public or to chance, while the open poetics of other theorists is largely about strategies that the reader devises to make the arrangements of a text's elements signify in accordance with his or her wishes. I am convinced that each of the two poetics of openness has its advantages and drawbacks. Reader-oriented openness enables us to produce unlimited new interpretations in our fashion-conscious society and academia but it may risk producing "overinterpretation" that proves far-fetched and unconvincing. Interactive openness born out of the transaction between the reader and text may seem at times less open, but it can overcome the drawbacks of unbridled openness in interpretation. In stressing the role of the author, interactive openness calls our attention to the signifying mechanism of a text, thereby probing into how a text is made.

Unbridled openness may be curtailed by considerations of making. In addition to stressing the role of the author and hence the importance of making, interactive openness intersects with practically all the key issues in the current debate of literary theories: meaning, making, author, reader, text, context, and so on. It may serve as a ground of compromise for both traditionalists and postmodernists.

Purely reader-oriented openness has a most vulnerable weakness. That is, it makes it difficult to determine what constitutes a good piece of work and what makes a reading a good reading. In extreme cases, readings conducted in the spirit of radical openness may run amuck and bring disrepute upon present-day theories. Moreover, I would raise an objection to radical reader-oriented openness from the perspective of making art. *When we look at a literary text from the perspective of verbal art, purely reader-oriented radical openness would produce an art, which is not so much the art of the author as the art of the reader. If a literary work is interpreted to be great, the great achievement is not so much the author's as the reader's. For this reason, we ought not to lose sight of the author's role in the making of a text. After all, it is not the reader's making but the author's making that decides whether a text will have a chance to become a piece of art. The reader's making can only discover but not create the art of a text. Otherwise there would be no distinction between the reader and author, artist and connoisseur.*

Le Mot Juste and Endless Meaning

Unrestrained hermeneutic openness in politics, law, and other fact-specific areas may spell disasters for people's lives, but in creative activities like literature and arts, it is a positive thing. Still, one may argue that to have meanings beyond words may not always be the objective in writing a poem or in creative activities, and in history, opposite impulses were stressed. For example, Fang Xun 方薰 (1736–99), a scholar of the Qing, once said: "Poetry attaches great importance to unlimited meanings, but it also requires adequate expression of meanings."[13] This idea is a different way of stating the Confucian saying: "When it comes to speech, all that matters is to get one's meaning through."[14] It is equivalent to the French expression, *le mot juste*. Thus, in the writing of poetry, there are a variety of creative motives in control of different aesthetic impulses. Two kinds of aesthetic impulses emanate from opposite directions. One impulse is to find the right word that will adequately express a scene, an object, a mood, or an emotion. The other is to locate a word that shall serve as a nodal point for several strands of thought, some of which are not always compatible and may be simply conflicting. Because of the different impulses, a writer must deliberate in order to find the most appropriate word or phrase that satisfies the diverse impulses. As a result, a poet's choice of words, phrases, and images is often a compromise formation resulting from competing impulses. With such compromises, a particular poem may have meanings beyond words by deliberate design.

Tuiqiao 推敲, the Chinese expression for "deliberation" exemplifies this sort of self-conscious making of poetic art in Chinese literary thought. This expression literally means "push or knock on the door." Its origin in a well-known literary legend has always been interpreted as an example of how careful ancient Chinese poets have been in their choice of words for making poetry.[15] If we examine the legend in terms of making verbal art, we will see that it represents a point at which the Chinese concern with suggestiveness and making converged. It not only embodies the ancient poets' desire to satisfy different impulses but also reveals their self-conscious desire to turn a text into an open space of signification.

The expression came from a poetic line, "A monk pushes at the door under moonlight" by Jia Dao (779–843), a Tang dynasty poet. Unsatisfied with this line, he changed it to "A monk knocks on the door under moonlight." Unsure of which was artistically more desirable, he sought the advice of another poet, Han Yu (768–824) who, after some consideration, recommended the second option. Scholars have come up with various ideas of why the second version is better. In my opinion, the second version is artistically more desirable because it gives the poetic line a much bigger space for imagination. In the first version, the interpretation would be that under the moonlight, a monk returns to his own lodging, most likely a temple. That he just pushed open the door suggests that he resided at this place. In the second version, whether he lived at this place or lodged at this place is not made clear. In fact, the place itself is indeterminate. That he knocked at the door suggests many possibilities. The monk may be returning to his own temple or his lodging place late; he may be going to visit someone else's house; he may be an itinerant monk seeking a place for the night; or he may be a symbolic figure seeking entrance into the home of being if we take into account the first poetic line of the same couplet, "(A) bird(s) perch(es) on the trees beside the pond." The case of *tuiqiao* is a typical example of deliberate making for the purpose of openness. Such instances abound in the history of Chinese poetry and poetic criticism and may shed light on the nature and function of openness in the making of verbal art.

The legend about *tuiqiao* illustrates two directions of conscious making by ancient poets. In one direction, they aspired to the aesthetic condition of "unlimited implications in limited words"; in the other they strove to find the exact word to convey their complex intentions and emotions.

My analysis shows that both *tui* (push) and *qiao* (knock) are apt choices of words depending on circumstances. This may be one of the reasons why the two characters must be combined into one word to mean "deliberation." In the *tuiqiao* legend, "push" and "knock" cannot appear in the same poetic line. The use of "knock," despite its larger hermeneutic potential, still leaves out a strand of meaning that can only be expressed by "push."

At times, however, intense self-conscious deliberation may enable a poet to find the right word that satisfies all impulses. Wang Anshi's 王安石 (1021–86) conscious search for the right word for his famous poem, "Mooring at the Melon Isle," is a case in point. Dissatisfied with a word in his four-line poem, he tried several different words until he hit upon the right one in the line "Spring wind again *greens* the southern bank of the Yangzi 春風又綠江南岸." According to an account in a poetic talk, a scholar kept the early draft of the poem, which showed that Wang Anshi first used *dao* 到 (arrive), then replaced it with a series of words including *guo* 過 (pass), *ru* 入 (enter), and *man* 滿 (fill). He finally settled upon the word *lü* 綠 (green), which gives his poem a lasting value.[16] The final choice is superior to all the other choices not only because it is more vivid and adequately conveys his impression of a spring scene but also because it gives the poetic line meanings beyond the page, a flavor beyond flavor. With the use of "green" as a verb, the spring wind was personified and given an open identity. It could be construed as a herald ushering in the coming of the warm season; or an angel in the service of a higher god who controls the four seasons, or a giant painter who treats the landscape as his canvas and paints it green.

In traditional poetic discourses, self-conscious reflection gave rise to instances of the so-called *yizi shi* 一字師 (a master who teaches one apt word). In most cases, these literary anecdotes and legends illustrate how poets made relentless efforts to seek the right word, phrase, or poetic line to capture a scene, an image, or a state of mind. On some occasions, their relentless efforts turned out to be deliberate striving for unlimited implications in limited words. Such deliberation on the choice of words constitutes an intriguing aspect in discussions of openness in Chinese literary thought. Yuan Mei, in his *Suiyuan shihua*, cited an example:

> When one word of a poem is changed, the altered artistic status is as different as that between the world of man and the realm of heaven. But this is not understandable unless one is an insider. Qi Ji (fl. 881) wrote "Early Plum-flower" which has these two lines: "In the deep snow at the front village / A few (or How many) blossoms burst forth last night.(?)" Zheng Gu (989–1061), [having read the poem], remarked: "If you change 'a few' to one, then the poem is truly about the early plum." Qi Ji bowed to Zheng Gu in grateful respect.[17]

Guo Moruo 郭沫若, the famous modern scholar and poet, does not agree with Yuan Mei. He has a number of reasons for arguing with the latter, but the major reason is that in his opinion, the change renders the poem aesthetically less desirable:

The word "ji 幾" (a few/how many) has a number of explanations. One of them is to raise a question; the other is to record a fact. If it was the first situation, to change "ji" into "yi (one)" is to turn a question into a state-ment, thus rendering a poetic line of liveliness (*huo* 活) lifeless (*si* 死). If one does not know whether the plum flowers have blossomed yet, how can he be sure that there is "one" flower. If it was the second situation, then the poet must have trodden in the snow in search of plum flowers and seen with his own eyes that "a few" flowers have come into blossom. "A few" flowers do not rule out the condition of early plum flowers. Why does one need to alter "a few" to "one"?[18]

What makes this case more interesting is that Guo Moruo later found out that Yuan Mei remembered wrongly the key word in the orig-inal poetic line. According to *Shiguo chunqiu* 十國春秋, it is not *ji* 幾 but *shu* 數 (a number of).[19] Although Yuan Mei's memory was amiss, his choice of *ji* gave Guo Moruo an opportunity to interpret the poem in a different light. Yuan Mei's change and Guo Moruo's reading have turned the poem into one with multiple possible readings: a factual observation, an imme-diate response to a real situation, an imaginative speculation, and so on. The alteration of a single word has blurred the distinction between what has happened and what may happen, fact and fiction, historicity and imag-ination. The ambiguity of *ji* leaves one wondering about the condition of the early plum flowers: have they blossomed? how many? one, two, a few or a number of? Although neither Yuan nor Guo was aware of the open-ness made possible by the change of a single word, the discussion of the key word offers us a valuable insight into the significance of conscious making for open representation.

Hermeneutic Openness Is a Positive Thing

In this study, I have dealt with conceptual, critical, and creative materials exclusive of the narrative tradition. In narrative criticism, insights of hermeneutic openness are legion. Some narrative scholars were even consciously aware of the significance of hermeneutic openness for the creation of narrative works. Zhang Zhupo 張竹坡 (1670–98) is one of them. In his comment on the *Dongyouji* 東游記, he wrote:

> A text has both entering strokes and departing strokes. An entering stroke enters my intention while a departing stroke deviates from my intention. An entering stroke must be tortuous and discriminating; a departing stroke must be devious and artificial. It is highly necessary for the reader to know how it enters but not to know how it departs, or to know how it departs but not to know how it enters. As for the location of the intention, a writer should frequently destroy the traces and hide the forms, or jumble up narrative threads so as to make it look disorderly, or totalize the story so as to make it ambiguous. The imperative is to make it seem indeterminate and to make it appear as though it could not be well understood. People feel happy about its being like a suspended river which pours out its inexhaustible water and about its rhetoric being like a sharp blade that displaces a hundred schools of thought. All they see is a vast ocean of free and unrestrained words; in no way would they discern any of the arrangements for structure and plot.[20]

What merits our attention in this passage is Zhang Zhupo's advocacy for deliberate efforts to conceal and reveal authorial intentions, to leave elements of narration in an indeterminate and ambiguous state, and to build an intricate network of interpretive possibilities. This passage as a whole anticipates what Eco advocates as "a conscious poetics of the open work."[21] The special mention of jumbling up narrative threads so as to make the text look disorderly reminds us of Eco's characterization of James Joyce's works as a chaosmos, or "*an original organization of disorder.*"[22]

Hermeneutic openness in literature and art is a positive aesthetic category. It is useful for both reading and writing, creation and appreciation. I wish to reaffirm the insight that has appeared again and again in this study: a self-conscious awareness of hermeneutic openness may not only help readers produce adequate and interesting readings but also benefit writers in their efforts to create masterpieces with enduring artistic value. Gadamer once defines the task of hermeneutics as "the bridging of personal or historical distance between minds."[23] In this study, apart from that task, I have attempted a task of a different dimension: the bridging of the gap between Chinese and Western hermeneutic thought. Whether or not my study has achieved any success on that dimension, I may close it with an optimistic prediction that a transcultural hermeneutics and an open poetics of reading and writing are not impossibilities.

Notes

Preface

1. I have especially benefited from these books: *Thinking through Confucius, Thinking from the Han, Anticipating China, Self and Deception: A Cross-cultural Philosophical Inquiry*, and *Self as Person in Asian Theory and Practice*, all published by the State University of New York Press.

2. Cunningham, *Reading after Theory*, 3–6, 87–121.

Introduction. Hermeneutic Openness

1. *The Cambridge Dictionary of Philosophy*, 323.

2. Hans-Georg Gadamer, *Truth and Method*, 319.

3. Umberto Eco, *The Open Work*, 1–23.

4. For this dating, see Liu Dajun 劉大鈞, *Zhouyi gailun* 周易概論, 14.

5. *Zhouyi zhengyi* 周易正義, *juan* 7, 66a–b, in *Shisanjing zhushu* 十三經註疏, 78.

6. Dong Zhongshu, *Chunqiu fanlu* 春秋繁露, *juan* 3, in *Ershi er zi* 二十二子, 775a.

7. Shen Deqian, *Tangshi biecai* 唐詩別裁, 1:1.

8. See Paul de Man, *Blindness and Insight*, 105–6.

9. Kongzi, *Lunyu zhushu* 論語註疏 *juan* 2, 5c, in *Shisanjing zhushu*, 2461.

10. Dong Zhongshu, *Chunqiu fanlu, juan* 3, in *Ershi er zi*, 775a.

11. All these ideas appeared before or around the sixth century.

273

12. Plato, *The Collected Dialogues of Plato*, 340.

13. Longinus, *On the Sublime*, VIII, 3, in *Critical Theory since Plato*, 80.

14. Philip Sidney, "An Apology for Poetry," in *Critical Theory since Plato*, 166.

15. Longxi Zhang, "The Letter or Spirit," *Comparative Literature* 39.3 (1987): 193–217.

16. Longxi Zhang, "The Letter or Spirit," 200.

17. See Empson, *Seven Types of Ambiguity*; Richards, *Practical Criticism*; Brooks, *The Well Wrought Urn*; Ransom, *The New Criticism*; Wimsatt and Beardsley, *The Verbal Icon*.

18. E. D. Hirsch, *Validity in Interpretation*, 1; Tzvetan Todorov, "Viaggio nella critica americana," *Lettera* 4 (1987): 12.

19. Introduction to *Poétique* 1 (1970): 1–2. The English translation is from Robert Scholes's forward to Todorov's *The Fantastic: A Structural Approach to a Literary Genre*, vii.

20. David Robey, introduction to Umberto Eco's *Open Work*, viii.

21. See Umberto Eco, *Interpretation and Overinterpretation*, 45–66.

22. See *Interpretation and Overinterpretation*, 109–23.

23. Mencius, *Mengzi zhushu* 孟子註疏, *juan* 9a, 71c, in *Shisanjing zhushu*, 2735.

24. Edmund Husserl, *The Idea of Phenomenology*, 33–51.

25. E. D. Hirsch, *Validity in Interpretation*, 31.

26. James J. Y. Liu, *Language—Paradox—Poetics: A Chinese Perspective*, 97.

27. For example, Zhu Ziqing acknowledges his indebtedness to Empson's *Seven Types of Ambiguity*. See *Zhu Ziqing gudian wenxue lunwenji*, 61.

28. Roland Barthes, *Empire of Signs* (New York: Hill and Wang, 1982).

29. Christopher L. Connery, *The Empire of the Text: Writing and Authority in Early Imperial China*, 1–18; Mark E. Lewis, *Writing and Authority in Early China*, 337.

30. See Josef Bleicher, *Contemporary Hermeneutics*, 1.

31. James J. Y. Liu, *Chinese Theories of Literature*, 1.

Chapter 1. Theories of Reading and Writing in Intellectual Thought

1. Mencius, *Mengzi zhushu* 孟子註疏, *juan* 9a, 71c, in *Shisanjing zhushu*, 2735.

2. Adapted from Arthur Waley's translation.

3. Mencius, *Mengzi zhushu*, *juan* 9a, 71c, in *Shisanjing zhushu*, 2735.

4. Mencius, *Mengzi zhushu*, *juan* 9a, 71c, in *Shisanjing zhushu*, 2735.

5. Roman Jakobson, "Closing Statement: Linguistics and Poetics," 353.

6. Mencius, *Mengzi zhushu*, *juan* 3a, 21c, *Shisanjing zhushu*, 2685.

7. Ibid., *juan* 3a, 22a, *Shisanjing zhushu*, 2686.

8. Ibid., *juan* 3a, 22a, *Shisanjing zhushu*, 2686.

9. Stephen Owen, *Readings in Chinese Literary Thought*, 22.

10. *Chunqiu Zuozhuan zhenyi* 春秋左傳正義, in *Shisanjing zhushu*, 1985.

11. Edmund Husserl, *The Idea of Phenomenology*, 33–51.

12. E. D. Hirsch, *Validity in Interpretation*, 31.

13. James J. Y. Liu, *Language—Paradox—Poetics: A Chinese Perspective*, 97.

14. Stephen Owen, *Readings in Chinese Literary Thought*, 35.

15. This shorter English translation is quoted from *Readings in Chinese Literary Thought*, 35–36. The second paragraph is a paraphrase of a longer version. For a complete version, see *Zhuangzi*, 160–61.

16. Zhuangzi, *Zhuangzi* 莊子, annotated by Guo Xiang 郭象, 160.

17. *Zhouyi zhengyi*, *juan* 7, in 18a, in *Shisanjing zhushu*, 70c.

18. Zhuangzi, *Zhuangzi*, 160.

19. Umberto Eco, *Interpretation and Overinterpretation*, 35.

20. Quoted from *Cambridge Dictionary of Philosophy*, edited by Robert Audi, 324.

21. Zhuangzi, *Zhuangzi*, 23.

22. Zhuangzi, *Zhuangzi*, 23–24.

23. Emile Benveniste, *Problems in General Linguistics*, 226.

24. For a brief account of the debate over the nature of meaning between the Husserlians and Heideggerians, one may read Eagleton's *Literary Theory: An Introduction*, 54–78.

25. Umberto Eco, *Interpretation and Overinterpretation*, 38.

26. *Mengzi zhushu*, *juan* 10b, *Shisanjing zhushu*, 2746.

27. Gu Zhen, *Yudong xueshi* 虞東學詩, requoted from Cai Zhongxiang et al, *Zhongguo wenxue lilunshi*, 1: 36.

28. *Zhongguo lidai wenlun xuan* 中國歷代文論選, 1: 17.

29. *The Hermeneutics Reader*, 83–6.

30. Gadamer, *Truth and Method*, 307.

31. Gadamer, *Truth and Method*, 300–7; and "Text and Interpretation," in *Hermeneutics and Modern Philosophy*, 377–96.

32. Martin Heidegger, *Being and Time*, 21–28.

33. Martin Heidegger, *Basic Writings*, 45.

34. Martin Heidegger, *Being and Time*, 25.

35. Martin Heidegger, *Being and Time*, 194.

36. Martin Heidegger, *Being and Time*, 192.

37. Edward Said, *Beginnings: Intention and Method*, 196.

38. Said, *Beginnings: Intention and Method*, 12.

39. Lu Ji, *Wenfu* 文賦, in *Wenxuan* 文選, *juan* 17, 224.

40. *Zhouyi zhengyi*, *juan* 7, in *Shisanjing zhushu*, 82c.

41. Ibid.

42. Ibid.

43. Zhuangzi, *Zhuangzi*, 184.

44. Liu Xie, *Wenxin diaolong*, 452.

45. Zhuangzi, *Zhuangzi*, chap. 25, 294.

46. Zhuangzi, *Zhuangzi*, chap. 26, 303.

47. Martin Heidegger, "The Nature of Language," in *Critical Theory since Plato*, revised edition, 1091.

48. Yang Xiong, *Fayan* 法言, *juan* 6, in *Ershi er zi*, 816a.

49. *Zhouyi zhengyi*, *juan* 7, in *Shisanjing zhushu*, 82c.

50. *Weishu* 魏書, in Lu Bi, comp., *Sanguo zhi jijie* 三國志集解, *juan* 10, 313.

51. Requoted from Hu Qiguang, *Zhongguo xiaoxue shi*, 118.

52. *Zhongguo meixueshi ziliao xuanbian*, vol. 2, 9.

53. Yang Wanli, *Chengzai ji* 誠齋集, *juan* 84, "Yilun 易論."

54. Ge Zhaoguang 葛兆光, *Zhonggu sixiag shi—Daolun* 中國思想史:導論, 61–62.

55. Xiao Tong, *Wenxuan* 文選, *juan* 17, 224.

56. Liu Xie, *Wenxin diaolong*, chap. 26, 365. English version is adapted from Vincent Shih's translation in *The Literary Mind and the Carving of Dragons*, 220.

57. Liu Xie, *Wenxin diaolong*, chap. 27, 368.

58. See Edmund Husserl, *The Idea of Phenomenology*, 33–51.

59. Vincent Shih's translation in *Literary Mind and the Carving of Dragons*, 372.

60. Liu Xie, *Wenxin diaolong*, chap. 48, 587. My own translation.

61. Guo Xiang's idea is expressed in his annotation of the *Zhaungzi*, chap. 17, 184.

62. Liu Xie, *Wenxin diaolong*, 552. Though *xiao* and *hui* both mean "understanding," *xiao* also means "to inform." I regard *xiao* as the writer's meaning and *hui* as the reader's understanding.

Chapter 2. Hermeneutic Openness in Aesthetic Thought

1. See Stephen Owen, *Readings in Chinese Literary Thought*.

2. Fung Yu-lan, *A Short History of Chinese Philosophy*, 12.

3. See relevant passages in Qian Zhongshu's *Tanyi lu* 談藝錄.

4. Shen Deqian, *Shuoshi zuiyu* 説詩晬語, 251.

5. Fung Yu-lan, *A Short History of Chinese Philosophy*, 12.

6. Yan Yu, *Canglang shihua* 滄浪詩話, in *Lidai shihua* 歷代詩話, 2: 688.

7. Zhong Rong, *Shipin* 詩品, in *Lidai shihua*, 1: 3.

8. Liu Xie, *Wenxin diaolong* 文心雕龍, 550.

9. Mencius, *Mengzi zhushu*, *juan* 14b, 114c, in *Shisanjing zhushu*, 2778.

10. *Zhouyi zhengyi*, *juan* 8, in *Shisanjing zhushu*, 77a–b.

11. Aristotle, *Poetics*, IX, in *Critical Theory since Plato*, 53.

12. Sima Qian 司馬遷, "Qu Yuan zhuan 屈原傳," in *Shiji* 史記, 8: 2482.

13. My translation is a synthesis of Shih-hsiang Chen's version in *Anthology of Chinese Literature*, 211, and Owen's version in *Readings in Chinese Literary Thought*, 164.

14. *Liji zhengyi* 禮記正義, *juan* 37, 300c, *Shisanjing zhushu*, 1528.

15. *Liji zhengyi*, *juan* 37, 300c.

16. Lao Zi, *Daode jing* 道德經, chap. 41, 24.

17. D. C. Lau's translation, in Lao Tzu, *Tao Te Ching*, 102.

18. Wang Bi, *Wang Bi ji jiaoshi* 王弼集校釋, 113.

19. Thomas Carlyle, *Sator Resartus*, 165–66.

20. Bai Juyi, *Bai Juyi xuanji* 白居易選集, 177.

21. Keats, *The Poems of John Keats*, 372.

22. Zhuangzi, *Zhuangzi*, 137.

23. Thomas Carlyle, *Sator Resartus*, 166.

24. See Lao Zi, *Daode jing*, chap. 35, 19.

25. English version is quoted from D. C. Lau's translation, in Lao Tzu, *Tao Te Ching*, 94.

26. *Liji zhengyi* 禮記正義, *juan* 37, 300c.

27. This view started with Li Shan's 李善 (c. 630–89) annotation in Xiao Tong, *Wenxuan*, *juan* 17, 226.

28. I am using Shih-hsiang Chen's translation, in *Anthology of Chinese Literature*, 211.

29. Lao Zi, *Daode jing*, chap. 41, 24.

30. Wang Bi, *Wang Bi ji jiaoshi*, 113.

31. Lu Xun, in *Lu Xun lun wenxue yu yishu* 魯迅論文學與藝術, 1: 410.

32. *Lu Xun: Selected Works*, translated by Yang Xianyi and Gladys Yang, 4: 143.

33. "Notes after Reading (I)," in *Lu Xun: Selected Works*, 4: 81.

34. Liu Xie, *Wenxin diaolong*, 482. English version is adapted from Vincent Shih's translation, p. 304, with the addition of sentences not found in Shih's version.

35. Liu Xie, *Wenxin diaolong*, chap. 26, 365.

36. Fan Wenlan 範文瀾, *Wenxin diaolong zhu* 文心雕龍註, 633.

37. Jiaoran, "Shishi 詩式," in *Lidai shihua*, 31–32.

38. James J. Y. Liu, *Language—Paradox—Poetics: A Chinese Perspective*, 62–66.

39. James J. Y. Liu, *Language—Paradox—Poetics: A Chinese Perspective*, 66.

40. Liu Xie, *Wenxin diaolong*, 490.

41. Fang Xuanling 房玄齡 et al., *Jinshu* 晉書, *ce* 8, 2377.

42. Zhong Rong, *Shipin* 詩品, in *Lidai shihua*, 1: 3.

43. Han Yu, *Han Changli wenji jiaozhu* 韓昌黎文集校註, 198.

44. Zhong Rong, *Shipin*, in *Lidai shihua*, 1: 3.

45. Liu Xie, *Wenxin diaolong*, 444.

46. Ouyang Xiu, "Liuyi shihua 六一詩話," in *Lidai shihua*, 1: 267.

47. Sima Guang, "Wen Gong xu shihua 溫公續詩話," in *Lidai shihua*, 1: 277.

48. Wei Tai, "Linhan yinju shihua 臨漢隱居詩話," in *Lidai shihua*, 1: 323.

49. Ge Lifang, "Yunyu yangqiu 韻語陽秋," in *Lidai shihua*, 2: 485.

50. Jiang Kui, "Baishi daoren shishuo 白石道人詩説," in *Lidai shihua*, 2: 681.

51. Yang Wanli, "Chengzhai shihua 誠齋詩話," in *Lidai shihua xubian* 歷代詩話續編, 137.

52. Zhang Jie, "Suihan tang shihua 歲寒堂詩話," in *Zhongguo meixueshi ziliao xuanbian*, 2: 56.

53. Yan Yu, *Canglang shihua* 滄浪詩話, in *Lidai shihua*, 688. English translation is requoted from James J. Y. Liu's *Chinese Theories of Literature*, 39.

54. Liu Zhiji, *Shitong* 史通, *Sibu congkan* edition, *ce* 2, *juan* 6, 16b.

55. Ibid., 12a–b.

56. Ibid., 15a–b.

57. Yang Zai, "Shifa jiashu 詩法家數," in *Lidai shihua*, 2: 737.

58. Liu Xizai, *Yigai* 藝概, *juan* 4, 1a.

59. Shen Deqian, *Shuoshi zuiyu*, 251.

60. Ibid., 219.

61. Yuan Mei, *Jian zhu Suiyuan shihua* 箋註隨園詩話, *juan* 2, 11.

62. Yuan Mei, *Jian zhu Suiyuan shihua*, *juan* 3, 7.

63. Ye Xie, *Yuanshi* 原詩, 30.

64. Jiang Kui, "Baishi daoren shishuo," in *Lidai shihua*, 2: 683.

65. Ye Xie, *Yuanshi*, 30.

66. Zhu Chengjue, "Cunyu tang shihua 存余堂詩話," in *Lidai shihua*, 2: 792.

67. Wang Guowei, *Renjian cihua xinzhu* 人間詞話新註, ed. Teng Xianhui 滕咸慧, 26.

68. Tan Xian 譚獻, "Futang cihua 復堂詞話," in *Xinyuan congke yiji* 心園叢刻一集, 1a–b.

69. T. S. Eliot, "The Music of Poetry," in *On Poetry and Poets*, 30–31.

70. Julia Kristeva, *Revolution in Poetic Language*, 25–30.

71. *Sui Tang Wudai wenxue piping ziliao huibian*, 252.

72. *Sui Tang Wudai wenxue piping ziliao huibian*, 254.

73. Yan Yu, "Canglang shihua," in *Lidai shihua*, 2: 687.

74. Requoted from Chen Linagyun, *Zhongguo shixue tixi lun* 中國詩學體系論, 414.

75. Yang Tingzhi 楊廷之 expressed a similar opinion. See his *Ershisi Shipin qianjie* 二十四詩品淺解, in *Sikong Tu Shipin jieshuo erzhong* 司空圖詩品解說二種, 102.

76. Herbert Giles, *A History of Chinese Literature*, 183.

77. Yang Hsien-yi and Gladys Yang, trans., "The Twenty-Four Modes of Poetry," in *Chinese Literature* 7 (July 1963): 65.

78. Wai-lim Yip, trans., "Selections from 'The Twenty-Four Orders of Poetry,'" *Stony Brook* 3/4 (1969): 280–81.

79. Pauline Yu, "Ssi-k'ung T'u's *Shih-p'in*: Poetic Theory in Poetic Form," in Ronald C. Miao, ed., *Studies in Chinese Poetry and Poetics*, 1: 99.

80. James J. Y. Liu, *Language—Paradox—Poetics: A Chinese Perspective*, 67.

81. Sikong Tu, "Ershisi shipin," in *Lidai shihua*, 1: 40–41.

82. Zhu Dongrun, *Zhongguo wenxue pipingshi dagang* 中國文學批評史大綱, 99.

83. See Qiao Li 喬力, *Ershisi shipin tanwei* 二十四詩品探微, 58.

84. J. P. Muller and W. J. Richardson, *Lacan and Langauge: A Reader's Guide to Écrits*, 2.

85. Su Shi, *Su Dongpo ji* 蘇東坡集, quoted from *Zhongguo meixueshi ziliao xuanbian*, 2: 34.

86. Roman Jacobson, "Closing Statement: Linguistics and Poetics," in *Style in Language*, 356.

87. Weng Fanggang, "Shenyun lun 神韻論," in *Zhongguo lidai wenlun xuan*, 3: 376.

88. Yang Tingzhi 楊廷之 expressed a similar opinion. See his *Ershisi Shipin qianjie*, 103.

89. Zhuangzi, *Zhuangzi yigu* 莊子譯詁 (Shanghai: Guji chubanshe, 1991), 29.

90. James J. Y. Liu, *Language—Paradox—Poetics: A Chinese Perspective*, 69.

91. Zhan Youxin 詹幼馨, *Sikong Tu Shipin yanyi* 司空圖詩品衍繹, 120.

92. Guo Shaoyu, ed., *Shipin jijie* 詩品集解.

93. Qiao Li 喬力, *Ershisi shipin tanwei*, 61.

94. For a full understanding of this term, refer to Derrida's *Margins of Philosophy*, 1–27.

95. Derrida, *Margins of Philosophy*, 18.

96. Roman Jacobson, "Closing Statement: Linguistics and Poetics," 358.

97. Sun Liankui, *Shipin yishuo* 詩品臆説, in *Sikong Tu Shipin jieshuo erzhong*, 27.

98. Roman Jacobson, "Closing Statement: Linguistics and Poetics," 358, italics original.

99. Sun Liankui, *Shipin yishuo*, 27.

100. Yang Tingzhi, *Ershisi Shipin qianjie*, 103.

101. Charles S. Peirce, *Collected Papers*, 2: 228.

102. James J. Y. Liu, *Language—Paradox—Poetics: A Chinese Perspective*, 67.

103. *Tao Te Ching*, translated by D. C. Lau, chap. 14, 70.

104. Liu Xie, *Wenxin diaolong*, 101.

105. Huang Ziyun, "Yehong shidi 野鴻詩的," in *Qing shihua* 清詩話, 857.

106. Liu Xie 劉勰, *Wenxin diaolong* 文心雕龍, 99–101.

107. Zhou Dunyi, *Zhou Lianxi ji* 周濂溪集, *juan* 1, 2; De Bary, *Sources of Chinese Tradition*, 1: 458.

108. Zhu Xi, "Taijitu shuo jie," in *Zhou Lianxi ji*, *juan* 1, 4.

109. Shao Yong, *Huangji jingshi shu* 皇極經世書, *han* 4, *ce* 16, 29a.

110. Ibid., 1a.

111. Zhu Bokun, *Yixue zhexue shi* 易學哲學史, 2: 98.

112. See Wing-tsit Chan, *A Source Book in Chinese Philosophy*, 758–59; Chinese Source: Feng Youlan's *Xin lixue*, 97–100.

113. Wang Bi, *Wang Bi ji jiaoshi* 王弼集校釋, 117.

114. Ibid.

115. D. C. Lau's translation of Lao Tzu's *Tao Te Ching*, 57.

116. D. C. Lau's translation of Lao Tzu's *Tao Te Ching*, 101.

117. D. C. Lau's translation of Lao Tzu's *Tao Te Ching*, 103.

118. *Hanshi waizhuan, juan*, 5, 191.

119. Xue Xue 薛雪, *Yipiao shihua* 一瓢詩話, in *Qing shihua*, 714.

120. Chen Tingzhuo 陳廷焯, *Baiyuzhai shihua*, 5.

121. Zhong Rong, *Shipin*, in *Lidai shihua*, 1: 8.

Chapter 3. The *Zhouyi* and Open Representation

1. Yang Xiong's and Ban Gu's remarks are requoted from Liu Dajun's *Zhouyi gailun*, 145.

2. Richard Wilhelm, *Heaven, Earth, and Man in the Book of Changes*, v–vii.

3. See Tang Mingbang 唐明邦, ed., *Zhouyi pingzhu* 周易評註, 7.

4. *Siku quanshu zongmu* 四庫全書總目, 1.

5. See San Quan 珊泉 and Chen Jianjun 陳建軍, *Zhonghua Zhouyi* 中華周易, 104.

6. See Hellmut Wilhelm, "Leibniz and the I-Ching," *Collectanea Comissiones Synodalis* (Peking) 16 (1943): 205–19.

7. *Zhouyi zhengyi* 周易正義, annotated by Kong Yingda, *Sibu beiyao* edition, *juan* 7, 19a.

8. *Zhouyi zhengyi, ce* 3, *juan* 7, 18a.

9. See Daniel J. Cook and Henry Rosemont's introduction to G. W. Leibniz, *Writings on China*, 16.

10. Zhang Binglin, "Shuzheng guwen bashi 疏證古文八事," *Taiyan wenlu xubian*, 1: 65–70.

11. August Conrady, "Yih-king-Studien," *Asia Major* 7 (1932): 409–68.

12. Ma Xulun, *Zhongguo wenzi zhi yuanliu yu yanjiu fangfa zhi xinqingxiang*, 4–5.

13. Chen Weizhan and Tang Yuming, *Gu wenzixue gangyao* 古文字學綱要, 19.

14. Ma Xulun, *Zhongguo wenzi zhi yuanliu yu yanjiu fangfa zhi xinqingxiang*, 4–5.

15. Zhang Binglin, "Shuzheng guwen bashi," 68.

16. Xu Shen, postface to *Shuowen jiezi* 說文解字, 314.

17. For a detailed list of phenomena depicted by the eight trigrams, please refer to the "Shuogua" chapters of the *Book of Changes*.

18. W. J. T. Mitchell, "Representation," in *Critical Terms for Literary Study*, 12.

19. Roland Barthes, *Elements of Semiology*, 11.

20. Guo Yong, *Guoshi chuanjia yishuo* 郭氏傳家易説, *Wenyuange Siku quanshu* 13: 8b.

21. W. J. T. Mitchell, "Representation," 13.

22. See Gu Jiegang, *Gushi bian* 古史辨, 3: 45–69, 84–88.

23. *Zhouyi zhengyi, juan* 8, 4a.

24. The first reading appears in *Zixia yizhuan* 子夏易傳, *Wenyuange Siku quanshu*, 7: 4; *Chunqiu Zuozhuan zhengyi* 春秋左傳正義, in *Shisanjing zhushu*, 1942a–b; Kong Yingda, *Zhouyi zhengyi* 周易正義, *juan* 1, 1a; Li Dingzuo 李鼎祚, *Zhouyi jijie* 周易集解, 5; Zhu Zhen 朱震, *Hanshang yizhuan* 漢上易傳, 635; Cheng Yi 程頤, *Yichuan yizhuan* 伊川易傳, 388; Zhu Xi 朱熹, *Zhouyi benyi* 周易本義, 1028; Lai Zhide 來知德, *Zhouyi jizhu* 周易集註, 1596; Mao Qiling 毛奇齡, *Zhongshi yi* 仲氏易, 1972; Hui Dong 惠棟, *Zhouyi shu* 周易述, 2240. Except for *Zhouyi zhengyi*, all page numbers referred to are found in *Yixue jinghua* 易學精華 (Jinan: Qilu shushe, 1990), 2 vols. The second reading can be found in *Guoyu* 國語, *juan* 10, 10b, *Sibu congkan*; the third reading in "Wenyan 文言," in Kong Yingda, *Zhouyi zhengyi, ce* 1, *juan* 1, 11a; the fourth reading in Wu Cheng's 吳澄 (1249–1333) *Yizuanyan* 易纂言, in *Yixue jinghua*, 2: 1241.

25. Li Jingchi, "Zhouyi Shici kao 周易筮辭考," 29–31. He acknowledges other readings in history in "Zuo Guo zhong Yishi zhi yanjiu 左國中易筮之研究," *Zhouyi Tanyuan*, 416–17.

26. Quoted from Kong Yingda's *Zhouyi zhengyi, juan* 1, 1a.

27. See Kong Yingda's *Zhouyi zhengyi, juan* 1, 1a.

28. *Chunqiu Zuozhuan zhengyi, juan* 30, in *Shisanjing zhushu*, 1942a–b.

29. "Wenyan 文言," in *Zhouyi zhengyi, ce* 1, *juan* 1, 6b.

30. Li Dingzuo 李鼎祚, *Zhouyi jijie* 周易集解, *juan* 1, 1a.

31. Cheng Yi 程頤, *Yichuan yizhuan* 伊川易傳, *juan* 1, 1a, in *Yixue jinghua*.

32. Zhu Xi 朱熹, *Zhouyi benyi* 周易本義, *juan* 1, 1a.

33. "Wenyan 文言," in *Zhouyi zhengyi, ce* 1, *juan* 1, 11a.

34. Xu Shen, *Shuowen jiezi, juan* 3b, 9a.

35. Wu Cheng 吳澄, *Yizuanyan*, juan 1, 1a, in *Yixue jinghua*.

36. See *Zhouli zhushu* 周禮註疏, *juan* 24, 165c, in *Shisanjing zhushu*, 803.

37. Li Jingchi, "Zhouyi Shici kao," 29.

38. James Legge, trans. *I Ching: Book of Changes* (New York: Bantam, 1964), 57.

39. Wilhelm, *The I Ching or Book of Changes*, 4.

40. Shchutskii, *Researches on the I Ching*, 138.

41. Ibid., 136.

42. Kunst, "The Original 'Yijing,'" 241.

43. Xu Shen, *Shuowen jiezi*, *juan* 1a, 1a.

44. See Lu Zongda 陸宗達 and Wang Ning 王寧, *Xungu yu xunguxue* 訓詁與訓詁學, 56–134.

45. *Zhouyi zhengyi*, ce 2, *juan* 3, 1a.

46. *Chunqiu Zuozhuan zhengyi*, *juan* 30, 1942a–b, in *Shisanjing zhushu*.

47. Zhao Rumei, *Yiya* 易雅, in *Tongzhitang jingjie* 通志堂經解, 10: 22a–b.

48. For a full account of Mao Qiling's case study, see Mao Qiling, *Chunqiu zhanshi shu*, *juan* 3, 5b–6a.

49. Li Jingchi, *Zhouyi Tanyuan*, 410.

50. See Zhang Zhenglang, "Shishi Zhouchu qingtongqi minwen zhongde yigua," in *Kaogu xuebao*, 4 (1980): 403–15.

51. Shao Yong, *Huangji jingshi shu*, 25a–b.

52. Han Yongxian 韓永賢, *Zhouyi jingyuan*, 632. See also his *Zhouyi tanyuan*, 467.

53. Charles S. Peirce, *Collected Works*, 2: 172.

54. For a quick reference of the three explanations, see Zhang Shanwen, *Zhouyi cidian* 周易辭典, 81.

55. Charles S. Peirce, "On the Nature of Signs," in *Peirce on Signs*, 141–43.

56. Shang Binghe 尚秉和, *Zhouyi Shangshi xue* 周易尚氏學, 339.

57. Cheng Yi 程頤, *Er Cheng quanshu* 二程全書, *Sibu beiyao* 四部備要, han 182, ce 3, 2a.

58. Zhu Xi, *Zhuzi yulei* 朱子語類, *juan* 66, 10b, 4: 2594.

59. Ibid., *juan* 67, 11b.

60. Ibid., *juan* 67, 13b–14a.

61. Aristotle, *Poetics*, 9, in *Critical Theory since Plato*, 53.

62. Zhu Xi, "Yixiangshuo 易象説," *Zhu Wengong wenji* 朱文公文集, *juan* 67, 1b.

63. Ibid., *juan* 67, 1b.

64. Ibid., *juan* 67, 2a.

65. Zhu Xi, *Zhuzi yulei*, *juan* 67, 9b.

66. *Lunyu zhushu* 論語註疏, *juan* 13, 50, in *Shisanjing zhushu*, 2506.

67. *The Analects of Confucius*, trans. Arthur Waley, book 13, 171.

68. Ferdinand de Saussure, *Course in General Linguistics*, 65.

69. Zheng Xuan, "Zhengshi Yizan Yilun," in *Zhouyi Zhengshi zhu jianshi*, *ce* 1, 1–6.

70. Lu Deming, *Jingdian shiwen* 經典釋文, *Sibu congkan* edition, *juan* 2, 1a.

71. Kong Yingda, preface to *Zhouyi zhengyi*, 1a.

72. *Zhouyi zhengyi*, 6a–6b.

73. See *Zhouli zhushu* 周禮註疏, *juan* 24, 165b, in *Shisanjing zhushu*, 803.

74. *Yiwei* 易緯, *Wuyingdian juzhenban quanshu* 武英殿聚珍版全書, *han* 3, *ce* 20, *juan* 1, 1a.

75. Zheng Xuan, "Yi Zan," in *Zhengshi yishu*, *juan* 9, 9b.,

76. *Zhouyi zhengyi ce* 1, 2b.

77. *Zhouyi zhengyi*, *ce* 3, *juan* 7, 6b.

78. *Zhouyi zhengyi*, *ce* 3, *juan* 7, 1b.

79. *Zhouyi zhengyi*, *ce* 1, *juan* 1, 3a.

80. *Zhouyi zhengyi*, *ce* 3, *juan* 7, 2a.

81. *Zhouyi zhengyi*, *ce* 3, *juan* 7, 2b.

82. *Zhouyi zhengyi*, *ce* 3, *juan* 7, 5b.

83. Xu Shen, *Shuowen jiezi* 説文解字, *juan* 9b, 7b.

84. Xu Shen, *Shuowen*, *juan* 9b, 7b.

85. Wei Boyang 魏伯陽, *Cantongqi* 參同契, 18.

86. For Yu Fan's remark, see Lu Deming, *Jingdian shiwen*, *juan* 2, 1a.

87. Sun Xingyan, *Zhouyi jijie* 周易集解, *juan* 1, 1.

88. Zhang Huiyan, *Zhouyi Yushixue* 周易虞氏學, 7.

89. Chen Menglei, *Zhouyi qianshu* 周易淺述, 13.

90. Yao Peizhong, *Zhouyi Yaoshixue* 周易姚氏學, 1.

91. Liu Shipei, *Liu Shenshu xiansheng yishu* 劉申叔先生遺書, 4: 2371a.

92. This is requoted from Cai Shangsi's *Zhouyi sixiang yaolun*, 7–8.

93. "Xicizhuan," *Zhouyi zhengyi, ce* 3, *juan* 7, 9a.

94. Xu Shen, *Shuowen jiezi, juan* 9b, 7b.

95. See Cai Shangsi, *Zhouyi sixiang yaolun*, 8.

96. Requoted from Han Yongxian, *Zhouyi tanyuan*, 444.

97. Yao Peizhong, *Zhouyi Yaoshixue*, 1.

98. *Liji zhengyi, juan* 37, 300, in *Shisanjing zhushu*, 1528.

99. *Zhouyi yanjiu lunwenji* 周易研究論文集, 4: 157–58.

100. Mao Qiling 毛奇齡, *Zhongshi yi* 仲氏易, *juan* 1, 1b–2b.

101. *Yiwei*, in *Wuyingdian juzhenban quanshu, han* 3, *ce* 20, *juan* 1, 11a.

102. *Zhouyi zhengyi, ce* 3, *juan* 7, 17a.

103. *Zhouyi zhengyi, ce* 3, *juan* 7, 9a.

104. Chen Menglei, *Zhouyi qianshu*, 13.

105. I have discussed this additional principle extensively in my article "Reconceputalizing the Linguistic Divide," *Comparative Literature Studies* 37.2 (2000): 101–24.

106. W. J. T. Mitchell, "Representation," 14.

107. Requoted from Bernard Faure, *Chan Insights and Oversights*, 198.

108. Bernard Faure, *Chan Insights and Oversights*, 198–99.

Chapter 4. Elucidation of Images

1. *Zhouyi zhengyi* 周易正義, *Sibu beiyao* edition, *ce* 3, *juan* 7, 18a.

2. *Zhouyi zhengyi, ce* 3, *juan* 8, 1a.

3. *Zhouyi zhengyi, ce* 3, *juan* 7, 18a.

4. *Zhouyi zhengyi, ce* 3, *juan* 7, 18a.

5. Kong Yingda's comment is found in *Zhouyi zhengyi, ce* 3, *juan* 7, 18a.

6. Guo Yong, *Guoshi chuanjia yishuo*, in *Wenyuange Siku quanshu*, 13: 8a.

7. Shang Binghe 尚秉和, *Zhouyi Shangshi xue* 周易尚氏學, 304.

8. Stephen Owen, *Readings in Chinese Literary Thought*, 33.

9. See Ferdinand de Saussure's *Course in General Linguistics*, 15–16.

10. See Roland Barthes, *Mythologies*, 109–58.

11. Wang Bi, "Mingxiang 明象," in *Wang Bi ji jiaoshi* 王弼集校釋, 2: 609. Henceforward, all quotations of Wang Bi's discourse are from this source.

12. *Zhouyi zhengyi, ce* 3, *juan* 7, 18a.

13. Ferdinand de Saussure, *Course in General Linguistics*, 65–67, 114.

14. Jacques Lacan, *Écrits: A Selection*, 149.

15. Stephen Owen, *Readings in Chinese Literary Thought*, 33.

16. Ferdinand de Saussure, *Course in General Linguistics*, 65.

17. For more information, see Chad Hansen's *Language and Logic in Ancient China*.

18. Compare Wang Bi's notion with the classical definition of poetry in the "Great Preface" to the *Book of Songs* in James J. Y. Liu's *The Art of Chinese Poetry*, 70.

19. Roman Jakobson, "Closing Statement: Linguistics and Poetics," 353.

20. Guo Yong 郭雍, *Guoshi chuanjia yishuo*, in *Wenyuange Siku quanshu*, 13: 8b.

21. Wang Yan, "Duyi biji xu 讀易筆記序," in *Wenyuange Siku quanshu*, 115: 723b.

22. Zhu Xi, "Yixiangshuo 易象説," *Zhu Wengong wenji* 朱文公文集, *juan* 67, 2a.

23. Ferdinand de Saussure, *Course in General Linguistics*, 111–12.

24. Mu Jianpu 莫儉溥, *Zhouyi mingxiang: Wang Bi mingxiang jishuo* 周易明象:王弼明象集説, 28–29.

25. Saussure, *Course in General Linguistics*, 113.

26. Shao Yong, *Huangji jingshi shu, juan* 13, in *Wenyuange Siku quanshu*, 803: 1067a.

27. Wang Yan, "Duyi biji xu 讀易筆記序," in *Wenyuange Siku quanshu*, 115: 723b.

28. Liu Xie, *Wenxin diaolong*, 359.

29. To differentiate the Chinese concept *yixiang* from the Western concept of image, I have coined this neologism.

30. Wang Yinglin, *Kunxue jiwen* 困學紀聞, *juan* 1, 5b.

31. Zhuangzi, *Zhuangzi*, 303.

32. Martin Heidegger, "The Nature of Language," in *Critical Theory since Plato*, revised edition, 1091.

33. Liu Dajun, *Zhouyi gailun*, 174.

34. This last sentence has variations. Some editions make no distinction between *yi* 意 (meaning) and *yi* 義 (significance). I am using the definitive version in *Wang Bi ji jiaoshi*, 2: 609.

35. E. D. Hirsch, *The Aims of Interpretation*, 2–3.

36. Jacques Lacan, *Écrits: A Selection*, 156.

37. Lacan, *Écrits: A Selection*, 157.

38. Lacan, *Écrits: A Selection*, 160.

39. Freud, *The Interpretation of Dreams*, 311–73 and 526–46.

40. Stephen Owen, *Traditional Chinese Poetry and Poetics: Omen of the World*, 18.

41. Lacan, *Écrits: A Selection*, 160 and 175.

42. Zhuangzi, *Zhuangzi*, 160.

43. Wang Bi, "Mingxiang," in *Wang Bi ji jiaoshi*, 2: 609.

44. See *Wang Bi ji jiaoshi*, 1: 321 and 351; 2: 459 and 468.

45. See *Wang Bi ji jiaoshi*, 2: 609.

46. Terry Eagleton, *Literary Theory: An Introduction*, 54–78.

47. Shang Binghe, *Zhouyi Shangshi xue*, 310.

48. Zhu Bokun, "Questions on the Mysteries of the *Zhouyi* 關于周易的奧祕問題," in *Yixue yu Zhongguo wenhua* 易學與中國文化.

49. Zhu Xi, "Yixiangshuo," *Zhu Wengong wenji*, *juan* 67, 1b.

50. Terry Eagleton, *Literary Theory: An Introduction*, 67.

51. Roland Barthes, "The Death of the Author," in *Image—Music—Text*, 145.

52. Roland Barthes, "The Death of the Author," 146.

53. Roland Barthes, "The Death of the Author," 146.

54. *Siku quanshu zongmu* 四庫全書總目, vol. 1, *juan* 1, 3.

55. Zheng Muyong 鄭慕雍, "Wang Bi zhuyi yong Lao kao 王弼註易用老考," in *Zhouyi yanjiu lunwenji*, 2: 220.

56. See "Tiandao pian 天道篇" in *Zhuangzi*, 160. See the English version in chap. 1.

57. Kong Yingda 孔穎達, "*Zhouyi* zhengyi xu 周易正義序," in *Zhouyi zhushu* 周易註疏, 1.

58. See Wang Bi's annotation in *Zhouyi shangjing* 周易上經, *juan* 1, 3b, *Sibu congkan*.

59. W. K. Wimsatt and M. C. Beardsley, "The Intentional Fallacy," in *The Verbal Icon*.

60. Huang Ze, *Yixue lanshang* 易學濫觴, in *Wenyuange Siku quanshu*, 24: 14.

61. Requoted from Mu Jianpu, *Zhouyi mingxiang: Wang Bi mingxiang jishuo*, 33a.

62. Zhu Xi, "Yixiangshuo," *Zhu Wengone wenji*, *juan* 67, 2a.

63. Zhu Xi, *Zhuzi yulei* 朱子語類, 4: 2664.

64. Wang Yan, "Duyi biji xu," in *Wenyuange Siku quanshu*, 115: 5723b.

65. Liu Dajun 劉大鈞, *Zhouyi gailun*, 174.

66. Zhu Xi, *Zhuzi yulei*, in *Wenyuange Siku quanshu*, 701: 352a.

67. Huang Ze, *Yixue lanshang*, in *Wenyuange Siku quanshu*, 24: 14.

68. Wang Yan, "Duyi biji xu," in *Wenyuange Siku quanshu*, 115: 5723a.

69. Zhong Rong, *Shipin*, in *Lidai shihua*, 3.

70. See Yan Yu's *Changlang shihua*, in *Lidai shihua*, 688.

71. Guo Yong, "Guoshi chuanjia yishuo zonglun," *Wenyuange Siku quanshu*, 13: 8a.

Chapter 5. The *Shijing* and Open Poetics

1. Kongzi, *Lunyu zhushu* 論語註疏, *juan* 17, 69b; *The Analects of Confucius*, 212.

2. See *The Analects of Confucius*, 208.

3. *Liji zhushu* 禮記註疏, *juan* 50, 381c, in *Shisanjing zhushu*, 1609.

4. *Maoshi zhengyi* 毛詩正義, *juan* 1, 2c, in *Shisanjing zhushu*, 270.

5. Huang Xun, "Yuanshi 原詩," in *Maoshi jijie* 毛詩集解, *Tongzhitang jingjie* 通志堂經解, *han* 31, *ce* 242, 3b.

6. Yao Jiheng 姚際恒, *Shijing tonglun* 詩經通論, 1.

7. *Hanshi waizhuan* 韓詩外傳, *juan* 5, 191.

8. *Maoshi zhengyi*, in *Shisanjing zhushu*, 270 and 273.

9. Ibid.

10. Cheng Yi 程頤, *Yichuan jingshuo* 伊川經說, *ce* 9, *juan* 3, in *Er Cheng quanshu* 二程全書, *Sibu beiyao* 四部備要.

11. Lü Zuqian, *Lüshi jiashu dushiji* 呂氏家塾讀詩記, *juan* 2, 6–9.

12. Chen Huan 陳奐, *Shi Maoshi zhuanshu* 詩毛詩傳疏, 1: 13–15.

13. Xu Qian 許謙, *Shijizhuan mingwu chao* 詩集傳名物鈔, *Wenyuange Siku quanshu*, 76: 8b.

14. Yan Can 嚴粲, *Shiji* 詩輯, *juan* 1, 14a–18a.

15. Shen Pei 申培, *Lu shigu* 魯詩故, *juan* 1, 1a, in *Yuhan shanfang ji yishu* 玉函山房輯佚書.

16. Han Ying 韓嬰, *Han shigu* 韓詩故, *juan* 1, 1a, in *Yuhan shanfang ji yishu*, 491.

17. Sima Qian, *Shiji* 史記, 2: 509.

18. Ouyang Xiu, *Shi benyi* 詩本義, *juan* 14, 3a.

19. Ouyang Xiu, *Shi benyi*, *juan* 1, 2b.

20. Wei Yuan, "Ernan shixu jiyi 二南詩序集義," *Shiguwei* 詩古微, *han* 1, *ce* 1, *juan* 2, 1a.

21. Hao Yixing, *Shiwen, Haoshi yishu* 郝氏遺書, *han* 2, *ce* 9, *juan* 1, 1b–2a.

22. Chen Huan 陳奐, *Shi Maoshi zhuanshu*, 1: 16.

23. Yao Jiheng, *Shijing tonglun*, 15.

24. Fang Yurun, *Shijing yuanshi*, 72.

25. Cui Shu, *Du Feng ouzhi* 讀風偶識, in *Cui Dongbi yishu* 崔東壁遺書, 10: 25.

26. Zhai Xiangjun, "Guanju shi qiuxianshi 關雎是求賢詩," *Tansuo* 探索 (1985), no. 2.

27. Hu Shi, "Tantan *Shijing*," in Gu Jiegang, ed., *Gushi bian*, 3: 585.

28. Wen Yiduo, *Fengshi leicao* 風詩類鈔, in *Wen Yiduo quanji* 聞一多全集, 47.

29. Yu Guanying, *Shijing xuan* 詩經選, 3.

30. Chen Zizhan, *Guofeng xuanyi* 國風選譯, 19.

31. Li Changzhi, *Shijing shiyi* 詩經試譯, 1–3.

32. Wei Ziyun, *Shijing yinsong yu jieshuo* 詩經吟誦與解説, 11–12.

33. See Hao Zhida 郝志達, ed., *Guofeng shizhi zuanjie* 國風詩旨纂解, 8.

34. Cheng Junying, *Shijing shangxiji* 詩經賞析集, 4.

35. Huang Diancheng, *Shijing tongshi xinquan* 詩經通釋新詮, 2.

36. Lan Jusun, *Shijing Guofeng jinyi* 詩經國風今譯, 64.

37. Chen Zizhan and Du Yuecun 杜月村, *Shijing daodu* 詩經導讀, 72.

38. Su Dongtian 蘇東天, *Shijing bianyi* 詩經辯義, 25.

39. See *The Cambridge Dictionary of Philosophy*, 29.

40. Aristotle, *Topics*, in *The Complete Works of Aristotle*, 245 and 273.

41. See Paul de Man's *Blindness and Insight*, 102–41.

42. *Maoshi zhengyi* 毛詩正義, *juan* 1, 2c, in *Shisanjing zhushu*, 273.

43. *Maoshi zhengyi* 毛詩正義, in *Shisanjing zhushu*, 273b.

44. Zhu Xi, *Shijizhuan*, *juan* 1, 2b.

45. Mou Yingzhen 牟應振, *Maoshi zhiyi* 毛詩質疑, 6.

46. Yao Jiheng, *Shijing tonglun*, 15.

47. Wen Yiduo, *Fengshi leicao* 風詩類鈔, in *Wen Yiduo quanji*, 48.

48. *Maoshi zhengyi* 毛詩正義, 273b, in *Shisanjing zhushu*.

49. *Maoshi zhushu*, *juan* 1, 25a–b, *Wenyuange Siku quanshu*, 69: 127.

50. *Maoshi zhushu*, *juan* 1, 24a, 69: 127.

51. Qu Wanli 屈萬里, *Shijing xuanzhu* 詩經選註, 31.

52. Liu Xie, *Wenxin diaolong*, "Bi and Xing" chapter.

53. Luo Binji 駱賓基, *Shijing xinjie yu gushi xinlun* 詩經新解與古史新論, 36–44.

54. Wei Yuan, *Shi guwei*, *ce* 2, *juan* 2, 1a–b.

55. *Maoshi zhengyi*, 273b.

56. *Maoshi zhengyi*, 273b.

57. *Maoshi zhengyi*, 273c.

58. Yao Jiheng, *Shijing tonglun*, 16.

59. Fang Yurun, *Shijing yuanshi*, 74.

60. Gong Yuhai 宮玉海, *Shijing xinlun* 詩經新論, 10.

61. Lu Ji 陸璣, *Maoshi caomu niaoshou chongyu shu* 毛詩草木鳥獸蟲魚疏, 3b.

62. *Maoshi zhushu, juan* 1, 27a.

63. Hao Yixing, *Shiwen*, 1b.

64. Cui Shu, *Du Feng ouzhi, juan* 10, 25.

65. Yao Jiheng, *Shijing tonglun*, 14.

66. Zhu Xi, *Shijizhuan* 詩集傳, *juan* 1, 2b.

67. Chen Zizhan, *Guofeng xuanyi* 國風選譯, 19–20.

68. Dai Jun'en, *Dushi yiping* 讀詩臆評. Requoted from *Guofeng jishuo* 國風集說, 17.

69. Traditional and modern fictional works are full of such examples. Suffice to cite one example: an old man who marries a young wife is called "an old ox that eats tender grass."

70. *Chunqiu Zuozhuan zhengyi, juan* 19a, 142a, in *Shisanjing zhushu*, 1844.

71. *Maoshi zhengyi, juan* 11a, 166b, in *Shisanjing zhushu*, 434.

72. See Ouyang Xiu, *Shi benyi, juan* 6, 12a; Zhu Xi, *Shijizhuan, juan* 11, 4a, 498; Yao Jiheng, *Shijing tonglun*, 198; Huang Diancheng, *Shijing tongshi xinquan*, 240.

73. Fang Yurun, *Shijing yuanshi, juan* 10, 380.

74. Mou Yingzhen 牟應振, *Maoshi zhiyi* 毛詩質疑, 6.

75. Yao Jiheng, *Shijing tonglun*, 15.

76. Jacques Derrida, *Writing and Difference*, 292.

77. See *Maoshi zhushu*, 69: 127–31.

78. Feng Fang, *Shishuo* 詩說, Requoted from *Guofeng jishuo*, 9.

79. Yao Jiheng, *Shijing tonglun*, 14.

80. Zhu Xi, *Shijizhuan, juan* 1, 3a.

81. Wei Yuan, *Shi guwei*, part 2, section 1, 12b.

82. See Luo Mi 羅泌, *Lu shi* 路史, "Gaoxin shi 高辛氏," in *Wenyuange Siku quanshu*, 383: 161.

83. See Chen Qiaozong 陳喬樅, *Lu shi yishuo kao* 魯詩遺説考, *juan* 1, 66–71.

84. See relevant pages in their respective works listed in the bibliography.

85. Wen Yiduo, *Shijing xinyi* 詩經新義, *Gudian xinyi* 古典新義, 69–70.

86. Wen Yiduo, *Shijing tongyi*, in *Gudian xinyi*, 108.

87. Yu Guanying, *Shijing xuan* 詩經選, 3.

88. Ming Dong Gu, "Fu-bi-xing: A Metatheory of Poetry Making," *CLEAR* 19 (1997): 6–7.

89. Lü Zuqian 呂祖謙, *Lüshi jiashu dushiji*, *juan* 2, 9a.

90. Zheng Qiao, *Shi bianwang* 詩辯妄, edited by Gu Jiegang, 13.

91. Su Zhe argued in his *Shilun* 詩論: "In looking at the *Shijing*, one must first know that a *xing* cannot be the same as a comparison." English translation is quoted from Panline Yu, *The Reading of Imagery in the Chinese Poetic Tradition*, 60.

92. Zheng Qiao, "Dushi yifa 讀詩易法," *Liujing aolun* 六經奧論, *juan* 1, 14b, *Tongzhitang jingjie* 通志堂經解.

93. Yao Jiheng maintained, "The *xing* only borrows an object to start [a poem]; it does not need to be related with the proper meaning [of the poem]." See his *Shijing tonglun*, 1.

94. Gu Jiegang argues that the function of *xing* is only to start the rhyme pattern of a song and that the starting line and what follows have no connection. See "Qixing 起興," *Gushi bian*, 3: 673–77.

95. Ji Ben 季本, *Shishuo jieyi* 詩說解頤, *Wenyuange Siku quanshu*, 79: 136b.

96. *Maoshi zhengyi* 毛詩正義, *juan* 2, 43, in *Shisanjing zhushu*, 311b–c.

97. See *Maoshi zhengyi*, *juan* 2, 43, in *Shisanjing zhushu*, 311.

98. Wen Yiduo, *Shijing tongyi* 詩經通義, in *Gudian xinyi*, 121–22.

Chapter 6. *Shijing* Hermeneutics

1. Yao Jiheng 姚際恆, *Shijing tonglun* 詩經通論, 7.

2. For a full account of the controversy, see Xia Chuancai 夏傳才, *Shijing yanjiu shi gaiyao* 詩經研究史概要; Lin Yelian 林葉連, *Zhongguo lidai shijing xue* 中國歷代詩經學.

3. See preface to Yan Can's 嚴粲 *Shiji* 詩輯, 1a.

4. Gu Jiegang, "*Shijing* zai Chunqiu zhanguo jiande diwei 詩經在春秋戰國間的地位," *Gushi bian*, 3: 309.

5. Zheng Zhenduo, "Du Maoshi xu 讀毛詩序," *Gushi bian*, 3: 383 and 385.

6. See Hu Shi, "Fakan xuanyan 發刊宣言," *Guoxue jikan* 國學季刊, 1.1 (Jan. 1923): 11.

7. Mengzi, *Mengzi zhushu*, *juan* 9a, in *Shisanjing zhushu*, 2735c.

8. Steven Van Zoeren, *Poetry and Personality*, 114.

9. Steven Van Zoeren, *Poetry and Personality*, 46.

10. Ouyang Xiu, *Shi benyi* 詩本意, *juan* 14, 6b–7a, in *Sibu congkan* 四部叢刊.

11. Fang Yurun, *Shijing yuanshi* 詩經原始, 1: 3. Italics mine.

12. Zheng Zhengduo 鄭振鐸, "Du Maoshi xu 讀毛詩序," in *Gushi bian*, 3: 385.

13. Marcel Granet, *Festivals and Songs of Ancient China*, 6.

14. Marcel Granet, *Festivals and Songs of Ancient China*, 17. Italics mine.

15. Zhao Zhiyang 趙製陽, *Shijing fubixing zonglun* 詩經賦比興綜論, 8.

16. Gu Jiegang, in *Gushi bian* 古史辯, 3: 367.

17. Lan Jusun, *Shijing Guofeng jinyi*, 6.

18. Chen Zizhan, *Guofeng xuanyi* 國風選譯, 11.

19. Niu Yunzhen 牛運震, *Shizhi* 詩志, requoted from *Guofeng jishuo*, 1065.

20. Lü Zuqian 呂祖謙, *Lüshi jiashu dushiji*, *juan* 12, 11b.

21. *Maoshi zhengyi* 毛詩正義, in *Shisanjing zhushu*, 372.

22. Zhu Xi, *Shijizhuan*, *juan* 6, 17b.

23. *Lunyu zhushu* 論語註疏, *juan* 9, 35a, in *Shisanjing zhushu*, 2491.

24. *Maoshi zhengyi*, *Shisanjing zhushu*, 1: 372.

25. Wen Yiduo, *Fengshi leicao* 風詩類鈔, in *Wen Yiduo quanji*, 27.

26. Xu Shen 許慎, *Shuowen jiezi* 説文解字, *juan* 1a, 6b.

27. See *Ciyuan* 辭源, 1466, 1467, and 987.

28. Zhu Xi, *Shijizhuan*, *juan* 6, 17b.

29. Ji Ben, *Shishuo jieyi* 詩説解頤, *Wenyuange Siku quanshu*, 79: 136b.

30. See, respectively, James Legge's "Prolegomena" to *The She King*, in *The Chinese Classics*, 4: 29 and Herbert Giles's *A History of Chinese Literature*, 12–14.

31. Marcel Granet, *Festivals and Songs of Ancient China*, 6.

32. See Arthur Waley, trans., *The Book of Songs*, 335–37; C. H. Wang, *The Bell and the Drum*, 1–3.

33. Andrew Plaks, *Archetype and Allegory in the "Dream of the Red Chamber."*

34. Pauline Yu, "Allegory, Allegoresis, and the *Classic of Poetry*," *HJAS* 43.2 (1983): 377–412.

35. Stephen Owen, *Traditional Chinese Poetry and Poetics: Omen of the World*, 53, 254–58.

36. Longxi Zhang, "The Letter or the Spirit," *Comparative Literature* 39 (1987): 193–217.

37. Haun Saussy, *The Problem of a Chinese Aesthetic*, 20.

38. Pauline Yu, *The Reading of Imagery in the Chinese Poetic Tradition*, 76.

39. Haun Saussy, *The Problem of a Chinese Aesthetic*, 28.

40. Hu Shi, "Tantan *Shijing*," in *Gushi bian*, vol. 3, 525.

41. Aristotle, *Poetics*, in Hazard Adams, ed., *Critical Theory since Plato*, 53.

42. Zheng Qiao 鄭樵, *Shi bianwang* 詩辯妄, 4.

43. Zhou Fu 周孚, *Fei Shi bianwang* 非詩辯妄, in Zheng Qiao, *Shi bianwang*, 24–25.

44. See Gu Jiegang's postface to *Fei Shi bianwang* 非詩辯妄, in Zheng Qiao, *Shi bianwang*, 59.

45. Longxi Zhang, *The Tao and the Logos: Literary Hermeneutics, East and West*, 195–96.

46. Stephen Owen, *Readings in Chinese Literary Thought*, 37.

47. Cai Zhongxiang 蔡鐘翔 et al., *Zhongguo wenxue lilun shi* 中國文學理論史, 1: 85.

48. Zhu Xi, *Shixu bian* 詩序辨, in *Zhuzi yishu* 朱子遺書, 1b–2b.

49. Stephen Van Zoeren, *Poetry and Personality*, 97.

50. For a fairly clear and systematic introduction of *xunguxue*, one can read Lu Zongda 陸宗達 and Wang Ning 王寧, *Xungu yu xunguxue* 訓詁與訓詁學.

51. For a detailed discussion of these two principles, please see Lu Zongda and Wang Ning, *Xungu yu xunguxue*, 56–134.

52. See Kristeva, *Revolution in Poetic Language*, 59–60.

53. Kristeva, *Revolution in Poetic Language*, 60.

54. See Roland Barthes, *The Pleasure of the Text*, 64.

55. See Jacques Derrida, *Positions*, 3–36.

56. The Chinese text of the Preface is quoted in full from *Zhongguo lidai wenlun xuan*, 1: 63–64. I have followed the paragraph division in the quoted source.

57. Kongzi, *Lunyu zhushu*, *juan* 12, 48b, in *Shisanjing zhushu*, 2504.

58. Tse-tsung Chow, "The Early History of the Chinese Word *Shih*," in *Wen-lin: Studies in the Chinese Humanities*, 151–209.

59. *Shangshu zhengyi* 尚書正義, *juan* 3, 19c, in *Shisanjing zhushu*, 131.

60. Lu Ji, "Wenfu 文賦," in Xiao Tong, *Wenxuan* 文選 *juan* 17, 225.

61. *Liji zhengyi* 禮記正義, *juan* 37, 299c; *juan* 39, 317c, *Shisanjing zhushu*, 1527 and 1545.

62. See *Liji zhengyi* 禮記正義, *juan* 37, 299b–c, *Shisanjing zhushu*, 1527.

63. See Xun Zi 荀子, *Xunzi xinzhu* 荀子新註, 332–42.

64. See *Zhouli zhushu* 周禮註疏, *juan* 23, 158a, *Shisanjing zhushu*, 796.

65. *Maoshi zhengyi, juan* 1, 3a–b, *Shisanjing zhushu*, 271.

66. Confucius, *Lunyu zhushu, juan* 12, 48b, in *Shisanjing zhushu*, 2504.

67. See Zheng Xuan's and Kong Yingda's annotations in *Maoshi zhengyi, juan* 1, 4c, in *Shisanjing zhushu*, 272.

68. Cao Pi 曹丕, "Dianlun lunwen," in Xiao Tong, comp., *Wenxuan*, 719–20.

Chapter 7. Open Poetics in Chinese Poetry

1. Requoted from David Spaeth, *Mies Van Der Rohe*, 8.

2. James Liu, *Language—Paradox—Poetics: A Chinese Perspective*, 56.

3. Martin Heidegger, "The Way to Language," in *Basic Writings*, 409.

4. Julia Kristeva, *Recherches pour une sémanalyse* (Paris: Seuil, 1969), 178–79.

5. See Roland Barthes, "The Imagination of the Sign," in *Critical Essays*, 205–211.

6. See *Ciyuan* 辭源, 1570.

7. Kao and Mei, "Syntax, Diction, and Imagery in T'ang Poetry," *HJAS* 31 (1971): 120.

8. Sigmund Freud, *The Interpretation of Dreams*, 317–18.

9. Xin Qiji, *Jiaxuan ji* 稼軒集, 91.

10. *Tang-Song mingjia ci xinshang* 唐宋名家詞欣賞, 208–9.

11. Zhu Qingyu, *Zhu Qingyu ji* 朱慶餘集, *Sibu congkan xubian jibu* 四部從刊續編集部, 33a.

12. Li Shangyin, *Li Shangyin shige jijie* 李商隱詩歌集解, 4: 1461.

13. James Liu, *The Poetry of Li Shang-yin: Ninth-Century Baroque Chinese Poet*, 66–67.

14. Barbara Herrnstein Smith, *Poetic Closure: A Study of How Poems End*, 188.

15. Xu Ling 徐陵, comp., *Yutai xinyong* 玉台新詠, *juan* 1, 4a–b, *Sibu congkan* 四部叢刊.

16. Tao Qian, *Tao Yuanming ji jiaojian* 陶淵明集校箋, 219–20.

17. James Robert Hightower, *The Poetry of T'ao Ch'ien*, 130.

18. Kao and Mei, "Meaning, Metaphor, and Allusion in T'ang Poetry," *HJAS*, 38 (1978): 322.

19. Zhu Ziqing, *Zhu Ziqing gudian wenxue lunwenji*, 68.

20. James Liu, *Language—Paradox—Poetics*, 43.

21. Said, *Beginnings: Intention and Method*, 196.

22. Owen, "The Self's Perfect Mirror: Poetry as Autobiography," in Shun-fu Lin and Owen, eds., *The Vitality of the Lyric Voice*, 71–102.

23. Tao Qian, *Tao Yuanming ji jiaojian*, 73.

24. For an account of this feeling, see Sigmund Freud, *Civilization and Its Discontent*, 11–12.

25. Sigmund Freud, *Civilization and Its Discontent*, 13–14.

26. Tao Qian, *Tao Yuanming ji jiaojian*, 73.

27. Tao Qian, *Tao Yuanming ji jiaojian*, 462.

28. Bai Juyi, *Bai Juyi shiji daodu* 白居易詩集導讀, 198.

29. *Quan Tan shi* 全唐詩, *juan* 84, 908.

30. Stephen Owen, *The Poetry of the Early Tang*, 175.

31. Requoted from Guo Shishan 郭石山 et al., *Zhongguo gudai wenxue jiangzuo*, 203.

32. Immanuel Kant, "Analytic of the Sublime," in *Critical Theory since Plato*, 396.

33. Immanuel Kant, "Analytic of the Sublime," 395.

34. *Chuci quanyi* 楚辭全譯, 121.

35. Stephen Owen, *The Poetry of the Early Tang*, 176.

36. *Quan Tan shi* 全唐詩, *juan* 128, 1239.

37. *Zhongguo lidai zuojia xiaozhuan* 中國歷代作家小傳, 110.

38. François Cheng, *Chinese Poetic Writing*, 25.

39. See Eliot Weinberger and Octavio Paz, *Nineteen Ways of Looking at Wang Wei*, 31.

40. See *Japanese-English Buddhist Dictionary* 日英佛教辭典, 71.

41. Su Shi, *Su Dongpo ji* 蘇東坡集, quoted from *Zhongguo meixueshi ziliao xuanbian*, 35.

42. Wu Zetian, "On Su Hui's 'Silk-Woven Palindromic Verse,'" in Chang and Saussy, eds., *Women Writers of Traditional China: An Anthology of Poetry and Criticism*, 670.

43. Quoted from *Women Writers of Traditional China*, 670.

44. Quoted from *Women Writers of Traditional China*, 676.

45. See Yi Boyin 裔柏蔭, ed., *Lidai nü shici xuan* 曆代女詩詞選, 16.

46. Umberto Eco, *The Open Work*, 220.

47. Joseph M. Conte, *Unending Designs: The Forms of Postmodern Poetry*, 24.

48. Robert Von Hallberg, *Charles Olson: The Scholar's Art*, 59.

49. Meng Haoran, *Men Haoran ji jiaozhu* 孟浩然集校註, 282.

50. Conte, *Unending Designs*, 24.

51. Conte, *Unending Designs*, 22.

52. Umberto Eco, *The Aesthetics of Chaosmos: The Middle Ages of James Joyce*, 66.

53. Conte, *Unending Designs*, 25.

54. *Tangshi sanbai shou* 唐詩三百首, 475.

55. This anecdote has been attributed to Ji Yun, but it has other sources. See Lu Jiaji 陸家驥, *Wenyi qutan* 文藝趣談, 294–95.

56. Ibid.

57. Pierre Boulez, *Relevés d'apprenti*, 297. English translation is from Eco's *Open Work*, 218.

58. Umberto Eco, *The Open Work*, 218.

59. Chang and Saussy, *Women Writers of Traditional China*, 670.

60. Quoted from *Women Writers of Traditional China*, 676.

61. Quoted from *Women Writers of Traditional China*, 670.

62. Barthes, *Critical Essays*, 210.

63. Barthes, *Critical Essays*, 210.

64. Conte, *Unending Designs*, 21.

Chapter 8. Linguistic Openness and the Poetic Unconscious

1. Zhu Ziqing, "Shi de yuyan 詩的語言," in *Zhu Ziqing gudian wenxue lunwenji*, 79.

2. Josef Bleicher, *Contemporary Hermeneutics*, 114.

3. Martin Heidegger, "The Way to Language," in *Basic Writings*, 424.

4. The English translation is requoted from Bleicher's *Contemporary Hermeneutics*, 115.

5. Martin Heidegger, "The Way to Language," *Basic Writings* 404.

6. Martin Heidegger, "The Way to Language," 410.

7. Hans-Georg Gadamer, *Truth and Method*, 338.

8. François Cheng, *Chinese Poetic Writing*, 24.

9. François Cheng, *Chinese Poetic Writing*, 25.

10. Peter Boodberg, "Philology in Translation Land," Cedules from a Berkeley Workshop in Asiatic Philology, 1954–55.

11. James J. Y. Liu, *The Art of Chinese Poetry*, 8.

12. Ernest Fenollosa, *The Chinese Written Character as a Medium for Poetry*, 25–32.

13. James J. Y. Liu, *The Art of Chinese Poetry*, 40.

14. Burton Watson, *Chinese Lyricism*, 7.

15. Burton Watson, *Chinese Lyricism*, 8.

16. Burton Watson, *Chinese Lyricism*, 8.

17. James J. Y. Liu, *The Art of Chinese Poetry*, 8.

18. Burton Watson, *Chinese Lyricism*, 8.

19. Ferdinand de Saussure, *Course in General Linguistics*, 123.

20. Roland Barthes, *S/Z: An Essay*, 13–14.

21. James J. Y. Liu, *The Art of Chinese Poetry*, 39–46.

22. See François Cheng, *Chinese Poetic Writing*, 23–42.

23. Kao and Mei, "Syntax, Diction, and Imagery in T'ang Poetry," *HJAS* 31 (1971): 132–33.

24. Kao and Mei, "Syntax, Diction, and Imagery in T'ang Poetry," 57.

25. Tsu-lin Mei and Yu-kung Kao, "Tu Fu's 'Autumn Meditations,'" 54.

26. T. E. Hulme, *Speculations*, 134–35.

27. Pauline Yu, *The Poetry of Wang Wei*, 25.

28. See Freud, *The Interpretation of Dreams*, 344–74.

29. François Meltzer, "Unconscious," in *Critical Terms for Literary Study*, 161–62.

30. Jacques Lacan, *Écrits: A Selection*, 147.

31. See Lacan's *Écrits: A Selection*. 81–82, 159–64, 234, 293–94, 509–15.

32. Claudé Levi-Strauss, *Anthropologie Structurale* (Paris: Plon, 1958), 224–25.

33. Freud, *The Interpretation of Dreams*, 647.

34. Jacques Lacan, *Écrits: A Selection*, 159.

35. See Lacan's detailed analysis in *Écrits: A Selection*, 147–61.

36. William Wordsworth, "Preface to *Lyrical Ballads*," in *Critical Theory since Plato*, 435.

37. Sigmund Freud, *The Interpretation of Dreams*, 347.

38. Kang-i Sun Chang, *The Evolution of Chinese T'zu Poetry: From Late T'ang to Northern Sung*.

39. Burton Watson, *Chinese Lyricism*, 16.

40. Sigmund Freud, *The Interpretation of Dreams*, 353–54, especially footnote 3.

41. Xu Shen, *Shuowen jiezi, juan* 15a, 314b.

42. See Liu Yuxi, *Liu Yuxi ji* 劉禹錫集, 253.

43. See François Cheng, *Chinese Poetic Writing*, 165.

44. Sigmund Freud, *The Interpretation of Dreams*, 388–89.

45. Ma Zhiyuan, *Ma Zhiyuan sanqu zhu* 馬致遠散曲註, 22.

46. Wang Guowei, *Renjian cihua xinzhu*, 104.

47. Wang Guowei, *Song-Yuan xiqu shi* 宋元戲曲史, 131.

48. Luo Jingtang 羅錦堂, *Zhongguo sanqu shi* 中國散曲史, 1: 57.

49. Freud, *New Introductory Lectures on Psychoanalysis*, requoted from *Dictionary of Psychoanalysis* (New York: Premier, 1965), 52.

50. Freud, *The Interpretation of Dreams*, 311–12.

51. Freud, *The Interpretation of Dreams*, 313.

52. Li Bai, *Li Taibai quanji* 李太白全集, 2: 837.

53. See Cheng, *Chinese Poetic Writing*, 37.

54. Roman Jacobson, "Closing Statement: Linguistics and Poetics," in *Style in Language*, 358.

55. Kao and Mei, "Meaning, Metaphor, and Allusion in T'ang Poetry," 347–48.

56. Lacan, *Écrits: A Selection*, 156.

57. Lacan, *Écrits: A Selection*, 157.

58. Lacan, *Écrits: A Selection*, 175.

59. T. S. Eliot, "Hamlet and His Problems, " in *Selected Essays*, 124–25.

60. Coleridge, "Biographia Literaria," in *Critical Theory since Plato*, 471.

61. *The American Heritage Dictionary of the English Language*, 1810.

62. Jacques-Alain Miller, "Suture (elements of the logic of the signifier)," *Screen* 18.4: 25–26.

63. Shen Deqian, *Shuoshi zuiyu* 說詩晬語, *juan* 1, section 5.

64. See *The Collected Papers of Charles Sanders Peirce*, 1: 171.

Conclusion

1. Terry Eagleton, *Literary Theory: An Introduction*, 85.

2. Requoted from E. D. Hirsch, *Validity in Interpretation*, 1. Tzvetan Todorov also subscribes to this idea; see his "Viaggio nella critica americana," *Lettera* 4 (1987): 12.

3. Stanley Fish, *Is There a Text in This Class?* 322–27.

4. Umberto Eco, *Interpretation and Overinterpretation*, 23–84, 38–40.

5. Umberto Eco, *Interpretation and Overinterpretation*, 23.

6. Umberto Eco, *The Open Work*, 4.

7. Umberto Eco, *Interpretation and Overinterpretation*, 66.

8. W. K. Wimsatt and Monroe C. Beardsley, *The Verbal Icon*, 5.

9. For scholarship on this subject, the reader can read Guo Chengkang and Lin Tiejun's *Qingchao wenziyu*, and Luther Goodrich's *The Literary Inquisition of Ch'ien-lung*.

10. Yang Fengcheng 揚風城 et al., *Qiangu wenziyu—Qingdai jishi*, 401–6.

11. See *Zaixiang Liu Luoguo* 宰相劉羅鍋, produced by Bejing Television, 1996.

12. Eco, *The Limits of Interpretation*, 6.

13. Fang Xun, *Shanjingju shihua* 山靜居詩話, in *Qing shihua* 清詩話, 964.

14. Slightly adapted from Arthur Waley's translation in *The Analects of Confucius*, 201.

15. See *Yunyu yangqiu* 韻語陽秋, *juan* 3, *Lidai shihua*, 502.

16. See Yuan Mei's *Suiyuan shifa conghua* 隨園詩法從話, *juan* 3, 15b.

17. Yuan Mei, *Jianzhu Suiyuan shihua* 箋註隨園詩話, *juan* 12, 7; 491.

18. Guo Moruo, *Du Suiyuan shihua zhaji* 讀隨園詩話札記, 38–39.

19. Guo Moruo, *Du Suiyuan shihua zhaji*, 39.

20. Zhang Zhupo, "Dongyouji pingyu 東游記評語," in *Jin Ping Mei ziliao huibian*, 208.

21. Umberto Eco, *The Open Work*, 8.

22. Umberto Eco, *The Open Work*, 63.

Works Cited

Works in Chinese and Japanese

Bai Juyi 白居易. *Bai Juyi xuanji* 白居易選集. Shanghai: Guji chubanshe, 1980.

Bai Juyi shiji daodu 白居易詩集導讀. Chengdu: Bashu shushe, 1988.

Cai Shangsi 蔡尚思, *Zhouyi sixiang yaolun* 周易思想要論. Changsha: Hunan jiaoyu chubanshe, 1991.

Cai Zhongxiang et al. 蔡鐘翔等. *Zhongguo wenxue lilun shi* 中國文學理論史. 5 vols. Beijing: Beijing chubanshe, 1987.

Cao Pi 曹丕. "Dianlun lunwen 典論論文." In Xiao Tong, comp. *Wenxuan* 文選. 719–20.

Chen Huan 陳奐. *Shi Maoshi zhuanshu* 詩毛氏傳疏. Taipei: Xuesheng shuju, 1981.

Chen Kui 陳騤. *Wenze* 文則. Beijing: Renmin wenxue chubanshe, 1962.

Chen Liangyun 陳良運. *Zhongguo shixue tixi lun* 中國詩學體系論. Beijing: Zhongguo shehui kexue chubanshe, 1992.

Chen Menglei 陳夢雷. *Zhouyi qianshu* 周易淺述. Shanghai: Guji chubanshe, 1983.

Chen Qiaozong 陳喬樅. *Lu shi yishuo kao* 魯詩遺説考. *Huang Qing jingjie xubian* 皇清經解續編. Taipei: Yiwen yinshuguan, 1965.

Chen Shou 陳壽. *Sanguo zhi* 三國志. Reprint. Beijing: Zhonghua shuju, 1981.

Chen Tingzhuo 陳延焯. *Baiyuzhai shihua* 白雨齊詩話. Beijing: Renmin wenxue chebanshe, 1959.

Chen Weizhan 陳煒湛 and Tang Yuming 唐鈺明. *Gu wenzixue gangyao* 古文字學綱要. Guangzhou: Zhongshan daxue chubanshe, 1988.

Chen Zizhan 陳子展. *Guofeng xuanyi* 國風選譯. Shanghai: Chunming chubanshe, 1955.

Chen Zizhan 陳子展 and Du Yuecun 杜月村. *Shijing daodu* 詩經導讀. Chengdu: Bashu shushe, 1990.

Cheng Junying 程俊英. *Shijing shangxiji* 詩經賞析集. Chengdu: Bashu shushe, 1989.

Cheng Yi 程頤 and Cheng Hao 程顥. *Er Cheng quanshu* 二程全書. In *Sibu beiyao* 四部備要.

Chuci quanyi 楚辭全譯. Guiyang: Guizhou renmin chubanshe, 1984.

Ciyuan 辭源. Beijing: Shangwu yinshuguan, 1988.

Congshu jicheng 叢書集成. Shanghai: Shangwu yinshuguan, 1935–37.

Cui Shu 崔述. *Du Feng ouzhi* 讀風偶識. In *Cui Dongbi yishu* 崔東壁遺書, vol. 10. Shanghai: Oriental, 1930.

Ding Fubao 丁福保, comp. *Xu lidai shihua* 續歷代詩話. Beijing: Zhonghua shuju, 1983.

Dong Zhongshu 董仲舒. *Chunqiu fanlu* 春秋繁露. In *Ershi er zi* 二十二子.

Du Fu 杜甫. *Qianzhu Dushi* 錢註杜詩. Annotated by Qian Qianyi 錢謙益. Shanghai: Guji chubanshe, 1979.

Ershi er zi 二十二子. Shanghai: Shanghai guji chubanshe, 1986.

Fan Wenlan 範文瀾. *Wenxin diaolong zhu* 文心雕龍註. Hong Kong: Shangwu yinshuguan, 1960.

Fang Xuanling 房玄齡 et al, comp. *Jinshu* 晉書. Beijing: Zhonghua shuju, 1974.

Fang Yurun 方玉潤. *Shijing yuanshi* 詩經原始. 2 vols. Beijing: Zhonghua shuju, 1986.

Feng Youlan 馮友蘭. *Xin lixue* 新理學. Changsha: Shangwu yinshuguan, 1939.

Ge Zhaoguang 葛兆光. *Zhonggu sixiag shi—Daolun* 中國思想史：導論. Shanghai: Fudan daxue chubanshe, 2001.

Gong Yuhai 宮玉海. *Shijing xinlun* 詩經新論. Changchun: Jilin renmin chubanshe, 1985.

Gu Jiegang 顧頡剛, ed. *Gushi bian* 古史辯, vol. 3. Beijing: Pushe, 1935.

———. "Lun Yi Xicizhuan zhong guanxiang zhiqi de gushi 論易系辭傳中觀象製器的故事." *Gushi bian* 古史辨. 3: 45–69.

Guo Chengkang 郭成康 and Lin Tiejun 林鐵鈞. *Qingchao wenziyu* 清朝文字獄. Beijing: Qunzong chubanshe, 1990.

Guofeng jishuo 國風集説. Zhang Shubo 張樹波, comp. 2 vols. Shijiazhuang: Hebei renmin chubanshe, 1993.

Guo Moruo 郭沫若. *Du Suiyuan shihua zhaji* 讀隨園詩話札記. Beijing: Zuojia chubanshe, 1962.

Guo Shaoyu 郭紹虞, ed. *Qing shihua xubian* 清詩話續編. 4 vols. Shanghai: Shanghai guji, 1983.

———, ed. *Shipin jijie* 詩品集解. Hong Kong: Commercial Press, 1965.

Guo Shishan 郭石山 et al. *Zhongguo gudai wenxue jiangzuo* 中國古代文學講座. Changchun: Jilin daxue chubanshe, 1987.

Guo Yong 郭雍. *Guoshi chuanjia yishuo* 郭氏傳家易説. In *Wenyuange Siku quanshu*, 13: 1–273.

Han Yongxian 韓永賢. *Zhouyi jingyuan* 周易經源. Huhehaote: Neimonggu renmin, 1991.

———. *Zhouyi tanyuan* 周易探源. Beijing: Huaqiao chuban gongsi, 1990.

Han Yu 韓愈. *Han Changli wenji jiaozhu* 韓昌黎文集校註. Hong Kong: Zhonghua shuju, 1972.

Hanshi waizhuan 韓詩外傳. Reprint. Taipei: Shangyu yinshuguan, 1972.

Hao Yixing 郝頤行. *Shiwen* 詩問. In *Haoshi yishu* 郝氏遺書. *Guangxu renwu kanben* 光緒壬午刊本.

Hao Zhida 赫志達. Ed. *Guofeng shizhi zuanjie* 國風詩旨纂解. Tianjin: Nankai daxue chubanshe, 1990.

Hu Qiguang 胡奇光. *Zhongguo xiaoxue shi* 中國小學史. Shanghai: Shanghai renmin chubanshe, 1987.

Hu Shi 胡適. "Lun guanxiang zhiqi de xueshuo shu 論觀象製器的學説書." In Gu Jiegang, ed., *Gushi bian* 古史辨. 3: 84–88.

———. "Fakan xuanyan 發刊宣言," *Guoxue jikan* 國學季刊 1.1 (Jan. 1923). 1–16.

Huang Diancheng 黃典誠. *Shijing tongshi xinquan* 詩經通釋新詮. Shanghai: Huadong shida chubanshe, 1992.

Huang Qing jingjie 皇清經解. Guangzhou: Xuehaitang, 1829.

Huang Qing jingjie xubian 皇清經解續編. Reprint. Taipei: Yiwen yinshuguan, 1965.

Huang Xun 黃櫄. "Yuanshi 原詩." In *Maoshi jijie* 毛詩集解. In *Tongzhitang jingjie* 通志堂經解, *han* 31.

Huang Ze 黃澤. *Yixue lanshang* 易學濫觴. In *Wenyuange Siku quanshu*, 24: 1–15.

Japanese-English Buddhist Dictionary 日英佛教辭典. Taitoo shuppansha, 1965.

Ji Ben 季本. *Shishuo jieyi* 詩説解頤. In *Wenyuange Siku quanshu*, 79: 1–504.

Jiaoran 皎然. "Shishi 詩式." In *Lidai shihua*, 25–36.

Katô Jôken 加籐常賢. *Kangji no kigen* 漢字、起原. Tokyo: Kadokawa shoten, 1970.

Kong Yingda 孔穎達. *Maoshi zhengyi* 毛詩正義. Beijing: Zhonghua shuju, 1957.

———. "*Zhouyi* zhengyi xu 周易正義序." In *Zhouyi zhushu* 周易註疏. Taipei: Zhonghua shuju, n.d.

Kongzi 孔子. *Lunyu* 論語. Shanghai: Shanghai guji chubanshe, 1987.

———. *Lunyu zhushu* 論語註疏. In *Shisanjing zhushu* 十三經註疏. 2453–2536.

Lan Jusun 藍菊蓀. *Shijing Guofeng jinyi* 詩經國風今譯. Chengdu: Sichuan renmin chubanshe, 1982.

Lao Zi 老子. *Daode jing* 道德經. Annotated by Wang Bi 王弼. Shanghai: Shanghai guji chubanshe, 1995.

Li Bai 李白. *Li Taibai quanji* 李太白全集. Beijing: Zhonghua shuju, 1977.

Li Changzhi 李長之. *Shijing shiyi* 詩經試譯. Shanghai: Gudian wenxue chubanshe, 1956.

Lidai shihua 歷代詩話. Ed. He Wenhuan 何文煥. 2 vols. Beijing: Zhonghua shuju, 1981.

Li Dingzuo 李鼎祚. *Zhouyi jijie* 周易集解. Beijing: Zhongguo shudian, 1984.

Li Jingchi 李鏡池. *Zhouyi tanyuan* 周易探源. Beijing: Zhonghua shuju, 1978.

Li Shangyin. *Li Shangyin shige jijie* 李商隱詩歌集解. Beijing: Zhonghua shuju, 1988.

Liji zhengyi 禮記正義. In *Shisanjing zhushu* 十三經註疏. 1221–1696.

Lin Yelian 林葉連. *Zhongguo lidai shijing xue* 中國歷代詩經學. Taipei: Xuesheng shuju, 1993.

Liu Dajun 劉大鈞. *Zhouyi gailun* 周易概論. Jinan: Qilu shushe, 1986.

Liu Shipei 劉師培. *Liu Shenshu xiansheng yishu* 劉申叔先生遺書. Taipei: Daxin shuju, 1965.

Liu Xie 劉勰. *Wenxin diaolong* 文心雕龍. Jinan: Qilu shushe, 1995.

———. *Wenxin diaolong zhu* 文心雕龍註. Annotated by Fan Wenlan 範文瀾. Hong Kong: Shangwu yinshuguan, 1960.

Liu Xizai 劉熙載. *Yigai* 藝概. Shanghai: Shanghai guji chubanshe, 1978.

Liu Yujian 劉玉建. *Liang Han xiangshu xue yanjiu* 兩漢象數學研究. 2 vols. Nanning: Guangxi jiaoyu chubanshe, 1996.

Liu Yuxi 劉禹錫. *Liu Yuxi ji* 劉禹錫集. Shanghai: Shanghai renmin chubanshe, 1975.

Liu Zhiji 劉知幾. *Shitong* 史通. *Sibu congkan danxingben* 四部叢刊單行本. Shanghai: Zhonghua shuju, n.d.

Lu Bi 蘆弼, comp. *Sanguo zhi jijie* 三國志集解. Beijing: Zhonghua shuju, 1982.

Lu Deming 陸德明. *Jingdian shiwen* 經典釋文. *Sibu congkan jingbu* 四部叢刊經部. Shanghai: Hanfenlou, n.d.

Lu Ji 陸璣. *Maoshi caomu niaoshou chongyu shu* 毛詩草木鳥獸蟲魚疏. Shanghai: Juzhen yinshuju, n.d.

Lu Ji 陸機. *Wenfu* 文賦. In Xiao Tong, comp., *Wenxuan* 文選. 224–28.

Lu Jiaji 陸家驥. *Wenyi qutan* 文藝趣談. Taipei: n.p, 1978.

Lu Xun 魯迅 (Zhou Shuren 周樹人). *Lu Xun lun wenxue yu yishu* 魯迅論文學與藝術. 2 vols. Beijing: Renmin wenxue chubanshe, 1980.

Lu Zongda 陸宗達 and Wang Ning 王寧. *Xungu yu xunguxue* 訓詁與訓詁學. Taiyuan: Shanxi jiaoyu chubanshe, 1994.

Lü Zuqian 呂祖謙. *Lüshi jiashu dushiji* 呂氏家塾讀詩記. Shanghai: Shangwu yinshuguan, 1934.

Luo Binji 駱賓基. *Shijing xinjie yu gushi xinlun* 詩經新解與古史新論. Taiyuan: Shanxi renmin chubanshe, 1985.

Luo Jingtang 羅錦堂. *Zhongguo sanqu shi* 中國散曲史. Taipei: Zhonghua wenhua chuban shiye weiyuanhui, 1956.

Luo Mi 羅泌. *Lu shi* 路史, "Gaoxin shi 高辛氏." In *Wenyuange Siku quanshu*, 383: 156–74.

Ma Xulun 馬敘綸. *Zhongguo wenzi zhi yuanliu yu yanjiu fangfa zhi xinqingxiang* 中國文字之源流與研究方法之新傾向. Hong Kong: Longmeng shudian, 1969.

Ma Zhiyuan, *Ma Zhiyuan sanqu zhu* 馬致遠散曲註. Ed. Liu Yiguo. Beijing: Shumu wenxian chubanshe, 1989.

Mao Heng 毛亨. *Maoshi guxunzhuan* 毛詩故訓傳. *Sibu congkan* 四部叢刊.

Mao Qiling 毛奇齡. *Chunqiu zhanshi shu* 春秋佔筮書. *Huangqing jingjie xubian* 皇清經解續編. *Han* 1, *Ce* 3.

———. *Zhongshi yi* 仲氏易. In *Yixue jinghua* 易學精華.

Maoshi zhengyi 毛詩正義. In *Shisanjing zhushu* 十三經註疏, 1: 259–629.

Maoshi zhushu 毛詩註疏. In *Wenyuange Siku quanshu*, 69: 43–991.

Meng Haoran 孟浩然. *Men Haoran ji jiaozhu* 孟浩然集校註. Beijing: Renmin wenxue chubanshe, 1989.

Meng Zi 孟子. *Mengzi zhushu* 孟子註疏. In *Shisanjing zhushu* 十三經註疏, 2: 2659–84.

Min Ze 敏澤. *Zhongguo wenxue lilun piping shi* 中國文學理論批評史. Beijing: Renmin wenxue chubanshe, 1981.

Mou Yingzhen 牟應振. *Maoshi zhiyi* 毛詩質疑. Jinan: Qilu shushe, 1991.

Mu Jianpu 莫儉溥. *Zhouyi mingxiang: Wang Bi mingxiang jishuo* 周易明象：王弼明象集說. Hong Kong: Dunmei zhongxue, 1962.

Ouyang Xiu 歐陽修. *Shi benyi* 詩本意. *Sibu congkan* edition 四部叢刊.

Qian Zhongshu 錢鐘書. *Guanzhui bian* 管錐編. 5 vols. Beijing: Zhonghua shuju, 1979.

———. *Tanyi lu* 談藝錄. Enlarged ed. Beijing: Zhonghua shuju, 1984.

Qiao Li 喬力. *Ershisi shipin tanwei* 二十四詩品探微. Jinan: Qilu shushe, 1983.

Qing shihua 清詩話. Comp. Wang Fuzhi 王夫之 et al. 2 vols. Shanghai: Shanghai guji, 1978.

Qu Wanli 屈萬里. *Shijing quanshi* 詩經詮釋. Taipei: Lianjing chuban, 1983.

Quan Tan shi 全唐詩. Taipei: Hongye shuju, 1977.

San Quan 珊泉 and Chen Jianjun 陳建軍. *Zhonghua Zhouyi* 中華周易. Beijing: Beijing shida chubanshe, 1993.

Shang Binghe 尚秉和. *Zhouyi Shangshi xue* 周易尚氏學. Beijing: Zhonghua shuju, 1980.

Shangshu zhengyi 尚書正義. In *Shisanjing zhushu* 十三經註疏, 1: 109–257.

Shao Yong 邵雍. *Huangji jingshi shu* 皇極經世書. *Wenyuange Siku quanshu*, 803: 29–1088.

Shen Deqian 沈德潛. *Shuoshi zuiyu* 說詩晬語. Beijing: Renmin wenxue chubanshe, 1979.

———, ed. *Tangshi biecai* 唐詩別裁. 4 vols. Beijing: Zhonghua shuju, 1964.

Shen Pei 申培. *Lu shigu* 魯詩故. In *Yuhan shanfang ji yishu* 玉函山房輯佚書. Taipei: Wenhai chubanshe, 1967.

Shisanjing zhushu 十三經註疏. Ruan Yuan 阮元. Ed. 2 vols. Beijing: Zhonghua shuju, 1980.

Sibu beiyao 四部備要. Reprint. Beijing: Zhonghua shuju, 1935.

Sibu congkan 四部叢刊. Reprint. Shanghai: Shangwu, 1919–36.

Siku quanshu zongmu 四庫全書總目. Beijing: Zhonghua shuju, 1965.

Sima Qian 司馬遷. *Shiji* 史記. 10 vols. Beijing: Zhonghua shuju, 1959.

Su Dongtian 蘇東天. *Shijing bianyi* 詩經辯義. Hangzhou: Zhejiang guji chubanshe, 1992.

Sui Tang Wudai wenxue piping ziliao huibian 隋唐五代文學批評資料匯編. Taipei: Chengwen chubanshe, 1978.

Sun Liankui 孫聯葵. *Shipin yishuo* 詩品臆説. In *Sikong Tu Shipin jieshuo erzhong* 司空圖詩品解説二種. Jinan: Qilu shushe, 1980.

Sun Xingyan 孫星衍. *Zhouyi jijie* 周易集解. Shanghai: Shangwu yinshuguang, 1927.

Tan Xian 譚獻. "Futang cihua 復堂詞話." In *Xinyuan congke yiji* 心園叢刻一集. n.p.: Zhonghua shuju, n.d.

Tang Mingbang 唐明邦, ed. *Zhouyi ping zhu* 周易評註. Beijing: Zhonghua shuju, 1995.

Tang-Song mingjia ci xinshang 唐宋名家詞欣賞. Taipei: Chaoye chubanshe, 1977.

Tangshi sanbai shou 唐詩三百首. Guiyang: Guizhou renmin chubanshe, 1988.

Tao Qian 陶潛. *Tao Yuanming ji jiaojian* 陶淵明集校箋. Shanghia: Guji chubanshe, 1996.

Tongzhitang jingjie 通志堂經解. Comp. Nalan Chengde. Reprint. Guangzhou: Yuedong shuju, 1873.

Wang Bi 王弼. *Wang Bi ji jiaoshi* 王弼集校釋. 2 vols. Beijing: Zhonghua shuju, 1980.

Wang Guowei 王國維. *Renjian cihua xinzhu* 人間詞話新註. Annotated by Teng Xianhui. Jinan: Qilu shushe, 1981.

——. *Song-Yuan xiqu shi* 宋元戲曲史. Shanghai: Shangwu yinshuguan, 1930.

Wang Yan 王炎. "Duyi biji xu 讀易筆記序." *Wenyuange Siku quanshu*, 1155: 722–724.

Wang Yinglin 王應麟. *Kunxue jiwen* 困學紀聞. Shanghai: Shangwu yinshuguan, 1935.

——. *Shikao* 詩考. In *Congshu jicheng* 叢書集成.

Wang Zhenfu 王振復. *Zhouyi de meixue zhihui* 周易的美學智慧. Changsha: Hunan renmin chubanshe, 1991.

Wei Boyang 魏伯陽. *Cantongqi* 參同契. Shanghai: Fanyi chuban gongsi, 1990.

Wei Yuan 魏源. *Shi guwei* 詩古微. In *Huangqing jingje xubian* 黃清經解續編, *han* 42–44.

Wei Ziyun 魏子雲. *Shijing yinsong yu jieshuo* 詩經吟誦與解説. Taipei: Juliu tushu, 1986.

Wen Yiduo 聞一多. *Gudian xinyi* 古典新義. Beijing: Guji chubanshe, 1955.

———. *Shijing tongyi* 詩經通義. Changchun: Shidai wenyi, 1996.

———. *Wen Yiduo quanji* 聞一多全集. Wuhan: Hubei renmin chubanshe, 1990.

Weng Fanggang 翁方網. "Shenyun lun 神韻論." In *Zhongguo lidai wenlun xuan*, 3: 67–71.

Wenyuange Siku quanshu 文淵閣四庫全書. Reprint. Taipei: Shangwu yinshuguan, 1983–86.

Xia Chuancai 夏傳才. *Shijing yanjiu shi gaiyao* 詩經研究史概要. Henan: Zhongzhou shuhuashe, 1982.

Xiao Tong 蕭統, comp. *Wenxuan* 文選. Taipei: Qiming shuju, 1950.

Xin Qiji 辛棄疾. *Jiaxuan ji* 稼軒集. Wuhan: Changjiang wenyi chubanshe, 1990.

Xu Ling 徐陵, comp. *Yutai xinyong* 玉台新詠. *Sibu congkan* 四部叢刊.

Xu Qian 許謙. *Shijizhuan mingwu chao* 詩集傳名物鈔. *Wenyuange Siku quanshu*, 76:1–259.

Xu Shen 許慎. *Shuowen jiezi* 説文解字. Ed. Xu Xuan 徐鉉. Beijing: Zhonghua shuju, 1963.

Xue Xue 薛雪. *Yipiao shihua* 一瓢詩話. Beijing: Renmin wenxue chubanshe, 1979.

Xun Zi 荀子. *Xunzi xinzhu* 荀子新註. Beijing: Zhonghua shuju, 1978.

Yan Can 嚴粲. *Shiji* 詩輯. Rep. Taipei: Guangwen shuju, 1950.

Yang Fengcheng 揚風城 et al. *Qiangu wenziy —Qingdai jishi* 千古文字獄一清代記實. Haikou: Nanhai chubanshe, 1992.

Yang Tingzhi 楊廷之. *Ershisi Shipin qianjie* 二十四詩品淺解. In *Sikong Tu Shipin jieshuo erzhong* 司空圖詩品解説二種. Jinan: Qilu shushe, 1980.

Yang Wanli 楊萬里. *Chengzhai shihua* 誠齋詩話. In *Lidai shihua xubian* 歷代詩話續編. Beijing: Zhonghua shuju, 1983.

Yao Jiheng 姚際恆. *Shijing tonglun* 詩經通論. Beijing: Zhonghua shuju, 1958.

Yao Peizhong 姚配中. *Zhouyi Yaoshixue* 周易姚氏學. Shanghai: Shangwu yinshuguan, 1935.

Ye Xie 葉燮. *Yuanshi* 原詩. Beijing: Renmin wenxue chubanshe, 1979.

Yi Boyin 裔柏蔭, ed. *Lidai nü shici xuan* 歷代女詩詞選. Taipei: Dangdai tushu, 1971.

Yiwei 易緯. In *Wuyingdian juzhenban quanshu* 武英殿聚珍版全書. *han* 3. *ce* 20. Guangxu edition.

Yixue jinghua 易學精華. 2 vols. Jinan: Qilu shushe, 1990.

Yu Guanying 余冠英. *Shijing xuan* 詩經選. Beijing: Renmin wenxue chubashe, 1990.

Yuan Mei 袁枚. *Jianzhu Suiyuan shihua* 箋註隨園詩話. Taipei: Dingwen shuju, 1974.

———. *Suiyuan shifa conghua* 隨園詩法從話. Taipei: Qingliu chubanshe, 1976.

Yuhan shanfang ji yishu 玉函山房輯佚書. Taipei: Wenhai chubanshe, 1967.

Zhan Youxin 詹幼馨. *Sikong Tu Shipin yanyi* 司空圖詩品衍繹. Hong Kong: Huafeng shuju, 1983.

Zhang Dainian 張岱年. *Zhongguo zhexue dagang* 中國哲學大網. Beijing: Zhongguo shehui kexue chubanshe, 1982.

Zhang Huiyan 張慧言. *Zhouyi Yushixue* 周易虞氏學. Taipei: Guangwen shuju, 1960.

Zhang Shanwen 張善文. *Zhouyi cidian* 周易辭典. Shanghai: Shanghai guji chubanshe, 1992.

Zhang Taiyan 章太炎. "Shuzheng guwen bashi 疏證古文八事." in *Taiyan wenlu xubian* 太炎文錄續編. Wuhan: Wuhan yinshuguang, 1938, 1: 65–70.

Zhang Xuecheng 章學誠. "Yijiao 易教." In *Wenshi tongyi* 文史通義. Shanghai: Shangwu yinshuguan, 1963.

Zhang Zhenglang 張政烺. "Shishi Zhouchu qingtongqi minwen zhongde yigua 試釋周初青銅器銘文中的易卦." In *Kaogu xuebao* 考古學報 4 (1980): 403–16.

Zhang Zhupo 張竹坡. "Dongyouji pingyu 東游記評語." In *Jin Ping Mei ziliao huibian* 金瓶梅資料匯編. Comp. Hou Zhongyi 侯忠義 and Wang Rumei 王汝梅. Beijing: Beijing daxue chubanshe, 1985. 208–209.

Zhao Rumei 趙汝楳. *Yiya* 易雅. In *Tongzhitang jingjie* 通志堂經解. *Han* 10.

Zhao Zhiyang 趙製陽. *Shijing fubixing zonglun* 詩經賦比興綜論. Xinzu, Taiwan: Fengcheng chubanshe, 1974.

Zheng Qiao 鄭樵. *Liujing aolun* 六經奧論. In *Tongzhitang jingjie* 通志堂經解. *han* 79.

———. *Shi bianwang* 詩辯妄. Beijing: Jingshan shushe, 1930.

Zheng Xuan 鄭玄. *Maoshi zhuanjian* 毛詩傳箋. *Sibu congkan* edition 四部叢刊.

———. "Zhengshi Yizan Yilun 鄭氏易贊易論." In *Zhouyi Zhengshi zhu jianshi* 周易鄭氏註箋釋. n.p.: n.p., 1911. *han* 1. *ce* 1. 1–6.

Zhong Rong 鐘嶸. *Shipin* 詩品. In *Lidai shihua* 歷代詩話, 1: 1–24.

Zhongguo lidai wenlun xuan 中國歷代文論選. 3 vols. Shanghai: Zhonghua shuju, 1962.

Zhongguo lidai zuojia xiaozhuan 中國歷代作家小傳. Changsha: Hunan renmin, 1981.

Zhongguo meixueshi ziliao xuanbian 中國美學史資料選編. 2 vols. Beijing: Zhonghua shuju, 1985.

Zhou Dunyi 周敦頤. *Zhou Lianxi ji* 周濂溪集. Shanghai: Shangwu yinshuguan, 1937.

Zhou Shan 周山. *Zhouyi wenhua lun* 周易文化論. Shanghai: Shanghai shehui kexueyuan chubanshe, 1994.

Zhouyi yanjiu lunwenji 周易研究論文集. Comp. Huang Shouqi 黃壽祺 and Zhang Shanwen 張善文. 4 vols. Beijing: Beijing shida chubanshe, 1989–90.

Zhouyi zhengyi 周易正義. Annotated by Kong Yingda. *Sibu beiyao danxingben* 四部備要單行本. Shanghai: Zhonghua shuju, n.d.

Zhu Bokun 朱伯昆. *Yixue zhexue shi* 易學哲學史. 4 vols. Beijing: Beida chubanshe, 1988.

———. *Yixue yu Zhongguo wenhua* 易學與中國文化. *Lun Zhongguo chuantong wenhua* 論中國傳統文化. Beijing: Sanlian chubanshe, 1988.

Zhu Dongrun 朱東潤. *Zhongguo wenxue piping shi dagang* 中國文學批評史大網. Shanghai: Gudian wenxue chubanshe, 1957.

Zhu Qingyu 朱慶餘. *Zhu Qingyu ji* 朱慶餘集. *Sibu congkan xubian jibu* 四部從刊續編集部. Shanghai: Hanfenlou, n.d.

Zhu Xi 朱熹. *Shijizhuan* 詩集傳. Photocopy ed. Beijing: Wenxue guji kanxingshe, 1955.

———. *Shixu bian* 詩序辯. *Zhuzi yishu* 朱子遺書. Taipei: Yiwen, 1969.

———. "Taijitu shuo jie 太極圖説解." In Zhou Dunyi, *Zhou Lianxi ji* 周濂溪集. *juan* 1.

———. *Zhouyi benyi* 周易本義. Photocopy ed. Tianjin: Tianjin guji shudian, 1986.

———. *Zhu Wengong wenji* 朱文公文集. In *Sibu congkan* 四部從刊.

———. *Zhuzi yulei* 朱子語類. Taipei: Zhengzhong shuju, n.d.

Zhu Ziqing 朱自清. *Shi yan zhi bian* 詩言志辯. Shanghai: Kaiming, 1947.

———. *Zhu Ziqing gudian wenxue lunwenji* 朱自清古典文學論文集. 2 vols. Shanghai: Guji chubanshe, 1982.

Zhuangzi 莊子. *Zhuangzi* 莊子. Annotated by Guo Xiang 郭象. Shanghai: Shanghai guji chubanshe, 1995.

Zu Baoquan 祖保泉. *Sikong Tu shipin zhushi ji yiwen* 司空圖詩品註釋及譯文. Hong Kong: Shangwu yinshuguan, 1966.

Works in Western Languages

Ames, Roger and Wimal Dissanayake, eds. *Self and Deception: A Cross-Cultural Philosophical Inquiry*. Albany: State University of New York Press, 1996.

Anthology of Chinese Literature: From Early Times to the Fourteenth Century. vol. 1. Ed. Cyril Birch. New York: Grove Press, 1965.

Aristotle. *Complete Works of Aristotle*. Princeton: Princeton University Press, 1984.

Barthes, Roland. *Critical Essays*. Trans. Richard Howard. Evanston, IL: Northwestern University Press, 1972.

———. *Elements of Semiology*. Trans. Annette Lavers and Colin Smith. New York: Hill and Wang, 1967.

———. *Empire of Signs*. Trans. Richard Howard. New York: Hill and Wang, 1982.

———. *Image Music Text*. Trans. Stephen Heath. New York: Hill and Wang, 1977.

———. *Mythologies*. Trans. Annette Lavers. New York: The Noonday Press, 1972.

———. *The Pleasure of the Text*. Trans. Richard Miller. New York: Hill and Wang, 1974.

———. *S/Z: An Essay*. Trans. Richard Miller. New York: Hill and Wang, 1974.

Benveniste, Emile. *Problems in General Linguistics*. Coral Gables: University of Miami Press, 1971.

Birch, Cyril. Ed. *Studies in Chinese Literary Genres*. Berkeley: University of California Press, 1974.

Bleicher, Josef. *Contemporary Hermeneutics: Hermeneutics as Method, Philosophy and Critique*. London and New York: Routledge, 1980.

Boulez, Pierre. *Relevés d'apprenti*. Paris: Seuil, 1966.

Brooks, Cleanth. *The Well-Wrought Urn*. New York: Harcourt, Brace, 1947.

Bush, Susan and Christian Murck, eds. *Theories of the Arts in China*. Princeton: Princeton University Press, 1983.

Carlyle, Thomas. *Sator Resartus*. Oxford and New York: Oxford University Press, 1987.

Chan, Wing-tsit, comp. and trans. *A Source Book in Chinese Philosophy*. Princeton: Princeton University Press, 1963.

Chang, Kang-i Sun. *The Evolution of Chinese Tz'u Poetry: From Late T'ang to Northern Sung*. Princeton: Princeton University Press, 1980.

Chang, Kang-i Sun, and Haun Saussy, eds. *Women Writers of Traditional China: An Anthology of Poetry and Criticism*. Stanford: Stanford University Press, 1999.

Cheng, François. *Chinese Poetic Writing*. Translated from the French by Donald A. Riggs and Jerome P. Seaton. Bloomington: Indiana University Press, 1982.

Chow, Tse-tsung. "The Early History of the Chinese Word *Shih* (Poetry)." In *Wenlin: Studies in the Chinese Humanities*. Madison: University of Wisconsin Press, 1968, 151–209.

Coleridge, S. T. "Biographia Literaria." In *Critical Theory since Plato*, 468–71.

Connery, Christopher L. *The Empire of the Text: Writing and Authority in Early Imperial China*. New York: Rowman and Littlefield, 1998.

Conrady, August. "Yih-king-Studien." *Asia Major* 7 (1932): 409–68.

Conte, Joseph M. *Unending Design: The Forms of Postmodern Poetry*. Ithaca and London: Cornell University Press, 1991.

Critical Terms for Literary Study. Ed. Frank Lentricchia and Thomas McLaughlin. Chicago: University of Chicago Press, 1990.

Critical Theory since Plato. Ed. Hazard Adam. San Diego: Harcourt Brace Jovanovich, 1971. Revised edition, 1996.

Culler, Jonathan. *Structuralist Poetics: Structuralism, Linguistics, and the Study of Literature*. Ithaca: Cornell University Press, 1975.

Cunningham, Valentine. *Reading after Theory*. Oxford: Blackwell, 2002.

De Bary, Wm. Theodore, comp. *Sources of Chinese Tradition*. 2 vols. New York: Columbia University Press, 1960.

De Man, Paul. *Blindness and Insight: Essays in the Rhetoric of Contemporary Criticism*. New York: Oxford University Press, 1971.

Derrida, Jacques. *Dissemination*. Chicago: University of Chicago Press, 1982.

———. *Marges De La Philosophie*. Paris: Editions de Minuit, 1972.

———. *Margins of Philosophy*. Chicago: University of Chicago Press, 1983.

———. *Of Grammatology*. Baltimore: Johns Hopkins University Press, 1976.

———. *Positions*. Chicago: University of Chicago Press, 1981.

————. *Writing and Difference*. Chicago: University of Chicago Press, 1978.

Dilthey, Wilhelm. *Selected Writings*. Cambridge: Cambridge University Press, 1976.

Eagleton, Terry. *Literary Theory: An Introduction*. Oxford: Basil and Blackwell, 1983.

Eco, Umberto. *The Aesthetics of Chaosmos: The Middle Ages of James Joyce*. Tulsa, Ok: University of Tulsa, 1982.

————. *The Limits of Interpretation*. Bloomington: Indiana University Press, 1990.

————. *The Open Work*. Cambridge: Harvard University Press, 1989.

Eco, Umberto et al. *Interpretation and Overinterpretation*. Cambridge: Cambridge University Press, 1992.

Eliot, T. S. *On Poetry and Poets*. London: Faber, n.d.

————. *Selected Essays,* new edition. New York: Harcourt, Brace, 1932.

Empson, William. *Seven Types of Ambiguity*. New York: New Directions, 1966.

Faure, Bernard. *Chan Insights and Oversights: An Epistemological Critique of the Chan Tradition*. Princeton: Princeton University Press, 1993.

Fenollosa, Ernest. *The Chinese Written Character as a Medium for Poetry*. Ed. Ezra Pound. San Francisco: City Light, 1968.

Fish, Stanley. *Is There a Text in This Class?* Cambridge: Harvard University Press, 1980.

Foucault, Michel. *The Order of Things: An Archaeology of the Human Sciences*. London: Tavistock, 1970.

Frankel, Hans. *The Flowering Plum and the Palace Lady: Interpretations of Chinese Poetry*. New Haven: Yale University Press, 1976.

Freud, Sigmund. *Complete Psychological Works,* 24 vols. London: Hogarth, 1953–74.

————. *Civilization and Its Discontent*. New York: Norton, 1961.

————. *The Freud Reader*. Ed. Peter Gay. New York: Norton, 1989.

————. *The Interpretation of Dreams*. New York: Avon, 1965.

————. *On Dreams*. Trans. James Strachey. New York: Norton, 1950.

Fung Yu-lan. *A History of Chinese Philosophy*. 2 vols. Trans. Derk Bodde. Princeton: Princeton University Press, 1983.

Gadamer, Hans-Georg. *Philosophical Hermeneutics*. Berkeley: University of California Press, 1976.

————. "Text and Interpretation," in *Hermeneutics and Modern Philosophy*. Albany: State University of New York Press, 1986. 377–96.

————. *Truth and Method*. 2nd edition. New York: Continuum, 1999.

Giles, Herbert. *A History of Chinese Literature*. New York: Appleton, 1923.

Goodrich, Luther. *The Literary Inquisition of Ch'ien-lung*. Baltimore: Waverley Press, 1935.

Granet, Marcel. *Festivals and Songs of Ancient China*. London: Routelege, 1932.

Gu, Ming Dong. "*Fu-bi-xing*: A Metatheory of Poetry-Making." *Chinese Literature: Essays, Articles, Reviews* 19 (1997): 1–22.

————. "Literary Openness: A Bridge across the Divide between Chinese and Western Literary Thought." *Comparative Literature* 55.2 (2003): 112–29.

————. "Reconceptualizing the Linguistic Divide: Chinese and Western Theories of the Written Sign." *Comparative Literature Studies* 37.2 (2000): 101–24.

————. "Suggestiveness in Chinese Literary Thought: Symphony of Metaphysics and Aesthetics." *Philosophy East and West* 53.4 (2003): 490–513.

Hall, David, and Roger Ames. *Anticipating China: Thinking through the Narratives of Chinese and Western Culture*. Albany: State University of New York Press, 1995.

Hansen, Chad. *Language and Logic in Ancient China*. Ann Arbor: University of Michigan Press, 1983.

Heidegger, Martin. *Basic Writings*. Revised edition. New York: Harper Collins, 1993.

————. *Being and Time*. New York: Harper and Row, 1962.

————. *Poetry, Language, Thought*. New York: Harper & Row, 1971.

Hermeneutics and Modern Philosophy. Ed. Brice R. Wachterhauser. Albany: State University of New York Press, 1986.

The Hermeneutics Reader: Text of the German Tradition from the Enlightenment to the Present. Ed. Kurt Mueller-Vollmer. New York: Continuum, 1985.

Hightower, James Robert. *The Poetry of T'ao Ch'ien*. Oxford: Clarendon, 1970.

Hirsch, E. D. *The Aims of Interpretation*. Chicago: University of Chicago Press, 1976.

————. *Validity in Interpretation*. New Haven: Yale University Press, 1967.

Holland, Norman. *The Critical I*. New York: Columbia University Press, 1992.

Hulme, T. E. *Speculations*. Ed. Sam Hynes. Minneapolis: University of Minnesota Press, 1955.

Husserl, Edmund. *The Idea of Phenomenology*. The Hague: Martinus, 1970.

Iser, Wolfgang. *The Act of Reading: A Theory of Aesthetic Response*. Baltimore: Johns Hopkins University Press, 1978.

Jakobson, Roman. "Closing Statement: Linguistics and Poetics." In T. A. Sebeok, ed, *Style in Language*. Cambridge, MA: MIT Press, 1960.

————. *Language in Literature*. Cambridge: Harvard University Press, 1987.

Johnson, Barbara. "Translator's Introduction" to *Dissemination*. Chicago: University of Chicago Press, 1981.

Kao, Yu-kung, and Tsu-lin Mei. "Meaning, Metaphor, and Allusion in T'ang Poetry." *The Harvard Journal of Asiatic Studies* 38.2 (1978): 281–356.

————. "Syntax, Diction, and Imagery in T'ang Poetry." *The Harvard Journal of Asiatic Studies* 31 (1971): 51–136.

Kant, Immanuel. "Analytic of the Sublime." In *Critical Theory Since Plato*. 391–99.

Karlgren, Bernard, trans. *The Book of Odes*. Stockholm: Museum of Far Eastern Antiquities, 1950.

Keats, John. *The Poems of John Keats*. Cambridge: Harvard University Press, 1978.

Kristeva, Julia. *Recherches pour une sémanalyse*. Paris: Seuil, 1969.

————. *Revolution in Poetic Language*. New York: Columbia University Press, 1984.

Kunst, Richard A. "The Original 'Yijing': A Text, Phonetic Transcription, and Indexes, with Sample Glosses." Ph.D. Dissertation. University of California, Berkeley, 1985.

Lacan, Jacques. *Écrits: A Selection*. London: Tavistock, 1977.

————. *The Four Fundamental Concepts of Psycho-analysis*. London: Tavistock, 1977.

Lacan, Jacques, and Anthony Wilden. *Speech and Language in Psychoanalysis*. Baltimore and London: Johns Hopkins University Press, 1981.

Lao Tzu. *Tao Te Ching*. Translated by D. C. Lau. Harmondsworth: Penguin Books, 1962.

Legge, James, trans. *The She King*. In *The Chinese Classics*, vol. 4. Reprint. Hong Kong: Hong Kong University Press, 1960.

Leibniz, G. W. *Writings on China*. Trans. Daniel J. Cook and Henry Rosemont. Chicago: Open Court, 1994.

Levi-Strauss, Claudé. *Anthropologie Structurale*. Paris: Plon, 1958.

Lewis, Mark E. *Writing and Authority in Early China*. Albany: State University of New York Press, 1999.

Lin, Shuen-fu, and Stephen Owen, eds. *The Vitality of the Lyric Voice: Shih Poetry from the Late Han to the T'ang*. Princeton: Princeton University Press, 1986.

Liu, James J. Y. *The Art of Chinese Poetry*. Chicago. University of Chicago Press, 1962.

———. *Chinese Theories of Literature*. Chicago. University of Chicago Press, 1975.

———. *Language—Paradox—Poetics: A Chinese Perspective*. Ed. Richard John Lynn. Princeton: Princeton University Press, 1988.

———. *The Poetry of Li Shang-yin: Ninth-Century Baroque Chinese Poet*. Chicago: University of Chicago Press, 1969.

Liu Hsieh. *The Literary Mind and the Carving of Dragons*. Trans. Vincent Yu-chung Shih. Taipei: Chung Hwa Book Co. 1975.

Lu, Xun. *Lu Xun: Selected Works*, 4 vols. Trans. Yang Xianyi and Gladys Yang. Peking: Foreign Languages Press, 1956.

Mei, Tsu-lin, and Yu-kung Kao. "Tu Fu's 'Autumn Meditations': An Exercise in Linguistic Criticism." *Harvard Journal of Asiatic Studies* 28 (1968): 44–80.

Meltzer, François. "Unconscious." In *Critical Terms for Literary Study*, 147–62.

Miao, Ronald C. *Studies in Chinese Poetry and Poetics*. San Francisco: Chinese Material Center, 1978.

Miller, Jacques-Alain. "Suture (elements of the logic of the signifier)," *Screen* 18.4 (1977/78).

Mitchell, W. J. T. "Representation." In *Critical Terms for Literary Study*, 11–22.

Muller J. P. and W. J. Richardson. *Lacan and Langauge: A Reader's Guide to Écrits*. Madison, CT: International University Press, 1982.

Olson, Charles. *Human Universe*. Ed. Donald Allen. New York: Grove Press, 1967.

Owen, Stephen. *The Poetry of the Early Tang*. New Haven: Yale University Press, 1977.

———. *Readings in Chinese Literary Thought*. Cambridge: Harvard Council on East Asian Studies, 1992.

———. *Traditional Chinese Poetry and Poetics: Omen of the World*. Madison: University of Wisconsin Press, 1985.

Peirce, Charles Sanders. *Collected Papers of Charles Sanders Peirce*. 8 vols. Cambridge: Harvard University Press, 1931–58.

———. *Peirce on Signs*. Chapel Hill: University of North Carolina Press, 1991.

Plaks, Andrew. *Archetype and Allegory in the "Dream of the Red Chamber."* Princeton: Princeton University Press, 1976.

Plato. *The Collected Dialogues of Plato*. Princeton: Princeton University Press, 1963.

Preminger, Alex et al., eds. *The Princeton Encyclopedia of Poetry and Poetics*. Princeton: Princeton University Press, 1993.

Puett, Michael. *The Ambivalence of Creation: Debates Concerning Innovation and Artifice in Early China*. Stanford: Stanford University Press, 2001.

Ransom, John Crowe. *The New Criticism*. Reprint. Westport, CT: Greenwood Press, 1979.

Richards, I. A. *Practical Criticism*. Reprint. London: Routledge and Kegan Paul, 1964.

Said, Edward. *Beginnings: Intention and Method*. New York: Basic, 1975.

Saussure, Ferdinand de. *Course in General Linguistics*. London: Peter Owen, 1960.

Saussy, Haun. *The Problem of a Chinese Aesthetic*. Stanford: Stanford University Press, 1993.

Sebeok, Thomas A. *A Sign Is Just a Sign*. Bloomington: Indiana University Press, 1991.

Shchutskii, Iulian K. *Researches on the I Ching*. London: Routledge and Kegan Paul, 1980.

Sidney, Philip. "An Apology for Poetry." In *Critical Theory since Plato*, 154–77.

Silverman, Kaja. *The Subject Of Semiotics*. New York: Oxford University Press, 1983.

Smith, Barbara Herrnstein. *Poetic Closure: A Study of How Poems End*. Chicago: University of Chicago Press, 1968.

Spaeth, David. *Mies Van Der Rohe*. New York: Rizzoli, 1985.

Todorov, Tzvetan. *The Fantastic: A Structural Approach to a Literary Genre*. Trans. Richard Howard. Ithaca and New York: Cornell University Press, 1975.

Van Zoeren, Steven. *Poetry and Personality: Reading, Exegesis, and Hermeneutics in Traditional China*. Stanford: Stanford University Press, 1991.

Von Hallberg, Robert. *Charles Olson: The Scholars's Art*. Cambridge: Harvard University Press, 1978.

Waley, Arthur, trans. *The Analects of Confucius*. New York: Vintage, 1938.

———, trans. *The Book of Songs*. New York: Grove Press, 1960.

Wang, C. H. *The Bell and the Drum: Shih Ching as Formulaic Poetry in an Oral Tradition*. Berkeley: University of California Press, 1974.

Warnke, Georgia. *Gadamer: Hermeneutics, Tradition and Reason*. Stanford: Stanford University Press, 1987.

Watson, Burton. *Chinese Lyricism: Shih Poetry from the Second to the Twelfth Century.* New York: Columbia University Press, 1971.

Weinberger, Eliot, and Octovio Paz. *Nineteen Ways of Looking at Wang Wei.* Mt. Kisco, NY: Moyer Bell, 1987.

Wilhelm, Richard. *The I Ching or Book of Changes.* Trans. Cary F. Baynes. Princeton: Princeton University Press, 1967.

Wimsatt, W. K., and Monroe C. Beardsley. *The Verbal Icon.* New York: Noonday Press, 1954.

Wordsworth, William. "Preface to the Second Edition of *Lyrical Ballads.*" in *Critical Theory since Plato*, 433–43.

Yang, Hsien-yi and Gladys Yang, trans. "The Twenty-Four Modes of Poetry." *Chinese Literature* 7 (1963): 65–77.

Yu, Pauline. "Allegory, Allegoresis, and the *Classic of Poetry.*" *Harvard Journal of Asiatic Studies* 43.2 (1983): 377–412.

———. *The Poetry of Wang Wei: New Translations and Commentary.* Bloomington: Indiana University Press, 1980.

———. *The Reading of Imagery in the Chinese Poetic Tradition.* Princeton: Princeton University Press, 1987.

Zhang, Longxi. "The Letter or the Spirit: The *Song of Songs*, Allegorisis, and the *Book of Poetry.*" *Comparative Literature* 39 (1987): 193–217.

———. *The Tao and the Logos: Literary Hermeneutics, East and West.* Durham and London: Duke University Press, 1992.

Index

acoustic image, 52–53
acoustics, 49
addressee, 20, 67, 123, 129, 147
addresser, 20, 67, 123, 129, 147
aesthetics, 46, 47; open aesthetics, 150;
    aesthetic agendas, 82; aesthetic condition,
    77, 269; aesthetic edifice, 210; aesthetic
    equivalence between architecture and poetry,
    210; aesthetic feelings, 220–223; aesthetic
    impulse, 268; aesthetic issue, 1; aesthetic
    object, 230; aesthetic openness, 224;
    aesthetic pleasure, 220; aesthetic principle,
    64; aesthetic suggestiveness, 72, 76, 77, 78,
    149, 223
agnosticism, 32
allegory, 57, 128, 193, 194; allegorical
    exegeses, 6; allegorical intention, 214;
    allegorical interpretation, 5; allegorical
    methodology, 185; allegorical reading, 6,
    193; allegorization, 6, 194
allusion, 48, 75, 199, 241, 254
ambiguity, 6, 12, 39, 56, 67, 87, 238, 239,
    241, 243, 244, 271; contextual, 237;
    linguistic, 236, 237; syntactic, 12, 242
ambivalence, 52
Ames, Roger, xii
analogy, 68, 69, 75, 136, 175; GRE analogy,
    175
anshi (suggestion), 47
aporia, 158–59, 161, 163, 166, 169, 170, 171,
    212, 213
apotheosis, 59, 62, 178
architecture, 210
Aristotle, 48, 102, 158, 195, 255, 291n40;
    view on metaphor, 255; distinction between
    history and poetry, 102; "law of probability,"
    195

art, 1, 3, 6, 9, 44, 46, 47, 64, 101, 204, 235,
    248, 265; verbal, 14, 209, 216, 268, 289;
    poetic, 269
artistry, 64, 71, 209, 211, 239
association, 43, 51, 62, 71, 86, 87, 89, 111,
    161, 193; acoustic, 248; affective, 50;
    cultural, 259; imagistic, 248; inspired, 258;
    readerly, 62; sound, 248; symbolic, 89
Audi, Robert, 275n20
author, xi, 2, 12, 13, 17, 21, 22, 25, 27, 31,
    39, 41, 163, 31, 140, 146, 171, 172, 182,
    195, 264, 268; death of, 22, 27, 143, 145;
    author-centered interpretation, 150; authorial
    intentions, 63, 138, 143; author-oriented
    paradigm, 116; author's intention, 8, 19, 20,
    21–22, 25, 27, 31, 41, 63, 138, 139, 142,
    146, 148, 172; author's locatedness, 30;
    author's pretextual intention, 265; author's
    representation, 130, 261; author's
    unconscious, 63; author-centered exegesis,
    139; authorial intention, 19, 21, 272;
    empirical, 265; implied, 172; original
    meanings of, 143; role of, 265, 268; shift of
    emphasis from author to reader, 130
authority of writing, 267
axis of combination, 70–71, 76, 232, 253, 254
axis of selection, 70–71, 76, 232, 253, 254

Babbit, Ervin, 246
bagua (eight trigrams), 84–86, 114, 129
Bai Juyi (772–846), 50, 220; "Pipa xing," 50, 58
Ban Gu (32–92), 81
Barthes, Roland, 9, 119, 140, 233, 240–41;
    "The Death of the Author," 22, 143, 145;
    "empire of signs," 9; "segmentational
    reading," 240–41; "syntagmatic
    imagination," 233; *S/Z*, 240

interpretive closure, 199; modes of, 8;
multiple, 2, 5, 11, 56, 176; multiplicity of,
3; nature and function of reading and, 263;
overinterpretation, 7; Peirce's conception of,
261; possible and impossible, 195–96;
scheme of, 161; textual, 1; theory of,
132–33, 146; unlimited, 7
intertextuality, 62, 199–220, 205
irony, 6, 7, 168, 199
Iser, Wolfgang, 139
Israel, 5

Jacobson, Roman, 10, 20, 67, 71, 211, 246,
254; model of verbal communication, 20, 67,
123; "poetic function," 71, 254; notion of
poetic language, 70, 211
Ji Ben (1485–1563), 177, 192
Ji Yun (1724–1805), 231–232
Jia Dao (779–843), 269
Jia Gongyan (fl. 650), 104–5
Jiang Kui (c. 1155–1221), 57, 58, 60, 62
Jiaoran (730–799), 56
Jin Ping Mei (*Plum in the Golden Vase*) 200
jing sheng xiangwai (scenes rise beyond images),
77
jingjie (idea-scene), 8
jingwai zhi jing (scenes beyond the represented
scene), 77
Joyce, James, 155, 272; *Finnegans Wake*, 231;
Ulysses, 155
Jung, C. G., 81, 246
juxtaposition, 110, 242, 244–45, 251, 252,
257, 260, 260

Kant, Immanuel, 222; "negative pleasure," 222,
297n32
Kao, Yu-kung, 212, 218, 241, 242–43
Kasyapa, 111
Keats, John, 50; "Ode on a Grecian Urn," 50–51
King Wen, 83, 104, 148, 149, 156, 157, 162,
169, 170, 171, 172
King Yao, 19
Kong Yingda (574–648), 50, 93, 104, 105,
117, 156, 160, 162, 163, 169, 171, 183,
191, 192, 202, 283n24
kongling (empty deftness), 77
Kristeva, Julia, 63, 199, 210, 211;
intertextuality as a permutation of texts,
199; notion of poetic language, 211;
"transposition," 199–200
Kunst, Richard, 94

Lacan, Jacques, 66, 136; kinship of poetry,
dreams, and the unconscious, 246; linguistic

notion of the unconscious, 245–46; Mirror
Stage, 219; model of the linguistic sign,
121; psycholinguistic redefinition of
metaphor and metonymy, 135, 255–56; "the
unconscious is structured like a language,"
245; view of poetry, 247
Lai Zhide, *Zhouyi jizhu*, 283n24
Lan Jusun, 157, 187
Langer, Susan, 241
language, 20–21, 23–25, 32–35, 43, 122; gap
between thought and, 27, 125; inadequacy
of, 39, 218; inertia of language habits, 211;
inflective, 249; codes, 43; representation, 36,
37, 38–39, 40–41; symbols, 110; system,
86; limitations of, 42; metalanguage, 67;
metaphorical nature of, 34; nature of,
25; origin of, 123; paradox of language
communication, 35; performative function
of, 38; relationship between language and
thought, 117–18, 121–22, 125–28;
relationship between language and ideas,
35, 127–28, 129–32, 134–36; relationship
between language and the unconscious,
245–46; Saussure's view of, 103; slippery
nature of, 33, 130, 146, 147; strengths and
limitations of language in communication,
42; suggestiveness of, 149; the container
theory of, 35, 129; view of, 129
language philosophy, 32, 113, 114, 115, 129,
149
Lao Zi, 50, 51–53, 54, 63, 68, 73, 119, 143,
177; the *Laozi*, 72, 74, 107, 143
Lau, D. C., 277n17, 278n25, 281n103,
282n115–17
le mot juste, 268
Legge, James, 94, 193
Leibniz, G. W., 81, 82, 84
Levi-Strauss, Claudé, 300
Lewis, Mark E., 274n29; "empire of writing," 9
Li Changzhi, 157
Li Chonghua, 64
Li Dingzuo (fl. eighth century), 93, 283n24
Li Jingchi, 93, 94
Li Shan (c. 630–689), 278n27
Li Shangyin (813?–858), 215, 248
Liji (*Book of Rites and Rituals*), 153, 201, 202
Lin Tiejun, 301n9
Lin Yelian, 293n2
linguistics, 8, 13, 17, 210, 245, 263, 246, 255,
263; linguistic aspects of openness, 61, 92;
linguistic basis, 76; linguistic economy, 209;
linguistic model of the unconscious, 12;
linguistic phenomenon, 23; linguistic sign,
120; linguistic skepticism, 32, 38, 44;